REDEEMED BY FIRE

LIAN XI

Redeemed by Fire

THE RISE OF POPULAR CHRISTIANITY IN MODERN CHINA

YALE UNIVERSITY PRESS   NEW HAVEN & LONDON

Epigraph on page vi: from T. S. Eliot, *Little Gidding*, No. 4 of *Four Quartets* (London: Faber and Faber Ltd., 1942), IV. © The Estate of T. S. Eliot.

Set in FontShop Scala and Scala Sans by Duke & Company, Devon, Pennsylvania.
Printed in the United States of America by Sheridan Books, Ann Arbor, Michigan.

Library of Congress Cataloging-in-Publication Data

Lian, Xi.
Redeemed by fire : the rise of popular Christianity in modern China / Lian Xi.
p.   cm.
Includes bibliographical references and index.
ISBN 978-0-300-12339-5 (hardcover : alk. paper)
1. China—Church history—20th century. I. Title.
BR1288.L55 2010
275.1'082—dc22

                    2009026503

A catalogue record for this book is available from the British Library.

This paper meets the requirements of ANSI/NISO Z39.48-1992 (Permanence of Paper).

10 9 8 7 6 5 4 3 2

*To Esther
and to Serena and Grace
with love*

The dove descending breaks the air
With flame of incandescent terror
Of which the tongues declare
The one discharge from sin and error.
The only hope, or else despair
    Lies in the choice of pyre or pyre—
    To be redeemed from fire by fire.

—T. S. ELIOT, *Little Gidding*

CONTENTS

Acknowledgments   ix

List of Abbreviations   xiv

Introduction   1

1   In Search of Chinese Christianity   17

2   The Lightning out of the East: The True Jesus Church   42

3   The Jesus Family   64

4   The Smitten Land: China in Revival   85

5   "Elucidating the Way": An Independent Preacher's Revolt against Mission Churches   109

6   "Flame for God": John Sung and the Bethel Band   131

7   Awaiting Rapture: Watchman Nee and the Little Flock   155

8 The Indigenous Church Movement through War
and Revolution 179

9 Cries in the Wilderness: The Underground Church
in the Communist Era 204

Afterword 233

Notes 249

Glossary 293

Bibliography 299

Index 325

ACKNOWLEDGMENTS

THE WRITING OF THIS BOOK has been a long journey, most of which was undertaken in solitude. I would not have been able to complete it without the kind and generous help given by many people along the way. At the beginning of this study in 1997, Peter Ng of Chung Chi College at the Chinese University of Hong Kong put me in touch with Tian Wenzai, the knowledgeable head of the library at the Shanghai headquarters of the Chinese Christian Three-Self Patriotic Movement Committee, who retrieved for me several dusty copies of the "pre-Revolution" church publications. They turned out to be indispensable to this study. Over the years, in Fujian province and in many other parts of China, I was fortunate to meet people who were able to provide the best oral history on the subject along with their personal collections of historical documents. These include Guo Jiande of Fuzhou and four other informants on the Little Flock from the same city who have since passed away—Zhang Qizhen, Ni Yulong, Zheng Zhengguang, and Chen Biyin. Zhou Xingyi of Shanghai (Watchman Nee's former secretary and stenographer), the Reverend Liu Yangfen of New York City, and Joseph Tse-hei Lee of Pace University also provided valuable sources on the church that Nee founded.

For my research on John Sung, I am especially indebted to the Reverend Yu Yucheng, of Putian, Fujian, and Song Tianzhen, Sung's daughter and editor of his published diaries. I also thank Zhang Biwu, who retrieved for me parts of John Sung's doctoral dissertation at Ohio State University, and Dee Breland, secretary to David Epstein of Calvary Baptist Church of New York City, who sent me a copy of *Tell It from Calvary*. The Reverend Yu Yucheng also helped my research on the True Jesus Church. Others who directed me to key sources on the True Jesus Church include Xu Benying and several other members of the church in Putian. Wang Tianduo, son of Wang Mingdao, and Zhang Guiyan sent me several photographs of Wang Mingdao and also furnished historical information on him.

Those who granted interviews or shared with me historical documents on the Jesus Family and the Spiritual Gifts Movement in Shandong include Li Ruijun at the Jesus Family's original settlement at Mazhuang, Wang Guancan of Shandong Theological Seminary, Gu Zhijie, Pei Yufang, Zhang Shuyuan, Zhang Yufang of Jinan, and Luo Xingsan and Yang Zhisheng of Yantai. Tao Feiya of Shanghai University sent me his doctoral dissertation on the Jesus Family before it was published by the Chinese University Press; his friend at Shandong University, historian Liu Tianlu, aided my archival research in Jinan in 2002. Jing Fuyin, nephew of Jing Dianying and a former member of the Jesus Family, endured more than two hours of interview with me in his dimly lit apartment in Jinan, sustained by an oversized Mao-era oxygen tank and by his glowing memories. Still others whom I interviewed and who are part of the history of contemporary underground Christianity still in the making, including those in Xiaoshan, Zhejiang, and others in the remote, mountainous parts of Fujian, must remain anonymous. Revealing their names here would only add to the inordinate hardships they already have to contend with.

Several friends also helped my overall research with their kindness: Du Changzhong arranged for my use of the special collections at Fujian Normal University; Kathleen Lodwick offered both advice and encouragement, and John L. Rawlinson sent me his father Frank Joseph Rawlinson's books on Chinese Christianity published in Shanghai in the 1920s. I am also grateful for the courtesy and help extended to me by the staff members of the Tai'an City Bureau of Archives, the Shandong Provincial Archives, the United Methodist Church Archives in Madison, New Jersey, and those of the libraries of Shandong University, Fujian Normal University, Hanover College, Louisville Presbyterian Theological Seminary, the Southern Baptist Theological Seminary in Louisville, and Union Theological Seminary in New York. It was my good fortune to discover what the professionalism of dedicated research librarians and archivists can accomplish: my inquiry about the 1927 medical records for John Sung, first put to Seth Kasten at the Missionary Research Library at Union, was kindly redirected, through his contacts, to Elizabeth Shepard at New York Weill Cornell Medical Center Archives, who located the discharge ledger for the period when Sung was at the Bloomingdale Asylum and sent me a summary.

Other debts were incurred over an extended period of time. In the past decade, Guo Shengguang arranged practically all the interviews I conducted with surviving Christian Assembly (Little Flock) leaders as well as informants on contemporary popular Christianity. I am grateful for both his help and his enduring friendship. I also thank Gu Changsheng, a pioneering historian of Christian missions in modern China and an important participant in the making of that history, for making available to me his wealth of knowledge, his life story, his writings, and several reference books from his collection. I have drawn much on our conversations through the years. During the same period, Daniel H. Bays and Jessie G. Lutz gave me the most generous support and constructive criticisms as my writing evolved. Both read my manuscript in its entirety and steered me clear of many pitfalls. Those who read various parts of my manuscript and gave valuable suggestions include Gu Changsheng, Daniel Overmyer, Rudolph Nelson, and Philip Barlow. G. J. Barker-Benfield, who furnished my training in history at the State University of New York at Albany and who has remained my advisor and friend ever since, also read and critiqued most of my chapters. Other influences on my writing and thinking stretch farther into the past. In Fuzhou, during the 1980s, the late William E. Rowley became my mentor and friend. A student of Perry Miller's and a scholar of American religion himself, Bill kept up an interest in my research and once expressed a wish to live to see some of my "later writings." He did read an early version of this work a few months before his death in 2003 and found it a "sad story."

Whatever sadness lies herein, I emerge from this study marveling at the human spirit that lifted millions of nameless people—whose collective story I have tried to tell in this book—above voiceless suffering and despair toward exultant hopes and radiant visions. Among them was my late father. In a sense, this book is also dedicated to them and their memory. They have lived and suspired, to borrow T. S. Eliot's words, "consumed by either fire or fire." I am grateful for the opportunity to give voice to some of them in this book. I also thank the outside readers for Yale University Press who provided critical comments on the manuscript while firmly endorsing its publication. It was a pleasure to work with Chris Rogers, my editor at Yale University Press, who offered consistent, heartening support—and demanded that I prune the originally much longer book to its current length. His assistant Laura Davulis led me skillfully through the acquisition of permissions and the preparation of illustrations. My gratitude also goes to Jessie Dolch for her expert and careful copyediting, which rid this book of errors that I would never have been able to catch. I admire both her fortitude and her unfailing astuteness. Just as important, research for this book was made possible by several faculty research grants from Hanover College and by two Summer Stipends awards from the National Endowment for the Humanities.

This book contains materials that were included in my article "The Search for Chinese Christianity in the Republican Period (1912–1949)," *Modern Asian Studies* 38 (October 2004); they are reprinted here with the permission of Cambridge University Press. A slightly different version of Chapter 2 was also published as "A Messianic Deliverance for Post-Dynastic China: The Launch of the True Jesus Church in the Early Twentieth Century," *Modern China* 34, 4 (October 2008). I thank both journals for their permissions for me to use those materials.

Last but not least, my thanks go to my family for enduring my decade-long bewitchment while this study was under way—with all the attending trances of my own and other lapses including my frequent absences from home during summer. I am grateful to my wife Esther for all the love and support she has given me, and to my mother, who transcribed for me most of the taped interviews. Serena and Grace have filled our house with their beautiful, though at times reluctant, music. With their giggles, hugs, skirmishes with me that they carried on with good humor, and downright tears, they have helped set the mundane rhythms of my life while bringing simple joys into it. They have, far more than they can imagine, lifted my spirit with their capacity for love, forgiveness, and fun. Although they were disappointed that this book is not populated with thoroughbreds, cairn terriers, and the like, they still cheered me on. Grace also asked me the ever pertinent question (to which I have no answer): "Daddy, what if nobody reads your book?"

Louisville, summer 2009

ABBREVIATIONS

CCP   Chinese Communist Party
CIM   China Inland Mission
LMS   London Missionary Society
NCC   National Christian Council of China
TJC   True Jesus Church
TSPM   Three-Self Patriotic Movement

MAP 1 Provinces of China.

Introduction

ON JULY 29, 2006, hundreds of paramilitary police descended on the construction site of a rural Protestant church in Xiaoshan outside Hangzhou, the capital of Zhejiang province in eastern China. They clashed with the estimated three thousand people, mostly members of the local, unregistered "Little Flock" congregations, who had gathered there to protect the building. Many of those who protested or resisted were beaten; several were seriously injured. Dozens were arrested. Then four excavators were brought in, and the church, with all but the roof in place, was razed. The incident was reported by several major international media, including the *New York Times* and the BBC, as yet another example of the continuing repression of unapproved religion by the Chinese government.[1]

On a different note, a *Time* magazine article found in the episode "unmistakable evidence" of the flourishing of Christianity in China. "After four failed attempts over a millennium and a half by foreign missionaries to gain a foothold in China," it continued, "Christianity is finally taking root and evolving into a truly Chinese religion."[2] Proof of the vibrancy and resilience of this domesticated faith abounds: a few months earlier, also in rural Xiaoshan, another illegal church, which had been torn down thrice by the local government and rebuilt as many times, finally opened its doors. The stadiumlike new building—in the middle of a village—has a capacity of more than five thousand.[3] The spate of church construction followed years of a phenomenal spread of Christianity in the area. In August 2004, a series of open-air evangelistic campaigns targeting migrant workers in Xiaoshan concluded with a night meeting of more than ten thousand people. For that event, the organizers, supported by a column of trucks and cars transporting everything from chairs to drums to power generators, set up a mobile stage off a highway and rolled out cinema-style speaker systems. Defying an army of security personnel who had blocked off the site, the local lay preachers cried out messages of repentance onstage while women holding babies were deployed as human shields against fire engines that the police had dispatched. In the end, the authorities let the meeting proceed without incident, and it did not make news.[4]

The current burgeoning of Protestant Christianity in China comes into sharper focus if we stand back in time. At the dawn of the twentieth century, there were only some eighty thousand baptized Protestant converts in a land of more than four hundred million. Today, there are probably more than fifty million Protestants in China, well over six hundred times the total figure for 1900. (Catholics number about seventeen million.) During the same period, the Chinese population has not yet quadrupled.[5] Key to this growth, as we shall see, was the transformation of Christianity during the same period from an alien faith preached and presided over by Western missionaries into an indigenous religion of the masses. With a predominantly rural and lower-class membership, the homegrown Christianity has been characterized by a potent mix of evangelistic fervor, biblical literalism, charismatic ecstasies, and a fiery eschatology not infrequently tinged with nationalistic exuberance. As both a religious and a social movement, it has emerged amidst the upheavals of modern China; it will likely also help shape the country's future. One of the greatest fears of the Chinese government, a *New York Times* report pointed out, was the "breakaway emergence of an unorthodox sect that might seriously challenge public order." The specter of the Taiping Rebellion of the mid-nineteenth century, which began as a "charismatic Christian sect," lingers beyond the contemporary flame of Christian redemption.[6] To better glimpse the future of Chinese Christianity, we shall look back on its rise during the past one hundred years.

The 2006 demolition of the church in Xiaoshan highlights an important shift in the dynamics of the modern Chinese response to Christianity. A century earlier, the roles of the state and the common people in attacks on church properties were reversed. In a memorial presented to the Guangxu Emperor in 1896, the Office of the General Management of International Affairs (Zongli Yamen) pointed to chronic, spontaneous, and rampant acts of popular hostility toward Christian missions, including "church demolitions and the killing of missionaries." It also cited the inevitable, stringent demands for punishment and reparations made by the gunboat-backed Western powers following those incidents. In view of such recurring crises, it stipulated that local officials would henceforth be punished for any failure to "protect [mission property] according to the treaties"—demotions of one to two ranks would automatically be meted out as "punitive admonition."[7] It is not an insignificant change in the fortunes of Chinese Christianity over the past century that, in many areas of the country, the rural masses have completed a journey from church demolishers to church builders and defenders.

THE BEGINNINGS

The journey of Chinese Christianity started more than a millennium earlier, in 635 CE, when Alopen (A'luoben), a missionary from the Syrian Church in Persia, reached Chang'an (now Xi'an), the capital of the Tang dynasty (618–907). In that "great international metropolis," and at the dawn of an age of unprecedented grandeur and openness in imperial China, the new "Luminous Religion" (as Christianity was called) found a quick, official reception. In 638, the Taizong Emperor decreed that "the Way has no constant name; the sacred has no constant form." Upon close examination of the doctrine brought by Alopen, he had found that it preached "mysterious and transcendent non-action . . . saves creatures, and is of profit to people. It is fitting that it should be propagated under Heaven." Accordingly, he instructed that a Christian monastery be built in the capital for those who had taken religious vows. In the decades that followed, more missionaries of the Luminous Religion from Daqin, or West Asia, arrived. Books were translated, and the new doctrine spread to major cities in the empire. The appeal of the religion arose in part from the reputed medical skills of the Daqin Christians, often referred to as Nestorians; Tang records reveal at least one instance of an emperor being healed by a "monk" of the Syrian Church.[8]

Christianity fell on hard times after 845, when the Wuzong Emperor, under the influence of a jealous Daoist monk, issued a decree banning Buddhism along with all other foreign religions. Some forty-five thousand Buddhist monasteries and private temples were destroyed; a quarter of a million Buddhist monks and nuns were returned to lay life, as were "more than 3,000" clerics of the Nestorian, Muslim, and Zoroastrian religions. Christianity disappeared almost entirely from China in the next three hundred years.[9]

The rise of the Mongols in the early thirteenth century precipitated new Christian missions to China. By 1241, the fearsome steppe warriors from the east had swept across some four thousand miles all the way into Poland and Hungary and threatened to sack Vienna. In 1245, Pope Innocent IV dispatched an Italian Franciscan, Giovanni di Plano Carpino, as an envoy to the Mongol court in an effort to convert the Great Khan and to make him "desist" from the "savagery" of invading Christian countries. That mission ended in failure. Guyuk Khan demanded instead the pope's "submission." However, by the 1290s, Latin Christianity had established itself in Khanbaliq (Beijing) under the Mongols, whose pragmatic policy included religious pluralism.[10]

Meanwhile, at least from the twelfth century, Syrian Christians had been found among the nomadic tribes to the north, northwest, and northeast of China. *The Travels of Marco Polo* contains an account of a failed revolt in 1287 by Mongol prince Nayan and his army of "Christians" against Khubilai Khan (himself born of a Christian princess).[11] It is also known that Christians of Turkish and Mongol extraction—known as *Arkagun* (blessed people), or *Yelikewen* in Chinese, whom the Franciscan friars dismissed as "Nestorians"—held high positions in both the military and the civil administration of the Yuan dynasty (1279–1368). Apparently, the blossoming of the Luminous Religion in China under Mongol rule rivaled that during the Tang period.[12] One Latin Christian source dated circa 1330 asserted, "These Nestorians are more than thirty thousand living in the said empire of Cathay."[13]

Roman Catholic missions, which secured a bridgehead in the capital in the late 1290s, continued until the 1340s. During that period, dozens of Franciscan friars and laymen reached China, and a handful of churches and Franciscan communities were established in Beijing, Zaitun (Quanzhou), Hangzhou, and Yangzhou. Those missions faded away after the 1340s. No new European personnel arrived; no Chinese clergy was installed. Among the factors contributing to the decline of Catholic missions were the Black Death in Europe and the unraveling of the Mongol Empire, which made passages to China unsafe. In 1368, the collapse of the Yuan dynasty, whose rulers had patronized both the Latin and Syrian Christians, spelled the end of the alien faith in China. As in the Tang era, Christianity had depended upon the favor of the emperors, who did not grant it the status of state orthodoxy. Since it remained predominantly foreign in its membership and never gained a significant popular following, there was nothing to prevent its demise after the expulsion of the Mongols.[14]

In the mid-sixteenth century, at the dawn of the modern age of European exploration and expansion, Christianity made its third entry into China. By 1555, the first Catholic priests had reached Canton (Guangzhou). With a Portuguese settlement in Macao approved in 1557 by the imperial court of the Ming dynasty (1368–1644), more missionaries arrived. The best known among them, the Jesuit Matteo Ricci, reached Beijing in 1601 and inaugurated the ambitious but doomed effort to Christianize China by converting its ruling elite.[15] In the course of the seventeenth century, Catholic missions weathered several persecutions instigated by elements of the officialdom; they also survived the fall of the Ming, in part because the expertise of the Jesuits in casting cannon and improving the imperial calendar proved equally valuable to the Manchu rulers of China after 1644. In fact, the Belgian Jesuit Ferdinand Verbiest became a tutor to the Kangxi Emperor and served as director of the Astronomical Bureau from 1669 to 1687.[16] In 1692, Kangxi issued the first edict of toleration of Christianity. By the end of the century, dozens of missionaries—Jesuits, Dominicans, Franciscans, Augustinians, and representatives of the Société des Missions Étrangères—were in China. Their converts numbered as many as three hundred thousand, most of them from the lower classes.[17]

Promising as they were, Catholic missions in China were soon to run aground on the "Rites Controversy." Issues such as the proper Chinese translation of "God" and whether or not ceremonies in honor of Confucius and ancestors constituted idolatry had divided the missionaries from almost the beginning. The Jesuits' willingness to adapt Christianity to the Chinese tradition had scandalized their Dominican and Franciscan counterparts, and the latter secured the first papal proscription of Jesuit accommodations in 1645. The controversy intensified during the 1690s.

In 1704, Pope Clement XI issued a comprehensive ban of Chinese rites. Kangxi responded with an expulsion of missionaries who were opposed to "the method of Matteo Ricci." In 1720, he issued his final decree on the matter: in a reversal of his earlier policy of toleration, he prohibited Christianity in order to "avoid unnecessary troubles." Actual suppression began under his successor in 1724 and continued for the next 120 years.[18] During that period, Christianity became one of the heterodox "sects" and was driven underground. Toward the end of the eighteenth century, as the community of converts declined "in numbers and morale," Kenneth Scott Latourette observed, "the Church seemed to be on the way to extinction."[19]

By that time, however, the Industrial Revolution was already helping generate religious revivals in the West and furnishing means by which evangelical piety, particularly that of the Protestants, could be exported to the rest of the world along with manufactured goods. In 1807 the first Protestant missionary, Robert Morrison of the London Missionary Society (LMS), arrived in Canton on an American merchant ship. Other missionary societies, American and European, soon sent their representatives to China as well. On the eve of the Opium War (1839–1842), some two dozen Protestant missionaries were found on the southern edge of the Qing Empire.[20] However, the "Canton System" of limited trade and the imperial prohibition of Christianity remained a formidable barrier to Protestant efforts. They also confined the Westerners for the most part inside the "thirteen factories" just outside the walled city of Guangzhou.

The Opium War changed all that. Following the war, China was forced to sign a series of unequal treaties that, after 1858, included official toleration of Christianity and granted Western missionaries broad access into the Middle Kingdom. In all, about eight thousand missionaries entered the country during the first one hundred years of the Protestant movement in China, the majority of them after 1860. In the half-century before 1949, an estimated twenty-three thousand missionaries, half of them Americans, worked in China for various lengths of time under more than one hundred foreign societies.[21] Besides evangelism, missionaries often pioneered in social reform and services and helped introduce modern medicine and education as well as Western culture. Missionary institutions such as St. John's University, Yenching University, and Xiang-Ya (Hunan-Yale) College of Medicine and Hospital, as well as Young

Men's Christian Associations (YMCAs) that dotted the urban Chinese landscape, became enduring symbols of the contribution of Protestant missions to China's modernization.

The prominent role of the missionary enterprise in the emergence of modern China belied the frustrations it experienced in achieving its primary goal of converting the Chinese. Antiforeignism bedeviled the Western evangelists from the start. As "part of the Western invasion," John King Fairbank notes, the missionary had derived "his privileged status and opportunity" from "gunfire and unequal treaties."[22] Not surprisingly, he was more likely to attract popular resentment and suspicion than mass conversions. One woman in rural Shanxi who had been the dressmaker for three generations of China Inland Mission (CIM) preachers confided that "there seemed little inducement to repent and be saved, if going to heaven would entail associating with foreigners for all eternity."[23] Such apathy paled, of course, beside the repeated, violent "missionary cases" (*jiao'an*)—of which there were more than four hundred by the end of the nineteenth century—that pitted the local people and gentry against Westerners.[24] Then, in 1900, the Christian community became the target of a bloody rampage by famished North China peasants known as the Boxers. Before foreign expeditionary forces quelled the uprising in August, hundreds of Western missionaries and untold thousands of Chinese converts had died.

In the early twentieth century, as rural xenophobia gave way to urban nationalism, Western missions continued to encounter periodic outbursts of hostility. In 1922, the Anti-Christian Movement, spurred by a general anti-imperialist mood, broke out in Shanghai and Beijing and spread through much of the country, generating student protests and boycotts in mission schools. In 1924, those agitations coalesced into a national campaign for the "restoration of educational rights," which demanded the removal of foreign control and the elimination of religious propaganda in mission schools.[25] Thereafter, popular opposition and occasional violence continued to be directed against Western missions as part of the broader anti-imperialist upheavals. In 1926, the Nationalist Party (Guomindang) in alliance with the Communists launched the Northern Expedition to eliminate warlords and to unify China. The following March, as the expedition reached Nanjing, radical elements in its ranks unleashed terror on the foreign community in the city, killing several Westerners, including the vice president of the missionary Nanking University (Jinling Daxue). The result was the exodus of more than five thousand of the eighty-three hundred Protestant missionaries from China, a blow from which the missions never fully recovered.[26] By the end of the Republican period (1912–1949), mission churches in China reported a total communicant membership of 623,000, which represented a little more than one-tenth of 1 percent of the Chinese population. Nearly a century and a half after Morrison arrived, it was "evident," Fairbank writes, "that the missionaries' long-continued effort, if measured in numbers of converts, had failed."[27]

THE CHAPTERS

Whatever influences the missionaries did have on the Chinese church, a significant part of the explanation for the subsequent flourishing of Protestant Christianity in China must be sought outside the missions and among indigenous groups. It is the latter that were chiefly responsible for turning Christianity from an alien faith into a spirited, popular religion. The pages that follow are dedicated to that search.

Chapter 1 begins in the nineteenth century, which saw a tantalizing potential for Western Christianity to become the faith of the Chinese through the Taiping Heavenly Kingdom. Though disavowed by most mainline Christians, the Taiping movement, with its proclamation of raw supernatural power and its messianic visions, foreshadowed the development of a viable Chinese species of Protestantism during the twentieth century. This chapter also explores the innovative opium-refuge churches of "Xi the Overcomer of Demons" in the 1880s, along with other forerunners of the mass Christianity of the Republican era. Woven into this and subsequent chapters is an account of the faltering efforts of Protestant missions to foster a Chinese Christianity, including the establishment of the interdenominational and nominally Chinese-led National Christian Council of China (NCC) and the Church of Christ in China during the 1920s.

In the early twentieth century, many denominational churches embarked on progressive efforts to make Christianity relevant to the struggles of modern China. They made symbolic accommodations to rising nationalism and often advocated a social Christianity to infuse Protestant spirit and values into Chinese attempts at nation-building. The results were often dubious. In contrast, self-proclaimed leaders of emerging, independent Protestant groups were gripped by an indefatigable, pre-millennial vision of the impending end of the world and of the Second Coming of Christ. Chapter 2 turns to the earliest of these groups, the True Jesus Church (TJC). Founded in 1917, the TJC became the first durable indigenous Protestant sect in China. It throve on its exuberant Pentecostalism, apocalyptic convictions, and opportune denunciations of missionary Christianity amidst mounting anti-imperialist sentiments. Despite its beginning as a pariah sect, the TJC went on to become the largest independent church toward the end of the missionary era in China.

Chapter 3 is the story of the Jesus Family, an independent Christian mutual-aid community formed in Shandong province during the 1920s against a bleak backdrop of natural disasters and a general breakdown of political order. Like the TJC, it was energized by end-time expectations. Its most distinctive feature, however, was a utopian pursuit of Christian communalism, one that found its triumph over poverty and wartime miseries in shared Pentecostal ecstasies. In fact, its rapturous worship and quest for a tight-knit community of love that shunned the world revealed a general bent of mass Christianity in China that continued well into the second half of the twentieth century.

Separatist as it was, the Jesus Family actually tapped into a broader stream of revivalism that spilled across North China and Manchuria during the 1930s, carrying with it the hopes and fears of displaced farmers and refugees. Chapter 4 traces the development that culminated in the so-called Shandong Revival. Complete with trances, visions, "tongues," and prophecies, such outbursts of piety, which bore an uncanny resemblance to spirit possession in popular religion, allowed for indigenous expressions of religious rapture in contrast to what Harvey Cox would call the "ecstasy deficit" in mainline denominational churches.[28] They also circumvented the authority and teachings of Western missionaries, catapulted lay Chinese into positions of spiritual leadership, and became a major catalyst in the emergence of indigenous Christianity.

Chapter 5 looks beyond the revivalist groups to the phenomenon of independent, itinerant preachers. It follows the rise of Wang Mingdao, whose unflinching, fundamentalist opposition to liberalism in Western-controlled churches endeared him to the grassroots Christians buffeted by surging antiforeignism. To what he termed the "fake medicine" of the Social Gospel, Wang opposed an individualistic Christianity of repentance and eschatological salvation, one that was in tune with the prevailing pessimism of the masses and their craving for spiritual and moral certainty. In this way, he exerted a broad influence on the Chinese church, which endured well into the Communist era.

Compared with Wang, a more colorful evangelist, in fact the most electrifying revivalist of twentieth-century China, was John Sung (Song Shangjie), the focus of Chapter 6. Sung was reputed to have proselytized one hundred thousand Chinese during the 1930s, about 20 percent of the half million Protestants estimated for 1935. Beyond his charisma, his flair for drama, and his alleged magic of faith healing, the paroxysms of mass conversions at his revival meetings pointed to the fathomless despair and agony of millions of his compatriots caught in the tumult of war and devastation. In the late twentieth century, long after Sung had passed out of the evangelistic scene, millions more would find themselves in similar convulsions under the spell of a steady procession of lesser charismatic preachers in the underground.

To average Chinese Protestants in the second quarter of the twentieth century, Wang Mingdao and John Sung were prophets gifted in jeremiads and apocalyptic utterances. But the one who mastered the syntax of prophecy—who discerned, beyond the myriad revelations, a coherent, complete, and majestic divine scheme of human destiny as it neared its finale—was Watchman Nee (Ni Tuosheng), the founder of the Little Flock. Chapter 7 traces the origin of Nee's sect and the development of his intricate eschatology. Often touted as the leading Chinese theologian of the twentieth century, Nee displayed his real genius in transmitting the premillennial dispensationalist teachings of the Plymouth Brethren. In contrast to the sometimes orgiastic religiosity of the revivalists, Nee's followers pined for a profound, numinous union with God. In the process, they achieved, like Daoist mystics, what Max Weber would call "apathetic ecstasy."[29] What Nee fashioned was a theology of triumph over the blight of existence, which came to dominate the Christianity of the Chinese masses as its chief source of inspiration.

In Chapter 8, I bring together the narratives of these various groups and follow their rise and fall in the tide of war and revolution toward the end of the Republican era. I also provide a brief account of what befell them, and Chinese Christianity in general, during the first decade of Communist rule. It was a development that, though grim at the time, actually primed the church for the explosive growth in the post-Mao period.

The concluding chapter explores the emergence of new, unauthorized "house churches" after the Cultural Revolution (1966–1976). In the last quarter of the twentieth century, leading indigenous sects of the Republican period completed their journey from revelation to institutionalization within the official Three-Self (self-government, self-support, and self-propagation) framework. Meanwhile, the original messianic flame passed on to new spin-off groups as fresh cycles of the sectarian evolution began. Far more animated and with a following much larger than the legitimate Three-Self churches, underground Christianity throve in the face of social dislocation and state repression and has acquired both the official designation and the temperament of sectarian heterodoxy—with manifest potentials for continuing, radical mutation. As it spills beyond the boundaries of Western Christianity in both theology and practice, it also helps form the contemporary tide of the Christianity of "the global South and East."[30]

THE SUBJECT AND THE PROPOSITIONS

It should be noted that, historically, the naturalization of Christianity in China first took place in the Roman Catholic Church. The first Chinese bishop, Luo Wenzao (Gregory Lopez), was appointed by Pope Clement X in 1674. At the grassroots level, as D. E. Mungello points out, Catholicism under state persecution in the eighteenth century "began to be absorbed . . . into the indigenous tradition of sectarian heterodoxies." Western clergy, who had been driven underground if not already expelled, were powerless to "control these forces of assimilation." As the Christians incorporated local shamanistic elements, they demonstrated the efficacy of their faith by summoning rain during a drought or generating miraculous sightings of the cross in the sky. After the 1720s, Catholicism survived as a popular religion, a Christian heresy in the eyes of Qing officials and, not infrequently, the European missionaries as well. Significantly, the dominance of the West after the Opium War and the new power of foreign missionaries "had the effect of weakening the forces of assimilation" and making Christianity "more foreign."[31] In any event, after Luo, no Chinese bishop was named until 1926 when, in response to nationalist upheavals in the country, Pius XI consecrated six Chinese bishops in

Rome. However, with ecclesiastic control and finances ultimately in the hands of missionaries, the Catholic Church, in the words of Jean-Paul Wiest, "remained, for all practical purposes, a foreign institution" down to 1949.[32]

In contrast to Catholicism, which is not included in this narrative, far-reaching adaptations of Christianity began in the early twentieth century among Protestants. Those efforts, initiated by local leaders, led to the emergence of a lively, indigenous Protestantism at the grassroots level— the subject of this book. Nevertheless, in referring to it, I make liberal use of the term "popular Christianity." Part of the reason for such liberality is historical: during the first half of the century, Protestants of various denominational backgrounds increasingly dominated the Chinese church and eclipsed the influence of the Catholics. In the process, they came to appropriate the word "Christian" in connection with what was often essentially Protestant work.[33] Consequently, in historical discourse in the Chinese language, *Jidujiao* (Christianity) is typically reserved for Protestantism, and *Tianzhujiao* (the Teaching of the Lord of Heaven) denotes Roman Catholicism. What, then, constitutes "popular" Christianity? For the Republican period, I find it mostly outside denominational missions, even though its influence also spread among them. After 1949, it retained its antiestablishment predilection and throve in opposition to the Three-Self churches, although the latter were not impervious to its irrepressible energy. During both periods, it captured the religious fervor and creativity of the masses that were excluded, for the most part, from the pursuits of the elite in Chinese society.

As we look into the emergence of popular Christianity in twentieth-century China, we can discern some of its general features. First, it began to ferment in the early Republican period in a climate of rising nationalism symbolized by the May Fourth Movement. With widespread, public resentment directed against the Western presence in the country, the Christian community as a whole came under intense pressure to dissociate itself from imperialism. For the committed followers of the Protestant religion, which was often denounced as the "vanguard of imperialism," independent Christianity was probably the utmost act of dissociation. In general, indigenous preachers and sectarian leaders chose to sanctify their revolt against Western control of the Chinese church as an uprising against spiritual decadence and evil. They envisioned unfolding cosmic

容真牧司大羅教主華一第國中

FIGURE 1 Luo Wenzao (Gregory Lopez, 1616–1691), the first Chinese priest and bishop. Source: *Chinese Recorder* 58 (September 1927).

dramas in which God's elect in China were assigned a central role in the redemptive scheme. Such self-assurance continues in today's underground churches. In fact, in proclaiming a messianic salvation launched from China, the indigenous church has continually exhibited the assertiveness, and at times the ethnocentrism, found in the broader patriotic movement. In many ways, it has also been a more persistent, and no less flamboyant, form of nationalism compared with some of the virulent outbreaks of antiforeignism in modern China.

On the other hand, it is important to note an earthy side to the nationalism of mass Christianity. During the first half of the twentieth century, much of its opposition to Western missions was grounded in local rivalries with established denominational churches over ecclesiastical power and the recruitment of followers from the existing community of converts. In that sense, its patriotism often failed to transcend its more immediate sectarian interests. More importantly, there were intrinsic limits to the ability of religious sects to participate in nationalist pursuits. Neither the establishment of a prosperous, sovereign state nor the construction of a just social order upon the foundation of political unity approximated the millenarian visions of indigenous sects. As Ernst Troeltsch reminded us, because of its revolutionary principle of "unlimited individualism and universalism," Christianity "has a disintegrating effect upon all undiluted nationalism and upon every form of exclusively earthly authority." In the case of apocalyptic Protestant groups fired by their "idealistic anarchism," the characteristic hostility toward the secular social order and indifference toward the worldly dreams of a nation would hardly be mitigated.[34]

Compared with nationalism, a more conscious and sustained, and more sustaining, drive in the Protestant movement in modern China came from messianic convictions. Ostensibly Christian in theology but no less traditionally Chinese in temperament, popular millenarianism came to define the indigenous, largely sectarian, Christianity in the twentieth century. Although the latter consisted of disparate, often competing, groups, its diverse components shared a basic trait of mass eschatological religion: the vision of an impending catastrophic end of this world and the redemption of the spiritual elite who were privy to the messianic scheme. Throughout the war-torn Republican period, when cosmic catastrophe loomed large on the Chinese horizon, independent evangelists were also able to combine collective eschatology with, to borrow Norman Cohn's phrase, "eschatology of the individual soul."[35] In this way they generated further urgency and dramatic tension—and assured relief through public penance and conversion—in their meetings. Likewise, in the last three decades, underground church leaders have had little difficulty fitting the social and economic dislocation as well as official persecution into an apocalyptic scheme.

Under certain conditions, as in the midst of postdynastic chaos during the first half of the twentieth century, some sectarian groups also offered the tangible benefits of mutual aid and protection through varying degrees of communalism. A more common feature of their end-time salvationism, however, was Pentecostal effervescence, including glossolalia, trances, and sublime visions of heaven, as well as miraculous healing and exorcism. This was generally the case with the TJC, the Jesus Family, and the revivals of the 1930s. Even the Little Flock, which proclaimed a more sublime eschatological revelation in its dispensationalist mysticism, also briefly adopted Pentecostal and communitarian practices. In contemporary China, the underground church has displayed an unabated vigor in a similar vein. Like the earlier groups, it has generated an intimate experience of the divine and found a way to open the floodgate of celestial power, to channel its flow, to deluge the world and its evils, and to drench oneself in heavenly ecstasies as one awaits the return of the Savior.

To a large extent, as we shall see, the millenarian quest that energized mass Chinese Christianity in the twentieth century was not indigenous but was adapted from the West. Its main features are consistent with those in the long tradition of the radical pursuit of the millennium in Western Christianity that has been unveiled by Norman Cohn and Paul Boyer among others.[36] On the other hand, they also accord with the characteristics of traditional millenarian sects in Chinese society that have been studied by C. K. Yang, Daniel L. Overmyer, Susan Naquin, and Jean Chesneaux, and by Ma Xisha and Han Bingfang. Those traits often include trances, miracles, exorcism, mass penance, and, above all, the anticipation of a period of great cataclysms followed by a perfect new world that a messianic deliverer will usher in (see the Afterword).

In a pioneering study more than two decades ago, Daniel H. Bays argued that a "sectarian-Christian fusion" had occurred in the late Qing period, which brought many adherents of salvationist Buddhist groups into Christianity.[37] As the new religion spread among the masses after

Qing, its messianic and ecstatic elements converged with those in the Chinese tradition. In fact, the emergence of homegrown churches since the Republican era points to an evolution of popular religion in modern China, when Christianity joined indigenous beliefs in supplying the core ideology of sectarian movements. Like most messianic convulsions in Chinese history, the drive toward a fiery, apocalyptic Christianity in modern China was largely induced by political, national, and environmental crises, and by momentous social change along with overwhelming personal distress; it has also brought forth a religious response on a matching chiliastic scale.

At the start of a new, still earthly, millennium, one cannot help wondering about the potential role of popular Christianity in shaping the future of the most populous country in the world. Despite all the secularist complacency of our time, religion remains, as Samuel P. Huntington contends, "a central, perhaps *the* central, force that motivates and mobilizes people."[38] This is a book about the gathering of some of that force. In the course of the past century, an alien faith that had accompanied the coming of the West and that had been a constant reminder of China's modern woes was transformed into a vibrant popular religion that promised deliverance from those woes. It offered redemption from the collapse of the imperial order, the fire of war and revolution, the social upheavals of today, and the perils of tomorrow. It has, in sum, fostered a new form of messianism in a country where millenarian movements have been one of the few possible ways to channel the aspirations and the discontent of the masses.

CHAPTER ONE

In Search of Chinese Christianity

IN AUGUST 1834, Robert Morrison died in his middle life, worn out by a quarter of a century of pioneering and consuming labors to bring "the light of science and revelation" to the "Eastern limit of Asia." At the time, those labors were not particularly promising: in some twenty-five years he and a handful of his missionary colleagues had baptized only about ten Chinese. By 1840, when war had broken out between the British and the Chinese and more than three decades after Morrison landed in Canton, the total number of converts in the Middle Kingdom was less than one hundred.[1] It was likely in light of such statistics from mission fields that, in the mid-nineteenth century, leading Anglo-American missionary administrators began to call for "self-support and self-government and self-extension" in order to facilitate "the healthy growth and expansion of the Native Church."[2]

Whether or not the goal of autonomy and self-support seemed possible at the time, Protestant missionaries did not fail to see that much of the actual work of proselytizing would have to be shouldered by local converts. It was Liang Fa (also Liang Afa), a printer who had been won over to the new faith while in the employ of the LMS missionary William Milne, who made the first attempt to reach the gentry. In 1830, Liang in the company of a fellow convert "itinerated 250 miles into the interior of China, following in the train of one of the public examiners. They

FIGURE 2 Dr. Robert Morrison and his assistants. From a painting by George Chinnery in 1828. The writer sitting is Mr. Le; the name of the one standing is unknown. Source: *Chinese Recorder* 65 (August 1934).

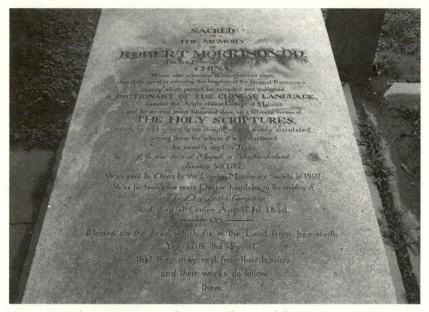

FIGURE 3 Robert Morrison's tomb, Macau. Photograph by Lian Xi.

thus had free access to the young literati at every examination center and distributed upwards of 7,000 tracts."[3] Among the Western missionaries, efforts to institutionalize such Chinese initiatives led to the formation of a widely acclaimed, and for a while promising, "native" evangelical enterprise known as the Chinese Union (Fuhanhui).

By 1844, with the recent conclusion of the Opium War and the signing of treaties that brought limited toleration of Christianity by the Qing court—which included the right granted to Westerners in the five treaty ports (Canton, Xiamen, Fuzhou, Ningbo, and Shanghai) to build hospitals, churches, and cemeteries—a new phase of Protestant missions in China had begun. On the other hand, the permission for Western evangelists to travel out of the treaty ports to propagate their religion would not be granted until a new round of treaties in 1858. To take full advantage of the historic opportunity and to raise an army of local evangelists to spread the Gospel in the meantime, the Chinese Union was formed in Hong Kong in 1844. Its founder was the independent Prussian evangelist-adventurer Karl Gützlaff, who had originally been appointed by the Netherlands Missionary Society in 1826. Following his daring trips during the early 1830s sailing up the coast of China (sometimes on board opium ships) to distribute Christian literature in defiance of Qing laws, Gützlaff had become known as "the apostle to China." (The less adoring Arthur Waley would later characterize him as "a cross between parson and pirate, charlatan and genius, philanthropist and crook.")[4]

At its inception, the Chinese Union consisted of nineteen Chinese and two Western missionaries, Gützlaff himself and Issacher J. Roberts, an "eccentric but earnest" American Baptist missionary who had arrived in 1837 and who was well known for his later connections with the Taiping Rebellion. The organization was placed nominally under the leadership of two Chinese converts but remained largely a Gützlaff enterprise. As a training center and headquarters for Chinese evangelists who would penetrate the interior, then still inaccessible to foreign missionaries, it embodied Gützlaff's dreams of bringing about mass conversions by making Christianity Chinese. A handful of missionary instructors and supervisors that Gützlaff recruited for the Chinese Union would dress, eat, and live like the Chinese. To advance the Gospel, Gützlaff had even had himself "adopted" into a clan in southern Fujian when he took Guo as his Chinese surname (Guo Shila, for Gützlaff), and at one point he made an evangelical trip to the Guo hometown near Amoy (Xiamen) under the pretense of making sacrifices to his ancestors.[5]

As Jessie G. Lutz has shown, the Chinese Union at first appeared to grow rapidly and soon reported hundreds of baptisms each year in contrast to the meager gains in the membership of denominational mission churches. By 1850 the organization counted (unreliably as it turned out) 1,871 members, of which 200 were itinerant preachers. A large number of those who joined the Chinese Union were "Hong Kong day laborers and drifters who had migrated from villages on the mainland." Filled with an apostolic zeal and ambition that was matched by his capacity for hyperbole, the exuberant Gützlaff sent back to Europe eloquent reports that gave rise to hopes that every province in China would be reached and millions would be saved in such a native evangelical operation. In reality, however, many of the preachers Gützlaff hired never left the Hong Kong area; they filed false reports of evangelical journeys to the interior in return for the stipends that Gützlaff provided. Some colporteurs for the Chinese Union "resold their tracts to book suppliers to be repurchased by Gützlaff." A number of Gützlaff's assistants had apparently joined the

Chinese Union for monetary purposes, often to maintain their opium habits or to repay their debts.[6] Hoodwinked by numerous Chinese Union members, the Prussian visionary missionary died a broken man in 1851, and the organization, whose reputation had suffered by then following investigations into its scandals, lingered on for another four years before closing its doors. Some of its members left to join the Triads (Tiandihui), the most widespread secret society that offered religious rituals and mutual protection. In the words of Lutz, the Chinese Union was "so much the creature of [Gützlaff] and his personality that it ceased to have life when the umbilical cord was cut."[7] Conditions for a real indigenous church were not there. Meanwhile, in the entire country, communicant membership in mission churches totaled just 350 in 1853 despite Gützlaff's earlier extravagant claims.[8]

THE TAIPING HEAVENLY KINGDOM

Yet by the time Gützlaff died, in the hinterland Thistle Mountain of eastern Guangxi province, mass conversions to Christianity were already taking place, with hundreds being baptized on some days and about twenty thousand "God Worshipers" under the banner of the Taiping Heavenly Kingdom when it was proclaimed in the spring of 1851.[9] The founder of the Taiping movement Hong Xiuquan (1814–1864) hailed from rural Guangdong. As a member of the Hakka ("guest people"), a minority ethnic group that had migrated there over the previous centuries from North and Central China, he was familiar with the hardships of village life exacerbated by an almost fourfold increase of population (to nearly four hundred million) since the beginning of the Qing dynasty. The chronic tension between the Hakka and the local people often flared up into deadly communal violence.[10] At the age of fifteen, Hong began taking the official examinations that, if passed at the prefectural level, would give him a licentiate's degree (shengyuan) as well as the privileged status of the gentry. He passed the preliminary test but never succeeded in the main licentiate's examination that was held in the prefectural capital Canton.[11]

In 1837, after failing the examination for the third time, Hong suffered a nervous breakdown. He was delirious for days, during which he proclaimed that he had been crowned "Heavenly King, Monarch of the Great Principle, Quan" and leapt about his room shouting orders to his invisible army to behead the demons who had brought "distress and suf-fering" to the world. In 1843, Hong made his fourth and final attempt at the prefectural examination in Canton, which he failed yet again. Shortly afterward, a Christian tract that he had received back in 1836 began to speak to him. Written by Liang Fa and titled "Good Words to Admon-ish the Age" (*Quanshi liangyan*), it quoted passages from the Christian scriptures and introduced to Hong a biblical world of divine creation and redemption, of God's wrath and punishment, and of the terrifying end of time as foretold in the Revelation. A year after the humiliating defeat of China by the British in the Opium War, the apocalyptic warnings and assurances of complete deliverance contained in Liang's tract struck a deep chord in Hong. He baptized himself one night with a basin of water set in his courtyard.[12]

It was a potent conversion, for the new faith brought order to the chaos that had ravaged Hong's crowded mind and the world around him. And it imparted clarity and meaning to the extraordinary experience he had had during his delirium in 1837: according to the Taiping's official account, numerous angels had descended at the time to escort Hong up to heaven in a sedan chair—with an "orchestra at the head of the proces-sion, followed by the God of Thunder, walking like a rooster."[13] In heaven, by imperial command, his stomach was cut open, removed, and replaced with a new one. His Heavenly Mother washed his "unclean" body in the river; his Heavenly Father, "the supreme Lord and Great God," who was "clothed in a black dragon robe" and had "golden whiskers which came down to cover his stomach," received him in sadness and anger. He told Hong that the people of the world had "lost their original hearts" and their awe and respect for him and had been deluded and misled by evil demons. (They had also been led astray by Confucius, whose books con-tained "extremely numerous errors and faults" and had confused people's minds.) The Great God then gave Hong "a golden seal and a sword" as well as a host of angels to drive all the demons from the "thirty-three levels of heaven" down into the world where Hong's heavenly army beheaded them in droves. God also ordered him to descend to the world to enlighten and save the people. And so he did, as "the true ordained son of Heaven," and with a conviction of his mission that would in time lead to the founding of the Taiping Heavenly Kingdom.[14]

By 1844, Hong had embarked on itinerant preaching among his relatives and members of his Hakka clan, which eventually took him to a village near Thistle Mountain in Guiping county, Guangxi province. There his followers formed the Society of God Worshipers in 1845.[15] As Hong Rengan, Hong Xiuquan's cousin and one of the later Taiping "kings," explained, "the displaced people, helping the old and carrying the young, all came to [the Society]." Constant intervillage fighting between the locals and the minority Hakkas at the time added a sense of urgency. In most cases, conversions were not of individuals alone; new congregations were often made of whole families and clans or whole occupational groups, such as charcoal burners and miners, or of entire villages.[16] To this Hakka nucleus was later added the displaced peasantry of South China. They in turn were joined by former pirates (driven inland after the British seized control of the Canton area), a few traders, unemployed porters, members of secret societies, occasionally wealthier peasants, local gentry, and deserters from the government's armed forces. To them Hong promised "myriads of years of eternal happiness and glory . . . in heaven."[17]

Having sprung from Hong's revelations, the Taiping movement would be borne also on the wings of continuous displays of unearthly power by Hong's lieutenants. According to Hong Rengan, "innumerable miracles were manifested by God and Jesus Christ. The dumb began to talk and the insane to recover." Prophecies of imminent pestilence and devastation and communal fighting with the locals abounded.[18] By 1848, as the Society of God Worshipers grew rapidly in rural Guangxi, trances were becoming routine among the believers. At prayer sessions, people would come forth and make strange utterances while in the state of spirit possession, a familiar local form of divination and sorcery.[19] Although most of the people who thus spoke up were "incoherent," a charcoal burner named Yang Xiuqing distinguished himself when he became possessed by the Heavenly Father himself. (Another God Worshiper by the name of Xiao Chaogui assumed the voice of Jesus, Hong's Elder Brother.)[20] In the years that followed (until his violent death in 1856), Yang would be the mouthpiece of the Heavenly Father, in whose name he issued proclamations, uncovered treasons, and, toward the end, chastised Hong and demanded to share his title of "Ten Thousand Years."

As Hong had only a brief brush with missionary Christianity—he had studied the Bible with the American Baptist missionary Issacher Roberts in Canton for a few months in 1847—he was quite free to develop a Chinese form of Protestantism that adapted well to local traditions. During services, which would include "incense-sticks and gold paper," two burning lamps were placed on the table (where an altar with a tablet dedicated to the ancestors used to stand), along with three cups of tea to make a simple offering; in prayer, the whole congregation knelt toward the sun. "Every new convert would kneel down, read aloud a written prayer of repentance, and burn it"—a common practice in popular religion when "memorials" were sent to the gods in flames. Then, "a bowl of water was poured over his head. After that he would rise, take and drink a cup of tea, and use a bowl of water to wash his chest around the area of the heart to signify the cleansing of the heart and the transformation of his body [*xixin gemian*]. . . . At dawn and dusk, the congregation would receive written prayers prepared by Hong . . . which they called memorials [to the Heavenly Father], and chant them."[21]

GOD'S LITTLE HEAVEN

From its beginning, the religion of the God Worshipers, set afire by Hong's fury against the imperial system that had thwarted his youthful dreams, remained iconoclastic. Its militancy, fostered by intensified conflicts with the locals and by government efforts at "bandit suppression," eventually erupted into an uprising against the Qing rule. In 1851, Hong declared the founding of the Taiping Heavenly Kingdom in the mountainous southwestern province of Guangxi. Over the next two years, the Taiping conquered much of Central China as well as the former Ming capital Nanjing and almost brought down the Qing dynasty. Its followers also grew to more than one million during the 1850s.[22] In Nanjing, after slaughtering some forty thousand Manchu "demons" trapped inside the city walls, Hong established "God's Little Heaven" in 1853. There, Hong and the other lesser Taiping "kings" sought to create a perfect world of equality, morality, and material abundance. They instituted a radical asceticism that included segregation of the sexes, for both the married and the unmarried, and bans on opium smoking, gambling, prostitution, dancing, and alcohol drinking.[23] In 1854, the Taiping published "The Land System of the Heavenly Dynasty" (*Tianchao tianmu zhidu*). Modeled after the legendary system described in the *Rites of the Zhou Dynasty* (*Zhouli*), the Taiping scheme mandated that land was to be divided equally among all the inhabitants of the Heavenly Kingdom and that public granaries and treasuries, where all the surplus from individual families was to be deposited, would provide for the needs of all: "There being fields, let all cultivate them; there being food, let all eat; there being clothes, let all be dressed; there being money, let all use it, so that nowhere does inequality exist, and no man is not well fed and clothed . . . for the whole empire is the universal family of our Heavenly Father."[24]

Such an egalitarian community was to be maintained, however, within a highly centralized and hierarchical political structure. Taiping's basic unit was the squad, made up of twenty-five families and administered by a sergeant. The latter organized household production—each family was to plant mulberry trees and raise five hens and two sows—settled disputes, presided over marriages and funerals, maintained the public granary, made sacrifices to the Heavenly Father, and led religious worship on the Sabbath. The regimentation of Taiping lives also led to the creation of battalions of specialized craftsmen, including carpenters and masons, goldsmiths, cobblers, and weavers, that at times numbered up to twenty thousand people.[25]

For the most part, however, "the land system of the Heavenly dynasty" remained an ideal that was not put into practice.[26] Its chief significance lies perhaps in its articulation of a utopian vision that was Chinese in its nature but Christian in its vocabulary. After the Taiping took Nanjing in 1853 and renamed it Tianjing, or Heavenly Capital, Hong sought to find in Christian eschatology proof that the rebellion fit into the millennial scheme of his Heavenly Father. In that scheme—which he uncovered in his "Annotations to the New Testament" (1853)—"The new Jerusalem sent down from heaven . . . is our present Heavenly Capital," the "divine kingdom on earth" and "God's Little Heaven." "The Great Heaven or heaven above is where souls return in glory," he wrote. "The Little Heaven among men is where physical bodies return in glory to God." In more traditional terms, one Taiping official explained, "Our Heavenly King, having personally received God's mandate, shall eternally rule over mountains and rivers. . . . thousands and hundreds of generations of boundless happiness should be founded for eternity."[27]

It is impossible to ascertain the degree to which such convictions were shared among the rank-and-file rebels, but it does appear that as a whole the millenarian hope both inspired and sustained the Taiping movement, so that even when it came to its fiery end in 1864, many of its followers retained their steeled tenacity. As Zeng Guofan, leader of the victorious suppression campaign, reported to the emperor, "not one of the 100,000 rebels in Nanjing surrendered themselves when the city was taken but in many cases gathered together and burned themselves and passed away without repentance. Such a formidable band of rebels has been rarely known from ancient times to the present."[28]

TOWARD AUTONOMY: "SELF-SUPPORTING" CHURCHES IN LATE-QING COASTAL CHINA

The Taiping Heavenly Kingdom was the only significant indigenous movement among Chinese Christians during the nineteenth century. After all, the imperial court, for all its ineffectiveness in dealing with the foreign menace and domestic problems, was intent upon nipping any popular religious movement and banned secret societies altogether. Because of the grand collapse of the Taiping rebellion and the overall control of the Protestant community by Western missionaries who were inclined more toward reform than revolution, Christianity did not rise again as a spontaneous mass messianic movement in the last decades of the Qing dynasty. Under the protection of the unequal treaties, and supervised by Western denominational missions, the Christian move-ment in China remained a subdued one—both in its numbers and in its capacity for indigenous initiative and innovation. It was only after the collapse of the central authority of Qing, along with the swell of Chinese nationalism in subsequent decades, that an ideal climate developed for popular Christian movements.

In a few isolated cases, however, we see late-Qing attempts at inde-pendent Christianity among Protestant converts. Typically they followed the emergence of small bodies of middle-class or wealthy members of mission churches in treaty ports or rose under the influence of ambi-tious leaders who enjoyed the gentry status. In 1862, union efforts under-taken by the (Dutch) Reformed Church in America and the English Pres-byterians in Amoy (Xiamen), Fujian, resulted in the formation of the Quanzhou-Zhangzhou Presbyterian Assembly (Quan-Zhang Zhanglao Dahui). The two missions granted the assembly a degree of independ-ence, and two of their churches in Amoy began to hire and support their own native pastors. A decade later, the LMS of Amoy also christened its first self-supporting Chinese ministers. Such experiments were limited, however, as the majority of annual funds, including salaries for the rest of the Chinese personnel, the expenses for the schools, and the rent for the church buildings, continued to come from the missions.[29] In the provincial capital Fuzhou, where the first representatives of the American Board of Commissioners for Foreign Missions (ABCFM) had arrived in 1847, the first call for self-support came from a Congregational minister in 1896, but it was not until 1911 that local Congregational preachers took the first symbolic step toward autonomy and formed a Preachers' Self-Governing Society.[30]

In Hong Kong, a handful of self-governing churches began to emerge during the 1880s, often with help from individual missionaries and sympathetic missions such as the LMS and the ABCFM. As the Qing political crisis deepened in the 1890s, some of the reformers and revolutionaries began to meet in autonomous Chinese churches to discuss the "new learning." It was the To Tsai Independent Church (Daoji Huitang)—the first self-supporting church in Hong Kong, which evolved out of an LMS mission during the late 1880s—that Sun Yat-sen attended while pursuing his education in Western medicine at a nearby school.[31]

In the northern province of Shandong, where American Baptist and Presbyterian missionaries arrived following the Tianjin Treaty of 1858, attempts at autonomy among local converts resulted in the formation of the Shandong Evangelistic Association of the Grateful (Shandong Chou'en Chuandaohui) in 1885. The association was made up primarily of students at the Presbyterian Tengchow College (Dengzhou Wenhuiguan) and dedicated itself to itinerant evangelism in the interior of the province on the principle of self-support. However, the association did not hold together for long; by 1904, it had rejoined the American Presbyterian mission.[32] In some rural areas of Shandong where the resources of foreign missions were stretched thin, local converts often practiced a degree of self-support by default, yet none of this blossomed into full-fledged independence. Invariably, the missionaries returned and brought such groups back within denominational bounds.[33]

XI THE OVERCOMER OF DEMONS

During the last decades of the Qing dynasty, only extraordinary circumstances coupled with rare personalities resulted in occasional genuine forms of Chinese Christianity untamed by the denominationalism of the missions. In the northern province of Shanxi, a charismatic leader styled Xi the Overcomer of Demons (Xi Shengmo) emerged after the great famine of 1877–1879, which claimed five million victims in that province alone, or one-third of its population. Xi was from a village near the prefectural capital of Pingyang (now Linfen City), the epicenter of the famine. Born in 1835 to a respected family of degree holders and practitioners of traditional medicine, Xi (original name Xi Zizhi) obtained the licentiate's degree (shengyuan) at the age of sixteen and, following the deaths of his parents, inherited a sizable amount of land. Before he reached the age of thirty, he was already a well-established member of the landholding gentry in southern Shanxi. The death of his wife, however, led to depression, which he sought to alleviate with the help of the "foreign smoke" (as opium was then called)—at a time when Shanxi province emerged as one of the largest producers of domestic opium. As Alvyn Austin put it, Xi was soon reduced to a "broken-down scholar" and an "opium sot" who "lay on his bed for a year and a half hallucinating that he had descended into hell."[34]

After he was converted by the renowned British Methodist missionary David Hill in 1879, Xi was cured of his drug addiction. His visions and dreams remained, however, and became the driving force for his evangelical work (as did his "imperious temper"). Like Hong Xiuquan, Xi would see himself "ascending into heaven, where the Holy Spirit sent him back to earth to save suffering humanity." He developed the gifts of healing and exorcism. The first demon he cast out was from his second wife, a "moody and restless" peasant woman who would sometimes break into "paroxysms of ungovernable rage." Soon Xi was going about the neighboring villages performing miracles of faith healing and exorcising demons.[35]

In 1886, Hudson Taylor, founder and director of the CIM, came to Pingyang and ordained Xi as a CIM minister and made him superintending pastor of three CIM districts in the area. However, in an unusual arrangement, most likely at his own insistence, Xi received no salary from the mission and was given a rather free hand in his work. In fact, the Cambridge Seven—the most celebrated recruits made by the CIM in 1884, including the stroke of the university crew and the captain of the cricket team—who had arrived in Pingyang the year before, refrained from claiming "the divine right" (as one of them put it) of missionaries and worked under Xi for a time as his "helpers."[36] As some of them found out, Xi's "exegesis of Scripture was often at fault and fanciful," yet the Overcomer of Demons believed that "God had given him a position like Moses . . . and in expecting the subjection of others to his authority, he thought he was carrying out the Divine Will."[37]

In the 1880s, after the recent famine, many peasants in Shanxi had turned to the cultivation of opium as a cash crop (which brought five times the price of wheat), and soon, in some villages, "eleven out of every ten smoked opium," as the local saying went. In 1881, two years after his conversion, Xi opened his first Opium Refuge, which doubled as a self-supporting mission station. When Western medicine for the treatment of opium addiction ran out, he received "through prayer and fasting" divine guidance on making effective but inexpensive "Life-imparting Pills" and "Life-establishing Pills" from traditional herbs. (The formula for the latter allegedly came from the Holy Spirit in a dream.) Xi also made other pills for a variety of ailments. One was called "Paradise Pill" (*leyuan wanzi*), a favorite prescription.[38] In time, he would open forty-five such refuges—which he called the Heavenly Invitation Office (Tianzhaoju)—in Shanxi as well as in the neighboring provinces of Henan, Shaanxi, and Zhili where he and his associates preached the "Holy Religion of Jesus" and dispensed medicines manufactured at Xi's home (which was renamed Zhong Leyuan, or the Middle Paradise). The CIM decided that while "the Mission as such has nothing to do with his Opium Refuge work," it would support such medical evangelism "on purely native lines."[39]

In its heyday, as M. Geraldine Taylor, CIM missionary and Hudson Taylor's daughter-in-law, put it, Xi's family compound and farm became "quite a School of Prophets. . . . At the present time two hundred of these are engaged in carrying on the work of the refuges."[40] However, while the missionaries rhapsodized about the "work of God" under "native leader-ship" in southern Shanxi and called Xi's Opium Refuge "an entering wedge" for the CIM, at least some who followed Xi and joined his enter-prise were driven by entrepreneurial ambitions. In fact, several of Xi's partners later broke up with him (and almost killed him) and set up rival refuges in scores of places and undersold Xi's prices for the medicines. Other impostors would arise and open refuges under Xi's name, making large profits before they "cleared out" and disappeared.[41]

Meanwhile, Xi persisted in producing his impeccably named pills and in building self-supporting native congregations centered on his Opium

Refuges in more than a dozen market towns and about thirty villages. By the time of his death in 1896, he had baptized about seven hundred people and had also written more than one hundred hymns, most of which he set to popular North China tunes.[42] Many of Xi's hymns were in the typical evangelical vein that would easily find approval among the missionaries; some borrowed Buddhist language to expose the "emptiness" of the dreamlike "red dust" of this world and to exhort sinners to enter into the "heavenly city . . . and the holy capital." Like the leaders of independent Protestant sects in the twentieth century, Xi was under pressure to assure his audience that Christianity was not a Western religion. One of his hymns explained that Jesus was "not the Westerners' sage, nor the Westerners' ancestor" but "the son of the living God who descended from the heavenly court."[43] In some of the most popular of Xi's hymns, one detects a flicker of millenarian flame that may have contributed to his reputation as a preacher "full of life and fire." The following lines from one of his hymns remind one of the ambitions of Hong Xiuquan a few decades earlier:

> When thou wouldst awaken the masses,
>   Then I would be the golden bell . . .
> When thou wouldst rid the world of the evil of the wolves,
>   Then I would be the spear and the sword . . .
>   to exterminate all the jackals and the wolves . . .
> When thou wouldst send the heavenly army,
>   Then I would be the command flag . . .
> Defeating all the demons, we will sing for eternity the song of
>   victory.[44]

It was a flame well contained, however, in the lampshade of the institutional and doctrinal safeguards of the CIM. In fact, during the last ten years of his life as an ordained CIM minister, Xi was always "advised" by D. E. Hoste, one of the Cambridge Seven who stayed with Xi as the local missionary-in-charge and who would later succeed Hudson Taylor as director of the CIM.[45] Hoste compared Xi to the "stroke," the pace-setter in rowing, and himself to coxswain: "It was a cox that was wanted, because Pastor Hsi was perfectly well able to stroke the boat. . . . What you wanted was a little man to sort of steer." In the end, Xi was steered clear of any material attempt to rid the world of evils, although he never ceased in his zealous campaign—at times joined by some of the Cambridge Seven—to cast out "demons" in the North China countryside.[46] After Xi's death in 1896, many of his followers returned to opium and became apostates. One close associate, who had succeeded Xi as an administrator of the Opium Refuges and had used his association with the CIM to win "law-cases and village disputes," also renounced Christianity and went back to opium smoking.[47]

AFTER THE BOXERS: THE RISE OF INDEPENDENT CHURCHES

By 1900, the year the Boxer Uprising broke out, it was clear that no significant independent Christian communities had endured in China. Almost one hundred years after the arrival of Robert Morrison, Christianity remained a foreign enterprise. D. E. Hoste, who in his ten years of association with Xi Shengmo had seen perhaps the most promising form of indigenous Christianity in late-nineteenth-century China, concluded nevertheless that "under the system hitherto generally in force the work has centred round the missionary; executive authority and financial control have been in his hands. For the most part, the native brethren engaged in it have been dependent upon funds administered by him for support, and have held their position at his discretion. . . . the system hitherto in general use . . . practically postpones indefinitely the independence and self-government in the native churches."[48]

For their part, most Chinese converts in the nineteenth century saw little need to dissociate themselves from missions or to form separate churches. In fact, affiliation with mission churches would bring tangible benefits in terms of social standing and educational and employment opportunities for the converts. As a result of the gunboat diplomacy after the Opium War, the prestige and influence of Western missionaries in China steadily increased until, in 1899, Roman Catholic missionaries were accorded official status by the Qing government, with the rank of a bishop corresponding to that of a viceroy or provincial governor and a priest being equal to a prefect. Under the "most-favored nation" clause in the treaties, the same official status applied to Protestant missionaries.[49] Western evangelists' assistance in lawsuits involving their converts was in much demand. As one missionary put it, one only had to "get hold of the missionary's card and take it into the Yamen on behalf of a litigant" to win a case.[50] Among those churches that achieved a degree of self-support, relationships with missionaries remained typically cordial and essentially subordinate. In general, Chinese Protestants felt no sense of urgency to cut their umbilical cords with Western missions.

The Boxer Uprising marked a turning point; it shattered any sense of security that Christian converts might have felt in the protective shadow of Western missions. As the culmination of nineteenth-century anti-foreign and anti-Christian agitation, the uprising drove home the point to Chinese Christians that, in the popular mind, their profession of the foreign faith and their membership in churches dominated by Westerners had turned them into disciples of the "foreign devils" and collaborators in a Western assault on Chinese tradition. The survival and growth of Christian communities in China now appeared to hinge on their ability to separate themselves from Western missions. In the decades that followed, a chief test of Chinese Christian leadership would be the ability to shake off the foreignness of their religion, to take control of the churches, and to fashion a viable indigenous Christianity that would respond to the needs of the country and its people.

The early stirrings of the independent Protestant movement were found in the years immediately after the Boxer Uprising. In 1902, several Shanghai YMCA activists led by Xie Honglai organized the Chinese Christian Union (Zhongguo Jidutuhui) after yet another "missionary case," in which the murder of two English missionaries in Chenzhou, Hunan, resulted in stringent British demands for punishments and indemnities. In the settlement, death sentences were meted out for about a dozen people, including local officials.[51] In forming the union, the group of Shanghai Christians attempted to sever their much-resented ties to Western imperialism. However, the organization primarily engaged in promoting the spirit of independence through a periodical called the *Chinese Christian* (*Zhongguo Jidutu bao*) and failed to establish its own churches. Although branches were formed in Hong Kong and in the provinces of Hunan, Shandong, and Zhejiang, they never coalesced into a permanent organization. By 1927, the union had become a "burst bubble."[52]

In 1906, Yu Guozhen (Yu Zongzhou), a Presbyterian pastor in Shanghai who had been one of the organizers of the Chinese Christian Union, declared his own Presbyterian church in the Zhabei district of Shanghai to be self-supporting, calling it the China Christian Independent Church (Zhongguo Yesujiao Zilihui). As Yu explained, the forming of the Independent Church was the result "of the anxieties of Chinese Christians . . . over anti-Christian cases, and of their sadness at foreign encroachments." To help prevent further outbreaks of anti-Christian violence and to stay clear of troubles caused by foreigners, the new Independent Church had brought together "those who devote themselves both to their faith and to their country and who are imbued with the spirit of self-support and self-government."[53] Yu's congregation drew many of its members from the emerging middle class in Shanghai. Several were employees of the Commercial Press; others were Shanghai merchants. Yu himself held a part-time job at a local utilities company. According to the *China Mission Year Book* of 1912, most members of the Independent Church retained their affiliations with denominational churches. By 1910, when several affiliated independent churches had sprung up around Shanghai and other coastal areas, Yu declared the formation of a national network of the Independent Church. Its official English name was the National Free Christian Church of China—deliberately shorn of separatist language that might alienate the missionary community.[54]

Until the fall of the Qing dynasty, however, the growth of Yu's church outside treaty port cities like Shanghai was slowed by imperial control of popular religion. In the 1900s, the new ministry of foreign affairs "forbade any Chinese to organize an independent church." Because of this and the continuing partial reliance on the missions' material support, many independent churches founded during the last years of the Qing rule chose to downplay their separatist intention and called themselves the Chinese Christian Church (Zhonghua Jidujiaohui, also Zhongguo Jidujiaohui).[55] In 1911, the revolution led by Sun Yat-sen brought an end to the old imperial order and gave birth to the Republic of China, whose new constitution granted broad religious toleration. Yet the new central authority soon fell apart. With the death of the strongman Yuan Shikai in 1916, the floodgate was opened for the militarists' unruly contention for lordship of the republic. One consequence of the political chaos was new opportunities for religious societies and ideas to flourish in relative freedom. Among the Protestants, independent Zhonghua Jidujiaohui churches began to multiply in major cities across China, including Tianjin, Beijing, Shanghai, Nanjing, and Changsha—often with the blessings of local mission churches and sometimes helped by grants of cash or land from local governments or warlords.[56]

By the end of the 1910s, many of the independent churches had entered into regional unions, most notably the North China Association of Chinese Christian Churches, with member congregations in major cities of Shandong and Zhili. However, the network remained loose and fragile, and no effective centralized leadership emerged. Financial weakness also doomed many of these early autonomous churches.[57] Within Yu's Zilihui system, 330 member churches (most of them small) were reported in 1926, yet many of them continued to depend on denominational missions, and most did not even maintain contacts among themselves.[58]

The faltering efforts among Chinese Protestants toward independent Christianity nevertheless reflected a growing realization—one that many missionaries shared—that for Christianity to take root in China, it had to shed its foreign image. It was a "truism," one missionary wrote, that "the masses in China must be evangelized by the Chinese themselves."[59] Although most missionaries at the time would not relish the prospect of independent churches, the Centenary Missionary Conference held in Shanghai in 1907 (one hundred years after the arrival of Robert Morrison) did for the first time call for the eventual formation of a "Chinese Church," which, "when the time shall arrive . . . shall pass beyond our guidance and control."[60]

In reality, it would take more than lofty visions or altruist intentions for missionaries to actually forego their dominance. For its part, the Chinese Protestant community had produced few educated leaders after a century of missionary work. There had been few incentives for educated Chinese to seek a clerical career during the nineteenth century; pastoral profession reminded most Chinese of the Buddhist and Daoist monks who were often held in low esteem by the elite. The majority of Chinese active in church work were relatively uneducated, poorly paid, and regarded as "helpers."[61] Effective indigenous Christian leadership awaited the emergence of educated youth in the church. In the early 1900s, this young group was being readied in mission schools whose rapid growth coincided with the demise of the imperial examination system in 1905. It was to them that the missionary establishment turned in an effort to cultivate a generation of native leaders with modern Western educations who could carry out effective evangelism, bridge the gap between the Protestant community and Chinese society at large, and help put a Chinese face on the church while maintaining the values and the practice of

Western Christianity. One of the first leaders of this kind to emerge in the early twentieth century was Cheng Jingyi (1881–1939).

CHENG JINGYI AND THE CHINESE HOME MISSIONARY SOCIETY

Cheng came from a Manchu family in Beijing. His father had been an ardent Buddhist before he converted to Christianity and joined the LMS, which had established its first station in the capital in 1863. He also became one of the earliest local preachers hired by the LMS and worked under it for twenty-five years. Cheng Jingyi himself attended the Anglo-Chinese College in Beijing and graduated from the LMS Theological School in Tianjin in 1900 shortly before the Boxers began their siege of the foreign legation quarter in Beijing. During the hostilities, Cheng's family sought shelter in the British Legation while Cheng became an interpreter for the foreign expeditionary forces who fought their way into the capital and put down the uprising. In 1903, he went to England to assist LMS missionary George Owen in the translation of the New Testament (as part of the "union" version translation project). He then studied at the Bible Training Institute in Glasgow for two years and returned to China in 1908 to become assistant pastor of an LMS church in Beijing located at Dengshikou. In 1910, Cheng was chosen as one of the handful of Chinese delegates to attend the World Missionary Conference in Edinburgh, at which he became famous for telling the missionary leaders, "your denominationalism does not interest Chinese Christians." He added that the Chinese "had never understood it, could not delight in it, though they often suffered from it." Meanwhile, despite his opposition to denominationalism, Cheng remained in the English Congregational mission and, later that year, was ordained as an LMS minister. Under his leadership, the LMS church at Dengshikou achieved a degree of self-support and autonomy.[62]

In 1913, John R. Mott, chair of the Continuation Committee of the Edinburgh Conference, arrived in China to preside over a national Christian conference and to organize the China Continuation Committee as a "consultative and advisory" organ for Western missions in the country. Cheng was named one of the two full-time secretaries of the committee (along with Edwin C. Lobenstine, an American Presbyterian missionary). The conference advised against the use of denominational names of mission churches in Chinese and called for the adoption of the name Zhonghua Jidujiaohui (the Chinese Christian Church) for all churches.[63]

For the next two and a half decades, Cheng would remain one of the most visible Chinese Christian leaders and worked tirelessly to bring about the Chinese church that the missionaries had called for. In 1918, he was put in charge of the Chinese Home Missionary Society (Zhonghua Guonei Budaohui), a nondenominational, "purely Chinese organization" that the visiting Frank Buchman, leader of the pietistic Moral Re-Armament movement in the United States, had backed.[64] The following year, Cheng helped launch the China for Christ Movement (Zhonghua Guizhu Yundong) with the Harvard-educated YMCA general secretary Yu Rizhang (David Z. T. Yui, 1882–1936) as chairman. It aimed at promoting religious education and ridding the church of the image of being unpatriotic and dependent on foreigners.

Within the next two years or so, the movement spread to about a dozen cities and echoed the dominant themes of the YMCA at the time in calling for "Christian involvement in forming public opinion and conscience as well as in delivering a practical and social message" in order to improve the moral character of the people and equip them for the task of nation-building. As a whole, both campaigns were carried out mostly on paper. The China for Christ Movement would lose its steam in less than three years and "was merged—logically—with the older and more representative China Continuation Committee." The Chinese Home Missionary Society would count a total of seventeen missionaries in its sixteen years of existence.[65] For their part, many mission churches remained unwilling to unite with others or to call themselves Zhonghua Jidujiaohui. Concerns over denominational finances aside, doctrinal anxieties also persisted. In the words of the Reverend J. F. Love, corresponding secretary for the Southern Baptist Mission Board, the union movement threatened to "break [our] denominational *esprit de corps* and weaken our defenses."[66] The "Chinese Church" envisioned at the Centenary Missionary Conference remained a distant goal within the missionary enterprise.

DING LIMEI AND THE CHINESE STUDENT VOLUNTEER MOVEMENT FOR THE MINISTRY

Meanwhile, missionaries did offer their blessings to local evangelists and revivalists who modeled themselves on their Western counterparts. In

1909, a revival broke out on the campus of Shandong Union College in Weixian under the leadership of Ding Limei (1873?–1936), an alumnus and a Presbyterian minister from Qingdao in eastern Shandong. Henry Winters Luce, a prominent Presbyterian educational missionary and then vice president of the college, had helped organize the revival. Like Cheng Jingyi, Ding was a second-generation convert and had received his early education at the Presbyterian Tengchow College founded by the American missionary Calvin Mateer. In early 1900, as the Boxer movement was brewing in Shandong, Ding narrowly escaped death by torture as a "secondary devil." After he was put into a prison hole in a magistrate's office, or *yamen*, near Qingdao, a German officer intervened to "pay his respects" to the magistrate—by ordering his men to blow up the city's closed gate, fight their way to the yamen, seize the magistrate, and drag him out in front of the mounted officer where he was reminded, "Next time a gentleman wants to call on you, don't forget!" Ding was promptly released.[67]

An articulate and fervent "modern man," Ding advocated the overthrow of Qing during the last years of the dynastic rule and had to flee Shandong when its governor issued an arrest warrant for him. In June 1910, under the auspices of the YMCA, Ding helped found the Chinese Student Volunteer Movement for the Ministry (Zhonghua Xuesheng Lizhi Chuandaotuan) at a Christian student meeting in Tongxian, Hebei province, with the ambitious goal of the "evangelization of our mother country and the world in this generation." The organization recalled the Student Volunteer Movement for Foreign Missions in the United States, and its motto echoed that of the American Student Volunteer Movement (SVM). In 1907, coinciding with the Centenary Missionary Conference, John R. Mott had come to China and led the first series of evangelistic meetings that targeted the burgeoning student body in modern government schools in several cities (forty-two thousand modern schools and "a million and a half students of western learning within their halls" by 1910).[68] The success of those meetings led the Chinese YMCA to develop "a movement to reach the students in the government schools and colleges." In time, Ding resigned from his ministry to become the first traveling secretary (*xunxing ganshi*) of the Chinese SVM. While indigenous in membership, the organization operated with help and guidance from the mission establishment. Its recruitment of volunteers was aided by the YMCA (often at its summer camps) in each city, and John Leighton Stuart, another influential Presbyterian missionary and later U.S. ambassador to China, served as its secretary during the early years.[69]

By 1914, the Chinese SVM had expanded to include branches in mission colleges and middle schools in thirteen provinces, mostly along the east coast and in the Yangzi River valley, and a membership of more than one thousand, half of whom pledged to become evangelists (the majority apparently did not). The society played a generally supportive role as American evangelists Mott and Sherwood Eddy conducted their whirlwind tours of major Chinese cities in 1913 and 1914 where each of their evangelistic meetings attracted thousands of young students eager to seek out the Christian formula for modernity and nation-building. When Eddy in the company of the science lecturer C. H. Robertson (who held his audience spellbound with demonstrations of a gyroscope, radio, monorail car, X-ray, and the like) conducted their meetings in Fuzhou, Fujian, Ding and other Chinese SVM leaders were asked to go to the secondary cities in that province to lead similar meetings—beginning likewise with science lectures on topics such as radio, telegraph, and lantern slides and proceeding to the Gospel. They, too, were carefully planned, with public notices and admission tickets distributed before the meetings and prayer groups, Bible study classes, and evangelical bands organized at their conclusion.[70]

Eddy's revivalist tactic was to present Christianity as the "fittest" religion, the basis for progress and national strength, and the "Hope of China," at a time when social Darwinism had acquired a predominating influence over a new generation of Chinese intellectuals. According to essayist Lin Yutang, who attended some of those meetings while a student at St. John's University in Shanghai, one of Eddy's evangelistic "tricks" was "suddenly to pull a Chinese flag (then of five colors) out of his coat pocket and declare that he loved China." (Lin added dryly, "Such melodramatics didn't go with us.")[71] Likewise, Ding would play into the rising nationalist sentiments. "To adjust to the psychology of the audience," Ding wrote, one should "first explain the individual's responsibility toward the country . . . and cite a few examples of social ills in our midst."[72]

FROM METHODISM TO INDEPENDENT REVIVALISM: YU CIDU

In 1909, at about the same time that Ding began his work among students in the north, a female revivalist known to missionaries as Dora

Yu (Yu Cidu, 1873–1931) emerged in the south. Based in Shanghai, Yu concentrated her work in cities in the lower Yangzi valley and along the South China coast and was among the first to introduce revival techniques such as teary public confessions.[73] Raised in the family of a Presbyterian preacher near Hangzhou, Yu attended the Soochow Hospital Medical School run by the Methodist Episcopal Church (MEC), South, from which she graduated in 1896. The following year, she accompanied an MEC missionary to Seoul as the denomination's work extended into Korea. Yu's life as a missionary in Korea was a difficult one. She was plagued by loneliness, depression, thoughts of suicide, and debilitating health problems that necessitated a return to Shanghai in 1899 for several months of treatment. In 1903, she ended her mission and went back to China.[74]

During the next few years, Yu gradually evolved from a Methodist preacher into a revivalist of national standing at a time when indigenous revivalism was just beginning in China. A woman of uncommon modern education and personal experience, she possessed both the refined manners of a cosmopolitan lady and an innate emotional intensity that was being channeled, through the influence of the Holiness movement (strong among MEC missionaries), into an ardent quest of higher spiritual life. While at medical school, she had lost both her parents, broken off an engagement, and experienced an unspecified emotional crisis that plunged her into overwhelming guilt and depression. During her years in Korea, she continued to be tormented by a sense of her own unworthiness (possibly as a result of a doomed romance there) and feared that she would be "left behind" when Christ returned.[75] Subsequently, she developed a tender and passionate kind of piety. Already in her thirties when she began itinerant preaching in 1909 (she would remain unmarried all her life), she perhaps exuded a maternal charm that helped capture young souls for Christ.

In 1909, Yu published her own translation of 160 English hymns as *Hymns of Revival;* she also began her own training of evangelists with an emphasis on holiness and millenarian themes. In 1910, she started a yearly two-week Summer Bible School (attended by dozens of church activists from various denominations) at a site made available free of charge by American Southern Baptists in Shanghai. By 1915, its dominant theme would be the "Lord's Second Coming." Subsequent meetings were renamed Summer Prophetic Conferences.[76] The following year, her modest attempts at theological education formalized into the Jiangwan Bible School, named after the part of the Shanghai suburb where the small school, with an initial enrollment of twelve, was located. In its mission statement, published in the *Chinese Recorder,* the leading missionary monthly in the country, Yu explained that there was no attempt on her part to undermine denominational churches—she promised to send all her trained students back to work in their home churches.[77] In those days, it was indeed characteristic of fledgling independent preachers to continue to seek the blessings of Western missions even as they sought to emerge from under their shadows. As we shall see, the greater significance of Yu's work was in sparking the spiritual quest of Watchman Nee in 1920, which would lead to a more radical departure from missionary Christianity.

Besides Ding Limei and Yu Cidu, other prominent young Christians were also active in mission-supported initiatives to cultivate indigenous Christianity. The Chinese SVM, for instance, attracted several influential Protestants, including Wang Zhengting (C. T. Wang, 1882–1961), former vice president of the first Republican Senate, who, upon the dissolution of the parliament by Yuan Shikai in January 1914, had taken a position as general secretary of the Chinese YMCA. Ironically, despite its name, the Chinese SVM depended mostly on financial contributions from Western sources.[78] By 1922, when the student-led anti-Christian movement broke out across China, the YMCA—along with its Mott-Eddy campaigns and its effort to equate national salvation with conversion and the development of Christian character—had been effectively rejected by Chinese students. The Chinese SVM had become a lost cause and would soon fizzle out. In that year, Ding began to withdraw from itinerant evangelism. He settled down to teach at the small North China Theological Seminary (Huabei Shenxueyuan) in Tengxian, Shandong. By 1927, he and most of the other early leaders had left the SVM. Ding died in 1936.[79]

Clearly, although early twentieth-century missionary efforts at bringing about an indigenous Christianity led to the creation of seemingly Chinese institutions, they did not give rise to a church beyond the "guidance and control" of Western missions. At best, Cheng Jingyi and his generation of Protestant leaders cultivated by the missionaries succeeded only in fulfilling the missionary vision of a native church safely within the limits of mainline Western Protestantism. And throughout the 1910s and 1920s, Ding and the other evangelists who joined the Chinese SVM and embarked on itinerant preaching continued to expound essentially a missionary Christianity. On the other hand, patriotic attempts at independent churches, whether as part of Yu Guozhen's Zilihui or within the loose Zhonghua Jidujiaohui confederation, often trickled into oblivion. Patriotism alone failed to attract either a sufficient and stable following or adequate funding. The indigenous church movement remained to be fired by more sublime visions. What emerged later as vibrant and enduring forms of Chinese Christianity invariably contained the ferment of antiforeignism and a spirit of independence but christened such attitudes as righteous indignation against the corruption and deviations of a worldly, and Western-dominated, church. Moreover, the movement would be energized by Pentecostalism and millenarian convictions that, despite the proclamation of the imminent return of Christ, led to the founding of earthly organizations that were here to stay. The first of these was the True Jesus Church.

CHAPTER TWO

The Lightning out of the East

THE TRUE JESUS CHURCH

The points of character which fit a man to be a good paid helper to
the missionary . . . are different from those essential to independent
leadership, with its burdens of responsibility and calls for initiative.
For the former position the qualities of tact, receptivity of mind, and
skill in details of business, without aspirations to command, are
especially needed. . . . Hence it will not be surprising to find that
many of these men will, in the new conditions, drop into the background; whilst others, whose very force and independence of character unfitted them for office under the old *régime*, will come to
the front.

—*D. E. Hoste (director of China Inland Mission), 1900*

[In spring 1917] I rose and . . . boldly proclaimed the gospel of
the Heavenly Kingdom. I was greatly moved by the Holy Spirit,
who clearly spoke to me (while I was praying): "In no more than
five years, but no less than four years, the end will come. . . .
The heavenly fire will consume the heaven, the earth, and all
the creatures and all the people." I earnestly asked the Lord:
"Is that so? But of that day and hour no one knows, not even
the angels of heaven, nor the Son." God said to me: "The Father
knows. This is the Father speaking in you." Then I wept and
said: "I dare not tell it to others, for fear that I may be wrong."
And the Holy Spirit strengthened me and said, "There is no
mistake, no mistake."

—*Wei Enbo, founder of the True Jesus Church, 1919*

LIKE ALMOST ALL THE OTHER LEADERS of major indigenous church
movements in China, the founder of the TJC, Wei Enbo (1876?–1919), be-

gan his religious career at a foreign mission church. In 1902, Wei, a poor farmer from the county of Rongcheng, some sixty miles south of Beijing, migrated to the capital and started a business dealing in silk and foreign merchandise. By his own accounts a "quarrelsome" man of "impetuous temperament," Wei got into a street fight one day during which he was helped by a member of the local LMS, whom Wei saw as upholding justice by coming to the defense of the migrant. Through him Wei came to know and then to join the LMS church at Ciqikou, which was a substation under the care of the nearby LMS church (at Dengshikou) where Cheng Jingyi became a prominent leader after 1908. It appears that Wei played a substantial role in the push for self-support and independence among local members of the LMS in 1912: he allegedly donated three thousand silver dollars (*da yang*), thereby becoming one of the founders of the independent church. His career as a respectable church activist was disrupted, however, when he, in his own words, "broke the Seventh Commandment against adultery" and was thrown out of the church. Wei's religious fervor was not dampened. He would later help organize an evangelistic band that took him to the Temple of Heaven, opened to the commoners after 1912, where local Protestant churches often joined forces to set up preaching booths and tents at the great annual temple fairs. Meanwhile, he continued at his silk business.[1]

A personal crisis in 1916 precipitated a new burst of religious energy in Wei and led eventually to the founding of the TJC. Early that year Wei came down with tuberculosis (whose effective treatment was three decades away), which led him to an encounter in autumn with a person from a local Pentecostal mission. The latter allegedly laid hands on Wei to administer miraculous healing, after which Wei became a Pentecostal and received the gift of the Holy Spirit and "tongues."[2] At the time, the transmission of that small flame of Pentecostalism could hardly have caught anyone's attention. Made up of a handful of largely independent evangels from the United States, the Pentecostal missions were new and small in China and scattered haphazardly in less than half a dozen places in and around some of the treaty ports. Yet that small flame of "tongues" and divine healing, passed along by Wei, would soon meet dry timbers in the country and help kindle visions of an end-time messianic scheme—one that also accorded with the rising nationalist sentiments among Chinese Protestants.

FIGURE 4 Wei Enbo. Source: Wei Yisa, ed. *Zhen Yesu Jiaohui chuangli sanshi zhounian jinian zhuankan* (1948).

THE COMING OF PENTECOSTALISM TO CHINA

The Pentecostal movement emerged from the late-nineteenth-century Holiness Revival in the United States, where radical evangelicals believed that as the Second Coming of Christ approached, the faithful were experiencing the "latter rain"—an outpouring of the power of the Holy Spirit prophesied by Joel (2:21–32) in the Old Testament—that corresponded to the "former rain," the signs and wonders described in Acts of the New Testament. On January 1, 1901, a student at Bethel Bible College in Topeka, Kansas, which recently had been founded by a prominent Holiness evangelist, was baptized by the Holy Spirit and received the gift of "tongues." Soon, most of the Bethel students were speaking in tongues. When glossolalia was followed by the gifts of divine healing, the movement spread quickly. In the spring of 1906, Pentecostalism came to Los Angeles where William J. Seymour, a black minister, led the famous Azusa Street Revival. The recent earthquake in San Francisco had stirred both apocalyptic fears and premillennial expectations, which likely contributed to the revival and helped turn the Azusa Street Mission into what Sydney E. Ahlstrom called "the radiating center of Pentecostalism." After 1906, the movement flourished across the United States and by the early 1910s had claimed between fifty thousand and one hundred thousand adherents.[3] It also quickly turned into an international phenomenon when Pentecostal missionaries, armed sometimes with hardly anything more than the conviction of their baptism by the Holy Spirit and their millennial hopes, sailed overseas.

By and large, Pentecostals combined a conservative stand on the inerrancy of the Bible and a puritanical moral code with a premillennial theology, according to which Christ would return after the fearful Last Days to establish a thousand-year reign on earth. For them, those days were approaching, signaled by the baptism of the Holy Spirit, chiefly in the form of "tongues" and divine healing. Reports on such miracles abounded. Stanley Frodsham recorded one in his popular book *With Signs Following: The Story of the Pentecostal Revival in the Twentieth Century*. At a Pentecostal convention sometime after the revival in Los Angeles, Frodsham noticed a young man at the back of the building: "His face was pale and emaciated, for he was far gone with tuberculosis. . . . [Later in the day] this young man . . . suddenly felt the power of God coming upon him. He got on his knees and in one moment he was speaking in other tongues as the Spirit gave utterance. Then thumping his lungs, he declared, 'I believe God has healed me.'"[4]

That young man, Frank Trevitt, went on to become a missionary to China. Others were empowered by a belief in "missionary tongues," the ability to speak unstudied languages, out in the field. Between 1906 and 1909, at least a dozen of these missionaries went out to remote parts of the world without language training, convinced that they would be enabled to preach in the native languages when they arrived.[5] According to Daniel H. Bays, pioneering Pentecostal missionaries who had received "Spirit baptism at Azusa" arrived in the Hong Kong–Macao area in late 1907 where they discovered that "far from being fluent in Chinese, they had not a word of the language." A few months later, however, one of them, Sophie Hansen, suddenly declared her ability to preach a sermon in Chinese. (She later stated, "Holy Spirit . . . speaks Chinese through me from heaven, without learning it.") In the North China province of Zhili (renamed Hebei after 1928), a Norwegian-American missionary named Bernt Berntsen, who first arrived in China in 1904 and who had returned to the United States in 1907 to receive his Spirit baptism at Azusa, set up a separate base of Pentecostalism in 1908.[6]

By the end of the nineteenth century, China had surpassed India and the entire Near East as the most promising of America's mission fields.[7] Therefore the choice of China for many Pentecostal missionaries was not unusual. In China, however, those missionaries, commonly referred to at the time as Apostolic Faith missionaries, were a novel phenomenon. By 1909, the Apostolic Faith Mission had emerged as a recognized missionary group in China with a total force of twenty-six, a loose association of mostly independent missionaries dispatched by the Holy Spirit rather than by established mission boards.[8] Like earlier independent "faith" missionaries, the Pentecostals belonged to what Kenneth S. Latourette characterized as a "usually picturesque, sometimes eccentric, and occasionally very able" group of foreign evangelists. "While some of them introduced a bizarre and often highly emotional type of Protestantism repulsive to the more intelligent and better educated Chinese," Latourette added, "many held their converts to exacting moral standards and emphasized an inward religious experience and a complete change of life."⁹ As we shall see in the development of the TJC and other similar groups, it was those converts, not the foreign missionaries themselves, who made Pentecostalism a defining feature of popular Christianity in twentieth-century China.

THE FOUNDING OF THE TRUE JESUS CHURCH

In 1916, when Wei Enbo encountered Pentecostalism in Beijing, the Apostolic Faith missionaries were still a small group, and stories of divine healing like that of Frank Trevitt may well have circulated among them and helped win the ailing Wei to the new faith. However, Wei went through only a brief period of tutelage under the Pentecostal mission before launching into an independent prophetic career on his own. In the early spring of 1917, he was "led by the Holy Spirit" to a river outside the city where he heard a loud voice from Heaven telling him to receive a "facedown" baptism by immersion. He promptly dived into the still icy water of March unassisted by any clergy and, emerging from the river, felt both his body and spirit "cleansed." Thereafter, in a revelation that recalls the Heavenly Father's command given to Taiping founder Hong Xiuquan to exterminate the Manchu demons, God announced that he would give Wei "a whole-body armor . . . and the sword of the Holy Spirit to kill the demons." Wei claimed that he was then given command of tens of thousands of heavenly soldiers, and he went on to fight with many "ferocious and . . . indescribably ugly demons," shouting and dancing and chasing them around "heroically." He was kept quite busy at this warfare, for he saw that "all those walking on the streets of Beijing were demons."

After a thirty-nine-day fast—discreetly one day shy of Jesus' record—Wei had sightings of Jesus, Moses, Elijah, and the twelve disciples, at which point the Lord commanded him, in slightly ungrammatical Chinese, to "correct the [Christian] Church [ni yao gengzheng jiao]." Jesus also gave him his new name, Wei Baoluo (Paul Wei). The "end-time apostle" soon went about the mission churches in and around Beijing, prophesying the imminent return of Christ ("between four and five years"), denouncing the corruption of Western Christianity, and calling for repentance and separation from foreign missions. He cited as evidence of the degeneration of Western Christianity the wealth of denominational churches supported by the rich and powerful, "the pampered wives" and "precious sons" of foreign Christians, the "silk and satin" that they wore, and their "extravagance and arrogance"—in contrast to the egalitarian communalism and simplicity of Jesus' followers at the time of the apostles. World War I, then raging in Europe among Christian nations, was further proof, he cried, that this corrupted, ungodly world was coming to an end.[10]

Closer to home, Wei found further signs of the impending apocalypse. The death of Yuan Shikai in 1916 had led to political chaos in the capital. The ensuing power struggle between the warlord prime minister Duan Qirui and the embattled president Li Yuanhong led in the summer of 1917 to the invasion of the "Queue Army" and the brief restoration of the deposed Qing emperor. As Beijing residents found themselves perilously caught in the political whirlwind, Wei and his handful of followers defied the earthly turmoil around them and were busy proselytizing among local Protestants and printing thousands of copies of a leaflet about his revelation titled "Articles of the Correction [Church]," which were sent out to select mission churches across the country. Wei was treated by many as insane and was twice jailed when missionaries, irritated by his intrusive and unrelenting "debates" on mission premises, called in police. Still, he was able to attract dozens who defected from denominational churches in the Beijing–Tianjin area, drawn to the new teaching by the promise of "instant healing of any disease upon baptism." In the winter of 1917, the group published its own "Hymns of the Holy Spirit" and raised a thirteen-foot-long banner bearing the characters "Zhen Yesu Jiaohui" (the True Jesus Church).[11]

In spreading the new teaching, Wei discovered that proselytizing among existing members of mission churches was far more effective than preaching to those outside the Protestant community. He also decided that mass mailing using the directory in the *China Church Year Book* was a quick way to reach beyond the capital and build a following. In late 1918, Wei began working on the official publication of the TJC that he called the *Universal Correction Church Times* (*Wanguo gengzhengjiao bao*). He lived to put together the first two issues of the periodical, published in the spring and the summer of 1919, in which he outlined the teachings revealed to him by the Holy Spirit.[12] These included the correct "facedown baptism," the baptism of the Holy Spirit evidenced by the gift of "tongues," the seventh-day observation of the Sabbath, the power of healing and exorcising demons, foot-washing among the members, and the offering of at least 10 percent of one's income in line with the principle of "sharing [material possessions] among the haves and the have-nots" (*youwu xiangtong*).[13]

In addition, the Universal Correction Church (an alternate name for the TJC) was to institute both lay leadership and a degree of egalitarianism. "Let there be no autocratic domination of meetings and prayers by any man," the church rules read. "Let all take turns to preach; let all pray aloud in meetings." Having been "instructed by the Holy Spirit" to become "bishop" (*jiandu*) of the TJC, Wei decreed a church organization with bishops, elders, and deacons—but no paid clergy. The new sect preached a confident exclusivism: only those who joined the TJC and received the baptism of the Holy Spirit could enter heaven; all other churches on the face of the earth belonged to the Devil. Wei also called on the mission churches in China to drop their denominational appellations, follow the teachings of the TJC and adopt its name, replace the clergy with lay leadership, reject the teaching of the Trinity (in favor of an undivided God), share material possessions, and "not rely on the foreigners' money and power." The early issues of the paper added a populist appeal to its proselytism. Since the "Holy Spirit of the 'latter rain' had descended," the *Universal Correction Church Times* was eager to hear from all readers who were willing to share "any hymns inspired by the Holy Spirit, any visions seen, any voices of God heard, and any ingenious methods of saving the peoples of this world"; it also called upon its readers to report all the "wrong teachings" found in mission churches.[14]

It is likely that Wei's unhappiness with foreign missionaries and the denominational churches they controlled had roots in personal grudges. About one year after the founding of the TJC, Wei had broken with the Pentecostal mission, citing the spiritual lapses and arrogance of its members.[15] His action probably reflected the sliding deference, and growing resentments, on the part of many converts toward Western missionaries and church leaders whose authority had rested in large measure on the popular belief in the superiority of Western civilization. As World War I dragged on, that belief was increasingly eroded, thereby preparing the ground for the swelling of anti-imperialist sentiments during the May Fourth era soon to dawn in China. In fact, Wei cited "this bloody war in Europe" that "has claimed tens of millions of lives" as "proof that [the missionaries] have got the [Christian] religion wrong," and he marveled that the

Westerners were still "shameless enough to preach in China." Meanwhile, the new church was soon able to fit both its own rise and the perceived decline of Western churches into an eschatological scheme. The TJC proclaimed that just as "the Lord Jesus had said, 'the lightning cometh out of the east, and shineth even unto the west'" in the Last Days (Matt. 24:27), he was "fulfilling his words" and was "revealing the truth about Jesus' salvation in the Republic of China in the East." He had also raised up an "unparalleled great man in the Chinese church. . . . The Lord Jesus has bestowed a sacred name on [Wei Enbo], saying, 'you are the second Paul.'"[16]

The first foothold that the TJC gained outside Zhili was in Shandong province. While proselytizing in Tianjin in the fall of 1918, Wei met a fellow Pentecostal from Weixian, Shandong, by the name of Zhang Lingsheng ("Zhang Born of the Spirit") and won him over to the TJC. Soon Zhang was back in Weixian, where he recruited new members including his relative Zhang Dianju (Zhang Banaba, or Barnabas Zhang), a dealer in antiques, who exchanged facedown baptism with him. By spring 1919, Wei himself was in Weixian, where he engaged in his characteristically aggressive proselytism among members of the Presbyterian churches there and set up local branches of the TJC, naming Zhang Lingsheng as the TJC bishop of Shandong and Zhang Dianju as an elder. The new church reported an outpouring of the Holy Spirit: "tongues," "visions," "spiritual singing," and "spiritual dancing" followed public confessions of unmentionable sins and fasts that sometimes lasted for weeks. Some were "caught up to the third heaven" where they remained for hours, visiting paradise and hearing voices telling them to "go down to spread the teaching" of the TJC.[17]

The movement throve on the relentless energy of Wei and his followers. By the fall of 1919, it had reached beyond the provinces of Zhili and Shandong to Shanxi, Jiangsu, and parts of Manchuria and claimed more than one thousand followers, made up largely of former members of independent churches, Pentecostal missions, the Seventh-Day Adventist Church, and some mainline denominations. At about the same time, some sixty TJC member churches scattered throughout those provinces united into one collective family, with all the members "offering their belongings to the Lord" and changing their family names to Ye (from Yesu, the transliteration of Jesus).[18] Zhang Dianju, for instance, became Ye Banaba Shensheng (Barnabas Ye Born of God). In one village near Weixian, Shandong, all the TJC members reportedly sold their belongings and moved to live together in a "Jesus Compound" (Yesu Dayuan)—an event that foreshadowed the start of the Jesus Family in the western part of the province a few years later. In southern Zhili, the sect members also began sharing their possessions, and the sound of their "singing in the morning and bells in the evening" could be heard in the neighboring villages. The practice, as well as the use of the sectarian surname Ye, appeared to have been broadly adopted within the TJC in 1920–1921, when drought and famine in North China left at least half a million people dead and close to twenty million destitute. Millions lived on ground wheat husks, ground leaves, corncobs, roots, bark, and sawdust.[19]

Despite the bleakness around them, TJC members were able to keep up an exuberant spirit by sharing testimonies of the efficacy of the new faith: the sick were healed, prophecies were made, demons were exorcised, and an illiterate farmer and night-soil collector would develop the uncanny spiritual gift—rivaling the ability of traditional fortune tellers—of enumerating people's past sins merely by holding their hands. The first national conference of the TJC that met in Beijing in 1920 reported that a mute man under the power of the Holy Spirit poured out "many words of repentance" (in the form of "tongues" that were interpreted by one endowed with such a gift) before "returning to the state of dumbness."[20]

THE SPREAD OF THE TRUE JESUS CHURCH

Wei himself did not live to see all the fruits of his labor. He died of tuberculosis in October 1919, three years after he contracted the fateful disease that had precipitated his embrace of Pentecostalism. However, in his two and a half years as the founder and leader of the TJC, Wei had brought forth a lively Chinese Pentecostal and millenarian sect that defied both the derision and opposition of mission church leaders and the scarcity of its means. By the early 1920s, the new faith had also spread to the North and Central China provinces of Henan, Hunan, Hubei, Jiangxi, and Anhui; it had reached down south to Fujian and up north to Jilin, often by way of mass mailings that targeted particularly the Seventh-Day Adventist churches, which could be found in many large cities in China.[21]

Compared with most denominational missions, the Adventists were a late arrival, having reached China only after the turn of the twentieth century. The first Adventist missionaries to China arrived in Hong Kong in 1902, but it was in the hinterland North China province of Henan in 1903 that the Adventists built their first mission stations. By the late 1910s, perhaps because of the outbreak of the war in Europe, the Adventists' message of the imminent return of Christ was gaining audience in China; their churches were already found in at least ten provinces in the country, with a total following of some three thousand. Despite the negligible size of its membership (which would total barely more than twenty thousand after half a century), the Adventist Church published a disproportionately influential and widely circulated monthly, *Signs of the Times* (*Shizhao yuebao*), which began spreading the church's apocalyptic prophecies in 1907.[22] Although the exact connection between Wei Enbo and the Adventists is unclear, it is almost certain that Wei derived many of his revelations from the latter, including Sabbatarianism and the eschatological teachings. The TJC therefore was able to speak the language intelligible to members of the Adventist churches, a language that was accentuated with nationalistic intensity. In several of the provinces where the TJC gained the largest followings, the spread of the new sect often began when members of local Adventist churches responded to free TJC publications such as the *Universal Correction Church Times* that were mailed to them and asked for a missionary to be sent to explain the new teaching. In due time, many of those Adventists defected to found TJC branches that became new centers for the sect.[23]

In Hunan, some members of an Adventist church in the provincial capital Changsha received the first issue of the *Universal Correction Church Times* in the spring of 1919. When they started praying according to the prescribed methods therein, "the Holy Spirit" broke loose upon one of them so that "his body shook violently and his 'tongues' rattled together with the earthen pots." Awed by the incident, the group chose one among themselves, an Adventist evangelist called Li Xiaofeng, and sent him to Beijing where he acquired the faith in person from Wei Enbo and brought it back to Hunan. Within a few months, the new teaching spread beyond Changsha into neighboring counties even as the area was ravaged by rivaling warlord armies and many Roman Catholic churches were burned during the fighting.[24]

In that hinterland area where peasants had for centuries sought the protective power of deities ranging from the Buddhist Goddess of Mercy (Guanyin) to apotheosized historical figures like Lord Bao (Bao Gong) and Guan Shengdi—as Mao Zedong pointed out in his famous investigative report on the peasant movement in Hunan—the TJC followers proclaimed a more potent divinity who could heal the sick; summon rain, lightning, and thunder; bestow the gift of "tongues"; and make prophecies through the mouths of virgin girls and boys. In one case, several girls and boys aged seven to fourteen "swooned and fell to the ground, crying out repeatedly in unison that the world would soon perish."[25]

In neighboring Hubei, which the TJC reached in late 1919, many rural substations and "prayer houses" were established when the word spread that the deity preached by the sect could "dissolve calamity and remove misfortune" (*xiaozai jie'e*), "cure a hundred diseases" (*xiaochu baibing*), and relieve people of "evil habits." Among those who joined the sect were opium addicts and people possessed by "disease demons." Most of the local groups held Spiritual Gifts Meetings (*ling'en dahui*) twice a year, in spring and fall, during the slack farming seasons to make new converts. Many TJC congregations in Hubei established distinctive baptismal rituals. In one area, new converts had to abstain from meat, wine, and smoking for seven days before baptism.[26] In another, two white flags each bearing a red cross were planted in a pool to form a "sacred gate" through which the convert passed. Two deacons stood behind the gate, one on each side, to receive him and then to plunge him facedown into the water. Then the neophyte emerged from the water to receive his "sacred name," which replaced his birth name.[27]

In Shanxi, the TJC soon won over an able Confucian scholar and educator by the name of Gao Daling. According to TJC records, Gao, a "presented scholar" (*jinshi*), had been a Chinese-language teacher for the prominent British missionary Timothy Richard and had assisted the latter in the establishment and supervision of what became Shanxi University.[28] After the Revolution of 1911, Gao became an advisor to the Shanxi warlord Yan Xishan; he also headed the Independent Chinese Church in the provincial capital Taiyuan, which had arisen with the financial support of Yan. Later, around the time when Wei formed the TJC, Gao also founded a New Jesus Church in Taiyuan with some three hundred members who had broken away from mission churches. By 1920, Gao had joined the TJC, bringing his entire congregation into its fold. In time, more than one hundred branches of the new church, with more than ten thousand members, would be found in Shanxi alone.[29]

In converting members of mission churches, TJC evangelists were able to harness the rising nationalism of the 1920s to their advantage. In 1922, Wei Yisa, son of the founder Wei Enbo, led a small group of TJC missionaries and went through the Seventh-Day Adventist churches in Henan province. Within three months, the TJC won over eighteen of the twenty-five churches that the Adventist missionaries had labored to build over two decades. When an Adventist missionary confronted an erstwhile church leader–turned–TJC elder and accused him of "stealing the sheep," the latter turned to the congregation and cried, "Whichever one of you is a foreign sheep can go back with him!"[30]

In the southeastern province of Fujian, which became one of the most important centers of the movement, the arrival of the new teaching followed a pattern seen in several other parts of the country. As early as 1919, the targeted mailings of the *Universal Correction Church Times* to Seventh-Day Adventist churches in Fujian had elicited inquiries and invitations for missionaries from many parts of the province. In October 1923, Zhang Banaba, probably the most effective evangelist of the sect, went to Fuzhou, the provincial capital, where within a few months he baptized hundreds of people into the TJC. One fifteen-year-old boy "ascended to the third heaven" and then became possessed by the Holy Spirit for several days, during which he poured out a stream of prophecies calling on people to repent as "the fire of the Last Days" and calamities were approaching. As in other cities, TJC's proselytism among fellow Sabbatarians and independents was particularly fruitful. Before long, an entire Adventist congregation in the city converted to the TJC.

After its establishment in the provincial capital, the sect began to expand south along the coastal area where a significant number of new converts, particularly those who later became local TJC leaders, joined it when they heard of its miraculous power to cure hopeless diseases like tuberculosis.[31] Among the appeals of the new church was its ability to dispense "holy water" (made sacred through prayers), which was used to cure the diseases of the believers and their poultry and pigs.[32]

The popularity of the new sect in coastal Fujian stemmed also from its reputed ability to rid people of opium addiction.[33] In the late Qing period, Chinese efforts to combat the narcotic had culminated in the anti-opium imperial edict of 1906, which was followed by a decade of remarkably effective suppression of the drug. It also helped to bring about the end of the British opium trade in 1917. Yet poppy cultivation reappeared in areas where government control was weak.[34] The erosion of central authority after the late 1910s exacerbated the problem. According to the 1924 issue of the *China Mission Year Book,* by 1923, China was producing no less than ten thousand tons of opium annually, about three times the production of the rest of the world. With the political disintegration of the country, many regional military authorities were promoting opium cultivation as "heavy taxation on poppy land, transit taxes, taxes for sales, permits, opium smoking den licenses, and taxes on individual pipes" became a major source of revenue supporting military campaigns. In Fujian, where the situation was "desperate," opium cultivation became compulsory.[35]

In Fuqing and Xinghua counties, where opium addiction was particularly widespread, many TJC churches doubled as opium refuges where broken addicts were cured of their "evil habit" through the "power of the Holy Spirit"—most likely a kind of shock treatment that utilized a combination of Pentecostal prayers, "tongues," and "spiritual singing and dancing." Likewise, in Zhangpu county in southern Fujian, the sect gained more than one thousand followers in the early 1930s after many opium addicts, some of whom had turned to the drug to alleviate pain from lingering illnesses, sought to "follow the religion to stop the opium." The TJC was accordingly dubbed "The Religion to Cure the Black Smoke" (Gaiwuyan Jiao) among the local people.[36] As in the case of Shanxi province in the 1880s, where the Heavenly Invitation Offices of Xi Shengmo were conduits to swift evangelism, the TJC's bold tackling of the opium problem along with a spectrum of ailments and demon possessions in coastal Fujian during the 1920s and 1930s resulted in rapid growth and the establishment of more than one hundred churches.[37]

One of the most important gains that Zhang Banaba made in Fuzhou in 1923 was the recruitment of a physician and former deputy head of a local hospital named Guo Duoma (Thomas Guo), who would soon emerge as a national leader of TJC at a time when the fledgling plebeian movement desperately needed educated and articulate spokesmen. On the initiative of Guo and several other local elders and deacons named by Zhang, the TJC faith would spread not only to the rest of the province, but also to Fujianese communities in Taiwan and Southeast Asia and beyond them to Japan and India. To its followers, all this fulfilled "the biblical prophecy that the true Word flashes like lightning out of the East and shines onto the West." In 1931, a year after the TJC was taken to a Chinese immigrant community in Hawaii, Guo would be sent to Honolulu as its first missionary to plant churches in the United States.[38]

In retrospect, the early death of the founder and leader of the TJC along with the sect's emphasis on direct communication with the Holy Spirit resulted in a tendency toward decentralization and democratization of the movement that in the long run helped its survival and growth. Efforts to counter the centrifugal forces of personalities and a wide range of Pentecostal practices following Wei's death also led quickly to a collective formulation of TJC principles, rules, and governance. At the first national conference of the fledgling TJC that met in Beijing in May 1920, Gao Daling from Shanxi, a new convert but one with unrivaled credentials (the lone holder of a *jinshi* degree) within the sect, was named to the top leadership circle. He apparently played a central role in hammering out the basic teachings of the TJC that later helped preserve the unity and identity of the church even as the spirit of the movement constantly defied any form of control. The emerging doctrines included most of the revelations of Wei Enbo and reaffirmed the position that as the Last Days approached, there was "no salvation" outside of the TJC. The principle of "self-support, self-government, and self-propagation" was instituted for all local TJC churches, which nevertheless required recognition and approval from provincial branches.[39]

In 1924, in an effort to institute theological discipline to contain unruly Pentecostal practices in some of its constituencies, particularly among its members in southern Zhili, the TJC began its first formal theological training program. It opened a Truth and Holy Spirit School in Tianjin—with Jesus as the president and Wei Yisa as his deputy. Such programs, under various names, were later conducted irregularly at several urban centers of the TJC and typically lasted from one to three months.[40] By 1926, the sect had developed a constitution that spelled out a five-tiered organizational structure starting with "prayer houses" at the bottom and reaching up through local churches, provincial assemblies, and national assemblies all the way to "the General Assembly," in line with the sect's global claims and ambition, which would oversee the envisioned international operation of the church. A corresponding ecclesiastical hierarchy included deacons, missionaries, elders, bishops, and a "general bishop." All bishops were to be elected by church elders. At the local level, members would elect officers to manage daily affairs, although their preacher, or "missionary," would be appointed or dispatched by the TJC elder responsible for the area. In finance, a more sustainable practice of tithes and special offerings replaced the initial call for "sharing [material possessions] among the haves and the have-nots." However, in many areas it was largely the donations of a few individuals with means that constituted "self-support." In Hunan, some TJC congregations supported themselves in part with revenue from church-run businesses and rental income. In rural Hubei, many TJC substations developed when a member donated or lent part of his property to be the prayer house, which would be renovated and furnished collectively by the group and maintained with the help of tithes, which were also known as "membership fees."[41]

TWO ROADS THAT DIVERGED: THE TJC AND THE NATIONAL CHRISTIAN COUNCIL OF CHINA

In 1922, when the China Continuation Committee called the National Christian Conference to promote cooperation among denominational missions and indigenization of Christianity in China, it extended an invitation to the TJC, one of the newest of all Protestant bodies, to send delegates to Shanghai for the meeting. By then, only five years after its founding, the sect claimed a membership of more than ten thousand, about three times the size of the Seventh-Day Adventist Church and rivaling the total of forty-two smaller Western missions. The TJC leaders saw in the conference "an exceptional opportunity to spread the [teachings of the Universal] Correction Church." In line with a plan of representation spelled out by the China Continuation Committee, they sent three representatives to the meeting, including Gao Daling, Wei Yisa, and Zhang Banaba. The committee claimed that the chief agenda for the conference was the organization of an interdenominational National Christian Council of China (NCC) (Zhonghua Jidujiao Xiejinhui), which was to "foster . . . unity of the Christian Church in China; to watch and study the development of the Church in self-support, self-government, and self-propagation; to encourage every healthy movement of the Church that leads to full autonomy; and to seek and work for the adaptation of the Church to its environment and for its naturalization in China at as early a date as practicable."[42]

The three TJC delegates to the conference, representing what they themselves called "the only truly indigenous church in China," had a more ambitious agenda. To them, what the National Christian Conference proposed for the future was already a reality among them. It would only take the correction of all mission churches—adopting the way of the TJC—to achieve that end. Therefore, the three launched a spirited crusade at the conference, "seizing the opportunity to preach the true way" and "bearing a beautiful testimony," as they put it, "among the 1,189 delegates." That "testimony" was a euphemism, however, for their denunciation of mission churches. The TJC's customary invective was more direct: it accused the numerous foreign churches in China of "hanging up a sheep's head but selling dog meat" and of "being used by the imperialists as the vanguard of their invasion, as proven by the 'missionary case' [Boxer Uprising] of 1900."[43]

The radicalism of the three delegates must have embarrassed the Chinese church leaders who helped organize the conference. According to TJC sources, the latter tried to silence them and threatened to expel them from the conference.[44] By 1922, a new generation of Western-educated, indigenous Protestant leaders had emerged within the missionary enterprise. One of the main organizers and keynote speakers at the conference was Liu Tingfang (Timothy Tingfang Lew, 1891–1947), who held a doctorate from Columbia University and was dean of the divinity faculty of Yenching University in Beijing. In contrast to the militancy of the TJC, Liu was attempting to set a cooperative and conciliatory tone for the conference when he urged delegates to "agree to differ but resolve to love."[45] The conference was chaired by Cheng Jingyi, who, although a partner with TJC's founder Wei Enbo a decade earlier in the push for independence from the LMS in Beijing, had traversed a very different path, one that was carefully balanced between patriotism and recognition of the reality of financial and administrative dependence on Western missions. As Cheng rose through the ranks within the Protestant establishment under the auspices of missionaries—becoming secretary of the China Continuation Committee and the de facto spokesman for Chinese Protestants in 1913, receiving an honorary degree of doctor of divinity from Knox College in Toronto in 1916, and attending the International Missionary Council meeting in Williamstown, Massachusetts, in 1919—he was identifying increasingly with an institution that represented Christianity in China.[46] Whatever resentment he had felt against foreign dominance of the Chi-

FIGURE 5   Retreat of staff members of the National Christian Council of China, 1925. *Back row, from right:* Cheng Jingyi (squatting), Yu Rizhang, E. C. Lobenstine, Y. J. Fan; *front row, from left:* T. K. Chung, H. T. Hodgkin, and Mrs. Hodgkin. Source: *Chinese Recorder* 64 (May 1933).

nese church would have softened in the face of moves missionaries had made since 1907 to put the Chinese, himself in particular, in the position of leadership.

For people like Cheng, a moderate, gradualist approach to church independence, one that would win the sympathy and support of most Western missionaries rather than alienate them, would therefore appear to be the only sensible one. With almost half of the conference's delegates being foreign missionaries who held real power in the churches, it was imperative for the organizers to contain the TJC's voices of discord. When the NCC was formed at the end of the conference, no TJC representative was nominated to the one-hundred-member council.[47] Chinese leaders of the newly organized NCC in fact took care to express their appreciation of the "altruistic motives" of Western missionaries who had come to China. In response, the TJC delegates lamented that those presiding over the conference "were all born of Western mommies and could not stop singing praises to them."[48]

From its inauguration in 1922 through the remainder of the Republican period, the NCC, the majority of whose members were Chinese, would serve as the most visible symbol of indigenous Protestantism. Though it did not have legislative or mandatory authority over denominational missions, it did claim to play an "advisory" role and to "act on behalf of the co-operating churches and missions," which included practically all the major mission churches, with the notable exception of the Southern Baptists and, a few years later, the CIM.[49] As the NCC replaced the China Continuation Committee, Cheng Jingyi was named general secretary of the new organization, and Yu Rizhang, a Harvard graduate and then general secretary of the national committee of the Chinese YMCA, became its chairman.[50]

The background of the modern urban elite like Cheng and Yu who made up the leadership of the NCC set them almost a world apart from the majority in the TJC. In 1902, when TJC founder Wei Enbo arrived in Beijing as a migrant from rural Hebei, Yu Rizhang, who grew up in the family of an Anglican minister, had just been admitted to St. John's University in the suburb of Shanghai (one of the most prestigious universities in the country with a student body drawn mostly from wealthy families), and Cheng Jingyi, already an activist in the LMS parish that Wei later joined, was about to leave for England to study at the Bible Training Institute in Glasgow.[51] While TJC leaders and activists included farmers, peddlers, shop owners, dealers in (mostly fake) antiques, artisans, fortune tellers, paid missionaries' helpers, and night-soil collectors, the NCC membership boasted of some of the best educated Chinese of the day. Besides Cheng and Yu, other prominent members included Liu Tingfang of Yenching University; Zhang Boling (Chang Po-ling, 1876–1951), founder and president of Nankai University in Tianjin, who had also been educated at Columbia University; and Zhao Zichen (T. C. Chao, 1888–1979), a graduate of Vanderbilt University and then professor of sociology at Soochow University.[52] Once established, the NCC adopted an organizational structure and agenda that reflected the progressive social concerns of influential liberal members on the council. It set up more than a dozen committees to deal with such issues as "church and home," emerging industrial problems, rural life, international relations, education, antinarcotic campaigns, work for the blind, and work among Buddhists and Muslims.

Among those committees set up by the NCC was one on the Indigenous Church, which went to work to propose a remedy for the "deplorable
fact" that, after more than a century since its introduction to China, the
Christian Church was "still referred to as 'that foreign sect.'" The findings
and recommendations of the committee, published in a report a few years
later, sketched out on paper a naturalized Chinese church with all the
urbanity and cosmopolitanism of a mellow liberal Christianity unhur-
ried by any eschatological exigencies: the "Indigenous Church" should
be a "member of the Church Universal" rather than "an Anti-Foreign
Church." It would aim at "bringing into fusion the best elements of both
the Western and the Eastern civilization." The committee's specific recommendations included the "building [of] the House of God . . . in bona
fide Chinese architecture," the use of "Chinese hymnology and Chinese
tunes" in church services, the "promotion of a modified Christian form of
ancestor-worship," and the "institution of Church festivals, partly western
and partly Chinese": there would be a day for "the Sweeping of Ancestral
Graves" and the "National Anniversary" (October 10), along with Easter,
Thanksgiving, and Christmas.[53]

THE SPILLOVER OF TJC REVELATIONS

For its part, the TJC had no time for such perceived trivialities. Those
who had rallied to the doomsday call of Wei Enbo preached a Christianity that was licked by the flame of an impending apocalypse. Frustrated
by its lack of success in converting mission churches en masse to their
teaching at the 1922 National Christian Conference in Shanghai, the TJC
withdrew into itself, cut off its contacts with the NCC, and continued its
crusade against mission-supported churches, vaunting its independence
and self-support and mocking those mainline Protestants who used to
boast about their membership in mission churches but had grown sheep-
ish about their reliance on foreign money at a time of rising nationalism.
In the aftermath of the May Thirtieth Incident of 1925, when British
police in Shanghai fired on unarmed Chinese demonstrators, the missionary enterprise came under increased nationalist pressure. During
the Northern Expedition (1926–1927), mission churches (particularly the
"British-flagged" ones) often attracted anti-imperialist propaganda and
harassment. Many of them rushed to declare independence from Western missions and to organize Chinese Christian unions. In contrast, the

TJC was in a coveted position of long-established autonomy and freedom from foreign domination. As a whole, it lay outside of the interest of the anti-Christian students of the 1920s who were chanting slogans against the more visible mission churches and their leaders and calling them the "running dogs" of British and American "imperialists."[54]

Throughout the 1920s, the TJC was rocked by its own explosive energy generated by a profusion of "revelations of the Holy Spirit" that, after the death of its founder, continually shook up the organization. At least fifteen splinter groups sprang up over the next two decades, under such impeccable names as the Church of God, the Church of Lord Jesus (led by a self-styled "Joseph the King of the Jews"), the Church of Jesus Christ, the New Jerusalem Holy City Church, and the Church of the Heavenly Mother (Tianmuhui), which was led by a woman who was apparently trying to fashion a Christian variant of the millenarian White Lotus belief in the Mother of No-Birth. Most of those breakaway groups led by alleged "heretics" were formed in the wake of power struggles within the TJC leadership. Zhang Lingsheng, the only TJC bishop named by Wei Enbo and a veteran Pentecostal who had sometimes contended the title of the founder of the sect, left the TJC after its sixth national meeting held in 1929 when he lost his position within the church. Other "heretics" denounced by the TJC included those who had tried to "fish in muddled waters," as some might say—people like Ye Fusheng ("Jesus Reborn"), a Shandong farmer and night-soil collector who had started the "Jesus Compound" in his village and later instituted the novel ritual of the "crucible" (lianlu), whereby women of all ages, especially the young, were to have sex with him.[55]

In the mid-1920s, the TJC went through a major crisis when Zhang Banaba, its most prominent and energetic evangelist, who had built up a large following in the south, tried to take control of the entire sect and founded a rival headquarters in Nanjing. The division lasted until 1930 when another national conference of the TJC excommunicated Zhang and reunited the movement under a collective leadership that included Gao Daling, Guo Duoma, and Wei Yisa.[56] Strengthened by the regained unity, the TJC flourished in the early 1930s. The China Christian Year Book of 1934–1935 reported that Central China was much affected by the spread of the TJC. In the city of Changsha, for instance, when most denominational churches were "sparsely attended" during the hot summer of 1934, "there were over a thousand people packed into a building where this sect was holding its worship." The report added that in its aggressive proselytizing, the TJC did have "the advantage of being a purely indigenous movement, not depending upon any foreign funds for support."[57]

Besides its nationalistic appeal, the TJC also continued to thrive on its end-time salvationism. As its theologians sought to systemize the eschatological teachings of Wei Enbo, they arrived at the "revelation" of a four-stage divine dispensationalism (hitherto hidden in the biblical story of Jacob's four wives) that started with the Pentecost in Acts. The fourth and the final stage—which began precisely in the year 1917 when Wei founded the TJC and which was represented by Rachel (listed as Jacob's fourth wife)—would culminate in the Second Coming of Christ. It was a time of special grace, for God had "sent down the Holy Spirit to establish the True Jesus Church as the end-time refuge" for humanity so that whoever joined the TJC "would be spared the catastrophe of the Last Days and enter into the Heavenly Kingdom of eternity."[58]

CHAPTER THREE

The Jesus Family

The Jesus Family is filled with love.
    The young are cherished and the old at peace;
The widowed and the widower, though alone, are at ease.
    The sick are cared for; the dead buried.
The guests are glad at home; the crippled grateful from their
    bosom.
    Isn't it the Great Harmony? Isn't it Communism?
.   .   .   .

The Jesus Family is filled with the Holy Spirit. There are the
    visions; there are the "tongues."
    There is the downpour of the Spirit as the Last Days come.
The spiritual dances, the spiritual songs—oh, what ultimate joy!
    Heal the sick, cast out the demons; show forth the power
      of the divine!
With the Holy Spirit bearing His own witness,
    Isn't it like a theater, a show, as if one is filled with the
      new wine?

—Jing Dianying, "The Jesus Family" (ca. 1930)

IN ITS EARLY YEARS, the TJC found several of its gifted leaders in
Shandong and brought a sense of personal power and security, albeit
mostly otherworldly and immaterial, to thousands of farmers in that
province which had suffered some of the worst scourges of natural and
manmade disasters in modern Chinese history. Fertile and heavily populated, Shandong province forms part of the Huaibei lowlands, a precarious
ecosystem plagued by both drought and flood. It was in Shandong after
a devastating flood in 1898 and then an even more agonizing drought
in the next two years that the hunger and restlessness of the peasants
fermented into the Boxer Uprising. In 1921, the drought of the previous
year in North China gave way to another major flood of the lower Yellow

River, and about three hundred thousand people in Shandong were displaced. Intensifying natural calamities and economic hardships since the nineteenth century resulted in a substantial migration of Shandong peasants to Manchuria and Inner Mongolia, with an estimated four million people leaving during the 1920s alone.

In addition to the unpredictable forces of nature, Shandong's strategic position at the mouth of the Yellow River and its relatively flat terrain condemned the area to hot military contests in times of war. In the warlord period, natural hardships and the general breakdown of the political order often led to desperate modes of survival. During the mid-1920s, bandit numbers in the province ranged between twenty thousand and thirty thousand and reached an estimated two hundred thousand by 1930. Such "predatory self-help," to use Phil Billingsley's words, only exacerbated the precariousness of life for the common people.[1] Accordingly, those who sought a peaceful alternative to predatory survival often formed themselves into communities of mutual support. Some of these were organized by eclectic religious societies such as the Jinan-based Society of the Way (Daoyuan). They ran their own small banks and offered credit to poor people.[2] Among the Protestant converts in Shandong, the search for communal self-help in the 1920s led to the formation of the Jesus Family, a sectarian mutual-aid community independent of mission Christianity and bound together by Pentecostalism and an ascetic pursuit of end-time salvation.

THE MAKING OF A SECTARIAN LEADER: JING DIANYING AND THE WESTERN MISSIONS IN TAI'AN

The Jesus Family was founded by Jing Dianying (1890–1957), who came from a learned, moderately prosperous gentry family near the village of Mazhuang, Tai'an county. During his early years, Jing had received a traditional education and was well versed in Confucian and Daoist classics. However, the abolishment of the civil service examination in 1905 thwarted his adolescent dream of becoming a Confucian scholar-official, and the death of both parents in his early teens may have traumatized him into certain disenchantment with this world. In his youth he had gone up the nearby Taishan Mountain where he "bared his chest in drifting snows and practiced sitting meditation" (in the manner of Daoist ascetics) before he was baptized into the Methodist Church in the county seat of Tai'an

FIGURE 6   Jing Dianying. Courtesy of Jing Fuyin.

in 1914. Jing's conversion followed a familiar pattern in the emergence of
the Protestant community in modern China, whereby fruitful encounters
with the alien religion often resulted from education in mission schools
or employment by missionaries. In 1912, the year of the demise of the
last imperial dynasty, Jing came to the city of Tai'an and, at the age of

twenty-two, enrolled in the newly opened Cuiying Middle School run by the American Methodist Episcopal mission.[3] As Perry O. Hanson, then principal of Cuiying, later recalled, "this young man was unusually mature, had unusual knowledge of Chinese, and was a devout Buddhist . . . [and] rather resented the idea of people coming from America to proselyte among his nationals."[4]

Although he initially detested the foreign religion and tried to separate it from the modern learning the school offered, Jing eventually yielded to the Christian faith after serving as the Chinese language instructor to an American Methodist Episcopal missionary by the name of Nora Dillenbeck (1883–1938).[5] An "altogether sweet and lovable girl" who was "very attractive in face and form" (as her recommendation letters to the Woman's Foreign Missionary Society noted), Dillenbeck had been appointed as a single woman missionary to the Tai'an station in late 1913.[6] As in many other such cases, a warm relationship developed between the missionary and the Chinese language helper. Before long, Jing fell in love with Dillenbeck, aged thirty, and was probably responsible for the far-fetched, flattering transliteration of her name into Lin Meili (Lin the beautiful), to which she did not object.

According to some accounts, the two exchanged engagement rings. However, it would have been hard for any such romance to be fulfilled under the circumstances. Dillenbeck's contract with her mission board stipulated "five years of continuous service as a single woman," and the prevailing racial attitudes among the missionaries alone would also have created an almost insurmountable barrier. It was a tortuous relationship. At one point, Jing was allegedly so tormented by the guilt over his desire for Dillenbeck that he went to a mission hospital and asked to be emasculated. She promptly arrived and "tearfully dissuaded him" from doing that. In any event, Jing's uncertain relationship with her plunged his own marriage into crisis. In 1919, he divorced his bound-feet wife.[7]

Jing was frustrated also in his quest of modern education, which could have brought him decent career opportunities in the cities. Cuiying Middle School was suspended temporarily in 1918 before he was able to complete his education there. At the age of twenty-eight, and still without a middle school diploma (despite his fine training in the classics), the best job he could find was that of a low-paid evangelist at a mission hospital in the provincial capital Jinan. Before long, however, Jing became disillusioned with what he saw as the predominance of the worldly power of money and diplomas ("especially those from America") in church organizations, which marginalized a rural convert like himself. By 1921, in the midst of continuing rural hardships in the area since 1918—a devastating flood of that year had been followed by two years of drought—Jing was back in the village of Mazhuang, where he founded a small Christian business cooperative called the Saints' Credit and Savings Society (with about a quarter of its total funds contributed by Dillenbeck), which dealt in textiles and grains and at the same time organized the local faithful in regular prayer and evangelism.[8]

The start of the Christian cooperative in Mazhuang did not immediately catapult Jing into sectarian communalism. In fact, he continued to be associated with the missionary establishment, returning briefly to the hospital in Jinan as an evangelist and then teaching for a while at the Cuiying Middle School. The early 1920s were unsettled years for Jing. In 1923, he took another step toward an eventual embrace of what Tao Feiya has called a "Christian utopia" when he sold his possessions and became briefly a wandering preacher—living by faith in the manner of begging monks, a familiar sight in the North China countryside—before he was again invited back to teach at the Methodist Episcopal middle school in Tai'an. Then came a decisive moment in his break with the missionary establishment. In 1924, Jing received his "baptism by the Spirit" while attending a revival meeting held at a Christian orphanage in Tai'an called the Home of Onesiphorus, alternatively known by its Pentecostal name Shenzhaohui (Assemblies of God), which had been founded in the mid-1910s by Leslie Anglin, an American Baptist–turned–faith missionary. Thereafter, Jing came under the sway of a form of Pentecostalism—complete with "tongues," visions, spiritual singing and dancing, and trances—that had already been practiced for some years among many local converts, including members of Jing's own business cooperative in Mazhuang.[9]

That was more than the Methodist Episcopal mission could bear. Jing was promptly fired by Perry Hanson, who later wrote unadmiringly of the Pentecostal wildfire that had spread through Jing into his mission. The staid Hanson detested the Pentecostalists' "loud weeping and shouting," which he compared to "a Chinese funeral," and told Jing to leave not only the school, but the mission church as well.[10] After he was expelled from the Methodist Episcopal church, Jing held on momentarily to the last string that tied him to the Western missions. In 1925, he went to work for a few months at the Home of Onesiphorus where he had been initiated into Pentecostalism the previous year. By the end of the year, Jing would be thrown out of that institution as well (for his role in the cover-up of an adulterous affair between an administrator and a female resident). However, during the few months that he worked there, Jing became acquainted with the orderly operation of Onesiphorus, which divided up the hundreds of orphans into occupational departments such as carpentry, cross-stitching, tailoring, shoe-making, masonry, and farming. As we shall see, when the Jesus Family started to emerge the following year, its organizational structure paralleled that of the well-established orphanage.[11]

"BAPTISM BY FIRE"

In early 1926, back in the village of Mazhuang (this time to stay), Jing started a Christian community of his own in a house donated by a relative and fellow convert, which he named the Silkworm and Mulberry-Tree House for the Learning of the Way (Cansang Xuedaofang), a charity house for widows who could grow mulberry trees, raise silkworms, and weave while learning the Christian Way. The following year the earlier Saints' Society was merged into the new, which was renamed the Jesus Family (Yesu Jiating).[12] For the fifteen or so initial members, the organization of this community had come at an opportune time. Under the corrupt warlord government in Shandong headed by the notorious "dog-meat general" Zhang Zongchang, banditry had spread out of control, and many farmers had had to fall back on whatever forms of mutual help they could find. A Tai'an branch of the popular self-defense society known as the Red Spears was formed in 1926, which became at least three thousand strong within a year and was able to overrun a bandit's den in the mountains. The Jesus Family, though less awe-inspiring than the Red Spears, provided a level of group security as well; its association (however weak) with the Christian church under the protection of foreign gunboats served as a possible deterrent to the lawless, and its self-proclaimed poverty would hopefully turn away any ambitious plunderers.[13]

In 1930, the group moved to a piece of land of about four acres that they had obtained, with some financial help from Dillenbeck, just outside the village of Mazhuang, where Jing and his followers farmed and also began to build their own communal settlement of straw huts and brick houses. Those who joined the Family were told to sell their possessions and either give the proceeds to the poor or bring them into the Family. It was a difficult life from the very beginning, for the small amount of land could not produce enough to supply the needs of the Family, which would grow to include more than forty people by 1931. The regular diet included a kind of thin gruel made of ground corn and ground beans (sometimes mixed with sweet potato) and ingeniously called *hutu* (muddledness)—which suggests a Daoist disdain for exquisite taste and worldly pleasures; the members were, in fact, often reduced to drinking the "four-eye *hutu*," so called because it was thin enough for them to see their own two eyes reflected in it.[14] But if food and other material provisions were not abundant, "spiritual gifts" and a host of immaterial blessings were. The song "Jesus Family" (excerpted in this chapter's epigraph), which Jing composed and set to a folk melody during the early years of the movement, celebrated the love, equality, and carefree life within the communitarian sect. Its members "love not food, nor clothing, and are not desirous of big mansions." Instead, borne by "visions," "tongues," and miracles, they "eagerly hope for the Coming of Jesus."

By 1933, the *China Christian Year Book* had already taken notice of this "communistic" group in western Shandong in which some one hundred members had "all things in common." It added that the religious life of the group was of the "extreme" Pentecostal type, "dancing being one of the main phenomena." To spread its influence, the Jesus Family regularly conducted semiannual revival meetings during the slack farming seasons in the first and sixth months of the lunar calendar. Each lasted from seven to ten days and typically attracted hundreds of admirers and fellow seekers of "spiritual gifts"—sometimes more than one thousand—from not only Shandong province but other parts of North China as well.[15] According to Zhu Xin, who attended some of those revival meetings in the 1930s while he was a student at the North China Theological Seminary in Tengxian some seventy miles south of Mazhuang, what distinguished the sect was its teaching that all should seek to be "filled with the Holy Spirit." He enumerated more than a dozen manifestations of such a condition, which included profuse sweating, a sense of being weightless, "weeping and howling," uncontrollable dancing and waving or shivering, sudden swooning and falling to the ground, rolling on the floor and "frothing at the mouth," numbness in the tongue and chattering of teeth, or an outpouring of incomprehensible glossolalia.

At one such revival, with three hundred to four hundred people standing in prayer, Zhu saw that only a few minutes into the meeting, "everyone started to cry out and wail, waving and dancing. There was the 'ba-ba-da-da' coming from one side and the 'wu-wu-wa-wa' from another, punctuated by the occasional 'dong-dong'—people all about were suddenly thumping stiffly to the ground. . . . The woman standing next to me went down. At first she was rolling and howling. Gradually she became stiff. I moved over and tried to help her up, but a brother standing to my left immediately stopped me and shouted into my ears: 'Her spirit has been raptured to heaven. Don't you disturb her!'" When the woman awoke from her trance half an hour later, those around her gathered to inquire about her celestial experience. She reported that Jesus personally gave her an audience in paradise, uttered words of admonition and encouragement, and took her on a tour of the heavenly court. In the "Garden of the Trees of Life," she saw names of people inscribed on the trees, some flourishing, others withering, each of which represented the spiritual state of a particular Christian on earth. Then she read out more than a dozen names and described the state of the trees they were inscribed on, to the thrill of some and the dismay of others.[16]

In the Jesus Family, rapture (*beiti*) was the highest state of "being filled with the Holy Spirit." The hierarchy started with "tongues" at the bottom and ascended through visions, dreams, and prognostication all the way to the top level, where one's spirit departed from the body and was "transported to heaven to meet the Lord face to face." Among those who were "raptured," adolescents accounted for the majority, followed by adult women and, last of all, adult men. While details of such unearthly experience were not always communicated to the earthbound—a fifteen-year-old boy who had the richest experience of rapture rarely went beyond the assertion that he had heard clearly Jesus' voice—its reality and sublimity was eagerly affirmed by all in the Family. In fact, to the members, such dramatic possession by the Holy Spirit, also called "baptism by fire," was proof that "the Family descended from heaven, and was never of man's design."[17]

For the members, who frequently ran out of food and had to "scrub the millstones" and flush out the residue for a meal, such a baptism must have been a vital source of strength and renewal. A poem Jing composed depicts the majestic realm of power and happiness into which one soars on Pentecostal wings (and empty stomach):

> Joy in poverty, joy in poverty;
>> Little to eat, nothing to drink.
> Laughing and clapping our empty hands. . . .
>> Seeking only to abide in Him.
> Who cares if there is anything to cook in the pot?
>> The Spirit lights the fire; tears steam the buns of life. . . .
> Spread your spiritual wings and the globe becomes small,
>> Let go your arms and dance, and the earth will tremble.
> Hook your swing to the moon,
>> And pluck the stars to taste the fruits from God!
> Pull up the rivers to gird your loins;
>> Shake the mountain and whip it like a top!
> The wind is our messenger; and our servant the flame. . . .
>> Misty and mysterious, the Lord in us abides.[18]

THE DESCENT OF THE SPIRIT: ECHOES OF PENTECOSTALISM AND MILLENARIANISM IN TRADITIONAL FOLK RELIGION

There is a striking resemblance between the state of "being filled with the Holy Spirit" experienced by the members of the Jesus Family and traditional spirit possession practiced in Shandong and other parts of North China. Both Joseph W. Esherick and Paul A. Cohen have given revealing accounts of spirit possession among the Boxers against the backdrop of widespread famine at the turn of the twentieth century. One former Boxer in Shandong recalled: "we requested the gods to attach themselves to our bodies [*qiushen futi*]. When they had done so, we became Spirit Boxers . . . [and] were invulnerable to swords and spears." Likewise, a gazetteer in Shanxi reported that the Spirit Boxers would chant an incantation and "suddenly fall to the ground. After a short while they get up and begin to dance in a frenzied manner and talk as if in their sleep." Then they would state that a god—usually one who had evolved from an ancient historical figure—had "descended" into their bodies. Other Boxers further believed that once possessed by the spirit "you'll go up to heaven."[19] As in the case of the Pentecostals in the Jesus Family and the TJC, male adolescents among the Boxers had a special propensity for spirit possession. One Qing official who watched "Spirit Boxing" at a temple in southern Zhili saw that the people "were all young lads of thirteen or fourteen." As Cohen points out, the preference for young males in spirit possession possibly arose from "the ancient Chinese notion that children who were still virgins possessed an undisturbed quality that made it easier for them to serve as mouthpieces of the gods."[20]

For the Jesus Family, the spectacular display of Pentecostal power served to confirm the core teaching that this world was coming to an end. However, unlike the TJC, which instituted theological education for its leaders out of which emerged a systematic eschatology, the community that Jing established had to cope with persistent material scarcity and did not develop a comparable program of theological education.[21] On the other hand, as a recent convert, Jing was not sufficiently accomplished in exegesis to unveil an elaborate divine scheme of the end of time. Nor did he experience as profound a personal crisis as Wei Enbo did when the latter received specific revelations about the timing of the apocalypse. Therefore, Jing and his followers did not go beyond a general conviction of the impending end of the world and a vague millennialism according to which the Family became the means of God's protection and salvation, a modern "Ark" that

> ferries [the saved] across the boundless sea
>   as hardships and afflictions fly wildly by.
> Outside the Ark,
>   The sea is ferocious and mankind cries in pain;
> Inside the Ark,
>   Animals dance and birds in unison sing.[22]

As an apocalyptic metaphor, the Ark must have been comforting to those who fled the calamities of the world into the Jesus Family. Though biblical in its reference, the image of a vehicle ferrying the faithful across the sea of suffering recalled the "Boat of the Dharma" (fachuan) that millions in the North China countryside had hoped would transport them to the "other shore" of salvation as they prayed for the speedy coming of the Maitreya Buddha. According to the teachings of the Eight Trigrams, a popular millenarian sect that emerged from the White Lotus tradition and arose in southwestern Shandong (not far from Mazhuang) during the Qing dynasty, humanity had to pass through three kalpa periods of great changes (*san jie*), also known as the "Three Suns"—the period of the "Blue Sun," or the past, ruled over by the Lamp-Lighting Buddha (Randengfo); that of the "Red Sun," the present and the age of Sakyamuni Buddha; and the period of the "White Sun," which would be ushered in by Maitreya, the Buddha of the future.

Presiding over these inexorable changes that were attended by great calamities was the Mother of No-Birth (Wusheng Laomu), who had always wanted her "children on the great earth to quickly return home" before they were forever lost to the cosmic disasters. In the Eight Trigrams tradition, the world was approaching the end of the second kalpa. Since humanity was "steeped in wickedness" and most of her children remained "lost" as calamities were closing in, the Mother of No-Birth had promised that "she would send down yet another god to lead men to salvation, the Buddha Maitreya."[23] The saved would return to the "Native Land of True Emptiness," beyond the cycle of life and death. In the late Qing dynasty, countless followers of the Eight Trigrams on the North China plain chanted the following lines as they anticipated the coming of their savior:

> True Emptiness—my native land;
>   No-Birth—my father and mother.
> For now—Tathagata;
>   My progenitor—Maitreya Buddha.[24]

The incantation would not have been unfamiliar to Jing Dianying, for in 1918—four years after his conversion to Christianity and about the same time as he became an evangelist in the mission hospital in Jinan—he briefly joined Shengxiandao (the Way of the Sages and the Worthies), a secret society that had spun off the Eight Trigrams.[25] When the Jesus Family came into being during the late 1920s, it must not have been too difficult for either Jing or his followers to be set aflame by the Christian millenarian and Pentecostal fire, for they had been licked by a similar fire before.

A HOME FOR THE VISIONARIES: THE GROWTH OF THE
JESUS FAMILY LEADERSHIP

In its formative years during the 1930s, the growth of the Jesus Family was helped by the addition of several able members who eventually formed a collective leadership centered around Jing. The first was Dong Hengxin (1907–1952), an opium smuggler from Shanxi province, where a ban on the drug had been enforced under the warlord governor Yan Xishan after the Revolution of 1911. However, during the same period, opium cultivation continued, even flourished, in the neighboring provinces of Shaanxi, Henan, Zhili, and Suiyuan, the administrative region just north of Shanxi. Therefore, Shanxi, clear of opium growing, became dependent on opium smuggling from neighboring areas.[26] Dong had stepped into this lucrative trade in his youth. According to David Vaughan Rees, an English surgeon and a CIM missionary who became a great admirer of the Jesus Family, Dong "substituted a smaller container for the usual large one in his thermos flask. It was easy for him to fill the large cavity left with opium." The penalty would have been death under Yan Xishan's government if Dong had been caught. Then, sometime during the late 1920s, he became a Christian, stopped his drug trafficking, and became the leader of Governor Yan's brass band. Later, he entered the Baptist Seminary in Kaifeng, Henan.[27] Eventually, in the early 1930s, the adventurous and restless Dong found his home in Mazhuang. There, he became a prolific songwriter and, before his suicide in 1952, set to music numerous verses that were either composed by Jing or evolved from spontaneous chanting of Family members as they applied themselves to departmentalized work such as masonry and tailoring.[28]

Also in the inner leadership circle were two women, Zuo Shunzhen (1907–1987) and Chen Bixi (1904–1980). Zuo was the great-great-granddaughter of Zuo Zongtang, the celebrated Qing scholar and governor general of Shaanxi and Gansu who was credited with the pacification of Muslim rebellions in the western parts of China during the 1860s and 1870s. Like many other children from families of means, Zuo Shunzhen had attended a Presbyterian ladies' school in Beijing before she became a nurse at the Beijing National School of Midwifery Hospital, where she met Chen Bixi, a fourth-generation Protestant and a doctor in the hospital's department of obstetrics and gynecology. In Rees's words, "They were both accomplished young ladies, and were noted in the social life of

Peking, especially in its dancing salons; both were prominent in skating and sport."[29]

All that changed, of course, during the early 1930s. In September 1931, the Japanese army occupied Manchuria after the staged "Mukden Incident." By late January 1932, Shanghai also came under attack from the Japanese and endured relentless aerial bombing. As Beijing became a likely target after Shanghai, the dancing salons and the skating rinks lost their charm; instead, eschatological revival meetings grew more pertinent. In that year, a Methodist minister named Wu Xikao led a series of Pentecostal meetings in the capital. There were "tongues" and prophecies, many of which were in fact announced in "tongues" and were then translated into Mandarin Chinese. (The ritual, though impressive, was not seamless. The evangelist who preached in "tongues" sometimes accused the translators of making up their own sermons that had nothing to do with the revelations he received.) The most alarming of those prophecies, which few could afford to ignore, was that "Beijing will come under great bombardments."[30]

In any case, both Zuo and Chen were converted to Pentecostalism during the revival and were "baptized in the Holy Spirit amid a flood of tears." Instructed by the Spirit to flee the city of destruction and to spread the message of salvation in remote areas of China, Zuo and Chen helped organize a group of young women in the hospital to "preach the Gospel and heal the sick in Mongolia." The two were women of both religious passion and pioneering spirit, for when they reached the city of Baotou in Suiyuan (now Inner Mongolia), they set up their evangelical base in one-half of a large building whose other half was being used as a brothel. In 1935, Zuo and Chen were "directed" by God to go to Mazhuang to attend the annual summer revival meeting that had gained considerable fame. Soon afterwards, Jing followed them to Baotou and persuaded them to join the Jesus Family, in which their medical expertise, no less than their organizational skills, came to play a vital role.[31]

By that time, Jing had also made impressive gains in winning over Nora Dillenbeck to his visions of a divinely appointed end-time community empowered by the Holy Spirit. Throughout the 1920s, Dillenbeck had given financial support to Jing at various stages of the evolution of the salvationist community that he started. During the same period, she had settled into the life of an educational missionary in Tai'an with occasional evangelical forays into neighboring towns and villages.[32] However, she became increasingly attracted to Jing's blend of fiery Pentecostalism, fundamentalism, and apocalyptism. According to Perry Hanson, who was in charge of the Shantung (Shandong) Annual Conference of the Methodist Episcopal Church in the 1930s and who retained a "personal friendship" with Dillenbeck even after she drifted away from the Methodist mission, Jing's "influence on her was strong. . . . [She] gradually got to the point where she would teach nothing but the Bible . . . and encouraged the free-for-all shouting, repetitious praying." In turn, Hanson added, "Miss Dillenbeck's influence was very strong with our pastors and several followed into the ultra-emotionalism which characterized the Jesus Home and was taken over by Miss D. in the work here in the Compound."[33]

In the early 1930s, Dillenbeck won over Lillian Greer, a fellow Methodist missionary, to the Jesus Family brand of Pentecostalism. Both withdrew from the Shantung Annual Conference of the Methodist Episcopal Church in 1934.[34] Early that year, Dillenbeck joined Jing and a few of his associates on an itinerant preaching tour that lasted several months and took them all the way to the remote Gansu province, relying, in Jing's words, on "the good earth as our mat and the blue heaven as our tent." The following year, Dillenbeck was back in the United States on furlough. Returning to China in 1936, she moved into the Jesus Family by the end of the year, where she stayed in a small Western-style house that Jing had built for her. There, the American missionary–turned–"Mother of the Home" (as she was called) lived, taught Bible classes, and shared both Pentecostal ecstasies and the "coarse food and the slim diet of the peasant" until she died of acute pneumonia on the fourteenth of the "hot and sultry" month of July 1938.[35]

THE EXPANSION OF THE JESUS FAMILY

With the help of a dedicated and gifted collective leadership, the Jesus Family flourished through the 1930s. During the same period, disasters, both natural and manmade, also drew many into the welcoming shelter in Mazhuang. (In 1933, yet another flooding of the Yellow River in North China left eighteen thousand dead and millions homeless.) Most of the new members were tenant farmers and quite a few were in wretched conditions—in Jing's words, "there were the blind, the lame, the crippled, and those seeking to fill their stomachs"; there were also small landowners, merchants, workers, teachers, and even doctors who were drawn to the vibrant and egalitarian religion of the community.[36] Others came to rid themselves of drug addiction, or, as in the case of the illiterate "parent" of one "subfamily" up in the mountains in southern Shandong who abandoned his precarious trade as a bandit leader, to start new lives.[37]

With the steady surge in membership, life in the Jesus Family became increasingly departmentalized. The organization was patterned after the Home of Onesiphorus, in which Jing had worked briefly in 1925. In addition to the farming department, which engaged in the most basic work of the community, fourteen other occupational units eventually were developed, including carpentry, blacksmithing, stone masonry, shoemaking, cooking, needlework, childcare, education, and health care, along with one charged with the care of draft animals.[38] Added to such organizational strength was Jing's undiminished vision of an authentic mystical communion with God as the basis of Family life. In a letter to the head of a "small Family," Jing wrote: "In the [Mazhuang] Family, we do not have set rules or conventions for clothing, food, and lodging. What we have in the Family is a genuine taste (mystery), a taste that can only be experienced but not communicated in words: it is 'the sacrificial love.'"[39]

Such a "taste" and down-to-earth organization led to major material achievements. Around their dwellings the members planted a row of cypress trees that in time formed a fifteen-foot-high "holy hedge" (*shengli*) within which they created an oasis of order and security. Inside the compound the Family members dug a big well, built a mill to grind the beans and the grains they grew, planted a vineyard, raised cattle and poultry, and set up looms where women turned their homegrown cotton into uniform coarse garments that, like other material possessions, were shared. And in contrast to the neighboring villages, where roads were in disrepair and bridges would disappear because the local population would "steal the wood and iron contained therein," all around the Jesus Family settlement "roads [were] improved, bridges built and kept in repair . . . and crops improved."[40]

By the mid-1930s, the Jesus Family had spread beyond Shandong and built similar settlements in Henan, Shanxi, and Jiangsu provinces, as well as in the far northwestern province of Gansu and in Inner Mongolia (possibly among some of the Shandong emigrants there). Many of those "subfamilies" started when local landowning converts or people of means

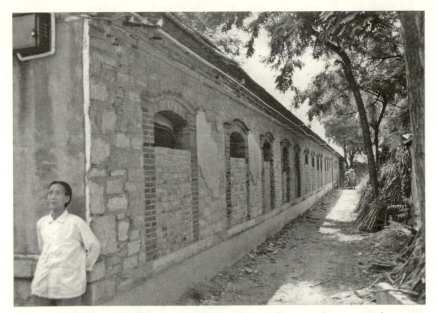

FIGURE 7   Li Ruijun, former Jesus Family member, at the original Jesus Family compound, Mazhuang, 2002. Photograph by Lian Xi.

donated their land or properties to the sect. Others were funded in part by individual missionaries such as Dillenbeck and Lillian Greer.[41] Theodore F. Romig pointed out that, as an expression of the drive to "divorce the Gospel from its Western trappings and to clothe it in native garb," the Jesus Family also "exerted considerable influence upon the regular churches in North China." He cited the example of Wang Changtai, a Methodist Episcopal clergyman and "one of the best educated ministers" in Shandong province. Wang had graduated from Drew Seminary and had spent "years of fruitless ministry" in the city of Jinan. After spending "some time with the Family of Jesus," he returned to the provincial capital to become "the strongest spiritual power in the city." (He played a central role in the founding of the independent Spiritual Gifts Society in Jinan.) The Jesus Family "gave him a sense of mission. They also stripped from him his cloak of false pride in his adopted Western culture. He literally threw away his Western clothes, his leather shoes, and his bottle of Kreml Hair Oil, and donned again his Chinese garments, put on the comfortable cloth shoes so typical of Chinese footwear, and shaved his head according to good Chinese style. No longer was Mr. Wang a disseminator of Western culture, but he was a preacher of the Gospel. His love for Zion superceded his longing for Madison, N.J."[42]

After July 1937, when Japan launched its full-fledged invasion of China, refugees poured into the Jesus Family settlements for shelter. During the eight years of resistance war, sixty-four smaller Jesus Family units sprang up across China. Within four years, the number of Family members at Mazhuang rose to about three hundred.[43] Throughout those years, Jing preached a moving gospel of "bankruptcy," or "broken property" (pochan), that was curiously soothing to both the haves and the have-nots. Not only should one not lament the devastations and the losses caused by the war, the faithful should in fact pursue a total "brokenness"—of their houses, belongings, learning, craft, know-how, and everything worldly they had relied upon. Members surrendered all their belongings upon joining the church. In return, they found within the Jesus Family the equality and warmth of communitarian life, the assurances of both eternal salvation and two meals a day, typically corn cakes or thin hutu. Any lingering hunger and other desires could be tamed by practiced fasting, which often lasted from one to three weeks. And if hunger still refused to go away, one could perhaps be reminded by the words of wisdom printed on the Jesus Family's "Worship Calendar" hanging on the wall in each room that "fat pigs die young while lean cranes live long."[44]

In time, the Jesus Family became in some ways a traditional family writ large. Members worked together on the Family farm and orchards at day and shared the oversized Family brick beds in segregated quarters at night. Natural blood relations were replaced by "spiritual relations and lineages" (lingtong), according to which a new generational order was created. The leaders became "parents" and were revered and obeyed as the "old people" even if they were still in their thirties. All newcomers quickly sorted out their standings within the community when they were accorded titles varying from uncle and aunt, to elder and younger brother and sister.[45] Inscribed on the wall behind the altar in the main church building (erected in 1931) was the passage from Matthew 12:48–50 that literally validated the new familial relationship: "Who is my mother? And who are my brethren? . . . For whosoever shall do the will of my Father which is in heaven, the same is my brother, and sister, and mother."[46]

As in traditional Chinese families, arranged marriages in the Jesus Family became routine. Before being admitted into the Family, young people, especially women, were asked to "surrender" their "rights of marriage." This might have become necessary because a disproportionate number of unmarried males were lame, blind, or decrepit. During the last decade of the Jesus Family, 211 of 216 marriages in the original settlement at Mazhuang were arranged by Jing and Zuo Shunzhen, to whom God allegedly revealed His will in such matters (often through dreams).[47] Married life was also carefully regulated. Husbands and wives lived separately most of the time, and cohabitation typically required approval by Zuo, who kept a record of the dates when couples lived together in one of the handful of private rooms in Mazhuang. Such periods of intimacy lasted for no more than two or three weeks at a time before the couple returned to their own segregated quarters. This was in part a matter of necessity: as late as 1949, after several single units were added, there were only a total of about two dozen private rooms for almost two hundred couples. The sexual segregation was important for the Jesus Family's reputation of virtue, and the resulting dissolution of natural bonds in the Family was central to its communitarian and egalitarian principle, which allowed no private ownership—of property, marriage, or children. The latter were entrusted to the nursery the moment after birth, were visited and breastfed by their mothers four times a day during infancy, and seldom saw them again after that. This would ensure that parents develop no special love for their own children, which would be "incompatible with their love of Jesus."[48]

Such practices were reminiscent of the social policies, including sexual segregation, in the ranks of the Taiping rebels of the mid-nineteenth century. Like the Jesus Family, Taiping policies had included the equal distribution of land, raising of chickens and sows by quota, planting of mulberry trees and spinning of silk by every household, and forwarding of all the fruits of such labor, except what each family needed for daily needs, to the public treasury. In the 1850s, Hong Xiuquan had also decreed the separation of the sexes into different camps and units to protect the God Worshipers' reputation for virtue, to allow the formation of women's army units, and to make procreation almost impossible until they established their projected Heavenly Kingdom.[49]

In the case of the Jesus Family, the breakdown of familial loyalties— to be rechanneled, along with the members' agricultural productivity, into the larger, and only, Family—was apparent. As Wang Xipeng, rural work secretary of the NCC, observed during a visit to the Jesus Family in Mazhuang, when husbands and wives met each other in the village, there were "no facial expressions exchanged between them. It was as if they were strangers. . . . Naturally, couples in the Jesus Family do not quarrel. There is nothing between them to quarrel about; there is only the religion of mutual love." The daily routine also helped to squeeze out any residual carnal desires. "Five to six hours of Pentecostal prayers, seven to eight hours of separate work, and one to two hours of communal dining" left little opportunity for couples to meet each other, let alone time for private intimacy.[50]

In the place of familial intimacy, the Jesus Family offered mutual support and protection at a time when individuals and natural families in rural Shandong were often incapable of providing or fending for themselves. Especially after 1937, as the terrifying waves of war surged around, it increasingly saw itself as the modern Ark to transport its occupants to the shore of Heaven. One song written by the Family members for "rural evangelism" was titled "The Last Days Are Here." It urged their "fellow countrymen" to "run fast . . . and flee the burning fire of Hell." Those who did by joining the Jesus Family would find in Heaven "manna and spiritual water, and fruits as many as you can hold." They would "live for ever" and would "not grow old."[51]

In the meantime, however, communitarian life within the Jesus Family still required discipline, for the promised picturesque pleasures in Heaven did not satisfy all earthly desires. Some apparently misbehaved, either by stealing food, using cosmetics, or contemplating desertion, as in the case of a young woman who became unhappy with her arranged marriage and was caught exchanging intimate letters with a young man in a nearby city. When such things happened, chastisement took the form of beating with a broom or spanking with a wooden slab, not unlike that practiced in traditional Chinese families. The slab used for such occasions had the characters *xiqi zhi ai* (wondrous love) written on it—in Jing's superb calligraphy.[52] In enforcing disciplines, both "familial" and spiritual, Jing and other leaders had the able assistance of dogs that "knew who was born again and who was not." Jing used to cite as an example "one of their brethren from an outlying home who was dreadfully upset because the dogs had growled at him," thereupon the terrified delinquent "confessed there was something wrong in his life and that he had grown lukewarm, and the dog knew it."[53]

The use of canine admonition and the recourse to the slab suggested that Jing's vision of a community of selfless love, moral purity, and higher purpose bound by a mystical "taste" was not easily translated into reality. In fact, both Jing and Zuo Shunzhen in the later years of the Jesus Family would find it difficult to abide strictly by the puritanical codes they themselves had established. They would withdraw to the "little house" (originally built for Dillenbeck) where a separate kitchen served more refined grains and spared them the coarseness and cheerlessness of the common *hutu*. Despite Jing's tribute that those who gave up personal property to enter the Family had "broken the net of selfishness and jumped out of the pit of self-interest," leaders in the Family would favor their own kin in the provision of food, lodging, medical care, and even burials. A former member recalled that, well before the Family's forced dissolution under the new government, different "classes" within the Family had already emerged as those with wealth and social standing demanded better treatment for their own children.[54] Moreover, at least three male "parents" of Jesus Family settlements, Jing included, would be accused of sexually exploiting female members.[55]

All this recalls the human foibles that had undermined the austere discipline in the Taiping pursuit of a virtuous and egalitarian Heavenly Kingdom. In the case of the latter, there were always those who defied Hong Xiuquan's stern edict that banned private hoarding of valuables and decreed their surrender to the "sacred [public] treasury of the Heavenly Court."[56] Taiping's forced separation of sexes had also led to homosexuality and to ingenuous subterfuges whereby men sneaked into female camps dressed as women and vice versa—and risked the punishment of beatings of up to 140 blows with a heavy pole (which could amount to a death sentence) or public beheading.[57]

Yet if the moral and spiritual lapses in the Jesus Family remind one of the failings of the Taiping Christians almost a century earlier, the utopian settlement that Jing built also points, beyond the Taiping, to a more ancient and enduring quest for the "Great Harmony" (*datong*) in Chinese history. In that vision, first articulated in the Western Han dynasty (206 BCE–9 CE) but attributed to Confucius, "when the Great Way was practiced, the world was shared by all alike. Thus men did not love their parents only, nor treat as children only their own sons. . . . They showed kindness and compassion to widows, orphans, childless men, and those who were disabled by disease, so that they were all sufficiently maintained. Males had their proper work, and females had their homes. . . . In this way [selfish] schemings were repressed and found no development. Robbers, filchers, and rebellious traitors did not show themselves, and hence the outer doors remained open, and were not shut. This was [the period of] the Great Harmony."[58]

Through the centuries, as the Great Way eluded the dynasties, and faded away during periods of political disintegration, the dream had endured among the populace and had kindled heroic, or desperate, attempts, including the Taiping Rebellion, to bring it to pass in a transformed China.[59] In times of hopeless disorder and decay, as toward the end of the Eastern Jin period in the early fifth century, it had also inspired poetic fantasies of a haven of peace and tranquility, or a land beyond the "spring of peach blossoms" with its "imposing houses, good fields, beautiful ponds, mulberry trees, bamboo, and the like," where men and women wearing exotic clothing worked side by side in the fields and where "the elderly and children all seemed to be happy and enjoying themselves," blissfully oblivious to the change of dynasties. The Jesus Family, drawn by its Christian millenarian hopes aboard an end-time Ark, remained heir to such a Chinese vision. And like the illusory land hidden by a mountain beyond the blooming peach trees, which vanished when the fisherman who first discovered it was sent back by a local official, the Jesus Family behind its "holy hedge" of cypress trees would also dissolve when centralized political authority reestablished itself at the end of decades of postdynastic turmoil.[60]

CHAPTER FOUR

The Smitten Land

CHINA IN REVIVAL

FOR ALL THE EXTRAORDINARY VIGOR in its religion, the communitarian and separatist Jesus Family was only one of the many conduits of indigenous Protestant revivalism in China. Throughout much of the 1930s, Pentecostal revivals erupted across the country. As in the Jesus Family, they typically took the form of a series of special meetings held over several days amidst floods of tears, holy laughter, "tongues," and cries for mercy; public confessions of sins and ecstatic shouts of joy were punctuated by the thumping sound of people being "smitten" by the Holy Spirit and "hurled down on the floor."[1] The movement first emerged in Shandong province as a result of a convergence of two streams of revivalism. One of these started within the mission churches during the late 1920s and was inspired in particular by Marie Monsen, a Norwegian missionary. The other, much greater in its influence, can be traced to a loosely organized indigenous Spiritual Gifts Society (Ling'enhui) that was founded in 1930 in Feixian in the southern part of the province.[2] Thereafter, the Shandong Revival, as it was often called, spread rapidly across the province as well as parts of North and Central China.

In one of the earliest reports on the movement, published in the *China Christian Year Book* of 1932–1933, Paul Abbott, chairman of the American (Northern) Presbyterians' Shandong Mission, wrote that the revival meetings were "pandemonium"; they routinely became "'a ritual of chaos' and a liturgy of disorder," filled with "dancing, jumping," ear-splitting "cacophonous praying," and "wild wailing." "Carried on often until the small hours of the morning," he wrote, "they degenerate into exhibitions of 'emotional debauchery' as the devotees abandon themselves to the floods of emotion. The bodies strained with fasting and loss of sleep react with jerks and the vocal organs with gibbering. Hysterical laughter makes the gathering uncanny. Many go into religious swoons and remain in such for long periods, sometimes indeed for twenty-four hours. A few have died as the result of the emotional strain; not a few have lost their reason."[3] Accompanying such outbursts of pious energy were often end-time revelations, visions of heaven and hell, and proclamations that "Jesus is coming back."[4] M. Searle Bates, educational missionary to China and church historian, noted that the revival in Shandong was not only "apocalyptic and premillenarian," but also "primitive, individualistic, and on the margins of superstition."[5]

While the revivals in China during the 1930s manifested some of the most prominent features of the modern Pentecostal movement that arose in America at the turn of the twentieth century, there is no indication that Western Pentecostal missions, which had reached China by 1907, were directly connected to or played any significant role in the eruption of those revivals. By 1915, the largest Pentecostal mission in China, the Assemblies of God, had a total foreign force of only thirteen men and women scattered in the provinces of Zhejiang, Zhili, Jiangsu, Shandong, Shaanxi, Gansu, Mongolia, Guangdong, and Yunnan.[6] A small surge in the number of Pentecostal missionaries was recorded after 1918.[7] In 1934, the Assemblies of God Mission, which included a consolidation of various previous Pentecostal groups in China, counted a total of seventy-five missionaries and a little over six thousand communicants for the entire country. Much of its work was based, however, in the remote northwestern province of Gansu, far from the hotbed of Pentecostal revivals in those days.[8]

In general, the revivals in Shandong were a spontaneous rural movement that Wiley B. Glass, who taught at a Baptist seminary in Huangxian in northeastern Shandong, compared to a "cattle stampede." Yet Glass also found it to be a genuinely "indigenous" Christianity in contrast to the liberal religion envisioned by the Shanghai-based leaders of the NCC (which he dubbed "a type of foreign-inspired modernism that the Chinese did not readily accept").[9] An article titled "Indigenous Revival in Shantung" published in the December 1931 issue of the *Chinese Recorder* also observed that the movement "spread without any direct organizational planning" and was often accompanied "by advance in self-support, self propagation and the development of lay leadership." It concluded, "Here, then, is an *indigenous* movement in the real sense of that much-used word."[10] In many ways, the Shandong Revival brought to a climax a sporadic Protestant grassroots movement that had been in the making since the dawn of the twentieth century.

EARLY TWENTIETH-CENTURY REVIVALS

The earliest Protestant revivals in China occurred within a few years of the Boxer Uprising. Li Shuqing, a physician in Jiangsu province whose message about the impending Second Coming drew large urban crowds, became the first notable indigenous revivalist. His brief stardom ended in 1908 when he died from illness at the age of thirty-four. By then, however, revivals had started in several parts of China. Some in the mission churches had learned about and were eager to duplicate in China the Welsh revival of 1904–1905, but it was the flame from Korea that more directly kindled the fire in China.[11]

The Korean Revival of 1907 broke out first among Protestant churches in Pyongyang—a city that had been ravaged by the Sino-Japanese War (1894–1895)—spurred in part by the news of the recent revivals in Wales and India. There were reports of "men . . . pleading for forgiveness and confessing their sins in great agony of spirit." Many confessed their "lack of love . . . for the Japanese" who had seized their country, others their resentment of Western missionaries. At one revival meeting in Pyongyang, a local convert rose to confess his grudge against a missionary, and a storm of emotions broke loose. "Some were springing to their feet pleading for an opportunity to relieve their consciences by making their abasement known, others were silent, but rent with agony, clenching their fists and striking their heads against the ground . . . and so it went on for several days."[12]

Within months of the outbreak of the Great Revival in the Korean peninsula, news of the unearthly work of the Holy Spirit had reached Chinese churches in Manchuria and beyond. A few Western missionaries and Chinese church workers were sent to Pyongyang to investigate. Upon their return, they started their own revivals, which became known as the Manchurian Revival and which spread to several other parts of the country. In the coastal province of Fujian, the Methodist Episcopal mission in the town of Xinghua orchestrated a series of short-lived revival meetings. Typically lasting seven to ten days and attended by thousands of people, they featured fasting, "weeping and wailing," public confession of sins, and restitutions.[13] Many came forth to surrender their instruments of sin, including an iron chain used by its owner, a bandit chief, for kidnapping people; opium pipes; opium-cure pills that contained morphine; and a "double-edged sword that flashed like frost" wielded by a would-be assassin—testimonies of lives that pulsated with violence, pain, and desperation. A major appeal of the revival in Xinghua was its campaign against opium, whereby hundreds of addicts, including officials and soldiers, quitted their habit "through the divine power of prayer." This led to the founding of the Xinghua Christian Stop-Opium Society in 1909. Overall, however, it was a limited mission-sponsored movement that had petered out by the time of the Revolution of 1911.[14]

The revivals in China that began in 1908 catapulted one missionary into evangelistic prominence. Jonathan Goforth (1859–1936), a missionary sent by the Presbyterian Church in Canada, had labored without conspicuous results in the hinterland province of Henan since 1888, "just touching the fringe," as he put it, "of the appalling multitudes needing Christ." In 1900, he and his family had survived the Boxer rampage in a harrowing escape southward through Henan province: he was struck on the neck by a blunt sword, and his skull was "dent[ed]" by another blow. In 1907, Goforth visited Korea, where the Great Revival was in full force. Returning from the trip via Manchuria, Goforth spoke about the Holy Spirit's work in Korea at several mission stations along the way. Such was the stir he created that Goforth immediately became convinced of his "call to Manchuria." The following February, he left Henan to conduct a series of revival meetings in Manchuria. In the words of his adoring wife, "Jonathan Goforth went up to Manchuria an unknown missionary. . . . He returned a few weeks later with the limelight of the Christian world upon him."[15]

His wife's boundless admiration aside, Goforth did become an evangelistic celebrity in China. He made a calculated decision to start a revival not "among the heathen but among the Christians." At the end of his sermons illustrated with stories from Korea, the congregation would launch into simultaneous prayer and open confession of sins mixed with anguished cries for mercy. Even the foreign missionaries would join in the prayer—"men and women, strictly Presbyterian, ordinarily restrained, with Scotch reserve sticking out at all points, raising their voices with the multitude."[16] In fact, the movement became so infectious that some were induced to fake the work of the Holy Spirit. On one occasion, Goforth decided that a man who "groan[ed] horribly and . . . threw himself full length upon the ground" during the meeting was only trying to "stage something really extraordinary" to impress others. The convulsion was cured almost instantly when Goforth "gave him a sharp slap on the side" and told him to "get up and pray decently," whereupon the man "shamefully slunk into his seat."[17]

In some of his later revival meetings, Goforth unwittingly provided a platform for the locals to vent their nationalistic sentiments in the guise of confessions. Once, the principal of a mission boy's school in Shandong took to the stage and made a public confession of his "great sin" of "hating the foreign nations without praying for them." He enumerated the wrongs heaped by Japan upon China and admitted that he had "hated the Japanese." He then went on to list the wrongs inflicted on his country by Germany (for occupying eastern Shandong), the United States (through its stringent, humiliating immigration laws), and Britain (which "forced that cursed opium upon us") before Goforth angrily stopped him, at which point the high school boys "rose in a fury. . . . Shouting and yelling and kicking they left the church." Such incidents notwithstanding, the revival spread through several provinces and led some missionaries to proclaim that they saw "the beginning of what might be called the Modern Pentecost in China."[18]

FENG YUXIANG AND HIS CHRISTIAN ARMY

Some of the most gratifying results of Goforth's revivalism were seen in the army camp of Feng Yuxiang (1880–1948). Feng was a peasant's son from Anhui province who had drifted into army life when he was only about twelve in search of a way out of grinding poverty. He attended a rally of John R. Mott's in Beijing in 1913 when Mott and Sherwood Eddy were making a thirteen-city evangelistic tour of China. Like thousands of young patriots in each city who were drawn to the message of Christ as "the Hope of China," Feng, by then already a major, signed a study card and was baptized the following year at a Methodist Episcopal church. He immediately began to try to convert his officers and soldiers, inviting chaplains, often assisted by missionaries, to his various camps. By 1918, Feng had become known as the Christian General.[19]

Goforth first met Feng in Changde, Hunan, in 1919 when the latter invited him to lead a ten-day evangelistic crusade among the nine thousand soldiers of Feng's Sixteenth Mixed Brigade stationed there. Two meetings were held each day in a large theater, and Goforth "baptized 507 officers and men" in all. Another evangelist, a Chinese Methodist minister from Hankou, Hubei, reached Changde shortly afterwards and at the end of his evangelistic campaign converted another "1,165 officers and men." G. G. Warren, chairman of the Wesleyan Methodist Missionary Society in Changsha, Hunan, who had been busy tending to "men clamoring to be baptized" in Feng's camp, found that although many of them had not heard either of the Ten Commandments or the Lord's Prayer, it was "impossible to doubt the sincerity of the applicants." Feng himself, Warren added, was "aggressively active and desires the salvation of all" under him.[20] At one meeting, Feng offered his prayer. His voice "quivered with emotion, and soon there was weeping aloud. . . . As he went on . . . the whole hall became a scene of loud weeping," one missionary recalled. "I could hear the sobs and ejaculated petitions of the men sitting there. . . . When the general went on to pray for his beloved China . . . he broke down utterly and wept."[21]

Feng's religion was not only emotional, but also pragmatic. Like the Taiping decades earlier, Feng put his newfound faith to much practical use. Goforth recalled that when threatened with drought at one point, "General Feng assembled his brigade and announced to all the city that they were going to pray for rain. . . . That night there was a great rain and famine was averted." By the summer of 1920, when his brigade left Changde, Feng probably counted as many as four thousand converts in his forces. During 1920–1921, when Feng was military governor of Henan province, he again arranged to have Goforth preach to his troops in a theater. At the end of one crusade, Goforth baptized 960 of Feng's men in an assembly-line fashion (not with a water cannon but with a colonel holding a bowl of water as Goforth passed down the line). A few years later, when Feng's army numbered tens of thousands, it was reported to be about 50 percent Christian.[22]

Army of the Open Bible—General Feng's soldiers holding up Testaments recently received.
SOME CHINESE ARMIES

FIGURE 8 The Christian Army of General Feng Yuxiang. Original caption reads: "Army of the Open Bible—General Feng's soldiers holding up Testaments recently received." Source: *Chinese Recorder* 58 (February 1927).

In late 1922, Feng was ordered to leave Henan and was moved to Nanyuan, just outside Beijing. The Christian General, now close to the center of China's unpredictable political life, became the object of fascination for missionaries in the capital. Feng himself enjoyed the warm relations with the missionary community. In an address in 1923 to new missionaries who were studying Chinese at the North China Union Language School in Beijing, Feng denied the accusation of his enemies that what he had done was "to bring 20,000 poor ignorant country people into his army and then pour some water on their heads and call them Christians." The fact, according to Feng, was that the soldiers were "perfectly free in making their own decisions. Now they rise in the morning and sing a national air; then when they have come back from drill and are ready for breakfast they always sing a grace. At twelve o'clock noon all work stops and every soldier is asked to stand with uncovered head and pray for his country."[23] Such an image stirred much enthusiasm among the missionaries. Even Frank Joseph Rawlinson, a veteran missionary and seasoned editor-in-chief of the *Chinese Recorder,* was swept off his feet when he visited Feng's parade ground outside the capital a week before Easter in 1923 and was told that "13,000 Christian soldiers" were to be in the parade the following Sunday. "What a sight this mass of men would be!" Rawlinson rhapsodized. "To see them would be to realise that in spite of government chaos, financial famine, and military jealousies, the Church in China is marching on and a new China is being born."[24]

Feng was promoted to marshal in late 1923. The following year, in a betrayal of his superior Wu Peifu (a leading militarist in China) that stunned the nation and only deepened the government chaos, Feng seized the capital and had himself appointed commander-in-chief of the newly organized National People's Army of the Republic of China (Zhonghua Minguo Guominjun).[25] A few months later, in spring 1925, Feng called a conference at Kalgan (Zhangjiakou) for the organization of a "Christian Council" for his army. Marcus Ch'eng (Chen Chonggui, 1883–1963) was named chaplain general in the First Guominjun and served as general secretary of the council. A plan was drawn up for aggressive evangelism in the army. In a decree that recalled the policy of the Taiping, there was to be "a chaplain for every 1,000 men and a secretary for every 10,000 who would be responsible to a Christian Council" in the army. Feng's wife, a secretary for the Young Women's Christian Association (YWCA) in Beijing whom he married in 1924 after the death of his first wife, helped establish schools for officers' spouses, who were required to attend a three-month course to be instructed in Christianity.[26]

While Feng's missionary friends were easily won over by his piety— Rawlinson had written that his "tall stature reminded us of Saul, his ruddy countenance of David, the roundness of his head of one of Cromwell's roundheads"—his contemporary detractors called his embrace of Christianity nothing but a cynical move to "ingratiate himself with foreign imperialists, who held the reins of power in China; and to manipulate his superstitious troops with the help of pseudo-Christian symbolism, after the manner of the Taiping leaders."[27] Yet Feng's closeness to the Western missionaries also put him in a quandary following the May Thirtieth Incident of 1925. Amidst a new wave of anti-imperialism and nationalism, Feng called his chaplains together to discuss Christianity and the Chinese church and urged, "We Chinese Christians must not fall behind the non-Christians in patriotism, in protesting against the injustice and inhumanity of the foreign powers."[28]

As Feng's biographer James E. Sheridan points out, the Christian General shifted to a more clearly anti-imperialistic stance after 1925.[29] He was open in his appreciation of the Russians' renunciation of extra-territoriality and the Boxer indemnity (which came in the Russian treaty of 1925) and incensed at the missionaries' comparative luxury and many Chinese pastors' emulation of it. In 1926, following his ouster from the capital as a result of the coalition between Wu Peifu and Zhang Zuolin, the Manchurian warlord, Feng left for a period in Russia. As Goforth observed a few years later, "The Soviet had done its utmost to fill Marshal Feng's mind with hatred against foreign nations." In March 1928, when Arthur N. Holcombe, professor of government at Harvard, visited Feng's headquarters in Kaifeng, the soldiers still began the day with song, but to the tune of doxology were now set nationalist lyrics reminding the troops of their "sacred duty" to serve the country and that "imperialism is the enemy of the nation." On his visit to Feng's camp in Shaanxi in 1929, Goforth found himself at times "in sharp disagreement" with the erstwhile evangelist-general. Goforth acknowledged, however, that "Marshal Feng is a true patriot. He loves his country. He keenly feels China's humiliation and shame." Feng insisted that he was still a Christian and continued to hold on to his Methodist abhorrence of gambling, smoking, and drinking. He explained that with his forces growing to several hundred thousand men, and with noted Muslim and Buddhist generals under him, he could not force his religion upon others. There were to be no more revivals.[30]

By that time, Feng had already fallen out of favor with most missionaries and had won the new nickname "the so-called Christian General." As Kenneth S. Latourette observed, "the clue to many of his actions seems to lie in his intense nationalism. . . . He probably looked upon the Gospel in part as a means of rescuing China from her ills: it may indeed have been that feature of Mott's appeal which finally won him." Feng himself had explained to Rawlinson in 1923 that the reason he believed that "China's greatest need is for Jesus" was that "all national greatness is really due to the presence of the spirit of God." In Latourette's view, "It may have been the failure of Christianity to achieve what he expected of it—constant victory for himself and the early unification of the country—which cooled his ardor."[31] Bates also noted that Feng's often harsh treatment of rich and influential men after 1926 led to accusations that Feng had turned red. He

added: "A later study suggests that Feng successively advocated the ideology of Christianity, of the Three People's Principles and of Communism.
His commitment was increasingly to the peasant masses, and later in life
it seems that he relegated Christianity to a position of personal preference,
but turned outside it for his political and social programs."[32]

After the Northern Expedition of 1926–1927 that culminated in a
nominal unification of China under the Guomindang, Feng, who had
borne the brunt of the fighting in Shandong, was briefly given authority over the province in addition to the three other provinces of Gansu,
Henan, and Shaanxi over which he had established control. By April 1929,
however, under pressure from Chiang Kai-shek, who grew increasingly
suspicious of Feng's personal ambitions, he was forced to withdraw his
troops from Shandong and retreat to his stronghold in Henan. In 1930, the
Nationalist government's Central Executive Committee dismissed Feng
from all government and party offices. Following his military defeat by
Chiang in 1930, Feng was forced to relinquish control of his troops. His
career as a militarist ended.[33]

For most of the time between 1932 and 1935, Feng stayed with his
family in a Buddhist temple at the foot of Taishan Mountain, where he
withdrew into a quiet life of painting, writing poetry, and studying classical works. In those days, he often visited the nearby Home of Onesiphorus
and became a friend of Leslie Anglin's as well as a leading philanthropist
for the institution. (The orphans there called him Grandpa Feng.) Feng
also urged Anglin to change the foreign name of the mission orphanage
to Taishan Jiaoyangyuan, or Taishan Court of Education and Nurture. The
latter obliged. There were no signs, however, that he was interested in the
Pentecostal revivals that had burst forth in the area and that were indeed
being held at the orphanage at times (featuring such revivalists as Jing
Dianying from the Jesus Family). Feng left Taishan for Nanjing in 1935
to become the titular vice chairman of the Military Affairs Commission
in January 1936. In late summer 1948, Feng, returning to China by way
of the Soviet Union after almost two years' sojourn in the United States,
died suddenly and mysteriously during a fire onboard the Russian ship
that carried him.[34]

MARIE MONSEN AND THE SHANDONG REVIVAL

By the late 1920s, as the Christian General turned lukewarm in his faith, mission churches in general were also at a low point. Years of anti-Christian agitation by students and other young urban patriots since 1922 (often at the instigation of Communist activists), along with widespread lawlessness in rural areas, had not been without damaging effects. The *Chinese Church Year Book* (*Zhonghua Jidujiaohui nianjian*), published by the NCC, lamented in 1925 the scourge of banditry in much of China, especially in Shandong, that disrupted the regular Christian work. It pointed out that in that province alone, there were scores of bandit groups, often led by diehards with flamboyant nicknames such as Xu the Big Nose and Caos the Two Tigers. One band was reportedly led by the cold-blooded Qiao the Old Mother under whom some one thousand outlaws roamed the countryside of the peninsula.[35] As the resentment against the unequal treaties spread, Westerners and their properties, including mission compounds, were no longer safe from civil strife and banditry and were in fact sometimes singled out for attack. After 1926, in areas controlled by the Guomindang, nationalistic sentiments would often lead to boycott, intimidation, and even violence directed against churches. In Xinghua, Fujian, where an awakening had broken out in 1908 in tandem with the Manchurian Revival and where the Methodist Episcopal mission was still reporting fast growth of membership in the mid-1910s, anti-Christian zealots tore down the walls of a local seminary in 1926 and opened a street through the compound, which they named the Non-Christian Road (Feiji Lu).[36]

By far the most serious attack on the foreigners occurred in late March 1927 when Nationalist troops, continuing their successful Northern Expedition, seized the city of Nanjing from the retreating northern warlord armies and terrorized the Westerners, killing several. As we have seen, the violence led to the exodus of thousands of Protestant missionaries from China. Ironically, some of the serious disruptions of missionary work in the north and the northwest were caused by Feng Yuxiang's soldiers, who in 1928 were occupying mission buildings.[37]

In that same year, Rawlinson reported in an editorial in the *Chinese Recorder* that following the destruction of the Northern Expedition, with banditry still rife and "economic destitution . . . appallingly widespread" and famine reported in at least ten provinces, there was "evident in some places spiritual lethargy."[38] In the words of some American Southern Baptist missionaries in Shandong, "After the Chinese Southern Army came in during the year 1928, and so much of our work showed up as 'hay and stubble,' most of us were willing to 'humble ourselves under the mighty hand of God.'"[39] The lethargy in established churches did not improve in 1929 when the Great Depression set in.

Yet, in Shandong province and many other parts of North China, the very frustration and setbacks that mission churches experienced spurred the more determined evangelists into action. Some, like the Norwegian Marie Monsen—who was later lauded by her fellow missionaries as the "pioneer of the spiritual 'new life movement'" of the 1930s—actually saw a rare opportunity for revivals in the midst of chaos and dangers. In rural Henan, where she had labored under the Norwegian Lutheran Mission since the early 1900s, "continual bandit attacks" forced people to flee from homes and villages. But by early 1927, Monsen saw for "the first time" how the unrest was turning into an opportunity for revivals: "It was in one of our out-stations [where some may have fled for relative safety]. What a sight it was! The congregation was five times as large as we had ever seen it, and three out of every five among them were women. . . . Political unrest had ploughed deep furrows across ancient traditions and prejudices."[40]

In spring 1927, Monsen and a fellow missionary were holding a series of Bible classes in their mission station with a group of sixteen women. On the fourth day, following discussions on infanticide, fourteen of the sixteen women broke down:

> "Oh, and I have killed three."
> "And I five. . . ."
> "I took the lives of eight of my children."
> "And I of thirteen, but they were all girls."

Monsen added, "It was the first time in over twenty years on the mission field" that those women yielded to missionary condemnation of infanticide and confessed to the sin. Monsen then had the women come in to talk to her one by one and "the whole group was at my heels immediately." After pouring out her confession, one woman described her feelings to Monsen this way: "It was just as if I were a great bandit and after hot pursuit the soldiers caught me and dragged me before the Mandarin; and instead of denying everything, I confessed everything, and the Mandarin did not say, 'Take her away and execute her,' but he said, 'She has confessed, it is no longer held to her account. Go home in peace.'"[41] Monsen had found the key, one that was soon used by many others, both missionaries and Chinese, to unlock the doors of private emotions for the rush of mass revivalism among converts. Leslie T. Lyall later credited Monsen as becoming "the handmaiden upon whom the Spirit was first poured out. . . . Her surgical skill in exposing the sins hidden with the Church and lurking behind the smiling exterior of many a trusted Christian . . . and her quiet insistence of a clear-cut experience of the new birth set the pattern for others to follow."[42]

In spring 1929, Monsen survived a twenty-three-day capture at the hands of pirates off the shores of northern Shandong, an experience that transformed her from a little-known missionary, at best a regional revivalist in the rural hinterland, into a hero. During her ordeal she reportedly "dispensed her motherly words" to the thieves, including the "chief of the pirates himself," about the "second coming of Christ and his promise to deliver the faithful from the tribulations to come." That summer Monsen was invited to address the annual missionary conference held at the seaside resort Beidaihe. The occasion brought her national prominence among Protestants. By autumn 1929, with the help of her friends among the American Southern Baptists in Chefoo (Zhifu, now Yantai), Monsen was organizing revival meetings that featured the hallmark "born again experience" of public confession of sins. According to Gustav Carlberg, president of the Lutheran Theological Seminary in Shekou, Hubei, Monsen was to set a sensational example herself of cataloging sin by publicly "'descend[ing] into the miry cess-pool of sin' in connection with the sixth commandment, against adultery."[43] The Shandong Revival had begun.

In meetings that typically targeted church members and drew large interdenominational audiences of pastors, evangelists, Christian workers, and students in mission schools, Monsen, reportedly eschewing overt emotionalism, preached about sins—one sin a day, including hatred, lying, stealing, coveting, and adultery. At the close of each session, she "took her stand at the door" and "press[ed] home" individually "the quiet question, 'Have you been born again?'" as people left. As her fellow missionaries recalled, "the evasion, the doubt, the conviction was terrible."

One young woman, who taught at a mission school, was "born again" after admitting herself to be a "lost sinner," for, in her words, "in the last years of High School anti-foreign propaganda reached us, and I came to believe that the Church was an 'Imperial Machine,' that prayer was empty, the Bible written by men only." Within a month after the meeting, the woman heard the call and enrolled in a seminary.

For a brief period after 1929, Monsen was the celebrated torchbearer of the awakening in North China. Under her influence, many missionaries rededicated themselves to fervent evangelism and started their own revivalist campaigns.[44] Yet Monsen's influence, and that of other missionaries, was quickly eclipsed as the movement gained its momentum and spread at the grassroots level, out of the missionaries' control. In February 1932, at the time of the Chinese New Year, a Baptist missionary from Laiyang in northeastern Shandong by the name of I. V. Larson went to neighboring Huangxian to lead a revival. On the second day, his preaching was interrupted by a confession. One missionary reported: "There were confessions every day, and Mr. Larson never preached after the first day. . . . The Holy Spirit conducted the meetings." One Southern Baptist missionary wrote from Chefoo in July 1932, "Again we find the laymen there [in the Laizhou area] preaching in tent and other meetings, while the missionary and evangelists are free to give their time largely to work elsewhere."[45] After examining reports on the Shandong Revival, an editorial in the February 1933 issue of the *Missionary Review of the World* concluded: "Several characteristics are noticeable. The Chinese preachers and elders, not foreigners, are the leaders."[46]

THE SPIRITUAL GIFTS SOCIETY AND THE SPIRITUAL GIFTS MOVEMENT

One development that helped turn Chinese laymen into revival leaders, and that constituted an unprecedented challenge to the dominance of Western clergy in mission churches in Shandong, was the formation of a loosely organized Spiritual Gifts Society (Ling'enhui) in Feixian in the southern part of the province in 1930. The society owed its inspiration to a Pentecostal named Ma Zhaorui who ran an orphanage named the Independent Assemblies of God in the Nationalist capital Nanjing. In 1928, Ma brought scores of Feixian orphans to Nanjing and was later invited back to Feixian to preach in the Presbyterian churches there. "This he did with much enthusiasm and emotional appeal," one article in the December 1931 issue of the *Chinese Recorder* noted. It added, however, that Ma's role in the launching of the Spiritual Gifts Society was "initiatory only." The actual formation of the society was the work of Yang Rulin and Sun Zhanyao, both of them members of the local Presbyterian church who, upon receiving the "spiritual gifts" at Ma's meetings, started proclaiming the work of the Holy Spirit in mission churches. When divisions regarding Pentecostalism arose, the two started a breakaway group that drew its membership primarily from Presbyterian missions in the area. They named it the Independent Chinese Christian Spiritual Gifts Society, commonly referred to as the Spiritual Gifts Society.[47]

From southern Shandong the Pentecostal outbreak in the form of the Spiritual Gifts Society quickly spread to other presbyteries in the province, including those in Yizhoufu (now Linyi), Qingdao, Dengzhou (now Penglai), the provincial capital Jinan, and the Presbyterian stronghold Weixian (now Weifang), where the TJC had built a fervent following a decade earlier. In those areas, local branches of the society were often organized; it also made inroads into many mission churches, particularly in rural areas, which came to adopt its practices. According to the *Chinese Recorder*, "about two-thirds of the pastors in the Weihsien Presbytery took it up." By late 1931, its effect had been felt "over an extensive part of Shantung. . . . It is the fruit of the work of indigenous zeal and Chinese zealots." One pastor from Dengzhou went to Weixian to investigate the movement and was promptly drawn into it, announcing, in the typical apocalyptic language of the society, that he had been "entrusted with the gospel for the end times."[48]

Before long, the movement had spread beyond the Presbyterian churches. Many other denominational churches in North China, including Baptist, Lutheran, Congregational, and CIM congregations, also reported revivals. By the summer of 1931, Baptist revivals—which, like their Presbyterian counterparts, were either directly led by society zealots or inspired by them—had broken out in Pingdu and Laiyang in eastern Shandong. This happened at a time when dozens of Baptist missionaries on furlough in the United States were unable to return to the mission field as a result of the Great Depression.[49] Once the Pentecostal fire was kindled, typically by public confession of sins, "tongues," dreams, swoons, prophecies, faith healing, and exorcism would follow. In late 1931, one

FIGURE 9   Revival meeting in Pingyuan, Shandong, February 1936. Source: *Chinese Recorder* 67 (April 1936).

Baptist missionary in Huangxian started a chorus of public confessions in his congregation with one of his own. For three days thereafter, he

> just sat there in the meetings sometimes as long as eight and
> ten hours a day. . . . It seemed like a strong electric current
> was going through my body. . . . Finally on the fifth night . . .
> we were praying about twelve o'clock and the Spirit came in
> mighty power. . . . He took right hold of me and shook me
> (physically) as I would shake a rag, then He opened my mouth
> so wide that my jaw bones seemed like they would break, and
> the room was filled with wind and it literally rushed into me
> until I felt that I would burst. . . . Then a great burst of joyous
> laughter that was different from any laughter that I had ever
> experienced, came right from deep down inside me.[50]

Such contemporary testimonies in the English language given by missionaries are among the available personal accounts that provide a window into the internal experience of those who were gripped by the Shandong Revival. Although it erupted primarily among local converts, Chinese sources from the 1930s are scarce. The illiteracy of the majority of the revivalists, the absence of any institutional practice of record keeping in the Spiritual Gifts Society, and the scourge of wars, banditry, and general poverty during that period help explain the rarity of contemporary Chinese-language accounts.[51] Given the fact that these Western missionaries had been drawn into a popular Chinese movement and that their experience was inseparable, and likely often indistinguishable, from that of the indigenous revivalists, we may picture a similar Pentecostal flame among those Shandong peasants who surrendered themselves to the "power of the Holy Spirit."

THE PENTECOST BEYOND SHANDONG

It should be noted that the revivals in Shandong coincided with a new spate of destruction and miseries in North China and beyond. Besides banditry, a massive civil war known as the Great Battle on the Central Plain broke out in North China in 1930 between Chiang Kai-shek's Nationalist troops and an alliance of warlords that included Feng Yuxiang. In that same year, the northwest was desolated by drought while the Yangzi valley and the northeast were ravaged by floods. Millions died that year alone. Then, in September 1931, came the Manchurian Incident and the Japanese occupation of the three northeastern provinces of China. Those calamities accentuated the message of the revivalists. A survey of "The Impact of Natural and Man-Made Disasters on the Church in the Last Two Years" published in the 1933 issue of the *China Church Year Book* reported that although regular church life was often disrupted in Communist-controlled, bandit-infested, and war-torn areas, "vigorous revivals" also broke out in such places as Shandong and Sichuan provinces.[52]

Outside Shandong, the revival movement was particularly strong in Manchuria and parts of North China. In Manchuria, which the Japanese occupied in September 1931, Chinese-led revivals started within months and were characterized by protracted, sometimes all-night, meetings of prayer and confessions (one nineteen-year-old woman "confessed to having taken opium to commit suicide"). In some areas, revivals took place when refugees from areas ravaged by flood or banditry filled the mission churches in larger towns. In one mission district, almost five hundred adult baptisms were reported in 1933—an addition of 30 percent to the church membership—in the same year during which some rural churches were commandeered by bandits and the roof of another mission building was blown in by cannon shells during fighting between bandits and Japanese troops. Not surprisingly, the apocalyptic theme was prominent at most of the meetings. Much of the teaching "emphasizes the speedy return of the Lord, and deliverance from this evil world," one missionary wrote. "Wars and rumours of war, brigandage, corruption, oppression, floods and famine, and widespread ruin are but the signs of His coming. . . . This gospel is very attractive to those who are harassed by doubts and fears, who are world-weary and well-nigh hopeless, and who seek a faith that abides through all changes."[53]

In Henan province, a number of women who had been the first fruits of Monsen's revivals in the spring of 1927 formed themselves into the "Widows Church" of some forty members—"a little church up among the mountains, where the bandits had ravaged wildly."[54] The Reverend William H. Nowack, head of the Ebenezer Mission in Miyang, reported in summer 1934 that a Chinese pastor called Liu Daosheng who was formerly Marie Monsen's chief helper at the Norwegian Lutheran Mission was leading a spirited revival there, with some "pounding the benches . . . and calling out, 'I am face to face with God'" and others screaming "I am going straight to hell, there is no hope for me" while striking their heads with their fists. On the fourth night of the revival, when Nowack entered the classroom of the mission orphanage, he found that "some stood pounding the walls; others were in a sitting posture, beating their desks; several were prostrate on their knees, while one little chap was in such agony of soul that he kept rolling around on the floor."[55]

As it developed, the movement came to feed on its own intensity and created a behavioral norm to which all came under pressure to conform—what some psychologists of revivals have called the force of "crowd suggestion" (or "herd suggestion").[56] Referring to sensational public confessions of sins "from childhood up," one missionary reported, "Those who do not fall in with these performances are accused of hindering the work of the Spirit." And it became widely accepted that "if one has not this 'spirit of exhilaration and spiritual fervor' then 'he is still in his sins' and a 'son of Satan.'"[57] Monsen herself witnessed the extent to which some revivalists would go to show that they were filled with the divine spirit; she wrote of an "ill-reputed group in the mountains" whose members "rivaled one another to see who could fast for forty days like Jesus, and had attempted to see which of them could lie for the longest time stretched out as Jesus was when He was nailed to the Cross. . . . Several in the congregation became demon possessed in the course of the [revival] meeting and had to be taken out."[58]

In most cases, the revivalists held themselves to a nerve-racking schedule. At a revival in Huangxian held in February 1932, "the meeting would last day and night, with intermission of only an hour more or less between," one missionary reported. "Every night some prayed all night. We were hungry, and God filled us. . . . Eating and sleeping were quite secondary."[59] Another wrote: "In some cases the meetings are prolonged until two a.m. with a call to prayer again at four a.m. Preaching, intermittent repetition of a few revival hymns, prayer in unison and hallelujahs occupy this time."[60] During a six-day spring revival meeting held in the Congregational church in Pingyuan, Shandong, in February 1936, "Every day there were four regular sessions of from one and a half to two and a half hours each with much singing and small group prayer meetings in between. How human nerves could stand it without being worn to shreds, one . . . cannot understand."[61]

"A SHIP WITHOUT AN ANCHOR"

During the early 1930s, the revival movement recorded impressive results. In the Yizhoufu field in southern Shandong, one of the first areas to come under the influence of the Spiritual Gifts Society, the number of baptisms in 1931 was "fifty percent over that of the previous years. Contributions have increased during the same period twenty-five percent." One Presbyterian missionary in Weixian reported: "Many opium addicts have also been given freedom from their dope—one of these was a man who had been for 35 years an addict. A 53-year-old Taoist became a believer. Bandits have come forward to confess their sins."[62] By late 1935, however, the Spiritual Gifts Movement in general had "moderated a great deal" according to the *China Christian Year Book* published for that year.[63] At around the same time, a degree of institutionalization was taking place: in the city of Qingdao, the local Spiritual Gifts Society completed its own church building in 1936 with funds contributed by a member who was manager of the North China Match Company. During that same year, the independent Spiritual Gifts Society congregation in the provincial capital Jinan also pooled enough resources to erect its own church. Upon its completion, it was proclaimed the site of the General Assembly of the Shandong Chinese Christian Spiritual Gifts Society. The new body proceeded to establish its bylaws and an ecclesiastical system that consisted of unsalaried elders, pastors, evangelists, and deacons. Although the organization did not exercise any real control over the various branches of the society throughout the province, it did maintain "ecclesiastical contacts" and a level of cooperation with the latter.[64]

Under the auspices of the General Assembly, the Court for Spiritual Retreat (Lingxiuyuan) was established outside the city of Jinan. Sun Zhanyao, one of the two founders of the Spiritual Gifts Society who had gone on to become an activist in the Jesus Family during the intervening years, left Mazhuang in 1936 to head the court. Modeled on the Jesus Family, which Sun had come to know well, the Court for Spiritual Retreat emerged as a scaled-down communitarian society that provided a sixty-*mu* (ten-acre) haven for those seekers of spiritual gifts who often came "carrying only a mouth on their two shoulders." Like the former, its dozens of members were organized into occupational departments including farming, tailoring, carpentry, and masonry and toiled to make the community self-sufficient. The court also adopted a Jesus Family slogan that trumpeted its egalitarianism: "The denominational boundary has been erased; the hierarchical order is removed." Throughout the remainder of the Republican period, the court was the site of biannual revival meetings that were timed around those held at nearby Mazhuang and that sometimes drew crowds of up to one thousand.[65]

In many areas, as the Pentecostal revival spilled into denominational missions, it helped "break down denominational lines," resulting, for instance, in collaborations between the Baptists and the Presbyterians in many parts of Shandong.[66] Yet it also created splits in other churches. The report in the December 1931 issue of the *Chinese Recorder,* which attempted an overview of the phenomenon in its early phase, found that as a predominantly rural movement, the revivals gained an ardent following in the countryside, while the city people, who tended to be "not so spontaneous and free as their rural brethren," were often "shocked" and inclined to discount the visions, revelations, and "tongues." In Dengzhou, divisions regarding the movement resulted in the revivalists splitting off from the Presbyterian mission and founding a rival group associated with the Spiritual Gifts Society. (They later received a "revelation" permitting them to return to the Presbyterian church.)[67] Ding Limei, founder of the Chinese Student Volunteer Movement who had led mission-sponsored revivals two decades earlier, reportedly resigned from the North China Theological Seminary in Tengxian, Shandong, when that institution closed its door to the Spiritual Gifts Movement.[68]

As a whole, the missionary community was divided on Pentecostal revivals. Some who were opposed to the outbreak detected in it a disguised challenge to the dominance of Western missionaries in Chinese Christianity. T. Ralph Morton, a missionary in Manchuria, wrote: "A 'revival' is almost always partly a protest. . . . It is protest against foreign theology, against the domination of foreigners and foreign-trained men. . . . So the 'revival' becomes a campaign and the enemy is not paganism but the foreigner and his colleagues. The desire is to drive out of power all those of whom they do not approve or, if necessary, to start an independent church. At the moment it is difficult to see more than protest and the love of power in such 'revivals' . . . Patriotism is now as a ship without an anchor."[69]

FRUITS OF THE REVIVALS

Others discounted the revivals on the ground that they were driven by forces closer to local religious traditions than to the Holy Spirit. Some pointed, for instance, to the claim of the revivalists that "at times they smell a 'divine fragrance.'" It was not uncommon for skeptical missionaries to view the movement as "a burst of primitive psychology" and to find the mystical experiences and revelations on the "verge [of] the superstitious."[70] At times the ardent revivalism carried a ghastly personal price, as in the case of the wife of a theology student in Shandong who became convinced that she had to "carry out literally the Scripture injunction that if her right hand offended her she should cut it off and cast it from her," whereupon she severed her own limb—an act that recalls the sacrifice of some Buddhist devotees who would wrap their fingers in oil-soaked bandages and set fire to them in homage to the Goddess of Mercy.[71] A. A. Fulton, a missionary in the Manchurian province of Jilin, lamented the "temptation" among native revivalists to "luxuriate in the emotional orgies into which revival meetings sometimes merge" and attributed what he called the "intellectual narrowness of many" to the "pathetic ignorance of most of the converts."[72] There were reports of "sexual excesses" practiced "under the guidance of the Holy Spirit": a preacher who grabbed a member's wife and started caressing and kissing her protested that he was bestowing "spiritual kisses." Others, in an eerie hark-back to the Boxers at the turn of the century, practiced "spiritual boxing" during the meetings.[73] According to Paul Abbott, chairman of the Presbyterian Shandong Mission, the revivalists' "undiscriminating acceptance of psychic phenomena as of the Holy Spirit, the undignified conduct of those seized by what many feel to be hysteria, the evident self-hypnosis in frequent instances and 'holy roller' character of a great deal of the phenomena, have led the missionary body in most cases to be wary of giving their sanction to [the Spiritual Gifts Movement]. Hence they have been willing to stand to one-side and let the movement run its course, feeling that the sooner the spasm is over the better it will be for the young Church."[74]

Seasoned missionary leaders who disapproved of the excesses decided that any attempt to maintain a degree of control over the riotous display of Pentecostal power by the converts required tact on their own part. Wiley B. Glass, for instance, tried to persuade his seminary students at the Baptist seminary in Huangxian that they "could use their strength and energy better in serving the Lord than in jumping up and down shouting 'Hallelujah.'" But he went on to caution them, "When cattle stampede you can't get in front and stop them, but by riding with them you can head them around and keep them from falling off the cliffs." For himself, he decided, "I wanted to ride with the herd."[75]

Perhaps it was more than judiciousness on the part of veteran missionaries like Glass and many other church leaders that explained their patience with the Pentecostal outbreak. Some had undoubtedly developed profound empathies for the congregations they shepherded. Behind "all the joy in the progress of the Church," one missionary in Manchuria wrote in 1933, "there is in the minds of the members of the Church an acute sense of tragedy."[76] Zhao Zichen, dean of the School of Religion at Yenching University, observed in 1931 that the "tongues" and the "so-called divine healing, casting out devils" addressed an "emptiness" in the hearts of the common people and the "disturbance in their lives." The Pentecostal groups also provided "a kind of 'mystical fellowship' that affords satisfaction in their social and spiritual life."[77] He added in 1935 that while the Pentecostalists were often "half insane," the movement was not without benefits; the church should "support any force" that could "bring people renewed hope and renewed life and help them endure the hardships of our times."[78] Even the staid Paul Abbott admitted that Pentecostalism was a kind of Christian faith that allowed the followers to "taste of a new joy in life, a loosening of the bonds of convention" and awakened "new and mysterious powers" in them, powers that emboldened them to confront the perils that otherwise would have rendered their hearts faint. As a result, even "delicate women have penetrated the dangerous haunts of bandits and the dens of vice to preach to hardened men."[79]

The revivalists themselves were, for the most part, blissfully oblivious to the judgments of church leaders and foreign missionaries. They heard instead hymns that beckoned them, for instance, to "Come and Eat Your Fill." At one rally, the faithful sang, prayed, and thrust their hands up into the air—where they allegedly caught sweet-tasting "manna from heaven," which looked like little white rice dumplings.[80] Others had, in their swoons and trances, savored the joy of being "caught up." Returning from their celestial journeys, the enraptured told "marvelous stories" of "all manner of delights" and reported on the sightings of "lofty and ornate buildings . . . good things to eat (peach being especially noted), fragrant and variegated flowers, beautiful clothes, music both instrumental and in song, social fellowship with heavenly beings, even the Trinity described as the Father, Son and Mother, and rest like that of a child in the bosom of Jesus."[81]

Those who recounted such excursions to the heavenly abode of the Trinity may not have realized that similar sightings had also been related by members of other religious sects in rural Shandong. In 1886, a Western missionary had taken note of the striking pictures of celestial happiness painted by members of the Eight Trigrams, the millenarian Buddhist secret society that had been involved in the failed uprising of 1813. For the sect's members, the "summit of reward . . . is entrance into the 'Palace of the King'" within which each "perfected spirit" was provided "a princely mansion, with courts and gardens" adorned by "flowers . . . fish ponds, and fountains" and populated by "birds of rare plumage." There were "'mountains of flour and mountains of rice,' the rice all of gold and the beans of jade and of pearl." And the celestial beings would dine with "golden bowls and silver cups," attended by "golden boys and pearly maidens" in great abundance.[82]

Back on earth, in the 1880s as it was during the 1930s, such heavenly abundance was much craved for. The mountains of flour and rice remained elusive, like the famed mirage of the Land of the Immortals (*Penglai xianjing*) off the shores of northeastern Shandong. And the peaches of bliss and longevity, plentiful in the Celestial City as they were in the Land of the Peach Blossoms pictured more than one thousand years before by the Jin dynasty poet Tao Yuanming (365–427), were hard to find.

CHAPTER FIVE

"Elucidating the Way"

AN INDEPENDENT PREACHER'S REVOLT AGAINST MISSION CHURCHES

> Like hearing, from behind the scenes in the theatre of life,
> the onstage symphony which blends laughter of vanity with
> screams of pain and despair, wild yell of rapine and massacre
> with shrill song of death wish and suicide;
> I have heard the chant of prayer and penitence in the Temple
> of Heaven's Stillness!
>
> . . . .
>
> Flow of joy from the source of Enlightenment, manifest now
> in this great, solemn calm, this calm of Release, harmonious,
> limitless calm!
> O hymn Nirvana! Extol Nirvana!
>
> —*Xu Zhimo, "Listening to the Chant of Prayer and Penitence*
> *in Changzhou's Temple of Heaven's Stillness" (1923)*

THE PENTECOSTAL ECSTASIES in the Spiritual Gifts Movement as well as in the TJC and the Jesus Family, while exhilarating to their followers, tended to enclose their communities and separate them from the larger Protestant body in China, estimated at about half a million during the mid-1930s. Outside these autonomous and often ostracized communities was the Protestant establishment still dominated by foreign missions. However, by the beginning of the Nationalist period (1928–1949), mainstream denominational churches were also increasingly coming under the influence of indigenous leaders. The growing antiforeignism of the 1920s had strengthened the desire of Western missionaries to present the Protestant church as a Sinicized enterprise in the country and had precipitated the formation, as we have seen, of Chinese-led interdenominational organizations, including the NCC. At the local level, mission churches also increasingly opened themselves to lay activists who were capable of invigorating church life in the face of antimission agitation and the resulting "spiritual lethargy." Thus the stage was set for the emergence of a prominent group of independent preachers. Typically conducting revival or evangelistic meetings in mission churches and schools, these lay itinerant preachers sought to generate a lively popular Chinese Christianity that would be unburdened by imperialist connections, unencumbered by ecclesiastical hierarchy, and that would offer a fundamentalist biblical solution to the crisis of their times.

As we have seen, a handful of itinerant lay preachers, both male and female, had emerged during the first decade of the twentieth century, but they did not become a significant phenomenon until the late 1920s. By the early 1930s, protracted meetings in the revival movement that started in North China created heightened demands for charismatic preachers and turned several of them into evangelistic celebrities. A report in the *China Christian Year Book* of 1932–1933 counted at least ten "national leaders" of revivals, some of whom would "go to the extreme in noisy, dramatic, sensational and [Billy] Sundayesque preaching, outdoing even their prototype in startling and unique features." It added, "There is little interest in the social application of Christianity. . . . Special stress is laid upon the deadly power of personal sin."[1] Another issue of the *China Christian Year Book* added that those "wandering evangelists" were generally able to secure with "ease" freewill offerings from the denominational churches they visited—"relatively large contributions . . . far greater in proportion than what the churches are giving to their pastors."[2]

Individually, many of those preachers made no more than a fleeting appearance on the scene; none of them occupied any position of power within the ecclesiastical structure of mission churches. Yet collectively, their simple, fundamentalist preaching on sin, repentance, and redemption helped shape a vital Christianity of the masses. Their repudiation of the Social Gospel appeared commonsensical at a time of political chaos and foreign aggression, and their eschatological proclamations spread hope even as war, random suffering, and gloom intensified. As a result, their influence on the Chinese church at the grassroots level far exceeded that of prominent denominational clergy and the leaders of national Protestant bodies such as the NCC and the YMCA who doggedly promoted a reformist Christianity. A leading figure among this group was Wang Mingdao (1900–1991).

THE ROAD TO INDEPENDENT EVANGELISM

Wang was born in July 1900 in the foreign legation quarter in Beijing when it was under siege by the Boxers. His father, most likely a rural migrant who had found employment at a Methodist Episcopal hospital in the capital, had joined more than three thousand Chinese Christian converts who sought shelter with the beleaguered Westerners. A month before Wang's birth, his father, fearing imminent death at the hands of the Boxers, hanged himself out of despair.[3] The circumstances of his birth would become a haunting reminder in Wang's later life of the predicament of Chinese Christians caught between their sometimes xenophobic non-Christian neighbors and the foreign missionary enterprise backed by Western gunboats. When he was about nine, his mother, a member of the LMS, enrolled him at a primary school run by the LMS church on Mishi (Rice Market) Street in the eastern part of the city where Cheng Jingyi, the future general secretary of the NCC, was emerging as a promising young church leader. The curriculum at the LMS school included core readings traditionally adopted in private academies—the Four Confucian Classics (*The Great Learning, The Doctrine of the Mean, The Analects of Confucius,* and *The Mencius*) along with *Zuozhuan* (a commentary on *The Spring and Autumn Annals*), much of which he was made to commit to memory.[4]

The classics evoked an orderly world populated with sages and scholars who presented a clear moral compass and offered inspiring examples of virtuous living. Yet it must have seemed a different land to Wang. The compound his family shared with nine other households (averaging some thirty people on a typical day) in the Dried Fish Alley in the eastern section of the capital was crowded with peddlers, rickshaw pullers, barbers, soldiers, and petty clerks, as well as unmarried women who furtively entertained a string of male visitors. It pulsated with life—noisy, sensual, filthy, often coarse and occasionally violent. There was constant gambling, stealing, and swearing. A woman spat into the wok while cooking for her mother-in-law; one husband beat up his wife and left bruises all over her, while in another family the lady routinely punished her husband by making him kneel for long hours on the ground. "Our compound was a

FIGURE 10 Wang Mingdao at the Christian Tabernacle in Beijing, circa 1950. Engraved on the wall are the following words: "He suffered for our sin; he was raised from among the dead; he has been lifted to heaven; he will come back to receive us—completed in summer 1937." Courtesy of Wang Tianduo and Zhang Guiyan.

model," Wang observed, "of the lower-class society in Beijing." Wang's later obsessive admonition in his sermons against moral disorders ranging from spitting, flirting, and chewing on raw garlic to brawling and fornication may have had roots in such childhood memories.[5]

Wang was also obsessed with death in his early life. He was a sickly child and had dreamed of going into the deep mountains to search for the "Way" of becoming an immortal. At the age of fourteen, while attending a mission boarding school, he was baptized into the LMS church. Wang credited the formative Christian influence on himself at the time to Xie Honglai, the Shanghai-based YMCA secretary whose translations and writings on the subject of model Christian living had inspired him. It is also possible that Xie, who had been a main force in the formation of the autonomous Chinese Christian Union back in 1902, had exemplified Christian patriotism as well. Wang became a YMCA activist, participated in the student-led boycott of Japanese goods in 1919, and, before his encounter with Pentecostalism, which radically reshaped his faith, would address mission school students on civic duties and the way to "save the country."[6]

During most of his remaining teenage years, Wang's greatest ambition, stirred by the steady decline of political order in the capital, was to study politics in college and prepare for a career as a statesman. He dreamed of becoming the "Lincoln of the East" and hung a portrait of his political idol on the wall. However, in his eighteenth year, an almost fatal illness forced him to surrender his political ambitions. He vowed to serve God instead if his life was spared. A year later, following the May Fourth rallies and boycott of classes by the Beijing students, Wang learned that his entire class of precollege students bound for what would become Yenching University was being relocated to Jinan, Shandong. Convinced that his widowed mother and his only sister needed him in the house, he made an anguished plea to a missionary administrator to allow him to matriculate directly as an undergraduate at Yenching. When that was ignored, he let loose a storm of fury at the missionary who had slighted "such an aspiring young Christian student" as he was.[7]

The obligation to stay near his family in Beijing having thwarted his university education, Wang accepted a low-paying teaching job at a Presbyterian mission school in Baoding, one hundred miles south of the capital. There, as in the other denominational schools he had attended, he found himself surrounded by hypocrisy, selfishness, snobbery, and low spirituality. He was convinced that the Chinese church needed a John Wesley to reform it and rid it of corruption. And that responsibility was "entrusted to none other" than himself. Within a year he had abandoned the various childhood names he had been given and adopted a new name—Mingdao ("elucidating the Way")—by which he came to be known, one with a moral and spiritual self-assurance that was characteristic of him in his later career.[8]

That assurance brought him into conflict, however, with his colleagues, the school administration, and eventually missionary Christianity itself. In December 1920, following a recent war between two northern warlord factions that weakened the central government and left many troops unpaid for months, rumors spread in Baoding that some of the soldiers stationed in the city were about to mutiny and to pillage the Presbyterian compound. When the missionaries there frantically assembled rifles and started arming themselves and some of the male students to prepare for what appeared to be an impending attack, Wang rose to oppose armed defense. With the recent outbreak of the May Fourth Movement still fresh in his memory, and amidst the continuing spread of antiforeign sentiments in the country, Wang's opposition was likely patriotic as well as instinctive. The danger and predicament he was contemplating must also have been painfully reminiscent of that faced by his father two decades earlier. His justification, however, was biblical; he reminded the missionaries that "all who take the sword will perish by the sword" and added that preachers should not be prepared to take human lives.[9]

In January 1921, Wang was expelled from the mission school after another clash with his superiors. Having lately been persuaded by a colleague who was associated with a small Beijing Pentecostal faith mission called Xinxinhui that baptism by sprinkling, the common practice in most denominational churches, was unbiblical, he insisted on having himself rebaptized by immersion along with five of his students. During that small crisis, we catch a glimpse of the personality that was fundamental to his later rise as an independent preacher. Not only did he flout the warnings of the school's principal that rebaptism spelled immediate expulsion, he also defied the frigid temperature of North China. There had been two days of heavy snow, and the river was under deep ice. Wang recalled that when he and his five students emerged from the only spot in the city's moat that was not frozen, his long hair turned into an icicle.[10]

"ELUCIDATING THE WAY"

The expulsion meant of course that Wang's future as a Christian leader lay outside the missionary establishment, with which he had become disillusioned anyway. On the other hand, in contrast to those who joined the TJC or the Jesus Family, the flame of Pentecostalism that Wang's colleague had passed on to him merely flickered and would soon die down, as it did in the case of many lone Pentecostals outside the sectarian furnace. The coal peddler–turned–Xinxinhui preacher who baptized Wang succeeded in making his five students speak in "tongues" after immersion, but the gift of glossolalia eluded Wang for days. When his incessant shouts of "Hallelujah" finally trailed off into "confused and indistinct sounds," he felt no exhilaration, even as the preacher announced that he had been filled with the Holy Spirit.[11]

Back home in Beijing, Wang's small act of martyrdom was not well received. His mother was convinced that he was under the spell of the Evil One to have given up his job; his relatives, who took notice of his depression, concluded also that he had gone out of his mind. The sputtering efforts at "tongues," which he kept up for the next two years, did not dampen such suspicions. The independent Pentecostal faith mission of some twenty people into which he was baptized met in the Beijing home of an old "eccentric" Norwegian lay preacher and filled their meetings with repetitive "mechanical" sounds of "ba-ba-ba-ba" and "da-da-da-da." Wang faltered at producing such sounds; later, he would also balk at the indecorous behavior of some Pentecostals who "danced, clapped, and shouted wildly" during revival meetings, took off their clothes, and went naked in a deliberate "loss of face commanded by the Holy Spirit."[12] The large dose of Confucian teachings he received in childhood had inoculated him against such exuberance. Yet he shared the Pentecostals' sense of eschatological urgency. His first sermon, preached in July 1921, announced that the "Kingdom of Heaven is near." He realized also that he had been thrust onto the path of a religious reformer: he would preach the original Gospel of redemption, the Second Coming, and resurrection—simple truths that had long faded away in the church. But now, like a secret message from heaven written with "invisible ink," they appeared before his eyes after passing over "the fire of tribulations."[13]

By 1923, Wang had parted with the group and with Pentecostalism. On the other hand, there was no return to mission churches. He had continued to clash with missionaries over matters of faith after his expulsion from the Presbyterian school. In the spring of 1924, while Feng Yuxiang's Christian Army was stationed outside the capital, some thirty local preachers, both missionary and Chinese, were invited to the army camp to lead a six-day evangelistic meeting that resulted in the baptism of more than three thousand soldiers. Wang was among the invited but, appalled by Feng's assembly-line approach to baptism—what to him was a pompous and "lamentable" farce with "little genuine repentance"—he left before the last day. In this way the frustrated young visionary drifted in and out of independent preaching, sometimes looking for jobs outside the church and occasionally driven by thoughts of suicide.[14]

For Wang, the turning point came in early 1925 when an elderly lady influential in Protestant circles in Beijing took a liking to the young man and recommended him as a speaker for various church meetings. At a time when "most church leaders in Beijing saw me as mentally abnormal," Wang wrote, that lady's "recognition that I was chosen by God . . . brought boundless comfort." He had finally gained a sizable audience. What followed was a preaching tour to the lower Yangzi valley that coincided with the outbreak of the May Thirtieth Incident in Shanghai. As we shall see in the case of the Bethel Mission, the wave of antiforeignism in the aftermath of the incident—and the exodus of thousands of missionaries amidst antimission disturbances over the next few years—hastened efforts by many denominational missions to thrust Chinese preachers into more visible positions and to deflect accusations that the Protestant church was an arm of Western imperialism.[15] In Nanjing, Hangzhou, and neighboring areas, Wang was asked to lead several protracted evangelistic and revival meetings in denominational churches over a period of three months. It was the beginning of his career as an independent. He was still without ecclesiastical status, but he now saw himself as a modern Gideon who, "though a commoner and rising from the fields, was sent by Jehovah" to lead a handful of soldiers, defeat "massive armies," and "save the Israelites who were oppressed by a mighty power." It was a potent self-image. Over the next two and a half decades, his itinerant preaching would take him to twenty-four of the twenty-eight provinces where he would be offered the pulpit in churches belonging to some thirty different denominations.[16]

By 1925, Wang had also gained enough following in Beijing to begin

FIGURE 11   Wang Mingdao administering baptism in a river close to the Summer Palace in Beiping, circa 1935. Courtesy of Wang Tianduo and Zhang Guiyan.

a congregation of his own that he later named the Christian Tabernacle (Jidutu Huitang). True to his anti-ecclesiastical convictions, he never assumed the title "pastor," preferring the simple solemnity of "Mr. Wang." The service likewise was carefully shorn of any ostentatiousness. There was no liturgy, nor would the preacher countenance a choir—"lest talented singers" would use the opportunity to showcase their voice and "debase true worship." Wang's message was consistent and plain. It dealt with sin, repentance, Hell, and Heaven and, in a reflection of his obsession with the perceived moral disorder that surrounded him, was filled with detailed mundane advice, including being timely, wearing proper attire, and observing traffic rules (his admonition was to keep to the right).[17] But he had his passions. Convinced of his call to be a modern prophet, to whom "God had given the commission once entrusted to Jeremiah," he began to crusade relentlessly during the late 1920s against a whole sweep of "evils" in Chinese Christianity, ranging from worldliness and lifeless formalism to theological modernism. He saved his harshest chastisements for liberal institutions such as the YMCA (which published writings that "destroyed young people's faith") and for mainline denominational ministers and church leaders, most of whom he dubbed "unbelievers" who preached for a living and who fawned on their missionary superiors to secure their turf within the church.[18]

THE "FAKE MEDICINE" OF SOCIAL CHRISTIANITY

Wang's berating of "unbelievers" in the church came at a time when theological liberalism among Western (especially American) missionaries in China had gained broad influence. Both mainline denominational missions and interdenominational Chinese institutions—notably the fledgling NCC and the Church of Christ in China founded in 1927, which sought to represent the entire Protestant community—produced vocal advocates of a progressive, social Christianity that would be responsive to both modern science and the nationalist awakening in China. But liberalism also threatened to undermine the certainty and urgency of the church's teachings and to cut the "nerve" of Western missions.[19] In the case of fundamentalist lay preachers like Wang, their sense of purpose and self-worth, as well as their livelihood, hinged upon a shared conviction of the supreme value of their undiluted Gospel. Their frustration and anger at their own exclusion from the establishment was now vindicated by the latter's apparent turn toward "unbelief." Theological modernism hardened their contempt for the missions.

There was a curious popular resonance to Wang's railings against missionary Christianity, for they echoed some of the invective of anti-Christian students and intellectuals of the May Fourth era who dismissed church leaders as the "running dogs" of Western imperialists. Even Chen Duxiu, dean of Beijing University and future founder of the Chinese Communist Party (CCP), who briefly advocated the adoption of Christianity in China, lamented in 1920 that "the YMCA [leaders] flatter the powerful, ingratiate themselves with the rich, gather converts as well as their wealth, and commit a host of other despicable acts. Real Christians should weep for them."[20] For Wang, the missionary establishment including the YMCA constituted a realm of ecclesiastical power from which he had been banished. It also represented a woeful compromise with the world that drained the church of its primitive spirit, leaving it an "eggshell" as when "both the [raw] yolk and the egg white" had been "sucked out" through holes made by needles. To the marginalized and disinherited in Chinese society at large, both inside and outside the Protestant community, such a compromise—glaringly symbolized in the baptism of the rich, the powerful, and the "corrupt officials" and their installation as church board members—must have implicated the established church in the evils of an unjust society.[21] Indeed, it was the NCC chairman Yu Rizhang who officiated at the wedding ceremony of the bigamous marriage of Chiang Kai-shek with the Wellesley-educated Shanghai YWCA activist Soong Mayling (Song Meiling) in 1927. In 1930, Chiang would be baptized into the Methodist Episcopal Church.

The vicissitudes of public perceptions of the YMCA and the Protestant church in general in the early twentieth century reflected in part the flux and chaos of the political life and the frustrations of patriots who had pinned their hope for nation-building on a cascade of Western beliefs, including liberalism, anarchism, and socialism as well as Christianity and Marxism. During the late Qing and early Republican years, some of the prominent reformers and revolutionaries had sought inspiration for a modern, revitalized China in the Christian religion. Sun Yat-sen had declared, for instance, that he belonged to "the Christianity of Jesus who was a revolutionary."[22] After the fall of the Qing dynasty in 1912, he attributed the "essence" of the revolution he had led to "the teachings of the Church" and added, "it is the Church, not my efforts, that is responsible for the Republic of China."[23] In the early 1910s, as we have seen, the YMCA also advertised Protestant faith as the fountain of Western progress and modernity to patriotic Chinese youths.

In fact, of all the Protestant institutions in China, the YMCA was perhaps most closely identified with the scheme of Christianizing and modernizing China. Yu Rizhang, who served as national secretary of the YMCA in China before the founding of the NCC in 1922, had articulated this dream when he prescribed the formula of "national salvation through individual [Christian] character" (renge jiuguo).[24] However, as the dizzying shifts of warlord politics continued through the 1920s and as the country relapsed into civil war after the Northern Expedition, the YMCA formula must have become a pious fantasy in the eyes of most patriots. To those who had flocked to the Robertson-Eddy lectures during the early, hopeful days of the republic, corruption in the government and the venality and brutality of the warlords had clearly outpaced any individual character-building championed by the YMCA. Not surprisingly, conservative independent preachers were eager to distance themselves from the Social

Gospel. In a diatribe written in 1928, Wang castigated the YMCA (and YWCA) as a prime case of adulterated Christianity: it had cast away the Gospel of salvation and preached a poor worldly substitute that was all about "improving character, promoting mass education, reforming the society, and serving the people." He insisted through the years that all the social evils and human suffering such as "war, murder, violence, theft, pains, and illness" came "entirely from human sin"; social reform was "irrelevant." Like a raging plague that would not yield to "fake medicine," he wrote, the evils of this perishing world could be countered only by the Gospel of individual repentance and acceptance of Jesus.[25]

One might note that such an individualistic spin on what constitutes pure and primal Gospel—and Wang's customary didacticism in general—was no less moralistic than the YMCA prescription, except that it was shorn of reformist social ambitions. On the practical level it was also hardly distinguishable from the injunctions of most secular traditionalists, who continued to see Confucian morality as the cornerstone of an orderly society. For instance, Wang's revulsion at the "licentiousness and filth" of the new urban life of the 1920s—a time when "new gentlemen of lofty ideals who sing loudly of [personal] liberation divorce again and again"—echoed similar sentiments of Liang Qichao, a hero of the Hundred Days' Reform of 1898 and then head of the National Beijing Library. In late 1926, officiating at the wedding of the beautiful singer Lu Xiaoman and the poet Xu Zhimo—an icon for liberated youths whose "Listening to the Chant of Prayer and Penitence in Changzhou's Temple of Heaven's Stillness" is excerpted at the beginning of this chapter—Liang had made a scene by openly chastising the couple's reckless romances and divorces (despite Xu's bouts of Buddhist piety) that had preceded the occasion. "The youth make such a thing of love; they show no sense of moderation," Liang said; they "smash through the protective nets of convention, and so fall into their own sorrowful snare."[26]

For those who were repulsed by the onslaught of unbridled modernity, inside as well as outside the Protestant community, such righteous indignation must have struck a common chord. In the case of those Christians who were drawn to Wang's confident fundamentalism, it was also reassuring to find a clear scripture-based moral compass even when the ship of the Chinese state had run aground on warlordism and civil war. In any event, "great tribulations" were about to "descend on this evil world,"

Wang cried. As the end time approaches, not only was society at large defiled, the church also "degenerates ever faster. What God does at this juncture is not to reform or rectify this chaotic and corrupted church, but to call those belonging to Him to come out of it."[27]

Within the Protestant establishment, however, the Social Gospel continued to be a centerpiece of the drive to make Christianity relevant to China's modern struggles. During the early 1920s, the national YMCA and YWCA began studying emerging industrial problems in major cities, including "the horrors of child-labor," long working hours, and unsanitary working conditions. The YWCA also continued its long campaigns against foot-binding and opium addiction.[28] Meanwhile, the NCC organized a string of committees devoted to "Anti-Narcotic" campaigns, "the Work for the Blind," "Rural Life," "Economic Relations," and the like. Mission churches in general also supported various reformist organizations ranging from the International Anti-Opium Association and the China International Famine Relief Commission to the Door of Hope in Shanghai, a refuge for brothel girls started by five missionary women in 1901. After the formation of the Nationalist government in Nanjing in 1928, the NCC pledged to "cooperate with the government in the building of a new nation."[29]

During the same period, denominational church leaders had blessed the Mass Education Movement launched by YMCA activist James Yen (Yan Yangchu) "to make China's illiterate millions reading and intelligent citizens." While a student in the United States during World War I, Yen had volunteered to aid the YMCA's work for the Chinese laborers in France. He compiled a list of one thousand basic Chinese characters and taught the largely illiterate laborers to read. Yen returned to China after the war and, under the auspices of the YMCA, introduced the same literacy program in a handful of urban areas where he was able to gain the support of the local elite and recruit teachers. He launched the first city campaign in Changsha in 1922 with some fourteen hundred students (of various ages ranging from the teens to the forties) completing the course. In August 1923, the National Popular Education Association (Zhonghua Pingmin Jiaoyu Cujinhui) was formally established in Beijing with support from both within and outside the Protestant community.[30]

It was the hope of the YMCA that the "Popular Thousand-Character Lessons" would become "the entering wedge for more intensive help to the economic life of the villagers." With Western agricultural knowledge and technology, farmers would reap a host of benefits ranging from better crop selection to improved livestock, better roads, and more efficient water wheels for farm irrigation. In addition, the organization of "community parishes" as part of rural reconstruction would introduce "a new era of principles of mutual helpfulness and . . . will to that extent be bringing in the Kingdom of God."[31]

THE QUEST FOR INDIGENOUS LITERATURE AND ART

Meanwhile, mainline churches were also accelerating their efforts in building an indigenous church. In their view, the Social Gospel as well as the cultivation of Chinese leadership and of native expressions of the faith would enable Christianity to take root in Chinese soil; such efforts would also be the best defense against antimission agitations generated by nationalist upheavals. As we have seen, the organization of the NCC in 1922 catapulted a new generation of Western-educated Chinese leaders into prominent positions. Soon after its formation, the NCC listed among its primary tasks the promotion of "indigenous Christian literature" and dreamed of Chinese authors "bringing with vivid and picturesque detail" their religious experience "to the minds and hearts of the rising generation in this land."[32] The child of the dream was the National Christian Literature Association (Zhonghua Jidujiao Wenshe, better known as Wenshe) formed in 1924, an elite organization composed of preeminent Christian writers in established churches. Needless to say, it had no place for homegrown, moderately educated lay leaders like Wang Mingdao.

Missionary efforts to cultivate idiomatic Chinese expressions of the Protestant faith can be traced back to 1832 when Liang Fa's *Good Words to Admonish the Age (Quanshi liangyan)* was printed under the auspices of the LMS. Liang's tract, particularly the terrifying prophetic proclamation of divine wrath and the impending fiery destruction therein, later inspired Hong Xiuquan's apocalyptic visions. Yet the overall failure of mission churches to win over the cultured elite during the nineteenth century and the lack of cooperation among various denominations resulted in a relative scarcity of indigenous literary talents whose writings could reach a national audience.[33] In the early twentieth century, the significant expansion of the educational enterprise of Protestant missions, helped in part by the abolition of the imperial civil service examinations in 1905, led

to the emergence of a group of articulate and increasingly influential Protestant members of the political and social elite. By the late 1910s, several
Chinese members of the faculty at Yenching, the preeminent Protestant
mission university, joined their missionary counterparts in organizing
what became known as the Life Fellowship (Shengmingshe). In 1919,
the group started a periodical called *Life Journal* (*Shengming*), published
primarily in Chinese. With editorials that grew out of the group's meetings, devotional literature, biblical interpretations, and literary pieces, the
journal marked a significant moment in the development of homegrown
Protestant writings.[34]

In 1922, the formation of the NCC opened a new phase in the cultivation of indigenous literature as it facilitated coordinated efforts among denominational churches toward that goal. When Wenshe came into being
in 1924, it counted among its small membership several familiar names in
the Protestant circle, including Zhao Zichen, Cheng Jingyi, Yu Rizhang,
and Liu Tingfang. Under its auspices, a total of ten books were published
by 1928 and featured such authors as Zhao, Xie Songgao, Jian Youwen,
and Wang Zhixin. Zhou Zuoren, brother of Lu Xun and himself an accomplished writer, was also recruited to prepare a new edition of the Chinese
Bible with modern punctuations. Like the *Life Journal,* most of those works
sought to present Christianity in the light of respectable philosophical and
ethical traditions and as a force for social progress and scientific inquiry.
During its brief existence, the association published twenty-eight issues
of the *Wenshe Monthly* (*Wenshe yuekan*). The articles primarily aimed at
promoting the Sinicization of Christianity and often lamented the crudeness of writing and the ignorance of Confucian basics in many Christian
works. One writer compared some church publishers to "firms" that dealt
in "imported goods" and condemned the resulting "cultural aggression."[35]

For all the impressive strides that Wenshe seemed to be making
toward indigenization of Christian writings, the financing of the organization revealed the characteristic fragility of mission-sponsored efforts
toward Chinese Christianity: in contrast to literary ventures undertaken
by independent church leaders such as Wang Mingdao, whose *Spiritual
Food Quarterly* (*Lingshi jikan*) began in 1927 and endured into the 1950s,
Wenshe was able to begin its work only after two American missionaries
supplied initial funds for its operation. The more crucial support came
from the New York–based Institute of Social and Religious Research

headed by John R. Mott. When Wenshe openly supported the cause of the nationalist revolution at the time of the Northern Expedition, many in the mission church denounced the "intellectual extremism" and "heresy" of the association. As a result, the institute cut off funding for Wenshe in 1928, which almost immediately forced it to shut down.[36]

Despite the failure of Wenshe, several other efforts within both the Protestant and Catholic establishments were under way by the early 1930s to cultivate Chinese Christian literature, art, and music. As early as 1920, photographs of a series of Chinese paintings on biblical subjects by a rural Protestant convert in northern Fujian had appeared in *Asia: The American Magazine on the Orient*. The collection includes a picture of Noah's ark in the shape of an ornate South China pleasure boat, beside which a procession of eight people in unruffled garb lined up in order of seniority (with the long-bearded Noah and his wife in the lead) patiently await their turn after the animals.[37] During the 1930s, several graduates of the new School of Christian Art of the Catholic University (Furen Daxue) in Beiping (renamed from Beijing after 1928) were commissioned to paint Christian pictures "in Chinese form." The result was some 150 Chinese Christian paintings, many of which were intended for the 1940 exhibit of indigenous Christian art in Rome. Two dozen of those works appeared in 1938 in a printed collection titled *The Life of Christ by Chinese Artists*. One picture features a haloed boy Jesus standing on a tiled "porch of a Chinese temple" preaching to a few bearded Confucian gentry. The latter look "entertained and amused" but unconvinced. Perhaps the most striking picture in the book is "No Room in the Inn," which portrays an imploring Joseph at the closed gate of a walled farmhouse guarded by a fierce dog. A dozen yards or so behind him stands a shivering, forlorn Mary in the snow with her "bright red and blue garments . . . blown by the wind." The nativity narrative aside, the painting captures the bleakness of a North China winter.[38]

The same decade also saw the appearance of the first significant collection of Chinese hymns. In 1936, a popular "union" hymnal titled *Hymns of Universal Praise (Putian songzan)* was published under the auspices of the Church of Christ in China, the union body that had come into being in 1927 to represent sixteen mainline denominations and about one-third of baptized Protestant communicants in the country. Edited by Liu Tingfang, former dean of the School of Religion at Yenching University and head of several national Christian organizations, it included 62 original Chinese hymns out of a total of 514 and was used by six leading denominational groups in China.[39] Set to familiar traditional tunes, many of those original Chinese lyrics evoke idyllic scenes and traditional values. One such verse, written in 1931 by Zhao Zichen, who had succeeded Liu as the dean of the Yenching School of Religion, was called "Tian'en ge" (Song of Heavenly Grace), set to the tune of "Chutou ge" (Song of the Hoe). It sings of the mercies and rich provisions of the Heavenly Father, who is "the spring wind, I the grass as I yield." It urges the faithful to look at the birds as they fly and "at the fields so white with lilies," to not let their hearts be troubled over clothes or food, and to rest in the assurance that "this wide world is now our home, mine and yours."[40]

Another song by Zhao Zichen, also written in 1931, is named "Qing-chen ge" (Song of the Dawn) and contains the following lines:

> Golden breaks the dawn;
> > Comes the eastern sun.
>
> .   .   .   .
>
> Birds above me fly,
> > Flowers bloom below.
>
> .   .   .   .
>
> Humbly guide our youth,
> > Honor old and weak.
>
> .   .   .   .
>
> Content in coarse clothes,
> > Disdain not half-ground grains.[41]

There was a tranquility, a gentle and mellow Confucian sensibility, in the commonplace Christian exhortations in such songs. One could picture Zhao or his Yenching colleagues humming those hymns under the willow trees beside the misty, placid lake on the campus of Yenching (now Beijing University). But the peaceful world depicted in such songs did not exist for the majority of the Chinese masses. After September 1931, it was Japanese warplanes, not birds, that many people saw above them. And in the heartland of China, the rampage of the warlords and bandits during the 1920s gave way in the early 1930s only to the seemingly unending Nationalist campaigns, backed also by warplanes, to "exterminate" Communist "bandits."

FIGURE 12 "No Room in the Inn." Painting by Lu Hongnian. Source: *Chinese Recorder* 69 (December 1938).

FIGURE 13 "The Adoration of the Magi." Painting by Xu Sanchun. Source: *Chinese Recorder* 68 (January 1937).

FIGURE 14 Liu Tingfang (T. T. Lew), from MRL6, T. T. Lew Papers, Series 1, Box 1.
Courtesy of the Burke Library Archives (Columbia University Libraries) at Union
Theological Seminary, New York.

◆ ◆ ◆

It is understandable, therefore, that hellfire evangelists such as Wang Mingdao had little sympathy for the visions and indigenizing attempts of the likes of Liu Tingfang and Zhao Zichen. Wang had always been suspicious of symbolic—and to him strained and superficial—efforts at naturalizing Christianity. For him, indigenization had nothing to do with "building a church that looks like a [Buddhist] temple; singing a few hymns in the native tune; [and] borrowing musical instruments from [Buddhist] monks and playing them a couple of times in a church." He cried that such attempts to blend local customs into church life, like the trend to turn "gospel churches" into "associations of social reform," were nothing but "secularization" and a "sure way to destroy Christianity." They were the work of Satan and of those church leaders who were "unbelievers." (It would only add oil to the fire of Wang's invective if he knew that the Beijing artist who painted "No Room in the Inn" remained a non-Christian after executing several famous pieces of sacred art.) He argued that "the real indigenous church is one that is set up in the manner of the apostles" and involves "neither Westernization nor Sinicization." It would be a church that preaches "redemption, resurrection, miracles, and prophecies," a church that breathes apocalyptic fire.[42]

Most of Wang's tirade against missionary Christianity was carried in his *Spiritual Food Quarterly,* which provided him with a platform for animating controversy. An article he published in it in 1935 accused "60 or 70 percent, even 80 to 90 percent, of the church leaders and preachers" of being "false masters," a kind of sweeping vilification that sometimes invited boycotts of his revival meetings by mission churches. The journal also contained literalist biblical exegeses and mystical and eschatological works by Western authors that he translated himself. The circulation of *Spiritual Food* never exceeded two thousand, but it was distributed across China and over time gained an audience belied by its limited subscription. Like his itinerant preaching, Wang Mingdao's writings spread his influence in the Chinese church and were chiefly responsible for preserving his legacy. During the 1930s, his own congregation in Beiping also throve: three weeks after the outbreak of the Marco Polo Bridge Incident on July 7, 1937, just outside the city, which triggered the full-scale Japanese invasion of China, the Christian Tabernacle moved into its own new building and held an eighteen-day rally attended by a spirited crowd of some five hundred.[43]

As we shall see in Chapter 8, when we return to the story of Wang Mingdao and other independents caught in the turbulence of the 1940s and 1950s, there would be drama—not of his own making—in his later life. He had come close to embracing Pentecostalism and may well have been swept into it had his own experience of "spiritual gifts" been more fulfilling or had his Confucian sense of decorum not been offended by the riotous exuberance of the movement. Overall, he was a staid, if quaintly unbending, personality and a man of usually impeccable integrity. Cheng Jingyi, general secretary of the NCC and former pastor of the LMS church in Beijing to which Wang's family had belonged, once bestowed mixed praise on Wang as a person, "good in every way, except for the bit of stubbornness."[44] Wang's fame as a "man of iron" lies as much in his unflinching opposition to the Protestant establishment, which he saw as having compromised with the evil world, as in his fierce apocalyptic fundamentalism. The reason that he appears among what Leslie T. Lyall calls "Three of China's Mighty Men"—a somewhat idiosyncratic short-list of Protestants who Lyall believes stand tall in Chinese Christianity—is that Wang's obstinance was to collide with powers far more threatening and overwhelming than the imagined goliath of mission churches.[45] On the other hand, he was not without a measure of charisma. At a time of rising nationalism, he made a triumph out of his expulsion from Western missions; he also countered the latter's idealistic yet meager attempts at indigenizing Christianity with a dark eschatology that was in tune with the prevailing pessimism of the masses. As the agony of war and turmoil gripped multitudes across China, the simplicity and certainty of Wang's fundamentalist faith was both steadying and inspiring for his followers. It exuded confidence and hope even as he proclaimed the bleak message of an impending fiery end to this world. For many, the otherworldly salvation that he promised was perhaps the only absolute that they were able to cling to.

CHAPTER SIX

"Flame for God"

JOHN SUNG AND THE BETHEL BAND

THROUGHOUT THE 1930S, as Wang Mingdao conducted his itinerant revivalism from his Beijing base, other notable independent evangelists flourished in Shanghai where nationalist spirit found its religious expression among the educated, young members of the Protestant community. Comparative urban affluence as well as the relative freedom and security of the treaty port, which had helped in the growth of Yu Guozhen's China Christian Independent Church in the pre-Revolution years, continued to provide fertile ground for the growth of independent evangelism. It was in Shanghai in early 1931 that a preaching band made up of four modern-educated young men, most of them in their twenties, sprang into prominence.[1] Calling themselves the Bethel Worldwide Evangelistic Band (Boteli Huanyou Budaotuan), the four young men, neatly attired in Western suits, brought a modern flair and high spirits to their religious campaigns as they traveled up and down the country. The *China Christian Year Book* soon took notice of the Bethel Band for its "skillful and well trained singers and musicians" who "set the people singing happy, catchy choruses. . . . Singing has become spontaneous in the meetings . . . and the crowds catch their contagious good cheer." In many coastal cities, "the churches were swept by the [band's] spirit of revival. Bloodthirsty bandits, rapacious officials, overbearing soldiers, anarchistic students, dishonest servants, communists, polygamists, sedate scholars, hardheaders, business men, rickshaw coolies, beggars, men and women, young and old, city dwellers and country folk were moved to confess and forsake sin, and to make reparation and restitution. In Peiping a total amount of more than twenty thousand dollars conscience money was returned."[2]

The Bethel Band was an outgrowth of the Bethel Mission of Shanghai founded in 1920 by Jennie V. Hughes, a Methodist Episcopal educational missionary, and Shi Meiyu (Mary Stone, 1873–1954), a pioneering female surgeon. Shi and Kang Cheng (Ida Kahn) had been brought by a Methodist missionary to study at the University of Michigan where they became the first two Chinese women to earn medical degrees (in 1896) from a Western university. Upon graduation, Shi and Kang received commissions as medical missionaries to China from the Woman's Foreign Missionary Society of the Methodist Episcopal Church. They returned to Jiujiang, Jiangxi province, where Shi became the superintendent of the Elizabeth Skelton Danforth Memorial Hospital, which opened in 1901. By the time of the Revolution of 1911, around three thousand patients were treated at the hospital each month during the busy seasons, and Shi's reputation spread. (After observing her in the operating room, Dr. Danforth claimed, "no Chicago surgeon is doing work superior to hers.") Besides her work at the hospital, Shi also supervised the training of hundreds of nurses and prepared Chinese translations of medical textbooks. She was the first woman in Central China to be ordained a minister and became the first president of the Women's Christian Temperance Union in China.[3] Over the years, Shi developed a close friendship with Hughes, then principal of a mission school for girls in Jiujiang. In 1920, Shi's "increasingly literalist religious views" led her and the like-minded Hughes to sever their ties with the Methodist Board of Missions. The two decided to move to Shanghai where they set up the independent Bethel Mission in a "large haunted house" they rented. During the 1920s, the mission grew to include both a primary and a secondary school, a chapel, a hospital, a nursing school, a Bible school, and an orphanage.[4]

Ji Zhiwen (Andrew Gih, 1901–1985), the organizer and leader of the Bethel Band, was a graduate of the Bethel Middle School. He had grown up in a small town three miles from Shanghai. His father died when he was twelve, and the family sank into poverty; his mother had to supplement farming with spinning and weaving as she struggled to bring up her children. Ji's childhood was "full of sorrow," punctuated by the deaths of all three of his younger brothers. At the age of nineteen, he enrolled in the recently opened middle school at the Bethel Mission, which attracted him because of its low tuition cost and because it offered English, an increasingly popular subject, taught by American missionaries. At Bethel, religious instruction was compulsory, so he went to chapel daily and studied the Bible. Eventually, he was converted at an evangelical meeting held at the mission by a CIM missionary. In 1924, he passed the Shanghai post office recruitment examination and obtained one of the most coveted and secure positions at the time.[5]

In 1925, shortly after the May Thirtieth Incident that had broken out in Shanghai's International Settlement and sparked another explosion of nationalist frustration across China, A. Paget Wilkes, an English missionary of the Japan Evangelistic Band, came to Shanghai and braved the city's antiforeignism by holding revival meetings together with Wang Zai (Leland Wang, 1898–1975), a naval officer–turned–revivalist. Wilkes, who had been in East Asia for more than a quarter of a century, saw a new urgency for indigenizing Christianity in the aftermath of the recent crisis. "The foreign missionaries can never reach the people as well as the Chinese themselves," Wilkes declared. "God wants to save China. He is waiting for the yielded instruments."[6] Roused by Wilkes's challenge, Ji resigned his postal job to become a full-time revivalist. He was joined by many Bethel students and teachers, who formed several preaching bands and embarked on itinerant evangelism during the summer months that targeted in particular teenage students.[7]

"OUT OF COMMUNISM INTO GOD'S FAMILY"

In February 1931, Ji organized a "permanent" Bethel Band that included three other young men who, to varying degrees, were all products of mission education. The group would remain perhaps the best-known preaching team in Republican China. One of the members was Nie Ziying (Lincoln Nieh), whose family converted to Christianity in the early 1920s after Nie's younger brother was cured of a serious illness at the Methodist Danforth Hospital in Jiujiang. Nie was then sent to attend school in Shanghai by his "adopted" mother Dr. Phoebe Stone (Shi Chengzhi), younger sister of Shi Meiyu. Phoebe had received medical training at Johns Hopkins University and was put in charge of the hospital after her sister's departure. In a twist that would become increasingly familiar

among mission school students and young converts in mission institutions—more than sixty orphans who had grown up at the Home of
Onesiphorus in Tai'an left to join the CCP's Eighth Route Army between
1937 and 1940—Nie in his own words turned into "one of the most hot-
headed agitators" after the May Thirtieth Incident and secretly joined the
CCP.[8] According to his autobiographical account "Out of Communism
into God's Family," Nie worked under cover for the propaganda wing of
the party in early 1927 and was probably directly involved in the party's
organization of general strikes by Shanghai's General Labor Union in
late March that mobilized some six hundred thousand workers on the
eve of the National Revolutionary Army's entry into the city. After Chiang
Kai-shek treacherously turned against the labor organizations in April,
arresting and killing hundreds of activists with the help of Shanghai's
underworld leaders, Nie fled to join up successively with the CCP forces
in Wuchang and Jiujiang, where he obtained "a high position" and "lived
at the Party headquarters."

By the end of 1927, however, several armed "uprisings" launched by
CCP troops in Central and South China against the Guomindang had
all failed. Thousands were dead. After Nie managed to evade a series of
hunts by Guomindang troops that left many of his comrades dead, the
CCP allegedly began to suspect him of being a traitor and "counterrevo-
lutionist" and decided to kill him. Nie was at the end of his rope when
Phoebe Stone returned from Korea (where she and other missionaries
had sought shelter after the Nanjing Incident of March 1927) and sum-
moned him back to Shanghai, "so I escaped from the devil's hand." His
"five escapes from death" during the months of bewildering and bloody
turns of events cured him of political activism and drove him back into
the fold of the church. By the spring of 1928, he had reenrolled in the
mission school and was "born again" the following year during a summer
Bible conference held at the Bethel Mission.[9]

One cannot help wondering what might have happened if Nie's career
within the CCP had gone well. There were certainly others who did not
come back to the church. In his *Red Star over China*, Edgar Snow told of
the CCP agent—fondly called "Wang the Pastor" among the Communists
—who arranged his secret passage to Yan'an in 1936. According to Snow,
Wang had attended a mission school in Shanghai and had gone on to

become a pastor and a "prominent" member of the Christian community. But then, likely in the early 1930s, he "deserted his congregation" to join the "Reds."[10] In his autobiography *Fifty Years in China,* John Leighton Stuart, president of Yenching University and later U.S. ambassador to China, recalled that when he met Mao Zedong in Chongqing in August 1945, Mao "greeted me with the remark that there were present many of my former students at Yenan." Stuart "laughingly replied that I was well aware of that and hoped that they were proving a credit to their training."[11]

There is perhaps no way of knowing exactly how many graduates of mission schools ended up joining the CCP. On the other hand, there were certainly other young patriotic Christians besides Nie whose idealistic ventures into the Communist movement ended in disaster and who poured their erstwhile revolutionary fervor into revivalism—as in the case of a less known preacher of the 1930s named Paul Xu (Xu Baoluo, 1906–1989). Xu grew up in Wuhu, Anhui; his father had brought the family into the local Christian and Missionary Alliance mission. In 1927, the young Xu joined the CCP, and soon afterwards, the Nationalist crackdown on the Communists began. Xu's wife and two concubines had recently died within months of one another. In his bereavement and also to flee for his life, Xu went to Taiquan Shan Mountain near Wuhu, where he became a monk at a Buddhist monastery. A few months later, Xu's comrades found him out and brought him back to work for the CCP.[12]

During the early 1930s, Xu continued his underground work for the CCP as he taught in mission schools. In August 1932, he received Liu Shaoqi—the leading CCP labor organizer at the time and future head of state of the People's Republic of China—in his residence in Nanjing, a few hours before Xu had to flee from police. He returned to Taiquan Shan as a monk, but his crisis was not yet over. In 1934, he suffered a mental breakdown, possibly from the stress he had come under, including friction with fellow monks. Later that year, he found himself betrayed by a former comrade and took to flight from Guomindang authorities yet another time. While he was hiding in a Buddhist temple in Shanghai, Xu saw visions of Jesus calling upon him to repent, and he decided to "flee from Buddha and return to the Lord." Within a year, he started an independent congregation of his own in Shanghai. He had finally completed his journey "from a Bolshevik to a servant of God" and would

FIGURE 15 The Bethel Band. *From left to right:* Li Daorong, Ji Zhiwen, John Sung, Nie Ziying, Lin Jingkang. Source: *Home and Foreign Fields*, June 1932. Used by permission, LifeWay Christian Resources, Nashville, Tennessee.

remain an evangelist, exorcist, and faith healer through the remainder of the Republican period.[13]

Conceivably, the background of such young revivalists as Xu, Ji, and Nie brought them close to their audience, many of whom could identify with the preachers' tortuous personal experiences. During an eight-day revival held among the students of two mission high schools in Xinghua in 1932, Li Daorong, another member of the Bethel Band, likened the nationalistic students of the day to Saul, who persecuted the church; he added that he himself had done the same. But now, as the Day of Judgment approached, he asked his audience to repent of the sin of godless nationalism and "ninety per cent of the students raised their hands! . . . Men and women were terrified and literally watered the altar with their tears as they made confession and sought the joy of forgiveness."[14]

Riding the wave of such emotional responses to their simple message of repentance and salvation, the Bethel Band held 1,199 meetings in one year alone during which they preached to 425,980 people in thirteen provinces and sixty-five cities and reported "18,118 souls saved or dedicated for [Gospel] service."[15] After a month-long revival conducted at the Beiping Presbyterian Mission in December 1932, during which the band moved "audiences of 1000 to 1500" to kneel in "united prayer," the resident missionary, James P. Leynse, rhapsodized: "The anti-Christian movement, once very much alive, has been drowned into an ocean of interest. . . . The Manchurian crisis, boycotts and the economic reprisals are helping to drive them toward something higher than common materialism. Even tanks, bombs, planes, and guns can be turned into implements of the Kingdom."[16]

"TO SAVE MY COUNTRY"

To a large extent, the success of the Bethel Band was the result of its effective organization (modeled after the Asbury College Evangelistic Team that visited Shanghai in 1930), its harnessing of modern music, and the band members' own former Communist or student rebel background, which endeared them specially to the young. However, its most significant appeal was the charisma of its leading member John Sung (Song Shangjie, 1901–1944). In spring 1931, Sung rose to the center stage of popular revivalism after a series of campaigns in the lower Yangzi valley during which he often moved his audience to choruses of uncontrollable sobbing and confession of sins. In May he was invited to join the Bethel Band.[17]

Unpolished in his manners and attire and speaking in a coarse voice with a strong Xinghua accent that made his Mandarin Chinese often incomprehensible, Sung nevertheless was a mesmerizing figure onstage. A man who converted during one of his evangelistic meetings in the early 1930s remembered him—"a small, dark-skinned man with a dusty look on his face"—standing on the platform in an undersized blue cotton gown. Vigorously waving a white handkerchief up and down, Sung led his audience in singing a short song called "Come Home!" "The uncombed hair on his forehead was starting to gray; he had a spirited and piercing look in the narrow slit of his eyes." However, a "childlike innocence" lit up his face when he smiled. Sung often preached three times a day, for which he needed a platform or stage: the pulpit was never enough. The stage props he used included a coal-burning stove, which he would fan to send sparks (lights of the Holy Spirit) flying in all directions. There was also a huge rock that he struggled to carry on his back to illustrate the weight of sin. He would then hurl the rock on the platform with a loud thump and break into ecstatic singing to show the joy of divine forgiveness. His favorite furniture onstage was a coffin, which he would jump into and out of as he cried out a message on sin and death. At the end of his revival meetings, he would call on his audience to come forth to the platform and kneel down—some on the platform, others in front of it, many others standing for lack of room—in prayers of repentance. "The repentant would beat upon their breasts in loud wailing; some would collapse on the floor."[18]

Sung's rise as the incomparable Protestant evangelist in twentieth-century China has drama of its own. Like Wang Mingdao's, Sung's life as an independent evangelist was shaped by the Christian tradition in his family as well as his youthful ambition and patriotism. It was also shaped by the hardship and pains of his fellow Chinese, for whom he sought complete, otherworldly deliverance. Sung's father was a Methodist Episcopal minister in the town of Xinghua, Fujian province, seventy miles south of the provincial capital Fuzhou, one of the five treaty ports opened to foreign trade and missions in the 1840s. In 1920, Sung went to the United States on a scholarship arranged with the help of a Xinghua missionary to study theology at Ohio Wesleyan University and to train for the career of a preacher upon his return to China.

Soon after he arrived, however, he changed his subject to chemistry and graduated summa cum laude in three years—not without cheating on his last examination, he admitted. He then pursued graduate studies at Ohio State University, focusing his research at one point on poison gas and tear gas.[19] He also became a student activist and was elected president of the international student organization on campus. In that capacity he hosted events that featured prominent figures such as philosopher John Dewey of Columbia University. (Dewey had recently made a highly publicized tour of China where he was treated as a messenger of the twin modern sages of "Democracy" and "Science.") Such contacts roused Sung's patriotic ambitions, which nevertheless pointed in different directions. One was to become "an inventor in the field of chemistry" and to "use all my talents to benefit my countrymen," he wrote in a letter. Another plan, which he revealed in a separate letter to his parents in the wake of the May Thirtieth Incident in Shanghai, was to "build an independent church not to be controlled by foreigners" upon his return. He also wanted to become a YMCA secretary to promote social progress in China. The tension between the "calling to be a religious revivalist and my simultaneous addiction to chemistry" was gnawing and possibly accounted for "an inexplicable melancholy and difficulty in breathing" when he received his doctorate in chemistry on March 19, 1926.[20]

Upon graduation, Sung received several attractive offers, including a well-paid faculty position to teach biochemistry at Peking Union Medical College, which after 1914 came under the wings of the China Medical Board of the Rockefeller Foundation and emerged in the 1920s as the country's center for medical research and teaching. However, the observation made by a local minister and representative of the Wesley Foundation that Sung "looked more like a preacher than a scientist" reminded him of his earlier religious purpose and rekindled his guilt at his change of course in America. So crippling was the guilt that his hands "shook uncontrollably" when he tried to sign the contract with the medical college. When an opportunity for him to study tuition-free (plus stipends) at Union Theological Seminary in New York presented itself, he gave up, permanently as it turned out, his career in science. His piety mingled with patriotism when he wrote to his parents about the decision, asking them to offer him as a living sacrifice to God and pray for him so that he could gain "the calling and the divine power to save my country." After he completed his theological studies, he added, he would return to become a self-supporting evangelist and would not "wag my tail and beg for pity" before foreign missionaries. "One who is truly dedicated to saving his country must first taste all the hardships of the common people."[21]

In New York, however, he went through a personal and religious crisis, which caused a nervous breakdown. He was allegedly attracted to a girl, a fellow Chinese student, despite his engagement (arranged by his parents in 1922) to a woman in his hometown whom he had never met.[22] At Union Theological Seminary, the reputed citadel of modernism, he was also briefly attracted to the liberal theology eloquently expounded by Harry Emerson Fosdick, professor of practical theology who also served as pastor at the nearby Park Avenue Baptist Church (soon to become Riverside Church). Fosdick, who came to be dubbed "modernism's Moses," had developed a keen interest in China. He had visited the country in 1921, where he saw "fundamentalism . . . in its full intensity." In 1922, a few months after his return from the trip, Fosdick delivered a sermon titled "Shall the Fundamentalists Win?" which was then published in the *Christian Century*. The famous response from John R. Straton of New

York's Calvary Baptist Church, one of the chief contenders for the mantle of "captain of American fundamentalism," was the no less defiant sermon "Shall the Funnymonkeyists Win?"[23]

Those were some of the early shots fired in the fundamentalist–modernist controversy, which Sung was unable to shun while at Union. In fact, such was the liberal influence on him that he soon buried himself in books on comparative religion. He even rendered his own English translation of *The Classic of the Dao* (*Daodejing*). "Before long," he wrote, "I had reached the conclusion that the various religions are the different paths to the same destination." But that realization only brought bewilderment and "despair" and intensified the bouts of "mysterious sadness" he had often experienced while in Ohio.[24] One could picture Sung caught in an internal theological debate and emotional turmoil when he went down to Straton's Calvary Baptist Church on West 57th Street in October 1926 to attend a series of revival meetings being held there. Straton had invited an evangelical prodigy—a fourteen-year-old girl from California named Uldine Utley—to lead the six-week revival campaign, which would culminate in a mass rally at Madison Square Garden attended by some twenty thousand people. Utley was capable of a dramatic presence. By her own account, she had experienced "baptism of the Holy Spirit" at a Pentecostal revival meeting in 1921 (at the age of nine), falling on her knees and weeping aloud at the altar. Clad in angelic white ("white socks, white shoes, and white gown," in the style of the sensational Aimee Semple McPherson), the "blue-eyed blonde," as Sung remembered her, was mesmerizing. She preached on the Cross and Spirit baptism, and she told her audience to lay aside their "doubts and fears and perplexities." In New York City, she exclaimed, "people need rest. They are worried and their nerves are on edge. . . . Yet, Jesus is able to give rest to this great city." When she called for a moment of quiet prayer, Sung felt himself "transfigured into a feathered immortal" amidst the "sacred silence."[25]

It is doubtful that Sung had been immediately won over to Utley's "kind and gentle" fundamentalism. In fact, Sung's emotional crisis would only deepen during the weeks that followed as he sought after the elusive "rest." "I wanted to commit suicide many times," he recalled. A letter to Rollin Walker, professor of Bible at Ohio Wesleyan University, appeared "incoherent and as the product of an overstrained brain."[26] Eventually, on February 10, 1927, Sung's depression erupted into "ecstatic joy." "Jesus found me in Room 405 of an atheistic seminary," he wrote. That night, "the Lord changed my name to John." Jesus also "explained" that, like John the Baptist, he had been called to be the "herald" and to prepare the way "for the imminent Second Coming of the Lord." (His Chinese name remained Song Shangjie.) Sung then burned his theology books as "books of the demons" and confronted Fosdick with the pronouncement: "You are of the Devil. You made me lose my faith."[27] Having seen in a vision of hell the "terrifying, beast-like" faces of "pastors, bishops, and professors at the seminary," he went around "weeping" for his Union professors and fellow students who had "enslaved themselves to Satan." For days, he alternated between "unstoppable wild singing" of praises and laughs and teary moaning over God's revelation of the truth of the Cross. A week later, the authorities at Union sent him to Bloomingdale Hospital, a psychiatric institution in White Plains, New York.[28] His diagnosis was "paranoid condition/paranoid dementia praecox."[29]

One would assume that Fosdick concurred in, if not urged, the decision to consign Sung to the mental hospital. It could scarcely have been imaginable to Fosdick that the tormented, "emaciated figure" with a "jaundiced look" (as Sung described himself) who was being expelled from Union would soon become the greatest evangelist of twentieth-century China. Ironically, in a letter written to a missionary friend in China at almost exactly the same time as this was happening, Fosdick was looking forward to the day when "the seeds of Christianity already sown in China will have a harvest in a native church."[30] Could he picture Sung reaping that "harvest"?

THE "HARVEST"

In October 1927, Sung returned to China after spending six and a half months at Bloomingdale. He insisted throughout his life that he had never lost his mind: his born-again experience had been mistaken for insanity. Later that year, he married the woman his parents had chosen for him and began itinerant preaching in various parts of Fujian.[31] Within months, however, he had drawn the ire of local Guomindang party head-quarters (*dangbu*) for his vehement denunciation of bowing before the image of Sun Yat-sen—a ritual that Chiang Kai-shek's new Nationalist government decreed in an effort to appropriate the legacy of the "founding father" of the republic and shore up its legitimacy. The nationalistic rites were particularly abominable to him because Sun, though a Christian, had been enshrined at the expense of Christ. Under the Nanjing regime, mission schools were required not only to register with the government but also to abandon compulsory religious instruction—a decree first imposed in 1925 by the warlord-controlled Beijing government. As a result, "Sun can be preached to the whole school, but not Christ." For his part, Sung had no faith in the Nationalist government's scheme of saving China (nor had he been interested in a lucrative offer allegedly made by the Manchurian warlord Zhang Zuolin to help with making bombs). He condemned the ritual as "idolatry" and urged Christians to "tear up" the printed portraits of Sun.[32]

By late 1930, Sung's work was also being constantly disrupted by the worsening banditry in the province, especially near the border with Jiangxi where Mao Zedong had established a base for his revolutionary force made up of disgruntled peasants and outlaws (and at times allied with "powerful full-time gangs"). The fledgling preacher decided to leave his home province. He had recently joined the Xinghua Conference of the Methodist Episcopal Church and secured a special mission to study theological education and literacy programs in North China. His travel took him to Shanghai, Nanjing, and Beijing, where he met with missionaries and Chinese church leaders.[33] In Dingxian, a county of four hundred thousand people in the south of Hebei province and the center of the Mass Education Movement, he had a brief visit with James Yen, who was using the "model villages" in the district as a "living social laboratory" aimed at "equip[ping]" the "rural masses . . . with modern knowledge and skills." Yen was convinced that education would enable a farmer to "remake his life and play a noble part in reconstructing his country." However, Sung saw little value in the education of illiterate peasants. He was also dismissive of foreign missions' educational enterprises such as Yenching University—the pride of the Social Gospelers—which he saw as resting on the shaky foundation of foreign money. Theological schools likewise introduced only Western "scraps" and catered to "fawning" Chinese churchmen. The command he received from the "Holy Spirit within" was to "revive the lukewarm churches throughout the country."[34]

In early 1931, Sung was invited to conduct revival meetings targeting students in Nanchang, the provincial capital of Jiangxi. (Some were conducted at the Hospital for Women and Children founded by Kang

FIGURE 16 John Sung. Courtesy of Song Tianzhen.

Cheng after she moved there from Jiujiang.) Those meetings marked the beginning of his nationwide revivalism. In what was becoming his signature rejection of worldly schemes of modernization and national salvation, he condemned the teaching of English, history, and mathematics in mission schools as "feeding husks to pigs" and told his audience to "seek God" instead as they faced "the Lord's imminent return." He called on all to repent. Soon the meetings turned into public confessions (with the principal of one mission school admitting to having been a "pig" herself) and choruses of spontaneous prayer mixed with "thunderous wailing and crying." Even "anti-Christian students" who had sought to create disturbance in the meeting "beat their breasts" and cried out their repentance.[35]

Like Marie Monsen, Sung had found the key to mass revivalism: a sweeping, unrelenting attack on sin and insistence on public confessions was the way to break down the guardedness and pride of individuals (what he called "the walls of Jericho") and force them into a complete surrender to God. As his revivals burned on through the 1930s, his litany of sins grew to become an all-encompassing net from which nobody could escape—Do you hate? Raise your hand! Did you steal? One cent? Did you take office paper for personal use? Did you commit adultery? Did you almost? With animals? Did you kill? Have you entered the Communist Party? Do you worship idols or ancestors or the picture of Sun Yat-sen? (He never spared Sun.) Do you gamble? Play mahjong, drink, use cigarettes, opium, or heroin? Do you dance or go to the movies? Did you want to commit suicide? Do you love the world?

To make sure that nobody could slip away and dodge his questions, Sung would order all the doors closed for the two- to three-hour meetings.[36] If his meetings generated crushing emotional crises, there was also no lack of theatricals and other innovations to provide relief and to keep the audience awake. He could howl and wail for the dead Lazarus "like those in a village funeral procession," or jump off the platform exactly seven times to illustrate how Naaman was healed of leprosy.[37] He would pour out onstage "agonized prayer and ecstatic praise," as one missionary observed, "all intensified by vivid acting, scathing sarcasm and exuberant humour." He tapped freely into the energy and good cheer of his audience, punctuating every few sentences of his preaching with a break for a short chorus, some of which he made up on the spot, others to

the tune of popular student songs of those days such as "Dadao lieqiang!"
(Down with Imperialist Powers). And he would make room for throngs
of people, at times numbering two or three hundred, to come onto the
platform to give individual sentence testimonials.[38] "After three days,
all the young people (whom he made to sit in the front rows) would lose
their voices like him."[39]

If Sung encouraged his audience to pile burdens of guilt upon themselves, he also led them to moments of catharsis, relief, and reconciliation
—with God, with themselves, and with others. Husbands and wives,
ministers and their congregations, missionaries and their Chinese subor-
dinates were reconciled publicly and tearfully, often ending years of feuds.
And there was always the unfailing solace that he could offer to troubled
souls. After their parents were killed by bandits, two sisters who were
schoolgirls in Jiangxi sold their bodies and became prostitutes. One of
the sisters was soon driven to insanity; the other came to Sung and asked
whether Jesus would save a girl like her. The assurance was complete and
simple: "Sister, if you repent, Jesus will save you!" By the time that Sung
left Nanchang, young students along with their teachers had repented en
masse (and vowed to never repeat the idolatry of bowing to Sun's image).
So had the local clergy. "All my preachers [were] born again," declared
William E. Schubert, the Methodist Episcopal missionary who had invited
Sung to Nanchang and who became his lifetime friend. In one mission
school for girls, practically all the students converted.[40]

In May, Sung joined the nondenominational Bethel Band, whose
fervent revivalism and independence coincided with his own leanings.
Perhaps the organization as part of the Bethel Mission headed by Shi
Meiyu (though effectively under the control of Jennie Hughes) offered
the best alternative to mission churches in those days. Sung had sometimes been warned, in response to his preaching, not to act as a "running
dog of the imperialists." In part because of his own implication in the
foreign-sponsored enterprise, he had become quite vocal in his criticism
of Western missions lately. Missionaries, he said, were a chief reason for
the spiritual depression in the church. They had grown used to personal
comfort while living in China, being carried around by their servants in
sedan chairs and "enjoying more pleasure than an emperor"; they put on
an "imperialist air" and had become a "stumbling block" because of their
reliance on foreign power and money. He especially abhorred the liberal

missionaries he met near Shanghai who questioned the literal truth of the Bible. He told one of them, "China needs a Savior, not a sage"; it had no need for "false prophets" to "proffer poison to the Chinese. God will raise His preachers in China." As for himself, Sung was convinced that God had "called" him to go through the country to give the "final warning" to the people. The Bethel Band must have seemed ideal for such a purpose. It was decidedly fundamentalist in its theology; by then well established in Shanghai, it also offered better financial prospects than what Sung had found thus far as a poorly paid evangelist in Fujian.[41]

"HEAVENLY HEALING"

Like Wang Mingdao, Sung crossed paths with Pentecostalists whose ecstatic spirituality represented an attractive form of indigenous Christianity. In the early summer of 1931, the Bethel Band visited Shandong province just as the peninsula was experiencing an outbreak of the Spiritual Gifts Movement. Sung was impressed with Pentecostalism, having recently experienced what he believed was a miraculous cure of his heart ailment through the laying on of hands by a faith healer. It must also have seemed a most potent endorsement of him as a man of God when, after he laid hands on each member of a Pentecostal congregation in Hebei, "three fourths" of them started to "tremble all over" and break into glossolalia. After such encounters, Sung found himself on a number of occasions "losing control over my lips" and uttering "tongues." However, he concluded that glossolalia benefited only oneself. A servant of God, like the Confucians of the past, "sought to benefit all under heaven." Perhaps he also instinctively understood the riotous and uncontrollable nature of the Pentecostalists' enthusiasm. Their ability to fire off a rapid succession of spirit-filled utterances "astounded me, so that I had to ring the bell to stop them." Their tendency to defy external spiritual authority, even his, was also irritating. In some places, the "self-styled spiritual Pentecostals" would snub him or boycott his revival meetings. Besides, how could he offer spiritual guidance to those like a woman in Linyi, Shandong, who claimed to have been "lifted" up to heaven forty times and was going for a total of sixty?[42]

While Sung remained ambivalent toward Pentecostalism overall, he did discover and make much use of his own "gift" of healing, one that proved essential to his revivalism. He had long known what miraculous healing could do for evangelism. When he was still itinerating in his home province, a woman had offered to accept Jesus as her Savior if Sung could cure the disease of her sow through prayer. In late 1931, a Pentecostal missionary in Pingdu, Shandong, pressed him to anoint and lay hands on dozens of sick people. He did it with trepidation, and an invalid of eighteen years who had been carried to the meeting "suddenly got up and walked." Thousands of such faith healings—of the blind, the deaf, the crippled, the hunchbacked, the insane, and those afflicted with cancer or addicted to opium—reportedly followed during the 1930s. The sick would be brought one by one to the platform, and Sung "anointed" each with oil and "smacked him smartly on the forehead." Sung also recorded numerous miraculous healings in his own diaries.[43]

Some were of a dubious nature. According to a report in the *China Christian Year Book* of 1934–1935, a boy blind from birth attended Sung's meetings and on the last day "mounted the platform and cried out that he could see" even though he could not identify objects presented to him. When he was later confronted by the local mission doctor, the boy admitted that he could not see but that "Dr. Sung had told him that he must say, 'I can see'; otherwise it would be a lack of faith and he would never be able to see. . . . There are many other stories of healing with just as little foundation."[44] Such unfulfilled miracles apparently did little damage to Sung's reputation as a faith healer, nor did the setbacks he experienced from time to time as an exorcist: he was beaten back one day by a woman "possessed of the evil spirit" who, instead of succumbing to his exorcism, gave him such a slap on his face that it knocked him numb and momentarily deaf.[45] Others complained that the "prophecies he is prone to utter are frequently not fulfilled!"[46] Still, reports of hundreds of miraculous healings at each of Sung's revival meetings continued to appear in personal witnesses and in church periodicals such as the Shanghai-based *Chinese Christian Intelligencer* (*Tongwenbao*). Together with his uncanny power for drama, Sung's "heavenly healing" was largely responsible for his alleged conversion of some one hundred thousand of his compatriots during the 1930s.[47]

Sung's launch into a career of itinerant preaching happened at a time when new outbreaks of war and natural disaster aggravated the precariousness and misery of life in much of China. In November 1930, the same month that Sung left his bandit-infested province and headed

north, Chiang Kai-shek launched a massive but unsuccessful "extermi-
nation campaign" (the first in a series of five between 1930 and 1934)
against the Communists in the border regions of southern Jiangxi and
western Fujian. Two more failed annihilation campaigns were conducted
in spring and late summer of 1931, each involving hundreds of thousands
of Guomindang troops and causing widespread miseries. In many cases
the fighting also disrupted the local power networks and exacerbated
the problem of predatory bandits (from whom some of the Red Army
soldiers were at times indistinguishable).[48] Naturally, the net result was
increased hardship and uncertainty for the common people. It is probably no coincidence that the Nanchang Pentecost, as Sung's 1931 revival
has been called, erupted close to the center of the violence. In May and
June of the same year, continuous monsoon rains brought one of the
most devastating floods of the Yangzi River in the twentieth century and
wreaked havoc and destruction on some fifty million people in the middle
and lower parts of the basin.

Then came the Mukden (Shenyang) Incident of September 18, the
Japanese occupation of Manchuria, and the flood of refugees. The Bethel
Band had been holding a revival among the Presbyterians and young
students in Mukden and left the city on the morning of September 18,
hours before the Japanese attacked. The Manchurian crisis helped create
a spirited audience for the band's message of redemption among students,
soldiers, and ethnic minorities in remote areas of the extreme northeast.
On the other hand, the grim events also deepened Sung's end-time convictions and hardened his opposition to any worldly schemes of salvation
—Communist, Nationalist, or those offered by other patriots. When a
high-ranking army officer in Manchuria tried to recruit him to "save the
country through science" and to help manufacture poison gas to fight the
Japanese, Sung responded with a sermon on saving his fellow Chinese by
means of "spiritual power."[49] Likewise, he dismissed what to him was the
misguided optimism and worldliness of the Social Gospelers. Twice in the
early 1930s, Sung confronted NCC chairman Yu Rizhang in Yu's home in
Shanghai and told him to repent of the sin of social Christianity. On the
second occasion, with Yu already incapacitated from cerebral hemorrhage
and nearing death, Sung managed to bring him to "repentance" along
with a promise to "uphold the Cross" thereafter.[50]

"SUNG THE MADMAN"

In the eyes of some missionaries and denominational church leaders, however, Sung was a self-proclaimed prophet with volcanic energy and a capacity for the "pulpit mannerisms of Billy Sunday" but one with eccentric, often fanciful and bizarre, exegesis. They were puzzled by Sung's insistence that Heaven is in the northern firmament where there are fewer stars and that Hell, or *diyu* ("the prison down under"), is in the flaming "center of the earth" (as it had been depicted in popular religious texts).[51] The author of one article published in the *Chinese Recorder* objected to Sung's use of a vision of the "new heaven" that he had had while "confined in a lunatic asylum in America" as evidence that the Book of Revelation was true in the minutest details. He also found it distressing that when some failed to believe in such a heaven (by holding up their hands), "Dr. S . . . began to send the unbelievers to a hell as hot and as black as he could paint it with words."[52] Other missionaries dismissed him as being possessed of an evil spirit. In fact, the unflattering nickname "Sung the madman" followed him almost everywhere he preached.[53] He may have spoken fluent English, but unlike the thousands of "returned students" from the United States, Europe, and Japan who adorned China's coastal cities with their Western attire, parlance, and polished manners, Sung wore a coarse cotton gown and was equally coarse in speaking. "You hypocrites of missionaries on the back seat" was how he addressed the less enthusiastic members of his audience during revivals.[54]

Sung's lack of personal grace aside, what deeply disturbed missionaries and denominational leaders was his reckless disregard for their authority and his contempt for the established institution of grace. While conducting his revivals in a major church in Shanghai, Sung "ordered the sale of wholesome books published by a well-established Christian publishing house on the premises stopped" to clear the way for his own autobiographical account of God's work in him titled *My Witness* (*Wode jianzheng*).[55] As an itinerant preacher, he would brush aside the rules in host churches. In September 1931, when a revival meeting led by Sung and his Bethel colleagues in Fenghuang, Manchuria, turned into anarchic public confessions, one missionary attempted to stop them but was told instead to "quench not the Spirit." The next day, a meeting of the missionaries in charge of the twelve local parishes reached a joint decision to expel the band. Sung protested that it was the Lord Jesus, not the

Bethel revivalists, that the missionaries were evicting and called on the Chinese church to "rapidly become independent" and rely no more on "Westerners' funding." In Sung's ranking of the five groups of people who might be receptive to the work of the Holy Spirit (and his chastisement), ordinary churchgoers were on the top, followed by female and male students. Preachers ranked fourth. At the bottom were the missionaries, whom he called "the least willing to repent."[56]

By late 1933, Sung's repeated, blunt attacks on missionaries were becoming intolerable at least for Jennie Hughes, who dissolved the Bethel Worldwide Evangelistic Band and organized a new band without him. Before that, the Bethel Band had already been reduced to three members (Ji, Sung, and Lin Jingkang): in early 1933, Li Daorong and Nie Ziying, the two unmarried members of the band who had often become the focus of young women's attention during the band's tours, were removed. (Li, the musician of the group, soon left for the United States to study music at the Moody Bible Institute.)[57] Hughes told Sung that many missionaries had complained about his "bad attitude in preaching." She was also angered by the fact that many of the gifts and monetary offerings were going directly to him rather than to the band and ordered all the mail that he received at the Bethel Mission (about ten thousand letters) impounded.[58] Thereafter, he was on his own, a fully independent itinerant preacher.

The expulsion from Bethel did nothing to moderate Sung's misgivings about established churches. His "narrow separatist view," missionary-historian M. Searle Bates wrote, "brought tension in some quarters" and alienated the "intelligentsia" in the Christian community. As one "directly instructed by the Spirit," he needed no theological training "at mortal hands."[59] In fact, as we have seen, he reviled such training. For his preaching he had the vivid "spiritual pictures" that floated across his eyes and "the things that God tells me" in secret—even though others "would surely think me crazy." In some cases, Sung's preaching and personal charisma did foster separatism. With his blessing, a group of more than three hundred enthusiasts in a Tianjin church broke off to form a new congregation in 1934. Some in fact warned that Christians all over China were fast turning into followers of the "Sung religion."[60]

But Sung also had to tread carefully on the matter, for like Wang Mingdao and most of the other independent preachers, he relied on invitations from denominational churches to the pulpit. The result, from the very beginning of his ministry, was a curious mix of antiestablishment jeremiads and pragmatic concessions to its dominance. Back in 1928, Sung had applied to the Methodist Episcopal Church in Xinghua for appointment as probationary preacher and had begun his slow ascent in the denomination's hierarchy. In 1930, Bishop J. Gowdy of Fuzhou made him assistant pastor (*fumushi*) despite the fact that he refused to read the assigned conference course books (in which he found "no taste").[61] He never left the denomination, even though he found it expedient at one point to let a missionary in Hong Kong rebaptize him by immersion so that he could satisfy those who asked to receive the Baptist rite from him.[62] After 1934, Sung was able to secure invitations from various denominations as his itinerant preaching took him through most provinces of China. Before long, his revivalism also began to spill into Chinese communities in Southeast Asia.

The first of his overseas trips took place in June 1935 when three different churches of Manila extended a joint invitation to him. About a dozen more such trips followed in the remaining four years of his traveling ministry. In the Philippines, Singapore, Malaya, the Dutch East Indies, Thailand, Vietnam, and Japanese-controlled Taiwan, Sung's faith healing and sensational campaigns for souls drew large crowds of local Chinese. In Singapore, one *Strait Times* report noted that, dressed "more like a tennis player than an evangelist," the "hot gospeler" of China "puts himself and Christianity into the news by his unorthodox ways, which always annoy the orthodox."[63] One of the annoyances pointed out by a missionary in Sarawak on the island of Borneo was that Sung had received "excessive" offerings in view of the low incomes of local people. Many sick people had come to the healing but "not a single one was healed." In Taiwan, his fervent admirers made large offerings of both cash and jewelry.[64]

In many parts of China, both missionaries and Chinese clergy were divided in their reaction to Sung. There were those who never forgave his abrasiveness, oddity, and challenge to their ecclesiastical authority. On the other hand, there were also those who accepted, even promoted, him for the cause of the Gospel. As William Schubert reminded a Methodist bishop in Nanjing (who had initially opposed Sung's revivals in the city), even the Catholics would use someone they did not approve of if the man could "fill their largest church." He added, "Why can't we be as wise as the Catholics?"[65] On his part, Sung would also soften his criticisms of Western missions in later years and, toward the end of his career as itinerant preacher, accept ordination as a Methodist Episcopal elder and pastor by Bishop Gowdy.[66]

After July 7, 1937, war engulfed large areas of North and East China and severely hampered Sung's work. On his preaching tour from Shanghai to Hangzhou in August, the only ride he could find was atop a box of coal in a train's locomotive as enemy warplanes roared overhead. Then, the railroad bridge was hit by a bomb the moment after Sung's train crossed it. But the hardship and the dangers also created a new hunger for his message. As Sung quickly discovered on a trip to Shandong, while the rich were fleeing west into the interior of the country, "the poor are fleeing to God." When air raid sirens sounded halfway through his sermon on Heaven and Hell one day, he assured the congregation that if the church was hit by a bomb, they would be "riding fire chariots and fire horses together and going directly to the heavenly home."[67]

Sung also followed the flood of refugees that poured inland, trudging along muddy mountain trails or riding on whatever vehicle he could find—a rickshaw, a wheelbarrow, or on top a munitions train. As the Japanese warplanes passed menacingly overhead and as bandits roamed the countryside robbing whoever they could and killing the hapless, Sung spread his message of divine redemption and salvation to the widowed, the orphaned, the homeless, and the starving who jammed into his revival meetings. A song that he taught numerous people to sing in those days must have found a ready echo: "East is vain, west is vain, south is vain, north is vain." Likewise, the invitation he extended in his favorite revival song was also hard to resist. "Come home, come home!" it implored. "No more wandering!" A group of three bandits in Henan province who robbed Sung told him: "We are of the same trade. You preach Heaven's will; we carry out Heaven's will."[68]

For Sung, the war had borne out the urgency of the divine mandate, and he abandoned himself to feverish castigation of the sinning and the suffering. For years, he had routinely had to change, after preaching, his sweat-soaked clothes—"three sets a day." Now he also had to change his blood-soaked underwear every time he cried or jumped around too much during the revivals. While a student at Ohio Wesleyan, he had had surgery for hemorrhoids that never healed completely. Throughout the years, as he leapt back and forth on the stage and thundered out his sermons, life had been draining out of him through the running anal fistulae. During a trip to Penang Island in 1938, he was "carried on to the platform on a camp-cot," from which he preached through an interpreter. In that state he also anointed the sick and "commanded the disease to leave the sufferer." In December 1939, on his last overseas trip to Singapore and Malaya, an assistant had to help Sung get dressed and carry the preacher, who was fighting five anal fistulae and a persistent nausea, on his back up and down the stairs on the way to the meeting.[69]

In early 1940, Sung's itinerant preaching came to an end. In the course of a decade he had indeed been the "flame for God," as Leslie Lyall called him, for hundreds of thousands of his compatriots. He had dominated the stage of popular revivalism in China with a form of consummate artistry, one with utter abandon as well as a directness and artlessness that had a force all of its own. He had given himself to a relentless drive to bring his audience to a moment of emotional crisis and collapse of the self, from which he released them through public confessions into God's forgiveness as well as the warmth and security of the community of the "saved." He did it with a force of personality of which only a genius, or perhaps a "madman" as his detractors called him, was capable.

Yet unlike his contemporary American revivalists Aimee Semple McPherson and the child prodigy Uldine Utley, whose theatricals helped turn the preaching of the Gospel into mass entertainment in the United States, Sung's art was for the afflicted and the desperate. It offered solace, hope, meaning for seemingly endless and senseless suffering, and assurances of deliverance—a simple way out of the tangled life of misery, guilt, and despair. It was also wrought out of the incalculable suffering of both his audience and himself. He paid dearly and willingly for his craft; he had ignored William Schubert's kindly advice given at the beginning of his tempestuous revivalist career that he should "conserve energy" in his preaching like John Wesley (1703–1791) and "live long," rather than burn himself out on emotions that were too strong for mortals—like Dwight Moody (1837–1899)—and "die young." When a fortune teller told Sung to his face in 1935 that he had an "unfocused look" in the dilated pupils of his eyes and would therefore die young, he responded that he was "already dead" in Christ and would labor for God as long as he was alive.[70] And his neglect of his own family was almost complete: while fleeing a sinking ship in the East China Sea in 1931, he jumped into the lifeboat with his Bible and diary carefully wrapped in oilpaper and strapped to his back—but forgot his wife and left her behind.[71]

In late 1940, Sung's fistulae were found to be cancerous. Several operations performed between 1940 and 1944 did not halt the cancer's advance. In his final months, he was convinced of the approach of both his own death and the end of time. He craved to be "raptured." God also revealed to him that the moment of "the great revival of the Chinese church" was soon to dawn. He died a painful death in the outskirts of Beijing in the summer of 1944, humming "in the Cross, in the Cross, be my glory ever."[72] His country was yet to be saved from the Japanese, and years of civil war awaited those who survived the invasion.

CHAPTER SEVEN

Awaiting Rapture

WATCHMAN NEE AND THE LITTLE FLOCK

DURING THE 1930S, when John Sung's miraculous healings electrified hundreds of thousands in China and Southeast Asia, he retained his dark, apocalyptic views and a clear conviction that neither the miracles he performed nor the revolutions that were brewing would save China. "The end of the world is here," he proclaimed, and the only salvation lies beyond.[1] Such doomsday pessimism was in fact widespread among indigenous Protestant groups and evangelists who, unlike the NCC and the YMCA and YWCA, felt little pressure and found little opportunity to address the political and social plight of the time. After the outbreak of war with Japan in July 1937, mainline church organizations responded with heroic but meager relief efforts such as the National Christian Service Council for Wounded Soldiers in Transit to bandage, clothe, and feed the tens of thousands of the wounded and dying.[2] Independent evangelists like John Sung and Wang Mingdao, on the other hand, withdrew deeper into their search for otherworldly salvation.

By far the most elaborate end-time theology that shaped Protestant thinking in China throughout the 1930s and 1940s—and well into the second half of the twentieth century—was expounded by Watchman Nee (Ni Tuosheng, 1903–1972), founder and leader of the Christian Assembly (Jidutu Juhuichu), commonly known as the Little Flock (Xiaoqun). It revolved around the "truth of the Cross": those who penetrate the mystery of God would understand that they are already dead with, and in, Christ and have been "grafted," through the Cross, onto a glorious, incorruptible, and bountiful life; it is only through "brokenness," "destruction," and "death" of the "self" (the work of the Cross) that the inner spiritual being springs to real life in Christ.[3] Such a new being is also impervious to the evils of this world. Yu Chenghua, an eye doctor who became one of Nee's lieutenants in the Little Flock church in Shanghai, had this reaction to the sight of truckloads of severed human limbs after a series of Japanese aerial bombings in Shanghai: "Let me be counted among the severed limbs on the trucks. Yes, I am already dead. I have been nailed to the Cross with Christ."[4]

According to Nee, one who further discerned the unfolding of God's scheme would also know that the invisible hand of the divine clock was moving toward the "Age of the Kingdom," when "he who conquers" would sit with Christ on his throne, when death itself would be vanquished.[5] What happened during the long war years only seemed to vindicate such end-time beliefs, which became the most enduring feature of popular Protestantism in twentieth-century China.

THE DIMMING OF THE LIGHT OF A "WORLDLY" CHRISTIANITY

Watchman Nee was born in 1903 into a respectable Christian family in Shantou, Guangdong, where his father, a holder of the *shengyuan* degree, was a junior officer in the imperial Maritime Customs. When Nee was six, the family moved back to their ancestral home in Fuzhou. There, more than half a century earlier, Nee's paternal grandfather had been converted at the Congregational mission and had become one of the earliest local ministers in China.[6] Nee's mother, Lin Heping, a poor farmer's daughter, had been taken into a Fuzhou merchant family when she was a child and educated in mission schools after her adopted parents became Methodist Episcopal converts. Nee's childhood was a genteel one, complete with a private tutor to school him in calligraphy, the Four Confucian Classics, and the like, and graced with both a piano in the house and important outside connections to the small but thriving middle-class Protestant community in that treaty port city.[7] There was no indication of any emotional tinder in the Nee family ready to catch the messianic flame.

In fact, the most hopeful sparks, visible in Nee's mother, had been decidedly this-worldly. In her youth, she had been inspired by the example of Xu Jinhong, the first Fuzhou woman (and the second in the country) to have gone to study in America. Xu was trained at the Women's Medical College of Philadelphia and returned in 1895 (a year before Shi Meiyu) as the first female Chinese missionary of the Methodist Episcopal Church.[8] By 1897, Lin Heping herself was attending the Chinese Western Girls' School in Shanghai in preparation for undertaking similar medical studies in the United States, but her ambitions were dashed when her parents called her back to Fuzhou for an arranged marriage in 1899. When the Revolution broke out in 1911, Lin discovered a fresh outlet for her ambitions and zeal, shaped likewise by her Protestant education and made possible by her Methodist Episcopal ties. She donated her jewelry to the revolutionary cause and organized a Women's Patriotic Society, with the wife of the provincial governor as its chairwoman and herself as the general secretary. When Sun Yat-sen visited Fujian in 1912, Lin was given an official role as a special guide for the Father of the Republic.[9]

By 1920, with Sun and his remnant Republican loyalists relegated to Guangdong province on the periphery of warlord-dominated politics, Lin's erstwhile worldly ambitions—both her medical and patriotic pursuits —had long dissipated; her primary devotion was to the mahjong table. That spring Yu Cidu, the Shanghai-based revivalist and perhaps the best-known female preacher of the day, led a series of meetings in Fuzhou. Lin had met Yu in Shanghai in 1897. More than two decades later, the evangelistic zeal in Yu had continued to burn on while Lin had only the ashes of youthful dreams. Yu's campaigns in Fuzhou brought about an emotional born-again experience for both Lin Heping and her seventeen-year-old son Ni Shuzu, who later adopted the name Ni Tuosheng, or Watchman Nee. Yu also introduced Nee to an English missionary named Margaret E. Barber (1869–1930) outside the city of Fuzhou, who turned out to exert the single most important personal influence on the development of Nee's theology.[10]

Barber, an "independent and dominating character" (as Leslie Lyall puts it), first came to Fujian province in 1899 as an educational missionary under the Church Missionary Society but severed her ties with the Anglican mission while on furlough in 1909. In 1911 she returned to Fuzhou as a freelance evangelist.[11] The separatist influence had come from David M. Panton, minister of Surrey Chapel in Norwich and editor of the *Dawn,* by whom she was rebaptized. Through him, she had discovered a radical tradition in missionary thinking that stretched back to the 1820s, one that was founded on the governing principle of faith whereby missionaries would go into foreign lands "destitute of all visible sustenance." It was a hardy, intrepid spirit of missions, one that would steel her for an austere, lonely life through the end. (The same teaching of living by faith had been the direct inspiration for James Hudson Taylor when he founded the CIM in 1865.)[12] Panton had also steered Barber into an exhilarating eschatological mysticism known as "partial rapture," in which a number of spiritual or "watchful" believers would be spared "the great tribulation" immediately preceding the Second Coming and lifted up to heaven.[13] A hymn that Barber later wrote in Chinese, and which rhymes in the Fuzhou dialect, was titled "Rapture." It begins with "Some have heard a quiet whisper: Christ is returning soon, maybe today"; its soaring refrain asks Jesus to "come early and rapture me home!" Meanwhile, she rented a bungalow at Baiyatan, across from Mawei (commonly referred to as Pagoda Anchorage by Westerners), some twenty miles down the Min River from Fuzhou. There, for the next decade, she held out in a determined but largely fruitless evangelistic operation. It was to her that Nee and his mother went in 1921 to be baptized by immersion, since he had rejected as unbiblical his childhood baptism by sprinkling in the Methodist Episcopal Church.[14]

By Nee's own account, he had been unusually sensitive and emotional as an adolescent and often given to violent swings of mood between the extremes of "great sorrow and great joy." The rebaptism by Barber almost instantly plunged him into a feverish search for a higher spiritual life than what he had previously found either in his mother or in denominational churches. He had seen Lin Heping's Christian social activism shrivel in the midst of political disintegration in the country; he had also found mission Christianity in general to be in a sorry state—as reflected perhaps in the pastor who used to call at his home seeking donations while his mother and friends were busy at the mahjong table. The gamblers would shove over to him some money on the card table, and the pastor would knowingly accept it. "I therefore felt," Nee wrote, "that pastors were truly a base sort of creature and cared only for money."[15]

KINDRED SOULS: THE BEGINNING OF THE CHRISTIAN ASSEMBLY

Before long, Nee sought out the company of a fellow young zealot named Wang Zai, also a Fuzhou native, who would rise to become a popular revivalist heartily endorsed by missionaries. Upon graduating from a middle school in Shanghai in 1915, Wang had entered the Chefoo Naval Academy (Yantai Haijun Xuexiao) and completed his training the following year. At the age of eighteen, he joined the navy. Soon afterwards he was married and converted to Christianity under the influence of his wife. In 1920, he was baptized by immersion in Xiamen where his small gunboat was based. Around that time, he was already serving as the first mate on the ship. In 1921, however, Wang heard the call to abandon his naval career through the words of Isaiah 52:11: "Depart, depart, go out thence . . . purify yourselves."[16] So he left and returned home to Fuzhou.

It was a dramatic turnaround in his career. Like John Sung's, Wang's later popularity as an independent evangelist rested, to a significant extent, on his famous surrender of worldly success to the service of God. But at the time, the career he ended had in fact lost much of its glamour. The Republic of China had inherited a weak and aging navy with few modern vessels. During the 1910s, the navy had a total of four old cruisers, three new Schichau destroyers, and three torpedo gunboats along with a medley of training cruisers, gunboats, and smaller ships, many of which were for river use. Its personnel consisted of about one thousand officers and fewer than five thousand sailors. Financial problems and political disintegration of the young republic hampered any effort at modernization and expansion of the navy. In 1917, as the country began its slide into warlordism, the republic's navy split into two when its commander-in-chief turned his back on the Beijing government and defected to Canton where Sun Yat-sen attempted to revive the republic. During the next decade, crippled by lack of funds, ammunition, and fuel for the ships, the navy's fleets remained mostly in harbor and in the shadow of warlord feuds. Patrolling the Yangzi River and China's coast were the warships of world powers. By 1922, not long after Wang Zai left his ship, payments for the navy were often "long in arrears." Under such circumstances, one could imagine that whatever adolescent ambitions Wang might have harbored when he joined the navy in 1916 had likely dissipated. In fact, as the navies of the northern and southern governments vied for control of Fujian province, life onboard the warships had become perilous. In 1923, the two navies would clash for the first time in Xiamen. In that conflict, both the forts and a gunboat in the harbor were shelled.[17]

In leaving the navy, Wang had been called to preach the Gospel. He had also made up his mind not to attach himself to mission churches as a "running dog of the foreigners." In 1922, the same desire to follow and preach a Christianity untainted by Western dominance brought him and Nee together in a symbolic creation of a Chinese Christian body—of three people, the third being Wang's wife—through the "breaking of the bread" in Wang's small house. That night, Nee later wrote, "Heaven was so close to earth."[18] Such enthusiasm could hardly be contained, and they were soon joined by half a dozen like-minded youthful converts, most of whom were fellow students at the Anglican Trinity College in Fuzhou located in the compound of the former Russian consulate.

Though staffed mostly by Irish missionaries from Dublin, Trinity College—an elite secondary school that also offered college preparatory courses—had developed a secularized curriculum that included classical Chinese, literature, history, geography, math, English, and even Greek in addition to the Bible. By the early 1920s, it was also promoting vernacular Chinese, a literary movement that Hu Shi spearheaded in the mid-1910s while a student of John Dewey at Columbia University. With only a fraction of the student body being baptized converts, there was no sign of any intense religiosity that would satisfy burning souls like Nee's.[19] Therefore, the group rented a house nearby in early 1923 and started their separate meetings as well as roadside evangelism, wearing white shirts splashed with slogans announcing: "You will die!" "Jesus is coming!" and "Believe in Jesus and live!" Such innovation must have given full vent to their proselytizing zeal while keeping at bay any suggestion that they were mere allies of the imperialists.[20]

This outburst of indigenous evangelism had come at an opportune moment. In 1922, the Protestant community in Fuzhou had been roiled by the first nationwide anti-Christian upheaval since the Boxer Uprising. In early March, news of the upcoming conference of the World Student Christian Federation in Beijing had provoked a group of Shanghai students, many of them members of the Socialist League of China, to form the Anti-Christian Federation. Its manifesto denounced Christianity as an ally of capitalism and imperialism and a means of oppressing weaker nations. Two weeks later, an Anti-Religious Federation sprang up in the capital, and the movement broadened into an attack on all religions as enemies of science. From the start, however, the campaign targeted Christian institutions and would eventually turn into a demand for the "restoration of educational rights" to the Chinese, elimination of religious propaganda in mission education, and removal of foreign control. It would be followed by waves of student walkouts and withdrawals from mission schools.[21] Trinity College did not escape all this turmoil. There had been sporadic closings of the school during the early 1920s; after the May Thirtieth Incident, it would be forced to hand over its administration to Chinese nationals. And in the wake of the Northern Expedition of 1926–1927, when the province came under the control of the National Revolutionary Army, some of the school buildings would be torched by zealous converts to nationalism and Communism.[22]

Nee's own adjustment to the rise of nationalism had been swift. In late 1922, he had "discovered through the scriptures" that denominational divisions of the church were unbiblical. He then prevailed upon his father to announce to the Methodist Episcopal Church, to which his family belonged, that since denominationalism was a "sin," they had decided to have their names removed from its membership roster (which was called the Book of Life, but which Barber had pronounced to be "full of dead people").[23] However, the small group of mostly student-evangelists, who came to be called the Christian Assembly, was soon divided on how far they should go to assert their independence.[24] Nee demanded a complete rejection of denominationalism and its ecclesiastical structure dominated by clergy and advocated a radical separation from Western missions. Wang Zai and the rest of the group, on the other hand, were disinclined toward confrontation with existing churches. By 1924, Wang's own initial roadside evangelism had already extended beyond Fuzhou. Under the influence of a Christian and Missionary Alliance missionary in Shanghai, he was ready to accept ordination as a pastor and to formalize the group's evangelistic drive into a new, indigenous denomination. The differences turned out to be irreconcilable. Nee left his comrades and rented a house near Pagoda Anchorage, across the Min River from Barber, where he published an irregular journal titled the *Present Witness and Testimony* (*Fuxingbao*) and distributed it free of charge in a lone crusade to reveal the principles of a true Christianity.[25]

The road that Wang Zai chose—the kind of independent preaching that sought to revitalize denominational churches and that gently crossed their paths—put him in good favor with the missionary establishment. As we have seen, after May 1925, Wang would be conducting revival meetings in Shanghai alongside A. Paget Wilkes, the veteran English missionary of the Japan Evangelistic Band. He was particularly well received among the CIM churches. In a preface to Wang's own collection of revival and evangelistic hymns published in 1926, CIM director D. E. Hoste praised Wang as the "type of worker" who, though "not officially associated" with "the Missions," was in "friendly touch with like-minded missionaries" and often rendered them "valuable aid." Not surprisingly, it was Wang Zai, not the likes of John Sung and Watchman Nee, who would be given the honor of baptizing by immersion some members of the missionary community, including Jennie Hughes of the Bethel Band and Ruth Bells, daughter of a missionary doctor stationed in the town of Qingjiangpu in the lower Yangzi valley, who later married Billy Graham.[26]

In contrast, Nee's future seemed less promising. His conviction of having been appointed for "a great use" by God remained unfulfilled; the world seemed a forlorn, inhospitable place, as he lamented in "Moanings of the Cross-Bearer." Those moanings were serialized in late 1923 in the *Spiritual Light* (*Lingguangbao*), a Chinese Christian journal sponsored by the American Presbyterian Mission and published in Nanjing. In these writings he ruminated upon his loneliness and frailty and mused on his love for a woman, which he had surrendered to Christ. He wrote tearfully, too, of his thwarted hope to go to America to study at the Moody Bible Institute in Chicago. That opportunity had slipped away the previous year, possibly as a result of his prickly attitude toward denominational missionaries, whose sponsorship and support in such an arrangement would have been indispensable. And he sang of his sole wish to love and obey God, for "the Lord will return soon, and the pains will be over."[27]

By 1924, he had already graduated from Trinity and dedicated himself to the service of God, but no paid job was in sight. Like Wang Mingdao in Beijing, who at the time was a frustrated would-be preacher without an audience, Nee's self-imposed exile from mission Christianity had shut the door to church employment, recognized ecclesiastical status, and a dependable income. For the next year or so, he launched into sporadic itinerant preaching in the coastal cities in the southern part of his home province. He even accompanied his mother on a short preaching tour to a Chinese church in Sitiwan, Malaya, where they found a lukewarm reception.[28]

SEERS OF THE ADVENT

The disappointments were not insignificant, but under Barber's guidance, Nee was now able to fit them into a cosmic scheme in which a minority of faithful believers were called to renounce both the decadent church and the perishing world, undergo "tribulations," and "bear the Cross"—before receiving their "crowns" in heaven.[29] In fact, having gained access to most of the books on Barber's shelves, Nee had become familiar with the works of several contemporary British nonconformists who pursued a purer spiritual life outside mainstream Christianity. In addition to Panton, Nee came under the influence of F. B. (Frederick Brotherton) Meyer (1847–1929), a Baptist minister and leading figure in the Keswick Holiness, or Higher Christian Life, movement, which began in the 1870s.[30] David W. Bebbington writes that, with its emphasis on the "rest of faith" and the abandonment of human efforts, Keswick "shaped the prevailing pattern of Evangelical piety for much of the twentieth century." To a large extent, Meyer embodied the Keswick leaning toward premillennialism. In 1917, he launched the Advent Testimony and Preparation Movement, which taught that Jesus Christ would soon return and inaugurate a millennial reign—a theme that would become central to the movement that Nee later unleashed in China.[31]

Even more inspiring than Panton and Meyer for Nee were the works of a contemporary Welsh mystic named Jessie Penn-Lewis (1861–1927), the most prominent female speaker at Keswick during the first decade of the twentieth century. Frail since the age of ten and plagued by chronic depression and "bouts of pleurisy and neurasthenia" in her youth, she burst upon the revelation one day that "it was dying not doing that produced the fruit" and that it was through "helplessness" and a "deeper understanding of SELF crucified" that one becomes "meet" for God's use. In 1892, when she was thirty-one, she declared her "liberty" from disease and felt her soul flooded with "a sweetness that made me feel almost sick." Thereafter, her public addresses and writings on the Cross gradually made her into a household name in North America and in mission fields in Africa, India, and China.[32] Her theology had an irresistible appeal: she invited those few Christians privy to God's purposes to "ascend into the secret place of the Most High, having boldness to enter the Holiest by the blood of Jesus, and look out with Him upon the world, and watch the movings of His Spirit among His people." In time she also became the "spiritual mother" to Evan Roberts, the uneducated coal miner who led and personified the Welsh Revival of 1904–1905, which reportedly reaped one hundred thousand saved souls across the country in five months.[33] Penn-Lewis's *Awakening in Wales* (1905), along with F. B. Meyer's report on the Welsh Revival in the same year, helped generate a worldwide Pentecostal movement that convulsed places from Azusa Street in Los Angeles to Pyongyang in Japanese-occupied Korea.[34]

After 1907, however, with Roberts reduced to "acute nervous prostration" and several prominent Holiness movement leaders warning that Keswick was "being threatened by the presence of mercurial and over-emotional Welsh people such as Evan Roberts [and] Jessie Penn-Lewis," the latter began to distance herself from, and eventually sever ties with, Keswick. Unendowed with the gift of "tongues" or healing herself, she would develop her own reservations about Pentecostalism and even published articles that attacked the deceptiveness, lawlessness, and confusion in the movement—a stance that later helped steer Nee's movement away, for the most part, from the pursuit of "spiritual gifts." With Roberts's help, Penn-Lewis started a publication of her own called the *Overcomer* and distributed thousands of copies across Britain, Europe, and North America, as well as mission fields in Africa and Asia. After 1913, the monthly became the chief forum from which Roberts preached the coming end of the world, urging people to be ready for the "final translation." Penn-Lewis herself was also increasingly drawn to the theme of tribulation and the end of the age, which found its way into two pamphlets she published in 1923—*The Time of the End* and *Signs and Wonders at the Time of the End*.[35]

In that same year, Penn-Lewis asked Margaret E. Barber to seek a Chinese translator for her works. Barber soon found an ideal Chinese messenger for the Welsh prophetess in Nee: he was versed in English, ardent in his newfound faith, restless and ambitious, and yet frail in body like Penn-Lewis herself.[36] However, the role of translator that Barber had conceived for him was too confining. As we have seen, by late 1923, Nee began putting out the *Present Witness and Testimony*, an irregular journal devoted to the "profound matters of God" and printed whenever funds were available. In 1925, Nee started another journal, the *Christian* (*Jidu-tubao*), to deal with "truths about church and matters of prophecy."[37] Also during that year, he changed his name to Ni Tuosheng—and rendered it as Watchman Nee in English—mindful of Penn-Lewis's prayer "for all the faithful watchmen on their watchtowers."[38]

Nee was sickly at the time. In 1924, he had developed tuberculosis, which debilitated him and cast a long shadow over his life for several years. In late 1926, he moved to the Nanjing area to recuperate from his consumption and to commit his newfound spiritual insights to a book of his own. Despite a dire prognosis from a German doctor, Nee came to his moment of triumph over the shadow of death while lying in his sickbed in 1927: it was the epiphany about "the truth of the Cross," which came to him one day while he was reading Romans 6:6, whereupon he cried out in wild joy, "I am dead!" With that he had transcended death.[39]

By 1928, he had completed his magnum opus, *The Spiritual Man* (*Shuling de ren*), a book that promised to lead Christians into the "inner-most part of one's being" where one encounters the "life of God." Such a journey would begin with the intricate and vital distinction between "soul" ("self-consciousness") and "spirit" ("God-consciousness"), one that almost all Christians had failed to make. The spiritual man, made alive by the "God-consciousness," leaves behind "useless" human efforts—driven merely by one's own will or emotions (the "soul") and manifested in profitless "zeal"—and enters into "the life of God Himself." In the concluding chapter, titled "Victory over Death," Nee exhorted the spiritual Christians to have faith "that we shall not die, that we shall live to see the Lord . . . and that that moment will not tarry for long."[40] Nee made no specific mention of the fact, however, that such teachings were already found in Penn-Lewis's *Soul and Spirit,* published a decade or so earlier, or that his foreboding of the impending end of time accorded with that of Meyer, Penn-Lewis, and other contemporary British seers of the Advent, and was likewise prudently shorn of a specific time.[41]

THE GATHERING OF THE LITTLE FLOCK

Not far from Nanjing where Nee worked feverishly on *The Spiritual Man* in early 1927, end-time tribulations may indeed have seemed to be loom-ing nearer. In March, the Northern Expedition, which Chiang Kai-shek

had launched in 1926, reached Nanjing. The ensuing looting of consul-
ates and killing of some Westerners, widely suspected to be the work of
Communist elements of the expedition forces, caused shells from British
and American warships to rain down on the city, resulting in some two
thousand casualties. As panic spread and refugees fled from the area,
Nee also decided to move to the safety of the International Settlement in
Shanghai.[42] There, he attracted a small but dedicated circle of followers
that blossomed into the Little Flock movement.

Chief among Nee's "co-workers" in Shanghai were Li Yuanru (Ruth
Lee) and Wang Peizhen (Peace Wang), two spirited and able single women
who, like the resourceful female associates of Jing Dianying in the Jesus
Family, played key roles in nurturing and energizing the new group. Both
were slightly older than Nee and, despite their impressive educational
and social backgrounds, would quietly remain in the shadow of Nee's
charisma in the years to come. Li was editor of the Nanjing-based journal
the *Spiritual Light* to which Nee had submitted his earliest writings. A
"small and pretty, energetic and discerning" woman, Li was a native of
Tianjin and an atheist in her early years. During the 1910s, she had taught
at a government normal school for girls in Nanjing. There, she embraced
Christianity under the influence of some Presbyterian missionaries and
of one notable recent convert named Cai Sujuan (Christiana Tsai), later
lauded as the "Queen of the Dark Chamber" after the publication of her
memoir under that title.[43]

Cai's father had been vice governor of Jiangsu in the final years of
the Qing dynasty. A timid girl beset with "a melancholy unrest," Cai had
"immersed" herself in "Buddhist classics" and had taken "vegetarian
vows" during her childhood. After the Revolution of 1911, she entered a
mission boarding school in Suzhou for "advanced studies in English and
music" where she was baptized and became a church activist. After her
own conversion, Li Yuanru resigned from the government school and was
hired as dean of the Presbyterian Mingde Girls' School where Cai was a
music teacher. The two worked together for "several happy years" but went
separate ways by the late 1920s. Cai retained her bond of friendship with
the American missionaries who had ushered her into a modern Christian
womanhood; Li, who had met Nee in 1923 when she went to Fuzhou to
lead evangelistic meetings, came under the latter's separatist influence.
After 1927, when publication of the *Spiritual Light* was disrupted by the

National Revolutionary Army's occupation of Nanjing, Li left the city and joined Nee in Shanghai.[44]

Wang Peizhen, also a first-generation Christian, hailed from a venerable family of government administrators. Her grandfather had been an official of the first grade under the Qing. When she adopted the new faith in 1918 at the age of nineteen, her father was serving as a county magistrate in Zhejiang province. Like Cai Sujuan, she had entered a mission school (Mary Vaughan Girls' School in Hangzhou) to pursue a modern education and was converted at an evangelistic meeting held there by Shi Meiyu. Not long afterwards, inspired by the revival teachings of Yu Cidu, she literally ran away from an arranged marriage—she scaled the wall of her family compound in Jiaxing and fled to Hangzhou to seek the help of her missionary teacher—and dedicated herself to the service of God. Her parents eventually relented, and she entered the Bible Teachers Training School for Women in Nanjing. There, she met Li Yuanru.[45] The two later developed a lasting partnership that was vital to the Little Flock.

Upon completion of her theological training in the early 1920s, Wang Peizhen joined the small, emerging circle of itinerant, indigenous preachers and, like Yu Cidu, was active in the lower Yangzi valley. At a time when the Protestant enterprise was experiencing its most rapid expansion since 1807—with the total figure of communicants exceeding four hundred thousand by 1924 and the number of ordained Chinese (more than thirteen hundred) already surpassing that of their foreign counterparts by 1920—Wang was poised to follow Yu Cidu into the stardom of indigenous evangelism under mission auspices.[46] However, the chaos that followed upon the heels of the Northern Expedition changed all that. As we have seen, the Nanjing Incident of March 1927 led to an exodus of missionaries from China. For Chinese preachers, the stigma of association with Western churches could no longer be brushed off. By May 1927, Wang had already distanced herself from denominational missions and was holding communion services with a small group of converts at her house in Shanghai. It was that group that Watchman Nee joined when he moved to Shanghai in late spring.[47]

Despite his weak constitution, Nee's magnetic personality and his remarkable ability to speak in the profound eschatological language of Western end-time mystics mesmerized the group, and he soon emerged as their indisputable leader. It had been three years since he dropped out of the initial Christian Assembly that he helped found in Fuzhou, and he had held on to his early vision with tenacity. Unlike Wang Zai and Wang Mingdao—the latter had paid Nee a visit in Fuzhou in 1925—he would seek a calling higher than that of an itinerant revivalist. Perhaps he had sensed the rootlessness and evanescence of the power and influence of evangelists without their own bases. The alternative was to build a system of independent churches throughout China. "I closed my eyes," Nee wrote, "and such a picture appeared before me." In early 1928, the group rented a house off Hardoon (Hatong) Road where Nee started pursuing his dream of building a church of God's elect.[48] Its foundation was a revelation of the hidden design of human history, which, like a majestic cosmic clock, ticked precisely and inexorably toward a divine-appointed, apocalyptic climax. That revelation rendered all the contemporary chaos and evil in the world intelligible. And for the "victorious" Christians— the "faithful Little Flock"—it also promised a most dramatic escape from end-time tribulations and from death itself through "rapture."[49]

Known as premillennial dispensationalism, the prototype of the teaching divides human history into three successive divine dispensations. The first, from Creation to the birth of Jesus, is the Age of the Law. The second period, which spans history from Jesus' crucifixion to the present, is the Age of the Church (or Grace). This will end with the Second Coming of Christ, who will usher in the Age of the Kingdom. In its earliest form, Christian dispensationalism was expounded by the twelfth-century Italian monk Joachim of Fiore (ca. 1135–1202).[50] Its most influential modern version, however, was the work of J. N. (John Nelson) Darby (1800–1882), a former Church of Ireland curate who became one of the founders and the most important inspiration of the Plymouth Brethren movement that started in the 1820s. From its beginning, the Brethren search for a genuine and primitive Christian unity—which dictated separation from the decadent world (and the "fallen" Christendom)—had proceeded amidst intense end-time speculations. By the 1830s, Darby had developed his intricate system of dispensationalism, which from a mystical reading of the Bible decoded a pivotal seven-year period preceding the Second Coming. In the middle of that period, Christ will appear quietly to gather the true believers to heaven in a "secret rapture." Then will follow three and a half years of "Great Tribulation," the final battle at Armageddon, and the triumphant return of Christ to inaugurate the Millennium.[51]

By the turn of the twentieth century, the divine "pattern for the ages" that Darby uncovered had been further penetrated and improved upon by Cyrus Ingerson Scofield (1843–1921), founder of the Dallas Theological Seminary and known for his enormously influential *Scofield Reference Bible*. Scofield distilled from the Book of Revelation a "prophetic" essence of the messages to the seven churches, which "represent seven phases of the *spiritual* history of the church" from the first century to the end. In that dissection of time, Pergamos, "where Satan's throne is," signifies the time "after the conversion of Constantine"; Thyatira is the "Papacy," and Sardis the Protestant Reformation, "whose works were not 'fulfilled.'" Like Darby, Scofield's commentaries on the Bible point to "the awful intensity at the end" when "Christ becomes the smiting Stone."[52]

There was no lack of terror in that scheme, but for Nee, who edited a Chinese translation of study materials for Scofield's Correspondence Bible School in 1926, the shaft of light that pierced the otherwise unrelieved gloom of the Brethren eschatology was the secret rapture that would shelter the faithful from end-time destruction.[53] An able transmitter of Brethren spirituality, he poured such teachings into his own writing. Out came a fierce, potent mix of fear and hope—in a steady stream of eschatological expositions that Nee published in his own journal the *Christian*. In 1926–1927, during the same period that he was working on *The Spiritual Man*, he put out a series of long articles detailing the prophetic significance of each of the seven churches in Revelation. There was no doubt, he wrote, that "in the last few pages of the history of the church" (and of humanity), the "Lord's eyes are fixed upon" the church in Philadelphia—the Little Flock. ("Fear not, little flock, for it is your Father's good pleasure to give you the kingdom" [Luke 12:32].) To that group bound by "brotherly love" and dedicated to keeping His word, God had given the "exclusive promise" of "rapture" before the Great Tribulation.[54]

By then, Nee's own identification with Philadelphia was unmistakable, as was his calling to gather the Little Flock in China. Equally evident to his audience was the sophisticated "light" he had shone on the divine scheme. Discreetly shorn of the exact date of the Second Coming, his eschatology stayed clear of the embarrassing pitfall of expired prophecies such as the one announced by the scantily educated Wei Enbo of the TJC. Still, Nee was able to develop from the Brethren tradition a blueprint of the end time with an awesome specificity that, as the pattern of things yet to come, was practically indistinguishable from precision. That blueprint, and the excited anticipation of its unfolding, rendered the political disintegration and social turmoil of the 1920s pregnant with hope. In Shanghai, he organized several "Overcomers' Meetings" (*desheng juhui*)—echoing the name of the journal the *Overcomer* that Penn-Lewis had founded two decades earlier—and attracted zealous souls, or spirits, from neighboring areas. In 1930, the group published *Hymns for the Little Flock* (*Xiaoqun shige*), following the identical title of an 1856 collection of hymns prepared by the Plymouth Brethren, and inadvertently (Nee insisted) gained that name for itself.[55]

THE SHEEP WITHOUT THE PEN

In 1932, the Shanghai-based *Chinese Christian Intelligencer* reported that dozens of Presbyterian and CIM churches in the neighboring areas had turned their back on those denominations and come under the banner of the Little Flock. Particularly "hard hit" were congregations under the CIM, whose austere faith-mission doctrines had affinities with Nee's teachings and among which Nee had missionary friends. By late 1933, Nee reported that there were already more than one hundred Little Flock assemblies.[56] As the new sect spread into major cities along the eastern seaboard, it drew "a high preponderance of educated men, doctors, university staff, businessmen, [and] army officers." In Beiping during the 1930s, the Christian Assembly consisted almost entirely of "top honor students from Yenching, Ching Hua, Peking Union Medical College, Peking University," along with nurses from mission hospitals.[57]

Nee was careful to dispel any notion that his emerging enterprise was the product of worldly drives such as antiforeignism or personal ambition. Antidenominationalism was evident among his followers, Nee admitted, but it was merely the outward expression of a profound inner life found in an unadulterated way of being Christian. The Little Flock was neither a new "movement" nor a "group," neither an "organization" nor a "denomination," but a gathering of those who would "bring God's plan to fruition."[58] That self-image, at once modest and extravagant and decidedly innocent, was not shared by the Protestant community at large. A report in the *China Christian Year Book* of 1932–1933 noted that while most revivals during the early 1930s helped to "break down denominational barriers and unite the churches on the basis of a common spiritual experience," the self-proclaimed "purified body called 'The Little Flock'" had "frankly declared their purpose to be the destruction of the present Church as moribund, corrupt, and apostate," which, wherever their influence spread, "has resulted in a group of earnest spirits withdrawing from the churches."[59]

The inherent appeal of Nee's message aside, the group also resorted to unchivalrous but clearly effective tactics. An article in the 1934–1935 issue of the *China Christian Year Book* reported that in the city of Suzhou, a "large group has split off from the Church of Christ in China." To the chagrin of many Westerners, the new Little Flock congregation "have rented a building opposite one of the Presbyterian churches, and they hold their meetings at the same time as the church services" in an unabashed bid to "attract members to their group."[60] One writer for the *Chinese Christian Intelligencer* observed that in the name of "non-denominationalism," the Little Flock had "enslaved" themselves "to the ideas of Penn-Lewis and formed an unnamed denomination" with the Welsh mystic as its "founder."[61] Commenting on the "disrupting influence" of the Little Flock, an article in the July 1936 issue of the *Chinese Recorder* lamented that even "in the business world, sensible people usually observe some code of professional ethics" such as "fair play" and would not "openly practise 'piracy' or 'sabotage,'" but "in the field of evangelism" some had resorted to "the tactics of a high-pressure salesman." Indeed, to many missionaries "Watchman Nee seemed but a sheep-stealer."[62] Little Flock zealots themselves, however, took pride in this relocation of the spiritual herd. As one early leader recalled, "the denominational churches had a sheep pen but no sheep; we had sheep but no pen."[63]

Nee's disdain for what he saw as the spiritual shallowness and naivety of established churches also extended to independent preachers such as Wang Mingdao, Wang Zai, and John Sung. He likened Wang Mingdao's Christian Tabernacle to a roadside "half-way house"; in 1931, he also made an unsuccessful bid to bring under his wings his erstwhile associate Wang Zai as well as the newly famous John Sung (whom he dismissed as a "childlike" figure).[64] Nor was he particularly impressed with Chinese incarnations of the Pentecostal spirit: the TJC, he wrote, was a mere "heresy" powered by "the evil spirit"; its exegesis was "far-fetched, hallucinatory, and not worth our ridicule." In the early 1930s, he saw the Spiritual Gifts Movement as likely the work of "the prince of darkness."[65]

To him, Pentecostalism could work like "spiritual opium," addiction to which would only compel "an ever-increased dosage."[66] In Keswick and Brethren traditions, and in the works of Penn-Lewis, he had discovered a more serene and majestic path to spiritual triumph and transcendence.

That attitude changed for a brief period after 1935. A year earlier, Nee suffered a setback in his leadership of the Little Flock movement. His marriage in 1934 to Zhang Pinhui had triggered a damning exposé in a Shanghai newspaper of his alleged romantic fickleness and questionable character (which included a broken engagement with a girl he had met in Malaya in 1925). His reputation tarred, Nee withdrew from his top position in the Christian Assembly, which was now placed under the supervision of several elders whom Nee had installed back in 1932.[67] In May 1935, Nee was in Shandong, the hotbed of the recent Spiritual Gifts Movement. There, he found himself under the spell of the very Pentecostal influences he had scorned a few years earlier. Those influences came in part through Thornton Stearns, a Presbyterian missionary physician in Jinan whose placid, down-to-earth research into the treatment of tuberculosis of the knee joint prevalent among farmers in North China did not deter him from an intense interest in the Pentecostal ecstasies around him.[68] In Chefoo (Yantai), Nee's spirits soared as he watched Elizabeth Fischbacher, a gifted CIM missionary, holding jubilant revival meetings and speaking in "tongues"; he found himself also "filled with the Holy Spirit" and breaking into "holy laughter." (Nee was never adept at "tongues.") With his unfailing flair for hyperbole, Nee sent a telegram to his comrades in Shanghai announcing, "I have met the Lord."[69] With that, he also signaled his return to the helm.

Nee's endorsement of Pentecostalism in 1935 rippled rapidly through the Little Flock congregations in various parts of China. Later that year, the Christian Assembly in Quanzhou, Fujian, held protracted Overcomers' Meetings dedicated to the infilling of the Spirit. However, it soon became clear that the much-sought-after spirit also defied any order that the local leaders wished to impose. During the meetings, some started to "howl and bang on the tables and chairs"; others "staggered up the platform" and, "foaming at their mouths, uttered incoherent, indecent words." The mother of the Christian Assembly leader in Quanzhou tried to jump out of an upstairs window; one evangelist from Xiamen "dashed out into the street all naked." Then Chen Zaisheng (Chen the Reborn), a prominent Little Flock leader in southern Fujian—who used to be his sorceress mother's helper—sent a chill down quite a few spines when, halfway through his praying and laying on of hands for others, he lapsed into a state of delirium and his voice "changed into that of a woman." (His frayed nerves never healed through the rest of his life.) The panic-stricken congregation filed an urgent report to Nee, who wired back his directive to stop the Pentecostal meetings.[70]

Though thus clipped of the wings of "spiritual gifts," the Little Flock by 1936 was already a full-fledged messianic sect. It had been drinking deep in the pool of dispensationalist teachings and was assured of its unrivaled place in God's end-time scheme. The abandonment of Pentecostalism was only a withdrawal into its most vaunted and unshaken eschatology. Nee himself stood tall among his followers: he had steadily gained stature after the deaths, in 1927 and 1930, respectively, of Jessie Penn-Lewis, his theological mentor, and Margaret E. Barber, his "spiritual mother."[71] And he had weathered the storms of both unflattering media exposure at home and a troubled relationship with the "Exclusive" Plymouth Brethren in Britain. The latter had been the main branch of the Plymouth Brethren movement after 1848, when Darby excommunicated those fellow Brethren, later known as the Independent or Open Brethren, who opposed some of his core teachings, including the secret rapture. In Darby's lifetime, the Exclusive Brethren grew to include some fifteen hundred assemblies worldwide. Nee began corresponding with, and purchasing books from, some Exclusive Brethren in England during the late 1920s. In 1932, a small Brethren delegation arrived in Shanghai to visit what appeared to be their spiritual progeny in China, and Nee returned a visit in 1933 to England and North America.[72]

The Brethren who visited China were the Ravenites, yet another faction within the Exclusive Brethren named after F. E. Raven, one of Darby's successors, whose elaborate dissection of "the great mystery of the Incarnation" had led to a fresh split in 1890. Those Brethren were clearly interested in taking Nee's sect under its global wings and expected Nee to abide by its strict code banning any fellowship with the Open Brethren during his visit.[73] But Nee had designs of his own. Although he desired the Brethren's recognition and support—spiritual as well as material—he had declared in 1932 that he had no interest in turning the Little Flock into an affiliate of a Western organization.[74] Eventually, he went beyond the Ravenites and sought out T. (Theodore) Austin-Sparks, a former Baptist minister whose engaging writings on the Cross had reached him via Barber.[75] Austin-Sparks had worked briefly under Penn-Lewis as one of the joint secretaries of her organization called the Over-comer Testimony. After 1925, however, he was "instructed" by God to set up his separate Honor Oak Fellowship in South London, diverting many of Penn-Lewis's former followers into a new revival marked by an ecstatic "living in the heavenlies."[76] In such a charged personality Nee found his new spiritual mentor, to whose authority Nee pledged "submission" and whose profound influence on the Little Flock would continue well into the 1960s.[77]

Nee's disregard for the rules of the Exclusive Brethren resulted in a bitter decision announced by the group in 1935 to expel the Little Flock (on whom they admitted having laid hands "too quickly") from its worldwide fellowship.[78] Nee later reciprocated with disdain for what he saw as the degeneration of the Brethren movement, even as he continued to build his own sectarian enterprise on Brethren innovations. One vital ecclesi-astical novelty introduced by Darby had been a paradoxical affirmation of one unified "true" church on earth—outside the allegedly corrupted "Christendom"—and the theoretical independence of each local assembly of believers (despite his own "tyrannical domination of the Brethren").[79] Nee began introducing the Brethren practice in 1932, when he installed elders and deacons in the Shanghai assembly and at the same time cre-ated a superstructure of apostolic "co-workers" that included Li Yuanru, Wang Peizhen, and above all, Nee himself.

In 1938, with the rapid expansion of the Little Flock, which counted more than two hundred local assemblies nationwide, Nee codified the basic principles of his organization in a book titled *Rethinking Our Mis-sions (Gongzuo de zaisi)*.[80] The true believers who constituted the Christian Assembly, he wrote, would return to the archetype, the "genesis," of the church. Administratively, each local assembly would be autonomous and led by its elders, who were installed by the "apostles." In spiritual matters and in the central mission of establishing churches, however, all the "Lo-cal Churches" *(Difang Jiaohui)*—the self-designation increasingly used thereafter—would be led by the "workers," or apostles, who were chosen by God to be His "overseers." There would be no salaried clergy or rigid centralization of finances, yet the faithful in each locality would support

1938 年 7 月倪弟兄與史百克弟兄於倫敦合影

FIGURE 17 Watchman Nee with T. Austin-Sparks, London, 1938. Source: Chen Zexin, *Ni Tuosheng dixiong jianshi* (1973). Used by permission of Tien Dao Publishing House.

their elders, and a "spiritually sound" local church "would certainly know how to supply the needs of the 'workers.'"[81]

It was a carefully articulated polity, one that Austin-Sparks praised as "very clever."[82] It granted an apparent autonomy and flexibility to the local assemblies while presenting submission to the higher authority of the "workers" (headed by Nee) as a matter of spiritual obligation. It also paved the way for later drastic centralization of power by Nee. In the meantime, it adapted well to the chaotic circumstances of the time following the full-scale Japanese invasion of 1937 and the frantic westward migration of people from the eastern seaboard, which in any event rendered ecclesiastical centralization impractical for the Little Flock.

SWEET SMELLING MYRRH

Unlike Wang Mingdao and John Sung, Nee made few forays into war-torn and poverty-stricken parts of China, relying instead on the power of his mystical, abstruse, and haunting teaching that he dispensed in the relative safety of the International Settlement in Shanghai, in unoccupied cities, and during his second trip to Europe in 1938. In that year, he traveled to England and attended the annual Keswick convention where, with the havoc of war (including the Rape of Nanking) "fresh in everyone's mind," he delivered a prayer onstage with his patent ring of sublimity. "The Lord reigns: we affirm it boldly," he said. "Therefore we do not pray for China." Neither would he pray for Japan, he added. "We pray for the interests of Thy Son. . . . We stand for Thy will."[83]

During the same year, the Little Flock published the first Chinese translation of *Sweet Smelling Myrrh,* the autobiography of Madame Guyon (Jeanne-Marie Bouvier de la Motte Guyon, 1648–1717). An enchanting French mystic and a prolific writer, who was once imprisoned in the Bastille for her role in the Quietist controversy, Guyon had long been popular among Pietists, Quakers, Methodists, and adherents of nineteenth-century revivalism in North America.[84] She yearned for the destruction of the "vain, pompous edifice [that] human art and power had erected." The "horrible ruins" that resulted would enable God, she wrote, to "rear His sacred temple in us." Such teaching found a curious resonance among the Little Flock. Equally appealing was her intoxication with physical pain for the love of Christ. "I so esteemed the cross," she wrote, "that my greatest trouble was want of suffering as much as my heart thirsted for."

Friedrich Nietzsche found in her passion "a womanly tenderness and ardor that modestly impelled toward an *unio mystica et physica*" (italics in original) that often appeared "in the guise of . . . puberty . . . even as the hysteria of an old maid."[85]

Guyon was "excessively ill" during her infancy and was neglected by her mother, who sent her away, at the age of four, to a Benedictine convent. Subsequently ravaged by unending misfortunes, including smallpox (which destroyed her legendary beauty) and the early loss of her husband and young children, Guyon developed a glowing love for Christ. It was a "fire which burned in my soul, which had all the fervor of what men call love." The "Well-Beloved," she wrote, "was Himself the only object which attracted my heart."[86] Nee had been introduced to the writings of Guyon in the 1920s by Barber, whose own fascination with Guyon had likely been kindled by Jessie Penn-Lewis.[87] In time, he cultivated a fervent adoration of Guyon among his followers. Under his direction, Yu Chenghua, an elder in the Shanghai Christian Assembly after 1936, completed a Chinese translation of Guyon's autobiography in 1938. Nee himself also became steeped in a Guyon-like piety and adopted her sensual language of love in many of the hymns that he wrote. In one song, he pleaded with the Lord to "bind my spirit, soul, and body with your romantic love [*aiqing*]." In another, he likened himself and his church to "the bride" who was "sick with love" and pining for the "day of union."[88]

This was potent spirituality, pulsating with longing and a rapturous joy. Yet the line between spiritual and physical abandon is an uncertain one. For Nee, it melted away one night when, on a trip to the beautiful city of Hangzhou to lead yet another meeting for the Overcomers, he checked into the same hotel room as his two accompanying young female assistants. More revelry of the same nature with the two women and with prostitutes, some of which was strangely recorded on Nee's own cinecamera, would be exposed later.[89]

In the meantime, for Nee's followers (some of whom read his writings on their knees during morning devotions), transports of heavenly bliss came through Nee's stream of "revelations." Not long after his return from his second European trip in 1939, Nee electrified his inner circle when he announced, "We have the blueprint of God's plan in our hand."[90] His new revelation expanded the Plymouth Brethren's elucidation of God's design. It is true, Nee noted, that the seven churches addressed in the second and third chapters of the Revelation signify seven historical stages into which the Age of the Church is divided. The Plymouth Brethren movement had initiated the beginning, dated precisely to the year 1825, of the sixth and the most perfect stage, named after the church in Philadelphia. Unfortunately, Nee pointed out, the Brethren movement had passed into the last, degenerate phase (the church of the Laodiceans) of complacency and lukewarm faith. At this juncture between the end of human history and the beginning of the Millennium, it was thrust upon those few whom Jesus praised as having "a little strength, and [having] kept my word"—those who were able to "walk the road of Philadelphia" and "overcome," as the true believers in the Little Flock clearly were—to stand at the center of God's created universe, complete His work, and become pillars in the temple in the New Jerusalem.[91]

As war engulfed increasingly large areas of China, as cities fell into ruins, and as the flood of refugees swept across much of the country, there was no lack of those having but "a little strength." For the Christians among them, the contrast between the ramshackle houses burned to the ground and the everlasting temple in the promised New Jerusalem must have been a stark one. Zhou Xingyi, Watchman Nee's stenographer and secretary for two decades, became a devoted follower of Nee in 1932 after the little retirement house outside Shanghai in which his father lived was bombed by a Japanese warplane. Together with Japan's seizure of Manchuria in 1931, the almost eight-week-long Japanese attack on Shanghai in early 1932 was a prelude to the horrendous destruction yet to come that claimed tens of millions of Chinese lives before the war ended in 1945.[92] During the turbulent years of the 1940s, some seventy thousand in China would find hope and solace in Nee's musings on the Cross as well as his prophecy of rapture and the approaching "Kingdom" and would join his Christian Assembly network in more than seven hundred locations across China.[93]

CHAPTER EIGHT

The Indigenous Church Movement through War and Revolution

[In Shanghai newspapers] an announcement of public expositions of sutras by a certain Buddhist organization would be placed next to a story of murder and dismemberment; below the caption "Argentine Night Club Casino Remains Open," one reads "The Salvation of Jesus and the Rapture of the Saints" and "Proclaiming Daniel's Prophecy: The Casting Down of the Dragon, the World War, and the Second Coming of Christ."

—*Yuan Shuipai, "Baofahu de Shanghai" (The Upstarts' Shanghai), 1941*

THE JAPANESE OCCUPATION of much of China between 1937 and 1945 seriously disrupted the work of mission-supported churches in the country. Most church organizations including the NCC, along with an estimated fifty thousand members of denominational churches, moved inland as part of an exodus of some fifty million people from coastal provinces.[1] In occupied China, denominational churches were crippled by widespread destruction or requisition of church property by the Japanese and increasingly came under Japanese domination. According to Frank W. Price, Presbyterian missionary and chairman of the Rural Church Department at Nanking Theological Seminary, "at least one-third of the mission and church property in China . . . was destroyed or badly damaged in fighting, looting, or occupation by military forces." In addition, rural churches lost an equal percentage of their leadership as a result of desertion or westward migration. Since almost two-thirds of the total income of denominational churches during the late 1930s came from Western missions, much of the work at the local level was paralyzed when communications with mission headquarters broke down and funds were cut off.[2] And after Japan's attack on Pearl Harbor in December 1941, almost all the remaining Western missionaries in occupied areas (about twelve hundred) were interned; mission churches had to submit to the new authority and enter into Japanese-supervised Christian "unions" and "federations."³ Of the thirteen Christian colleges, eleven—including Yenching, Shandong Christian (Cheeloo) University, and the University of Nanking—were moved to hinterland cities such as Chengdu, Chongqing, and Kunming where they struggled to continue operation; practically all mission publications in Japanese-controlled areas ground to a halt.⁴

In Western China, major denominational churches as well as inter-denominational organizations such as the NCC and YMCA/YWCA doggedly carried on their work even as the majority of Western missionaries evacuated the country. (Of the 2,500 Protestant missionaries listed in "Free China" before the outbreak of the Pacific War, only 850 remained.)⁵ The exigencies of the war spurred a new level of cooperation among different denominational organizations. Their joint efforts were most visible in the areas of war relief, including social services for refugees, collection of donations for soldiers at the front, and medical aid—offered at some 250 mission hospitals throughout the country. In addition, around thirty mobile units operated under the direction of the National Christian Service Council for Wounded Soldiers in Transit formed in early 1938. Mainline Protestant bodies also appealed to Western church organizations and the international community at large for moral and financial support for China. Within one year of the Marco Polo Bridge Incident, the NCC raised two hundred thousand yuan in relief funds, most of which came from abroad. With the influx of members from the east, the Church of Christ in China even organized a "service department" to begin medical, educational, and social work for the ethnic minorities in the impoverished border regions of western Sichuan, eastern Tibet, Yunnan, and Guizhou.⁶

Upon the Japanese surrender in 1945, denominational churches embarked on ambitious efforts at reconstruction and revival of the Protestant enterprise in China. Missionaries returned in significant numbers, bringing the total to about four thousand by 1949. The NCC moved its headquarters back to Shanghai in July 1946, but by the end of that year, the country was descending irreversibly into civil war. The NCC attempted to steer clear of the Nationalist–Communist rivalry; it launched yet another "Forward Movement" to call for "repentance" of the whole country and to promote the evangelistic and social work of the church amidst intensifying chaos and destruction.[7] Nationwide, communicant membership of mainline churches—predominantly rural, female, and illiterate—rose to more than 623,000 toward the end of the Republican period, an increase of about 15 percent compared with 1936.[8] Under the auspices of the board of trustees of Nanking Theological Seminary, a group of Protestant scholars led by American Presbyterian missionary Francis P. Jones also embarked on a massive project, originally conceived in Sichuan during the years of Japanese occupation, to complete a Chinese translation of fifty-three volumes of classics of Christian literature. According to Xie Fuya (N. Z. Zia), a secretary of the national YMCA who later played a dominant role in the project, such an effort would be comparable to the work of Kumarajiva and Xuan Zang, whose monumental translation and introduction of Buddhist sutras (during the Northern Wei and Tang dynasties, respectively) made possible the indigenization of Buddhism in China. However, because of the disruptions of the civil war, not a single volume was produced before the collapse of the Nationalist government in 1949.[9]

As a whole, efforts of mission-supported churches between 1937 and 1949 were characterized by a progressive spirit and a tenacious search for a Christian solution to the political, social, and national crises of modern China. During the period of Japanese aggression, the NCC characteristically sought to infuse Christian ideals and morals into the fight for national survival. It affirmed that the Gospel of Christ was "a summons to struggle against the forces of evil in the lives of men and of nations," and it called for increased "devotion and sacrifice for the welfare of society and the state" and for "the world-wide Kingdom of God."[10] There was, however, an occasional slide in such Christian patriotism toward noble impertinence. Earlier, a small group of Shanghai Protestant intellectuals and YMCA secretaries also formed a short-lived Northeast Society (Dongbeishe) to work for the recovery of Manchuria in the wake of the Mukden Incident. However, the most potent expression of their Christian patriotism was three minutes of silence in front of a Chinese map laid out on a dinner table in a restaurant (with the three lost northeastern provinces covered in red). The somber party also placed an order for individual bowls of bitter broth made of Chinese goldthread—a symbolism that was lost on a bemused servant, who promptly dumped the soup.[11]

During the four years of Chinese civil war that followed Japan's surrender, the NCC, though largely anti-Communist and supportive of Chiang Kai-shek's Nationalist government, vowed to transcend the politics of the time as it worked for the Kingdom of God to be revealed in a reformed human society. The resolution of the NCC national conference held in Shanghai in late 1946 affirmed that the church could not "be blind to the dangers which threaten the foundations of the country" (a reference to the Communists); neither could it "refrain from passing moral judgment on social and political evils"—a slap on the wrist of the Guomindang. Instead, it called on Christians to be "united in opposition to all corruption, to all types of human bondage, inequality, unrighteousness . . . lawlessness and Godlessness."[12]

Leading missionaries also championed "rural construction" modeled on the campaigns of James Yen during the 1920s and 1930s. The aim was to improve life in the vast Chinese countryside and to cultivate a responsible citizenry as the foundation of a just society and an alternative to the violent Communist revolution—a scheme of which even Yen was skeptical.[13] In their continued search for an indigenous form of Christianity, Western-educated church leaders displayed the same mellow and refined, but frequently impractical, predilection shaped by Confucian sensibility. A proposal made in 1947 by Francis Wei (Wei Zhuomin), president of Central China College (Huazhong Daxue), called for a "four-center church" in China that would include centers of social service, Christian thinking, and Christian pilgrimages ("hundreds of them") situated in beautiful mountains for religious recreation and retreat. Each center of pilgrimage would be complete with a "cathedral" for worship, a cemetery, a library, and a hotel to attract both farmers and scholars in search of "illumination and inspiration." By then, the tide of war was already turning against the corrupt and demoralized Nationalist regime. With the populace stricken by massive destruction and by the panic of skyrocketing inflation, one would likely find in Wei's vision an intellectualism as high-minded as it was irrelevant to the struggles of the common people.[14]

THE TRUE JESUS CHURCH DURING THE WAR YEARS

Compared with mission Christianity, independent Protestant groups had neither the ability nor the inclination to save their country through ambitious human undertakings. To them, hope came in the form of messianic assurances. In addition, prophecies, prognostications, and visions—especially those that carried promises of divine protection amidst random death and destruction—brought much-sought-after relief and helped the continued growth of those sects.[15] After 1937, the TJC was forced to suspend its official periodical the *Holy Ghost* (*Shengling bao*) in Shanghai as a result of Japanese censorship. The sect was also forced to move its headquarters (located in Shanghai after the late 1920s) inland to Chongqing. In his flight from advancing Japanese armies, Wei Yisa displayed a resilience that was typical of his sect. He and his associates "followed the directives of the Holy Spirit," proselytized along the way, and succeeded in founding dozens of new TJC churches in the hinterland provinces of Shaanxi, Sichuan, Gansu, and Yunnan after 1938.[16] In western Hubei, near the entrance to the first of the Three Gorges on the Yangzi River, rural TJC stations reported a surge of new members, most of them urban refugees, in the early 1940s.[17] According to the TJC, during the ten years of war between 1937 and 1947, "tens of thousands" who had "seen through the red dust" and awakened to the "emptiness" of the world were led by the Holy Spirit into its fold. In 1942, dedicated TJC evangelists from Taiwan even succeeded in bringing the end-time message of the sect to Japan and established branches among Chinese expatriates in Tokyo and Osaka.[18]

By 1947, when it celebrated the thirtieth anniversary of its founding at a conference held in Nanjing, the TJC had spread to eighteen provinces. In addition, it had established itself in Taiwan and Southeast Asia and founded small communities in Hawaii, southern India, and Japan. It had also survived numerous internal splits and the excommunication of at least fifteen leaders of "heresies." The main strongholds of the sect, each with thousands of members, were to be found in Henan, Hunan, Hubei, and Fujian provinces and Taiwan. Nationwide, the TJC reported forty thousand active members in some 570 churches and "meeting places" and claimed a total following that was likely "three to four times higher" than the reported figures, or "over 100,000 people in more than 1,000 congregations" (including those living "under the Red Terror" in Communist-controlled areas).[19] Much of this gain came at the expense of Western denominations, which dismissed the work of the TJC and other Pentecostal groups as "reconversion" and deplored their "arrogant hostility" toward mission churches. Yet for the TJC, the "sad harvest of disrupted churches" decried by the missionaries and the NCC leaders remained, nonetheless, a harvest.[20] Among those who joined in the celebration of the TJC achievements at the Nanjing conference was Li Zongren, soon to be the acting president of the Nationalist government. In an inscription displaying his own calligraphy, Li wrote, "Since the European wind began sweeping the East, Christianity has thrived [in China] and the missionaries . . . have rivaled one another in attacking the traditional faith of our country." While most Chinese converts beset with low self-esteem had rushed to "curry favor with the foreign churches," Li added, Wei Enbo "succeeded in melding Chinese and Western traditions and, in the spirit of independence and self-determination, accomplished the pioneering deed of founding the autonomous [True Jesus] Church."[21]

A PENTECOSTAL SURVIVAL: THE JESUS FAMILY AND THE SPIRITUAL GIFTS SOCIETY AFTER 1937

Similarly, during the war years the Jesus Family saw a dramatic increase in the number of its settlements, in its total membership, and in attendance at the biannual revival, or "spiritual gifts," meetings in Mazhuang. There was an almost twentyfold surge in the number of people in the "original family" (laojia) during the eight years of Japanese occupation, and a total of sixty-three new "small families" were formed. Most of them were in Shandong province; other settlements were scattered over parts of the north, northeast, and northwest of the country.[22] In Shandong, the Japanese authorities exercised less supervision over small rural indigenous groups such as the Jesus Family than over Western denominational churches, which they forced into the North China Christian Union (Huabei Zhonghua Jidujiaotuan). During the occupation, each Family member in Mazhuang was in fact entitled to a "good civilian certificate" (liangmin zheng) issued by the puppet government of Shandong to ensure safe passage through Japanese checkpoints.[23] For the Jesus Family, mutual support and protection remained its main appeal: one Russian woman born in Siberia and married to a Chinese landowner on the Manchurian border joined the sect after the Japanese killed her husband and her father-in-law, an opium smoker, threatened to sell her to a brothel. (One of her sons sought out a different haven and joined the CCP.)[24]

During the civil war years, the Mazhuang Family again offered a rare tranquility even as the county of Tai'an repeatedly changed hands between the Nationalists and the Communists. In its embrace of poverty and egalitarianism and its pursuit of indiscriminate love—it provided refuge and medical care to wounded soldiers from either side of the conflict— the Jesus Family found itself in a coveted, though precarious, middle ground.[25] At times, however, one finds a curious echo of Communist land reform slogans in the Family. An inscription by Jing Dianying in 1946 called out:

> Down with clothing, food, and lodging;
> Bid farewell to riches, fame, and glory!
>
> Stand up to violence and oppression; love peace!
> Liberate the oppressed masses, and lead our society into the
> Great Harmony![26]

In the meantime, Jing and his followers displayed an inspiring nonchalance toward the fighting that raged on all around. "Cannons and guns are but firecrackers," a popular Family song during this period declared, "and warplanes are our paper kites. . . . Isn't this the land of the immortals? . . . isn't this the world beyond the 'spring of the peach blossoms' [shiwai taoyuan]?"[27]

As Tao Feiya shows, the period between 1946 and 1949 saw the most rapid expansion in the history of the Jesus Family. Thirty-nine new small settlements were founded in those four years, including about a dozen new "families" in wealthier urban areas to generate income and to fund the continued growth of the sect.[28] In 1949, in an isolated area south of Nanjing made quite inaccessible by "rivers and swamps," where people lived in "little huts built on huge dikes constructed a thousand years or so ago," an American missionary found "eight very active [Jesus Family] Christian communities" that had been established by a member of the Jesus Family from nearby Wuhu, Anhui.[29] According to a 1948 report published in the National Christian Council Monthly (Xiejin yuekan), membership of the Jesus Family totaled more than ten thousand in that year.[30] By the end of the Republican era, the Jesus Family counted 113 subfamilies in eight provinces. The original Jesus Family in Mazhuang had also grown to include about 140 mu of land (about twenty-three acres), a church, and nineteen brick buildings to house some five hundred members.[31]

Compared with the Jesus Family, the Spiritual Gifts Society was poorly organized. One of its own leaders likened the society to the Israelites who, before Saul and David, were "without a king."[32] The founding of the Shandong General Assembly of the Spiritual Gifts Society in the provincial capital in 1936 had been a nominal attempt at maintaining "ecclesiastical contacts" among various independent congregations of the seekers of "spiritual gifts." Information on the society remains scanty. By the end of the Republican period, when the paroxysmal "infillings" of the "Holy Spirit" of the 1930s had subsided, the total numerical strength of the group was probably in the low thousands. Larger Spiritual Gifts congregations, each with hundreds of people, could be found in a few main cities in Shandong.[33] Some of these had actually sprung up after 1937 when wartime Pentecostal "visions" of the final defeat of the Japanese helped generate new energy at least in certain parts of the province.[34]

There was a special affinity between the Jesus Family and the Spiritual Gifts Society. To a large extent, this was because of their shared Pentecostalism and apocalyptic messianism and because they both introduced lay leadership and claimed to have dissolved the denominational boundaries and abolished distinctions of status when they broke away from mission churches. Both groups frequently featured leaders and activists from the other group as guest revivalists.[35] In central Shandong, after the spasms of the Pentecostal movement in the early 1930s, some followers of the Spiritual Gifts Society, unwilling to return to the denominational churches that they had left (and offended), joined the Jesus Family where institutionalized Pentecostalism continued.[36] In Yantai, the local Spiritual Gifts Society church, which had been established in 1943, organized its own small Jesus Family in 1949 headed by a woman who, during the war, had famously turned away a squad of Japanese troops from her village when she shouted out a stream of "tongues" (allegedly in Japanese). Most members emerged from dire poverty, but the community also included a former nurse at the Peking Union Medical College hospital. Among those that the Yantai Jesus Family took in was a two-week-old orphaned baby girl, who was nourished with milk while the rest of the Family subsisted on rations of millet porridge and salted vegetables. (She grew up to become a woman of robust health and spirit.)[37]

By the end of the Republican period, the influence of the Jesus Family and the Spiritual Gifts Movement was likely more extensive than contemporary statistics would suggest. For example, in the provincial capital of

Gansu, a church completed and dedicated in 1942 was registered under the name of Lanzhou Zhonghua Jidujiaohui, or the Church of Christ in China at Lanzhou. However, the church was built by the local Jesus Family and consisted mostly of its members. In that urban setting, its communalism was incomplete, yet its Pentecostalism and antagonism toward Western missions were unmistakable.[38]

"FREE-LANCE" PREACHERS AND "SPORADIC EVANGELISTIC MOVEMENTS"

On the whole, most independent church groups that did not rely on Western funding or leadership and whose congregations were able to meet in informal places of worship suffered relatively minor disruptions amidst the chaos of war. For instance, the China Christian Independent Church, the oldest indigenous Protestant group founded in Shanghai in 1906, would claim a following of more than ten thousand members in hundreds of churches and meeting places nationwide by the end of the Republican period.[39] During the same period, a new generation of homegrown preachers—some independent but most of them supported by conservative missionary groups—rose to join the ranks of earlier revivalists and spread the simple but rousing message of divine deliverance. This happened at a time when the dominance and influence of foreign missionaries were fast receding as a result of either repatriation or internment. Meanwhile, Western-educated Protestant leaders in national church organizations were sometimes put out of action—Zhao Zichen and his Yenching colleagues were interned by the Japanese after Pearl Harbor—or forced to make unseemly compromises as they struggled to come to terms with shifting political powers. Jiang Changchuan (Kiang Ch'ang-ch'uan), who had baptized Chiang Kai-shek in Shanghai in 1930 and who became bishop of the United Methodist Church in China in 1941, was prevailed upon by the Japanese to head the North China Christian Union in 1942.[40]

In comparison, popular preachers of the war time, both inside and outside the mission churches, were more in touch with the masses, assumed greater spiritual authority, and were more responsible for shaping the theological temperament of an emerging Chinese Christianity. None of them had the charisma of John Sung or the stature of Wang Mingdao and Watchman Nee, yet they still became, in their own right, religious semi-heroes produced by the times. One often detects in them an attitude that mingled evangelical self-confidence with patriotic opposition to the dominance, the "sense of racial superiority," or the "oppression" of missionaries.[41] Moreover, they furthered an already apparent trend in Chinese Protestant Christianity—arising out of avowed biblical literalism—toward apocalyptic gloom and messianic fervor.

By the late 1930s, some of the earlier preachers were exiting the main stage of Chinese revivalism. Among them was Wang Zai, who joined the Chinese Overseas Mission (Zhonghua Guowai Budaotuan), the first organized Chinese mission abroad, which was founded in 1928 by Robert A. Jaffray, a Canadian Christian and Missionary Alliance missionary. At first, Wang was unable to speak Cantonese, the dialect of most Chinese expatriates in Malaya and the Dutch East Indies. He would preach in English, which Jaffray translated into Cantonese—a spectacle in itself. During the next four decades, Wang Zai personified the Chinese Overseas Mission, which gained a membership of some five thousand in Southeast Asia.[42]

Inside China, wartime chaos created new opportunities for "sporadic evangelistic movements," as a September 1938 report in the *Chinese Recorder* noted. At a time when "mobile bands" of evangelists proved "superior" to "installed" clergy, "lesser known itinerant preachers and revivalists of the 'free-lance' variety" sprang up to meet the demand.[43] Many of them were no more than passing figures; others were content to preach their way from one meal (or donation) to the next and vanished when such precarious living was no longer attractive or viable.[44] There were, of course, preachers of more established reputation. Among them was Chen Chonggui, the ex-chaplain of Feng Yuxiang's Christian Army. A convert of the Swedish Covenant Missionary Society (Xingdaohui), Chen had taught at the society's seminary in Jingzhou, Hubei. In June 1925, at a time when antiforeign sentiments ran high in mission schools, Chen was kicked out of the Jingzhou seminary for clashing with his missionary superiors over its foreign control. For the next two years he served under the "Christian General," leading evangelistic meetings and orchestrating mass baptisms of Feng's soldiers. In 1926, however, Feng was defeated by more powerful warlords and left for Russia. Chen sought asylum the following year in a secret hideout at the residence of a missionary in Suiyuan.[45]

In 1928, having survived the vicissitudes of warlord politics, Chen reemerged in the limelight of mission Christianity. He had recently become managing editor and leading author of a new journal, *Evangelism* (*Budao zazhi*), sponsored by the Stewart Fund for Evangelical Work in China, which would be one of the most widely read Protestant periodicals in China for the next two decades. The journal also became a major disseminator, besides Watchman Nee, of the "higher life" teachings of Jessie Penn-Lewis. As one of the better-educated conservative preachers (he had studied for a year at Wheaton College), Chen was chosen as a member of the Chinese delegation to the Jerusalem Conference of the International Missionary Council held that year. Shortly after his return, he joined the faculty of Hunan Bible Institute in Changsha, which was founded in 1917 and supported by the Bible Institute of Los Angeles. He soon gained a reputation as an "outstanding evangelical" and was a popular speaker at retreats and Bible conferences across China.[46]

During the 1930s, Chen was only one of several conservative preachers of growing national reputation. That group included Zhao Shiguang (S. K. Chow, Timothy Chao), a Christian and Missionary Alliance minister in Shanghai; Cheng Jigui, who hailed from a CIM church in Yangzhou and also taught at the Hunan Bible Institute; and Zhou Zhiyu, who succeeded Ding Limei in the Chinese Home Missionary Society.[47] Other rising stars included Zhao Junying (Calvin Chao), who grew up under strong Presbyterian influences but later worked for the CIM, and Gu Ren'en (John Ku), a Pentecostal preacher based in Qingdao and a former film actor who would captivate his audience with theatricals and with no less dramatic faith healings onstage. Like John Sung and Wang Mingdao, they itinerated in major cities, leading evangelistic meetings, Bible conferences, or spiritual retreats (*peilinghui*) in mission churches, at times reaping hundreds of conversions.[48] Another conservative—of more formidable stature (and with a longer, more dignified beard) than most—was theologian Jia Yuming (1880–1964). Jia was not a revivalist himself. A graduate of the Presbyterian Tengchow College, Jia had served as vice principal of the fundamentalist North China Theological Seminary in Tengxian, Shandong. In 1936, in an effort to train conservative preachers to counter the growing liberalism in leading mission seminaries, Jia started the independent Christian Bible Institute (Jidutu Lingxiuyuan) in Nanjing and served as its principal.[49] Their different personalities and denominational backgrounds notwithstanding, many of these preachers shared a vibrant nationalistic spirit as well as premillennial exuberance. According to Yu Ligong, himself a rising young evangelist at the time, most of the newcomers "sought the magnitude of the Shandong revivals" and craved "the liveliness of John Sung, the emotional appeal of Ji Zhiwen, and the spiritual profundity of Watchman Nee."[50]

WARTIME CRUSADES AND THE INTER-VARSITY CHRISTIAN FELLOWSHIP OF CHINA

After the outbreak of the war in 1937, there were few opportunities for large-scale revivalism in Japanese-controlled areas. In Western China, however, the influx of fifty million refugees, including tens of thousands of destitute, frustrated, and agitated students (whom one article in a Chongqing newspaper likened to trucks rumbling recklessly ahead with no drivers on board), created a new audience for eschatological messages—as well as new messengers. Many of the younger preachers in Nationalist-controlled hinterlands had student backgrounds and were cultivated by conservative (especially CIM) missionaries to work among the migrant student population. The best known among them was Zhao Junying. Zhao had been a promising student and a basketball star at Hangchow Christian College (Zhijiang Daxue) and, not atypically, a proponent of the Social Gospel. In 1928, three months before his graduation, he became sick with tuberculosis and forfeited whatever youthful dreams he had had. Three years later, he dedicated himself to the service of God at a Bethel Band revival meeting led by Ji Zhiwen. In 1938, already recognized as an energetic young conservative (he had shed his erstwhile liberalism with vehemence), Zhao proselytized his way inland as he fled the war in the east. He soon became popular among refugee students and found among them an unprecedented receptiveness to Christianity—a striking contrast to the anti-Christian zeal of students during the 1920s.[51]

Like many other popular evangelists of the time, Zhao inherited the burning premillennial dispensationalism as well as the robust revivalism of the early 1930s. He recalled having "perused" *The Spiritual Man* by Watchman Nee "several times"; he had also been overpowered by the magnetism of Bethel Band's emotional preaching. He entered his prime years as an evangelist among students toward the end of the resistance war when a handful of wealthy conservatives in Seattle led by a disaffected former CIM missionary offered to fund a small Chinese Native Evangelical Crusade (Zhongguo Budao Shizijun) and asked him to be its general secretary.[52] Zhao proved to be both a capable preacher and an effective organizer. He recruited several Christian officials in the Guomindang government to serve on the board of trustees of the new organization; set up its headquarters in Chongqing, the wartime capital; and conducted rousing campaigns that featured simultaneous prayer, public confession of sins, and howling and weeping that would leave "puddles of tears and snivel" on the ground. During the war, a steady stream of people were eager to unload the burden of sin: many repented of adultery, theft, incest, or murder; one confessed publicly that he used to serve as a CCP doctor in the Eighth Route Army and had dissected captured Nationalist soldiers live—and couldn't rid himself of the sound of their screaming.[53]

In contrast to prewar revivals, which typically took place in denominational churches and mission schools, the Chinese Native Evangelical Crusade took advantage of its connections to Guomindang officials in the wartime capital and proselytized vigorously on the campuses of universities that had been relocated to the Chongqing area. Those campaigns not only won fresh converts but also produced some of the popular church leaders of the second half of the twentieth century.[54] In July 1945, with the end of war in sight, the Chinese Native Evangelical Crusade convened the first summer conference of "national" university students. Its novel revivalist techniques included a parade of converted government officials onstage. Among them was Yin Renxian, a Harvard graduate and a senior ministry of finance official, as well as his eloquent wife, who was Ding Limei's daughter and also a returned student from the United States. The Yins had been "born again" after the tragic deaths in July 1934 of their two college-age children, whose train was blown up by a bomb that an anti-Japanese group had planted in an effort to sabotage the opening of railway services between North China and Manchuria.[55] Riding the high tide of youthful zeal after the conference, Zhao Junying organized the Inter-Varsity Christian Fellowship of China (Quanguo Jidutu Daxuesheng Lianhehui) (named after its American prototype), which became a major channel of student revivalism in the late 1940s.[56]

During the four years of civil war, denominational churches in the countryside often languished under "bitter persecution" by the Communists. By 1948, as Frank W. Price reported in *The Rural Church in China*, "hundreds of pastors and Christians have been killed and thousands have been driven from their homes by the threat of mob trials." The rural church in "most Communist areas," Price observed, "covering about one-fourth of China, is being driven underground."[57] However, in major cities in the east, which remained under Nationalist control until the very end, popular revivalism continued and, in fact, throve on the gathering apocalyptic gloom. The Inter-Varsity Fellowship, sporting its indigenous leadership, its alleged independence of mission churches, and its staunch fundamentalism and anti-Communism, scored its own victories among patriotic—and often anxious and bewildered—students in the cities.[58] In 1947, "truck-loads" of Beiping Protestant students attended a summer conference held in some "ramshackle buildings which had once been the Emperor's stables" beneath the walls of the Imperial Summer Palace. During the winter of 1947–1948, as the ancient capital was flooded with refugees from Communist-occupied areas, the city's "Youth for Christ Committee arranged what was possibly the largest evangelistic campaign ever to have been held in Peking—an open-air mat stadium was erected on the former polo ground of the foreign embassies and the Gospel was faithfully preached to large numbers of people."[59]

Those winter and summer student conferences held in Nanjing and Beiping typically featured well-known conservative preachers of the day, including Zhao Junying, theologian Jia Yuming, and Ji Zhiwen. After 1937, Ji had rechanneled much of his former evangelistic energy to the tending of orphans left in the care of the Bethel Mission. In the process, he had receded into the background of revivalism and, with a visible decline in his charisma as a preacher, was brought back onstage on only a few occasions during the late 1940s.[60] There were new preachers, however, who carried on the revivalist tradition of the early 1930s, proclaiming a total end-time salvation undiminished by meager attempts at wartime relief or social reform. One of them was Yang Shaotang (1900–1966), who hailed from Hongdong, Shanxi. In the early 1930s, Yang had organized a Spiritual Action Team (Linggongtuan) of twenty men and women (including a handful of young CIM missionaries) who lived a communal life of devotion and itinerant evangelism, often speaking in "tongues" and "laughing without restraint." In 1939, Japanese armies marching through the Fen River valley in southern Shanxi "burned the Spiritual Action Team premises to the ground." The team dispersed, and Yang fled. He ended up in Beijing, where he developed close ties with Wang Mingdao and John Sung (who was living out his last days outside the city) and, after the Japanese defeat, emerged as a popular revivalist.[61]

Meanwhile, Wang Mingdao himself, the preeminent popular preacher in the country (after the death of John Sung in 1944), was nearing the pinnacle of his influence. He and his Christian Tabernacle had survived the Japanese occupation of Beiping with fortitude and a stroke of good luck. In 1942, Wang resisted a Japanese order to bring his independent congregation of some five hundred people into the League for the Promotion of Church Union in North China (later renamed the North China Christian Union), which he regarded as a defiled "Babylon." Somehow, he was spared by the Japanese; his Tabernacle remained independent—the lone exception among all the churches in Beiping.[62] As a result, Wang's reputation soared. Toward the end of the civil war, at conferences organized by Beiping's Fellowship of Christian Students and held in the shadow of an impending collapse of the Nationalist government, Wang preached to eager crowds the same steadying Gospel of "The Cross," "The Resurrection," and "The Second Coming."[63]

In the Protestant community of Shanghai, the air was also thick with prophecies and calls for end-time repentance. Much of the eschatological fervor there was generated by the Seventh-Day Adventist Church, whose mission headquarters were based in the city. In the late 1940s, the church secured Chinese translations of two popular books by Adventist writer Arthur S. Maxwell—*So Little Time: The Atom and the End* (1946) and *Time's Last Hour* (1948). According to historian and then Adventist member Gu Changsheng, who translated both of the books, one hundred thousand copies of each title were printed.[64] In that cauldron of East and West, a city of solemn church spires thrusting through the smoke of incense wisping from crowded back alleys, the hunger for apocalyptic literature was by no means limited to Christian converts. In fact, a fresh craze for ancient prophecies had started in 1932. In the aftermath of fierce Japanese attacks on the city, bookstalls were filled with such titles as *Seven Chinese Prophecies* (*Zhongguo yuyan qizhong*). Numerous hawkers were also selling new versions of ancient prophecy works, including the *Sesame Seed Cake Song* (*Shaobing ge*) and *Back-Pushing Sketches* (*Tuibei tu*)—attributed to an illustrious advisor to the first Ming emperor and two Tang-dynasty seers, respectively—at Shanghai street corners.[65]

In the 1940s, independent Shanghai preachers freely drawing upon premillennial dispensational teachings appeared among the major purveyors of a redemptive eschatology. There were dozens of new indigenous, separatist (and frequently Pentecostal) Christian groups in the city. The best known among them was the Spiritual Food Church (Lingliangtang) founded by Zhao Shiguang. Zhao had been pastor of a Christian and Missionary Alliance church in the city. After the Japanese seized control of the International Settlement in Shanghai in December 1941, identification with Western missions was no longer profitable. The following June, Zhao founded his own church. Within a few years, the group had erected its own buildings, established several branches throughout the city, and attracted a following of more than three thousand. After the mid-1940s, Zhao's itinerant preaching led to the founding of several Spiritual Food churches in cities near Shanghai and overseas in Taiwan, Jakarta, and Calcutta. In the late 1940s, the Spiritual Food Church responded to wartime needs by developing its own network of educational and social services, including schools, orphanages, and nursing homes. Zhao combined such services with his own eschatological teaching—in pamphlets such as *Teaching Materials on the Book of Revelation* and *The Seven Dispensations*— and secured for the Spiritual Food Church an indisputable place among notable indigenous Protestant groups of twentieth-century China.[66]

THE LITTLE FLOCK DURING THE LATE REPUBLICAN PERIOD

The Little Flock movement also throve during the war years as expected. In 1942, however, Watchman Nee suffered a second setback in his leadership of the sect he had founded: his sex scandal involving the two young female co-workers was exposed, as were his questionable business dealings. After 1938, he had increasingly involved himself in a pharmaceutical venture of his chemist brother and had used his English connections to help create the China Biological and Chemical Laboratories (Shenghua Yaochang). Nee served as chairman of directors of the company and allegedly defrauded investors, many of whom were his own Little Flock followers.[67] Others accused him of "leaving Golgotha in neglect, propagating DDT instead." Nee's otherwise adoring biographer Angus I. Kinnear reveals that Nee's "boredom" with his "mediocre" followers (who eagerly idolized him as the end-time "seer") had been partly responsible for his turn from Gospel to business.[68] In 1943, Nee left Shanghai. In a parting letter to his associates, he asked to have his name "blotted out" from the church "register" in order to "give peace to many hearts, and to avoid bringing shame to the name of the Lord."[69]

Nee's self-imposed exile from the Little Flock was not to last for long, however. In his absence and under the restrictions imposed by the Japanese occupation, the Shanghai congregation had languished (even as Christian Assembly churches elsewhere continued to grow).[70] By 1946, Nee was already maneuvering to rally some of his devoted supporters for an eventual comeback, and in early 1948, he was brought back as the sect's undisputed leader. Playing a central role in Nee's reinstatement was Li Changshou (Witness Lee, 1905–1997), a devoted lieutenant after the 1930s, a gifted organizer, and future founder of Little Flock's spin-off sect known as the Shouters (Huhanpai). Li, a native of Chefoo (Yantai), Shandong, had spearheaded in 1943 an "evangelistic migration" (*fuyin yimin*) movement among Little Flock followers there. During that year, he mobilized many to give up "all their possessions" in support of some one hundred families of the Chefoo Christian Assembly, who were dispatched to found gospel communities in Manchuria and Suiyuan beyond the Great Wall.[71] The venture recalls the practice in the Jesus Family, with which Li was undoubtedly familiar. In 1947, Li began to introduce a similar communalism into the Christian Assembly in Shanghai, which soon received Nee's blessings and spread to other parts of the country.

In what became known as the "hand over" (*jiaochulai*) movement, Nee preached a doctrine of "submission" to the "authority" in the church. He also spread the new "light" of what he termed the Jerusalem Principle, whereby a communistic life would equip "workers" for subsequent individual evangelism. In Fuzhou, the birthplace of the Little Flock, a frenzy of *pochan* (breaking property) took hold as Nee's followers sold their land and other belongings. One turned over his automobile dealership to the church.[72] Elsewhere, members of the Christian Assembly donated significant quantities of cash, jewelry, and gold as well as shops, companies, and stocks. In Shanghai alone, the value of items that were "handed over" totaled an equivalent of US $500,000 by 1948. Nee himself "handed over" the ownership of his pharmaceutical company to the Christian Assembly. Such scorn for worldly possessions was egged on by the steady advance of CCP forces through North China, which entered Beiping in January 1949 and seized Shanghai four months later. As one Shanghai businessman and Little Flock devotee publicly warned, all the property that was not "handed over" to God would eventually be "redistributed" by the Communists.[73]

The Jerusalem Principle also entailed the submission of previously autonomous Assembly churches to central control by "Jerusalem," over which Nee presided.[74] In a particularly rancorous power struggle in Fuzhou in 1948, Nee's followers fought to take over churches that were loyal to Nee's estranged former cofounders of the Christian Assembly.[75] The new concentration of wealth and power in the Little Flock was accompanied by steady gains in its following. In 1948, the Shanghai Assembly registered a membership of close to seventeen hundred, 30 percent of which was made up of students, teachers, and medical professionals. Another 30 percent consisted of roughly equal numbers of workers and merchants. To accommodate them, Nee and his Shanghai associates ordered the construction of a new church on Nanyang Road with a capacity for some twenty-five hundred people. The expansion of both membership and resources fed a new euphoria. Nee began to call, in a militant language, for an evangelical campaign to "conquer all of China."[76] The central strategy, which Nee and his associates developed during the next several years, was "evangelistic migration." It would lead to the creation of new Little Flock communities in inland provinces, including the communistic Christian Faith Collective Farm (Jixin Jiti Nongchang) in Yiyang, Jiangxi, which counted more than two hundred members and was modeled on the Jesus Family.[77]

By the late 1940s, Nee's network of antidenominational and anticlerical Local Churches had become one of the best organized, and also ironically one of the most sectarian and tightly controlled, in China. It had a strict internal hierarchy that began with "young" Christians at the bottom, progressed through "brothers" and "sisters" of varying spiritual ages (at the ranks of "deacon," "elder," and "worker") and ended with "our brother"—the pontifical Nee himself—at the top. One missionary observed that the "clicking sound" Nee made while praying (a result of "imperfectly fitting dentures") was widely imitated; a disaffected former follower sneered that Nee was "swaggering like a goose" on the road of spirituality.[78] Others might also have objected that Nee's sporting of a donated Fiat (which he would sometimes drive out to the scenic Hangzhou) was a flashy display of style even by Shanghai standards. Yet it was also clear that, thanks to Nee's theology, the Little Flock influence had become widespread in denominational churches, particularly the CIM, which formulated a new policy during the war to facilitate greater autonomy of its various congregations.[79] In Sichuan, Guizhou, and Gansu provinces, a number of CIM churches became Local Churches of their respective areas after resident missionaries read Nee's *Rethinking Our Missions*.[80]

Meanwhile, in 1948, the approach of the People's Liberation Army ignited plenty of apocalyptic fervor in the Christian Assembly. In a parallel to student revivalism in Nanjing and Beiping orchestrated by the Inter-Varsity Christian Fellowship of China, Little Flock activists at a Shanghai university took the fire and brimstone to the city streets. Their burning evangelism recalled the picturesque beginning of the Little Flock movement in Fuzhou a quarter of a century earlier. Wearing "gospel shirts" splashed with words such as "Turn back, turn back! Why perish?" Nee's young followers marched through the commercial center of the city, chanting "Repent, Oh Shanghai!" In spring 1949, with the People's Liberation Army poised to cross the Yangzi River, Li Changshou invoked the majestic power of Moses' God to "drown the entire Communist army in the Yangzi River" as he did the "army of the Pharaoh."[81]

THE CHURCH AFTER 1949

The Communist victory in 1949 did not immediately lead to nationwide suppression of Christianity, although sporadic "persecution" that had been reported in CCP-controlled areas during the civil war continued. In May 1950, the new government began orchestrating a movement to promote "self-government, self-support, and self-propagation" (*zizhi, ziyang, zichuan*) in the Protestant church (which would gain new urgency following the outbreak of the Korean War a month later). A Christian Manifesto was proclaimed in the name of dozens of church leaders selected by the CCP. It called on all churches to sever their ties with foreign missions and to promote "anti-imperialistic, anti-feudalistic and anti-bureaucratic-capitalistic education" in their work.[82] In 1951, the government dictated the creation of the Three-Self Committee as the new national organization representing the Protestant church. As a result, the NCC was marginalized and would dissolve in 1955. (For the Roman Catholics, a separate Catholic Patriotic Association would be created in 1957.) Also in 1951, the government began expropriating all the Protestant educational, medical, and publication enterprises. By 1952, almost all foreign missionaries had left the country.[83]

Leading the Three-Self movement was Wu Yaozong (Y. T. Wu, 1893–1979), general secretary for publications of the National Committee of the YMCA after 1938, whose search for a messianic redemption of Chinese society had led him from the Social Gospel to Communism by the mid-1940s. Frank W. Price likened him to an "Old Testament prophet" whose "soul is seared by the social sins and injustices."[84] Wu Yaozong was not alone in the quest for an unlikely union between Christian faith and Marxist belief. During the last years of the anti-Japanese war, pro-Communist sentiments had run high among many Christian students in Nationalist-controlled West China. Earlier, progressive Christian intellectuals such as Wu Leichuan (1870–1944), chancellor of Yenching University, had also sought the Kingdom of God in a "new social order" and claimed that Jesus was a "revolutionary."[85] By the late 1940s, even Chen Chonggui, the popular conservative preacher of the 1930s, had become increasingly vocal in his sympathies for the CCP, which he saw as representing the poor, the vast majority of the Chinese population. In 1950, a senior CIM missionary in Central China lamented that Chen, "a CIM protégé . . . has gone for the new regime hook, line, and sinker." In 1954, Chen would become the vice chairman of the national Three-Self Committee.[86]

As a whole, the Three-Self movement in its early stage targeted mission-supported denominational churches and did not immediately threaten independent Protestant groups. Conversely, the typical initial response among the latter was to seek the tolerance—even court the favor—of the new government by openly supporting the Three-Self campaign (and gingerly citing their long-established practice of self-support). The Jesus Family not only eagerly endorsed the Christian Manifesto, it also dispatched a "Jesus Family Resist America-Aid Korea Medical Team" to the war front within months of the outbreak of the Korean War.[87] In 1951, while it remained in the good favor of the state, the Jesus Family, further tightening its own belt, even provided financial support to the School of Religion at Yenching University when the latter lost American funding. As a result, it won admirers in that unlikely place long known for its modernist disdain for the "spirituals." As Zhao Zichen recalled, some students "started to swoon and fall on the ground, shaking and screaming, and were 'filled with the Holy Spirit.'"[88]

FIGURE 18 Wu Yaozong (Y. T. Wu), from MRL6, D. W. Lyon Papers, Box 2. Courtesy of the Burke Library Archives (Columbia University Libraries) at Union Theological Seminary, New York.

In the early 1950s, the TJC was also left alone by the government. In 1952, its leader Wei Yisa wrote an abject "self-examination" admitting that the "self-support" often touted by the sect had actually come from the "exploiting class" of "bureaucrats and capitalists." He pledged that the TJC would reform itself and "accept the leadership" of the Three-Self movement.[89] So did the Little Flock. In fact, Watchman Nee publicly "repented" of the "sin" of the ineffective Three-Selfs—a mere "theological" but not "political" independence—that the Little Flock had practiced during its thirty years of existence and added that he had come to realize that "foreigners that are not imperialists are hard to find."[90] Wang Mingdao, on the other hand, offered a daring resistance to the Three-Self movement. In a long article titled "We, Because of Faith" published in June 1955, Wang contended that the Three-Self Committee headed by Wu Yaozong was made up of modernist "unbelievers" with which a fundamentalist like him had nothing to do. Wang later admitted that he had been emboldened in such defiance because of his previous "victory" in the "spiritual battle" with the Japanese in 1942. If he had not "bent" before the Japanese who "did not speak Chinese," why should he fear the Communists with whom he could "reason" in a common language? (He added, "How did I know that the Communists would not reason with me? They pointed a gun to my head and scared the wits out of me.")[91]

With the launch of successive mass campaigns through the 1950s to eliminate enemies of the revolution and to consolidate CCP rule, it became clear that independent, organized religion was not to have the sufferance of the state. After all, indigenous Protestant sects had all prophesied the coming of a different kingdom from what the Communists ushered in. In 1952, the Jesus Family—whose communalism entailed a tighter organization than other groups and whose millenarian exuberance was deemed politically subversive and "reactionary"—became the first to be forcefully disbanded. Jing Dianying was denounced at the mass "reform" meetings staged by the government and subsequently imprisoned; his close associate Dong Hengxin, the gifted songwriter, committed suicide. Almost all the subfamilies were disbanded. Jing himself died of cancer in 1957. In line with the ascetic ideal he had upheld since the 1920s, he instructed his relatives to wrap him only in a straw mat for a "plain burial."[92]

In August 1955, at the start of a nationwide movement to "eliminate counterrevolutionaries" (and just weeks after the publication of his defiant article), Wang Mingdao's independent ministry also came to an end. He was arrested on counterrevolutionary charges; his Christian Tabernacle was closed down.[93] At about the same time, Gu Ren'en, the flamboyant actor-turned-preacher who had taken after John Sung in his riotous revivalism, was also silenced. Gu was known to have brandished a sword onstage and vowed to kill the "great red dragon" (Rev. 12:3). At one of his evangelistic meetings that featured faith healing, two Public Security agents feigning illness went up on the platform to receive the laying on of Gu's hand. Then, as the evangelist pronounced them healed and the congregation chanted "Praise the Lord!" the two produced their police identification cards, proclaimed him a swindler, and arrested him.[94]

The crackdown on the Little Flock came in 1956, when it had gained a following of at least eighty thousand members in 870 congregations nationwide. Watchman Nee had been arrested in 1952 on charges of tax evasion and theft of state property by his pharmaceutical company. His incarceration came in the heat of the "five-anti" campaign launched in January 1952 against the economic "crimes" (bribery, tax evasion, fraud, the stealing of state property, and the theft of economic secrets) of the still active industrialists and business leaders from the Republican period and was unrelated to his leadership of the Christian Assembly. In 1954, with Nee in prison, the Little Flock leadership decided to pull out of the Three-Self movement. In January 1956, the government rounded up most of the sect's leaders throughout China—members of the "Ni Tuosheng Counterrevolutionary Clique"—and sentenced them to long prison terms. The authorities also installed a new leadership for the Christian Assembly, which promptly "expelled" Nee from the church.[95] Both Li Yuanru and Wang Peizhen, Nee's chief associates after 1927, reportedly apostatized while in prison.[96] Nee himself would die of heart failure in a labor camp in 1972, six months after the death of his wife. In his last letters addressed to her kin, he wrote of his "grief" and "regret" as he "looked back on the dust of the past." Longing to "return like a fallen leaf to its root," he pleaded with one of them to take him in when he left the camp. He never did.[97]

The ordeal for the TJC began in 1957 when Wei Yisa became the first TJC leader to be arrested. As the Anti-Rightist campaign that had started in the summer of that year extended into the "religious circles," dozens of TJC leaders were also arrested as counterrevolutionaries in 1958 on vague charges that the apocalyptic teaching and Pentecostal practice of the sect had been unruly and reactionary and that their faith healing practice had resulted in many deaths.[98] Nationwide, some two thousand Protestant leaders became Rightists, including Chen Chonggui, Jia Yuming, and Yang Shaotang, all of whom had served as senior Three-Self movement leaders during the early 1950s. With the start of the Great Leap Forward in 1958, denominational leaders throughout the country were urged to participate in productive labor and to hold only joint interdenominational worship on Sundays. The result was the closing of more than twenty thousand churches.[99] The numerically modest congregations of the Spiritual Gifts Society, which had held on to a subdued Pentecostalism during the early 1950s, were also dissolved in the merger of denominational churches that year. Fewer than one hundred churches remained open in the entire country. By 1966, at the start of the Cultural Revolution, they too were closed.[100]

For the indigenous church movement, the two decades of war and revolution that began in 1937 was a period of unprecedented growth. But by 1958, it had come to an abrupt, distressing end. In the early 1950s—before they were swept away by mass political campaigns—various independent groups counted a total following of some two hundred thousand, or about one-fifth of the estimated one million Protestants in China.[101] During the same period, leadership in denominational churches increasingly passed into Chinese hands. The Three-Self movement orchestrated by the new government after 1950 merely hijacked a locomotive that had already departed the old train station. The vigorous expansion of indigenous sects, often at the expense of Western missions, underscored a growing nationalistic assertiveness of Chinese preachers. At times it was strident and antagonistic toward denominational missions. More often it masqueraded as fundamentalist self-assurance, which swelled at a time when Western missionaries were being forced out of China by forces beyond their control.

Ecclesiastical developments during this period also accentuated both Pentecostal tendencies and the dominance of conservative theology among indigenous groups and—at the grassroots level—within mainline Protestant Christianity as well. Even Zhao Zichen, the Yenching theologian and preeminent liberal of the 1930s, came to echo Watchman Nee's teachings of the Cross and yearned for a "union" with Christ in "his death." A brief period of solitary confinement under the Japanese in 1942 had broken his modernist spirit and brought him, momentarily, to the realization of the "emptiness" and "arrogance" of a reformist Christianity of "character."[102] As Zhao Junying observed, "the hunger in the human heart and the spiritual vacuum" during the war years "could not be filled with a humanistic Christianity."[103] In the late 1940s, a minority of radical patriotic Protestants looked to Communism for a new heaven and new earth. Most popular preachers, including Zhao Junying, fed that hunger with an undiluted end-time salvationism instead. In doing so, they stamped a distinct apocalyptic character on Chinese Christianity that would remain striking in the decades to come. The tempest of the revolution may have subdued the eschatological fire by 1966, but the smoldering premillenarian anticipation of the Second Coming continued. Fresh messianic and Pentecostal flames awaited the first change of political wind.

CHAPTER NINE

Cries in the Wilderness

THE UNDERGROUND CHURCH IN THE
COMMUNIST ERA

WHEN THE CULTURAL REVOLUTION began in 1966, Christianity in China was facing a bleak and uncertain future: having been abruptly weaned from Western missions, it now found itself in the hands of an enraged state. For many, the reassertion of central authority in 1949 after four decades of postdynastic chaos had also altered the eschatological landscape. The "last hour" that in the first half of the twentieth century had been heralded by warlordism, banditry, foreign invasion, civil war, and the attending miseries was now manifested in the hostilities of an atheist government—the new Antichrist. In its moments of revolutionary ecstasy, the new regime had also been forthright about its enmity toward religion. At the start of the Great Leap Forward in 1958 and during the Cultural Revolution, the CCP twice attempted to "wipe out all forms of religion in China."[1] Such strident language in fact paled beside the actual violence unleashed against the guardians and practitioners of various faiths in the country. After August 1966, when the Red Guards spearheaded the campaign to destroy "old customs, old habits, old culture, and old thinking" (the "four olds"), church leaders joined hundreds of thousands of other "ox demons and snake gods" at the receiving end of the wrath of revolutionary exorcists. Historian Gu Changsheng estimates that between 1950 and 1978, some five hundred thousand Christians, both Catholic and Protestant, died from CCP persecution, half of those during the Cultural Revolution.[2]

The effects of the antireligious policies of the CCP on the Christian church were perhaps most visible in bonfires made of Bibles and hymnbooks, in decapitated cathedral spires, in sealed doors of church buildings and their conversion into government offices or warehouses, and in parades of "reactionary" priests and ministers, wearing dunce caps, through city streets. Throughout the country, church leaders were dragged into public "struggle meetings" to be humiliated or beaten; countless were sent to "cowsheds" (improvised places of confinement for the "ox demons") and labor camps or driven to suicide or apostasy. Yang Shaotang, former leader of the Spiritual Action Team in Shanxi who had become a senior member of the national Three-Self Committee, was reportedly ordered by the Red Guards to shovel ice from the road and died of a heart attack on the street. Zhu Dawei (David Zhu), a prominent Shanghai pastor, not only renounced his faith but also etched his break with Jesus in a new name. He became Zhu Dage, or Zhu the Great Revolutionary.[3]

As the Cultural Revolution raged on, Zhang Chunqiao, CCP head in Shanghai and later a member of the "Gang of Four," declared that the Red Guards had "wiped out" all religions in the Shanghai area "overnight." Party leaders in other parts of China likely made similar claims at the time.[4] Yet evidence has emerged that Christianity did not suffer the same fate as it did under the imperial suppression of foreign religions during the late Tang dynasty or at the collapse of the Yuan order when the alien faith was extirpated along with the Mongol rulers. As in the case of the Qing ban on the Catholic faith after the 1720s, Christianity was merely driven underground during the 1960s and 1970s. In a parallel to Roman Catholicism, which had long struck root among the rural masses, Protestant Christianity also produced its indigenous leaders and messengers of God as well as tens of millions of devotees in the twentieth century. The forced departure of Western missionaries during the 1950s hastened the transformation of Christianity into a Chinese faith, and the ruthless suppression by the state helped cast this faith firmly into the mold of end-time messianism. After the opening of China in 1979, Christianity made a startling comeback. By 2000, there were fifteen million registered Protestants along with five million members of the official Catholic Church. By some estimates, an additional thirty million Protestants and several million Catholics joined underground churches. Within five decades of the departure of Western missionaries, the Protestant population in China increased almost fiftyfold.[5]

During the last two decades of the twentieth century, the vigorous resurgence of Protestant Christianity was most visible in reopened Three-Self Patriotic Movement (TSPM) churches in cities across China that overflowed with worshipers. The authorities' close supervision of religion also resulted in a prescribed official Protestantism that preached moderate, evangelical doctrines along with the virtues of being "modest, honest, patient," and patriotic. On the other hand, a very different Chinese Christianity persisted in the underground through the political turmoil and religious persecution of the Mao years and remained beyond the control of the Communist state afterwards. At once more spontaneous, fervent, and unruly, it maintained the characteristic fiery spirit of the independent churches of the Nationalist period. In fact, the unabated hostility of the authorities toward unregistered churches would fill popular Protestantism with dark, apocalyptic beliefs that periodically spawned new millenarian sects. It was in the unofficial churches where one would find the heartbeat of the Christianity of China's masses and glimpse the future of Chinese Protestantism, which, at the turn of the twenty-first century, was already poised to rival the CCP in total membership. By then, it was probably also bringing more people into church on any given Sunday than in all of Europe.[6]

As we survey major developments in underground Protestant Christianity under Communist rule and particularly after the late 1960s, several features are discernible: by and large, it grew out of independent church groups of the pre-1949 era. From the beginning, those groups had typically rejected formal theological education as mere human contrivance and therefore devoid of divine sanction or spiritual value. The antinomian attitude only deepened when such education came under the direction of what they called Three-Self "unbelievers." In the absence of institutionalized theological training, ecclesiastical authority often derived from individual charisma and "spiritual gifts." It also tended to be passed along in a patron-client, or master-disciple, relationship that is reminiscent of the transmission of the "mantle and alms bowl" (*yibo*) in the Chan (Meditation) School of Chinese Buddhism.

While house churches typically developed hierarchical, sometimes elaborate, organizations, the beliefs and practice of those groups have been subject to idiosyncrasies and a degree of unpredictability. The multiplying of spin-off sects has taken on a life of its own. The Pentecostal exuberance that was never enervated by the CCP repression of religion has readily reawakened to confirm the potency of the Christian faith and of each of its new sectarian variations. As socialized health care degenerated and increasingly disappeared during the reform era, the "gifts" of healing and exorcism, which resonated profoundly with magic and sorcery in folk religion, came to play a vital role in the life of the Christian masses. What has also endured in the evolution of popular Protestantism is its apocalyptic disposition—inherited from the teachings of the major indigenous groups and, above all, from the works of Watchman Nee. By the late twentieth century, a Chinese Christian eschatology had already come of age and started to procreate. Meanwhile, the militancy of popular Christianity that had earlier targeted Western missions was increasingly redirected toward the Communist state. Each new crackdown on illicit religion only confirmed the reality of the Antichrist and the approach of the cosmic end.

THE 1970S AND 1980S

In a broad sense, underground Christianity has existed since the 1950s, when various groups rejected compromises with atheist authorities and practiced their faith outside the Three-Self establishment. During the Cultural Revolution, the only Christianity that remained was underground.[7] In the late 1960s, some twenty thousand Little Flock followers were reportedly active in Fuqing county, Fujian province, near the provincial capital Fuzhou. In Fuzhou itself, unauthorized Little Flock "house" meetings also began in 1970. In the early 1970s, "possibly 50,000 Christians" were holding illicit meetings in the Wenzhou area in the south of Zhejiang province. During the same period, Seventh-Day Adventists in South and Southeast China also maintained small "house churches."[8]

Also in Fuqing, "more than ninety percent" of the TJC congregations that had been disbanded between 1958 and 1966 were reportedly revived by 1973. The resurgence was spurred on by the testimony of an eighty-one-year-old woman who fell into a trance and, guided by an angel who spoke in Fuqing dialect, attended a series of "Kingdom of Heaven gatherings" in a celestial hall. With the publication and dissemination of her visions in an underground booklet, as many as one thousand people were baptized into the local TJC house churches each year. In 1978, on the eve of the official reopening of churches, a Jiangsu TJC faithful and a former sailor on inland waterways named Wang Yuansong, who had been diagnosed with lung cancer, burst into the murky religious underworld as a carrier of the TJC flame: he went through more than twenty cities and counties in seventeen provinces and almost single-handedly reconnected the sect's scattered congregations and their former leaders. In doing so, he helped prepare the ground for the mushrooming of TJC churches after 1979.[9] In Weishan county in south Shandong, a small Jesus Family persisted through the 1950s and early 1960s even after the dissolution of the original settlement at Mazhuang. During an unlikely period from the end of the 1960s to the early 1970s, a "spiritual revival" was also reported in the hinterland province of Gansu. Some saw "in a dream that the old vines along the sides of the Yellow River were sprouting new leaves and prophesied that the Lord would himself open the door of the church." A leader of that revival was a former general in Feng Yuxiang's Christian Army who had turned into a preacher after leaving Feng's army.[10]

In Henan during the early 1970s, the Fangcheng Church (Fangcheng Jiaohui), named after its county of origin in the southwest of the province and which would become the largest underground church network by the century's end with millions of followers, began to take shape in defiance of the strict ban on religion. Historically, the area was a CIM mission field; however, after the departure of Western missionaries around 1944, some groups came under the banner of the Little Flock. By the early 1970s, a new generation of freelance evangelists had emerged under the influence of older Little Flock and other indigenous preachers, including Li Tian'en (Li Musheng, 1928–), who had spent his early years in the Jesus Family and had been arrested in 1960 as an independent evangelist. After his release from a labor camp in 1970, Li returned to Fangcheng, his home county, where he helped build the Fangcheng Church. Among the young zealots he cultivated was Zhang Rongliang (1951–), the future Fangcheng leader. Zhang had barely survived the famine during the Great Leap Forward. He was secretly baptized in 1969 but carried on as a CCP deputy secretary of his production brigade during the early 1970s until his arrest as a "religious counterrevolutionary" in 1974. In those days, many illegal Protestant groups in rural Henan in fact throve under the protection of commune or production brigade cadres whose family members were believed to have been cured of their diseases by Jesus "the Great Healer."[11]

Elsewhere in China, the search for Christian faith healing and exorcism—an appealing substitute for similar practice in folk religion—likewise emboldened people to flout the atheist rules of the state. During the 1970s, Protestantism also found an earnest following among the traditionally Hakka population in Meixian, Guangdong, where sorceresses had been doing "a flourishing business." Some reportedly turned to Christianity for more efficacious healing and casting out of demons, prompting a few of the sorceresses themselves to "believe in Jesus." By the end of the decade, some local women were known to belong to one "Holy Spirit Church"; they spoke in "tongues" and "trembled" when they prayed.[12] Among ethnic minorities in southwestern China, evidence that Christianity had not been suppressed during the Cultural Revolution can be gleaned from reports of continuing campaigns against "counterrevolutionary" Protestant groups. In 1973, an underground pastor active in northern Yunnan "was executed at a mass rally before more than 10,000 people, most of them Christians forced to attend." The following year, "a secret Christian meeting of Miao people" in Guizhou was broken up "by armed militia," ending in "a bloody incident." In that Miao community on the periphery of Han-dominated society, which had long faced a hostile world of poverty and "demonic oppression and possession," and which had been "periodically . . . swept by pagan 'messianic' movements promising a king as a deliverer," the Christians "drew great strength from biblical teaching on the second coming."[13]

Until political and economic liberalizations began to be introduced in the late 1970s, however, the occasional, spontaneous flare-up of banned Protestant Christianity remained isolated and mostly contained. Financial constraints aside, the household registration (hukou) system restricted personal mobility and rendered itinerant evangelism impractical. Large gatherings (except on such occasions as funerals and weddings) were prohibited. Any significant expansion of religious activities would be swiftly brought under the iron hand of local governments. In late 1978, at the start of the Deng Xiaoping era (which lasted until 1997)—and as part of the CCP effort to regain popular support and reclaim its legitimacy after decades of destructive political campaigns—the party leadership moved to implement more moderate policies that included guarantees of the "freedom of religious beliefs." The reopening of churches began in 1979, as did the release and rehabilitation of imprisoned religious leaders. (Wang Mingdao, who refused to leave prison unless the government admitted that it had wrongfully incarcerated him as a counterrevolutionary, was tricked out of prison without the apology he demanded.) The new religious policy was spelled out in what became known as Document No. 19 issued by the CCP Central Committee in March 1982. It classified religious problems as "contradictions among the people" and decreed that religious and ethnic communities were to be brought into a "patriotic political alliance" to further the struggle for China's modernization.[14]

To maintain supervision and control of various religious groups, the state brought back the mechanism that had been in place before the Cultural Revolution. For the Protestant community, the TSPM Committee was revived in 1979. The following year, the government also sanctioned the creation of the seemingly less political China Christian Council (Zhongguo Jidujiao Xiehui). While the function of the TSPM was defined as uniting Christians "so as to take an active part in socialist construction," the new Christian Council would focus on "improving the pastoral care of Christians all over China."[15] Presiding over both organizations from 1981 to 1996 was Ding Guangxun (K. H. Ting, 1915–), an Anglican bishop and president of Nanjing Theological Seminary after 1952. Like his predecessor Wu Yaozong, Ding became the symbol of Protestant efforts to gain official tolerance even as the church was compelled to conform to the demands of the Communist state. On one hand, he led a determined TSPM struggle, often with support from various levels of the People's Congress and the People's Political Consultative Conference, to pressure local governments to "implement" the CCP's new religious policy and to reclaim confiscated church properties; on the other hand, he also attempted a liberal "reconstruction" of Chinese theology that would bring the church in line with the party's endeavor to build a modern socialist, and worldly, kingdom. Not surprisingly, he preached a "confluence" of "all the progressive, democratic, and humanitarian movements of humankind" (of which socialism in China was one) with "the redemptive work of Christ."[16]

In the last two decades of the twentieth century, under the auspices of the TSPM, sixteen thousand churches and thirty-two thousand registered "meeting-points" were established (an average of about six new congre-

gations added each day).[17] Since the state had forcefully ended denominationalism in 1958, Protestantism reappeared in the open theoretically
as a "postdenominational" faith with "unified" worship services. Most
of the former mission churches did seem to lack enthusiasm for their
denominational identities and allowed themselves to be designated Three-
Self churches. For their part, smaller independent groups such as the
Spiritual Gifts Society and the Spiritual Food Church were unable to gain
official recognition as distinct entities. There was also no room for Jesus
Family's communalism in the post-Mao era. Of its former settlement
in Mazhuang, only the original chapel was reopened as a TSPM church
in which the members' lively religion was well contained.[18] In Weishan
county, the local Jesus Family community reestablished its settlement in
1983 when the new "production responsibility system" gave peasants the
opportunity for privatized agricultural production and a degree of freedom. However, that attempt at revived Christian communalism turned
out to be short-lived: instead of being dissolved by the government, it
disintegrated by itself when economic opportunities bred individualistic
pursuits of wealth.[19]

The two largest indigenous sects, the TJC and the Little Flock, were
removed from the list of illegal organizations. Because of their numerical
strength, both were granted a degree of recognition as distinct groups
within the Three-Self structure. In Hunan, where TJC members accounted
for 110,000 of an estimated total of 150,000 Protestants in the province by
the mid-1990s, a TJC leader was in fact installed as head of the provincial
TSPM committee.[20] In 2002, Ji Jianhong, a Little Flock elder whose father
(a "close associate" of Watchman Nee) had opposed the Three-Self movement, became chairman of the national TSPM.[21] Co-opted by the state,
the approved TJC and Little Flock churches would increasingly be drained
of the kind of apocalyptic fervor that had fueled their earlier growth.

FLEEING "BABYLON": HOUSE CHURCHES DURING THE REFORM ERA

Although many people did flock into and fill up reopened churches to
taste a regained freedom of worship, a significant majority, particularly
those with sectarian backgrounds, failed to find satisfaction in what was to
them a diluted and "woefully compromised" faith. Eventually, they came
to reject the TSPM as an institution where Christ allegedly was no longer

FIGURE 19   Boyan Church, Yongkang, Zhejiang. Source: *Bridge: Church Life in China Today* 73 (October 1995). Used by permission of the Christian Study Centre on Chinese Religion and Culture, Hong Kong.

the undisputed "head" and had indeed been dethroned—TSPM churches typically were led by government-approved clergy who sometimes appeared more eager to please officials of the Religious Affairs Bureau than their own congregations. The result was the rise of competing house churches, which often decried their official counterparts as "Babylon" and "the whore" and featured their own independent preachers whose spiritual authority had not been sapped by any perceived conformity to the world. Those preachers, mostly itinerant, also took advantage of a more basic deficiency of the TSPM: the opening of approved churches, largely concentrated in cities and towns, could not keep up with the rapid expansion of the rural Protestant population, which made up around 70 percent of the national figure. Neither could the number of trained clergy. Only a few thousand graduates of theological seminaries were produced during the 1980s and 1990s. The result was a dire shortage of pastors. Since many remote villages were dozens of miles from the nearest church or minister, the void was often filled by those with the greatest zeal and the strongest, though not always the most predictable, convictions.[22]

FIGURE 20 A woman prays at her husband's grave in remote northwest China.
Source: *Christianity Today*, July 13, 1998. Courtesy of Tony Carnes, Image and
Memory Project.

As we have seen, the phenomenon of illegal churches was not new, but the new government policy of the late 1970s—which both opened the floodgate of religious fervor and attempted to direct it through the narrow channel of state-supervised worship—resulted in an overflow of unapproved piety. The release and reactivation of imprisoned or otherwise persecuted Protestant leaders also guaranteed an abundant supply of explosive evangelistic energy in underground Christianity. Their fierce religious devotion and fundamentalist opposition to the TSPM now appeared vindicated, and their martyrdom had become a spiritual asset. In its early stage, the house church movement of the post-Mao period was spearheaded by those with intimate ties to the indigenous sects or the independent preachers of the pre-1949 period.[23] In many cases, their sectarian backgrounds provided them with a well-developed eschatology that was radically opposed to the existing political and social order. Among rural congregations in particular, poverty, insecurity, and powerlessness in the face of widening income gaps and the rapacity of corrupt officials produced a restless and expectant underclass thirsty for spiritual solace and ready for millenarian deliverance; the reform policy of the Deng Xiaoping era, which at first benefited the peasants with its "production responsibility system," gradually left them behind and exposed them to new threats ranging from inflation and environmental degradation to land seizures.

Meanwhile, the Pentecostal tradition handed down from the Republican era readily rekindled ecstasies in the underground and brought triumphs over sickness, poverty, and other evils of the world. The common practice of lay leadership and emphasis on "spiritual gifts" allowed for the rapid ascendance of charismatic figures to the center stage of unofficial Protestantism; widespread illiteracy and the customary submissiveness of the masses molded by an ageless authoritarian tradition facilitated their easy transformation into messianic, cultic figures. Typically furnished with minimal education, many of the sectarian leaders hailed from the class of "lumpen proletariat," a dubious distinction granted by the country's top Religious Affairs official, but rose to attract hundreds of thousands of followers.[24] They promised divine favors, group solidarity, and exclusive salvation—and demanded loyalty, tithes, and unconditional obedience. The same religious culture ensured their swift replacements after government crackdowns.

In the early 1980s, unregistered TJC congregations accounted for much of underground Christianity. As many TJC devotees in Hunan found out, it was only outside the Three-Self churches that they were able to maintain the intensity of their apocalyptic fervor, their preference for healing with "a cup of cold water" given "to the little ones," and their "great water baptism" (in a natural body of water such as river, stream, or lake) decreed by the sect. Such insistence on "legitimate" baptism would create suspicious scenes of furtive gatherings with women "coming out of a river in dripping clothes."[25]

The TJC tradition also gave rise to one of the earliest illicit church networks in the post-Mao period. Known as the Spirit-Spirit Sect (Ling-lingjiao), it was founded in 1983 by Hua Xuehe, a TJC activist and an elementary school teacher in northern Jiangsu. Like its prototype, the sect distinguished itself with spiritual singing, dancing, trances, faith healing, and exorcism. Hua, whose name allegedly missed a perfect correspondence to the Chinese transliteration of Jehovah (Yehehua) by only one character, was proclaimed the Savior (Hua Jiuzhu) and the Christ of the Second Coming. His hometown in northern Jiangsu was renamed the Jerusalem of the East, and his birthday was celebrated as Christmas. Throughout the 1980s, the Spirit-Spirit Sect flourished on a rich Pentecostal diet as well as dire warnings of earthquakes, pestilence, flood, famine, and other tribulations. By 1990, it had spread to more than ten provinces as far as Gansu and Yunnan, prophesying both flood and fire as well as the collapse of heaven and earth. Specific dates for the cosmic catastrophe were announced, when "fire will burn out the old world; the Kingdom of Heaven will come."[26]

PROGENIES OF THE LITTLE FLOCK IN THE LATE TWENTIETH CENTURY

In the 1980s, many apocalyptic, sometimes obscure, groups gathered around charismatic figures of various backgrounds and convictions. Among tribal minorities in southwestern China, for instance, "false cults" with shamanistic features would sprout from congregations of Western denominational origins.[27] However, by far the most important inspiration for the underground church movement came from the Little Flock, whose followers retained their eschatological temperament and varying degrees of opposition to the TSPM. In the coastal provinces of Zhejiang and Fujian, the illegal church primarily consisted of unregistered Little Flock groups. In Zhejiang during the 1980s, nearly all those opposed to the Three-Self churches (estimated at around 120,000 of the total Protestant population of 700,000 in the province) belonged to the sect. Many early reports on the unofficial church in hinterland Henan during the same period also revealed the predominant influence of the teachings of Watchman Nee.[28] Nee's call for an individualistic, mystical union with Christ; his assurances of "higher [or deeper] life" and "rapture" for the Christian Assembly "overcomers"; his contempt for the organized church and formal theological training; and, above all, his uncovering of the premillennial, dispensationalist "blueprint" of God generated seemingly endless sectarian, and cultic, energy. In fact, a significant evolution of the Little Flock occurred while Nee was still alive but locked away in a labor camp. It began in Taiwan, under the leadership of Li Changshou, one of Nee's former lieutenants. With Nee and his chief associates in mainland China put out of action by the mid-1950s, Li emerged as the new patriarch in overseas Little Flock assemblies. After the late 1960s, Li took the Local Church (the Little Flock's preferred self-designation) down a new path— in quest of what he called the "release of the spirit" by way of "shouting." His followers later became known as the Shouters (Huhanpai).[29]

The Shouters' pursuit of a spirited form of worship unencumbered by either ecclesiastic formalism or neighbors' objections to nighttime noise can be traced back to 1931 when Li's hometown Yantai in northeastern Shandong was in the grip of riotous Pentecostal ecstasies. During that summer, an "explosion" inside Li had sent him dashing up a hill and "shouting" the name of Jesus. Li carried that energy with him when he later joined the Little Flock, but as long as Nee reigned in the sect, Li's Pentecostal predilection was held in check.[30] By the late 1950s, Li was already impatient with the theological rigidity within the Little Flock; he also appeared to have felt an increasing hollowness and irrelevance of Nee's teachings of the Cross for the sect's overseas (and increasingly affluent) followers. Although he inherited Nee's eschatology and continued to inculcate a worship of Nee as the end-time "seer of the divine revelation," Li also employed Nee's dispensationalist language to justify his own innovation, declaring that the "age of the Word" had passed, giving way to the "age of the Spirit," over which he presided. Accordingly, he preached a turn from "teachings" to the "Spirit," by means of which one "eats, drinks, and enjoys the Lord" with vehement shouting. In 1962, Li made a permanent move from Taiwan to Los Angeles, where he eventually established the Living Stream Ministry to oversee dozens of Little Flock congregations in a few U.S. cities. With a total following of only about five thousand in North America by the 1970s, Li's scattered, though animated, congregations faced almost certain oblivion.[31]

The "opening" of China and the lifting of the CCP ban on religion during the Deng Xiaoping era also lifted the Shouters of Southern California and their kin in Taiwan out of anonymity. As early as 1979, their evangels began to join the throngs of overseas Chinese and other foreign tourists who crossed into the mainland from Hong Kong. The bagfuls of Bibles and Shouters' tracts (as well as occasional stacks of cash) that Li Changshou's messengers carried were limited in amount. However, in the early 1980s, they represented spiritual, and material, fortunes to those underground church leaders who linked up with the overseas brethren. After Nee's death, Li enjoyed an unrivaled prestige among the sect's followers in China. As a result, his doctrines struck fire almost overnight in underground congregations that were already disillusioned with the TSPM's perceived adulterations of the Christian faith. In both the southeastern coastal provinces and the rural hinterland of Henan— two separate strongholds of the underground church that were linked together in 1980 by Little Flock networks—the Shouters built their major bases of operation.[32]

There was obvious buoyancy and vigor in the movement: the magic of "shouting" was simple and easily acquired; Li's urge to physically consume the divine was intoxicating. Likewise, there was an infectious revolutionary spirit in Li's call (directed particularly at the young) for a "break" with "old religion," including all the "organizations . . . and teachings of Christianity" (as Jesus himself had done with Judaism).[33] In many rural Little Flock congregations in coastal China, "shouting" broke out daily from 3:00 a.m. to 5:00 a.m. and resumed in the evenings. In the Wenzhou area, many young Shouters stopped their work and "met as often as fifteen times a week."[34] In Henan, where the influence of the Shouters remained strong throughout the 1980s, many were baptized in the name of Li Changshou, who they claimed was the "victor from the east" prophesied in Isaiah, the "successor to Jesus," and the one foretold in the Book of Revelation who would "open the scroll and its seven seals."[35]

In incidents in Zhejiang that recalled the Red Guards of the Cultural Revolution, Li's devotees armed with "big character posters" stormed official churches, denouncing the TSPM as "the great whore" and pledging themselves to a battle with "the powers." Others invoked the militant language that Watchman Nee had adopted in the late 1940s and vowed to "conquer" all of China within two years; the diehards were also prepared to "oppose Communism to the end." Some went insane, and sexual scandals of late-night Shouters were also reported. The crackdown on the group as a "heretic cult" (*xiejiao*) came in 1983 when, according to the government, the Shouters had already built a following of more than two hundred thousand "deluded people" in twenty provinces. Across China, the "meeting points" of the Shouters were raided and shut down; hundreds were arrested. In what became a pattern of police violence against "cult" members, many were beaten and tortured in prison; some died.[36]

The banning of the Shouters marked the start of nationwide campaigns against a string of "heretic cults" in the post-Mao era. It was an ominous beginning: the wrath and violence that the state unleashed validated the apocalyptic vision that lay at the heart of sectarian movements; it also started a cycle of suppression and defiant resurgence, each reigniting the other. The organizational flexibility and adaptability of underground groups aided their survival in an increasingly mobile society. Despite its ferocity, the clampdown on illegal religious groups proved to be largely ineffective and may indeed have spurred the sectarian proliferation and mutation since the 1980s. As a result, the state often appeared to be losing ground in the battle between earthly power and unearthly visions. Two decades after it was outlawed, the Shouters sect reportedly grew to include five hundred thousand followers.[37]

The suppression also accelerated the emergence of its offshoots. The first to appear was the Weepers (Kupai), formed in central Henan in 1984 and named after their distinctive practice of teary, even howling, repentance and public confession of sins. Its leader Xu Yongze was born in 1940 into a family of Lutheran converts who had come under the Pentecostal influence of Marie Monsen. Xu had had "a vision of God at the age of five." During the early 1970s, like Zhang Rongliang of the Fangcheng Church, Xu was apprenticed to the recently freed Li Tian'en, an experience that reinforced his Pentecostal leaning and turned him subsequently into a prominent underground preacher in Henan. In 1980, Xu and Zhang

Rongliang traveled to Guangzhou to meet with the messengers of the Shouters. They brought back the teachings of Li Changshou, which spread through the Fangcheng Church as well as other underground groups in Henan. After the crackdown on the Shouters in 1983—dozens were arrested in Fangcheng county alone—many went into hiding. With the Shouters in disarray, Xu took the opportunity to launch his new evangelistic venture from Pingdingshan near central Henan the following year.[38]

Among the Weepers, each believer was encouraged to be an "imitator" of John Sung, whose theatricals became a standard of sanctification. Sobbing accompanied their preaching and hymn singing and punctuated their meetings. Protracted weeping would culminate in visions of divine forgiveness, especially the sighting of a person in a white robe appearing in a blinding light to cross out one's sins from a list. Many went to extremes of remorse and self-inflicted pain—slapping their own faces, beating their chests, rolling on the ground, or kneeling in rain-drenched fields—in quest of such moments of spiritual sublimity. The emotional crisis both generated and relieved through weeping undergirded the group's claim to exclusive salvationism, for those who had not properly wept had not been "born again." Many took vows of chastity in view of "the coming of the great tribulation"; others forsook their families "for the Kingdom of Heaven."[39] Meanwhile, many sought the miracles of healing. According to the government, within a few years, the Weepers developed an extensive network across fifteen provinces and autonomous regions with "tens of thousands" of members. In 1988, the clampdown on the group started, but in a sign of the weakening of the party-state's control apparatus, Xu was able to elude authorities for several years. By the time of his arrest in 1997, the sect claimed to have five hundred thousand members.[40]

By most accounts, several major networks of unregistered churches in the 1990s remained within the bounds of evangelical Christianity. These included the South China Church (Huanan Jiaohui), an offshoot of the Weepers, and the Blessed Church of China (Zhonghua Mengfu Jiaohui), centered in Fuyang, Anhui. By far the largest networks were the Fangcheng Church and the China Gospel Fellowship (Zhonghua Fuyin Tuanqi), both of which were based in southern Henan, the "Jesus Nest" of China (a title bestowed by exasperated local officials).[41] A poor, overcrowded province in the rural heartland with a population approaching one hundred million, Henan was also the center of the AIDS epidemic in the country, with an estimated five hundred thousand to seven hundred thousand people infected with the human immunodeficiency virus in the late 1990s after selling their blood under poorly protected conditions.[42] Not surprisingly, among Christians, the fierce rural desperation there cried out for an urgent, manifest divine intervention. Outside the Weepers, the emotional spiritual quest in the underground found a seemingly orthodox channel in Pentecostal worship.

Although Pentecostalism in its modified, sectarian form—especially the Jesus Family and the TJC—had persisted in the country throughout the early decades of Communist rule, it was gifts such as faith healing, exorcism, and visions, rather than exuberant and clamorous worship, that had been most avidly sought after. In the late 1980s, however, a Hong Kong–based American Pentecostalist named Dennis Balcombe reintroduced "tongues" as part of an emotional, charismatic worship to the house churches in southern Henan. Within years, holy laughter along with spiritual crying, singing, and jumping became widespread in many Fangcheng congregations. After Zhang Rongliang was won over to Pentecostalism, a follower of his named Lü Xiaomin, a young peasant girl in southern Henan, began having visions of heaven (with Zhang and several other house church leaders hoeing in a lush celestial field).[43] Lü was from a minority Hui Muslim family. She had recently dropped out of middle school because of illness and had "contemplated suicide" in her depression. In 1989, she converted to Christianity and soon was inspired by "God's spirit" to compose hymns that were based on folk tunes. Unable to read musical notes herself, she would eventually produce more than one thousand songs, which sang of the loving care of Jesus the "dearest companion" who "raises us from the dust," of "the desert that is no longer desolate," of the "imminent return of the Lord," and of God's protection as the "end-time . . . tribulations" neared. Other songs urged God to "set the Chinese heart on fire" and proclaimed that "one day China will rise." Those lyrics, which alternated between tenderness and flaming revivalist zeal, were later collected into the popular *Songs of Canaan*.[44]

THE ESTABLISHED KING AND THE LORD GOD SECT

For the most part, the emotional intensity among many house churches found its way into lively but uncontroversial worship, which featured local innovations such as the *Songs of Canaan* while clinging to theological orthodoxy. Zhang Rongliang and some other Henan leaders would even seek out anti-TSPM evangelical patriarchs such as Wang Mingdao for their teachings and blessings. (Despite his old age and declining influence, Wang remained an unrivaled symbol of uncompromising faith until his death in 1991.)[45] For other groups, the increased secrecy and isolation after 1983 created an ideal climate for the spread of virulent sectarian and cultic strains of indigenized Christianity. The hostility of the atheist regime against the house church, often accompanied by the excessive use of state violence, only deepened the apocalyptic gloom. Not long after the rise of the Weepers, a Christian group led by the "Established King" (Beiliwang) Wu Yangming (1945–1995) arrived on the scene.

Wu, a farmer from western Anhui, had been arrested four times during the 1980s as a Shouters activist. Upon his release in 1988, he founded a network of his own based in Fuyang, Anhui. Having discovered a reference to himself in Luke 2:34, he styled himself as the Established King, the reincarnated Jesus. He also built an underground theocracy centered on himself as the "father king" (fuwang): it consisted of a five-tiered organization that included offices with such irresistible names as "pure gold," "pearl," and "rose" and that dispatched evangelists two-by-two to proselytize and offer miraculous healing.[46] In worship meetings, Wu sat in a chair covered with a red cloth and placed at the center of the hall while his followers knelt on the ground to pay homage to him. With only a middle-school education, Wu wrote almost twenty religious tracts that developed the mystical and apocalyptic themes of Li Changshou and Watchman Nee. As with the TJC in its early days (and parallel to a similar practice in Buddhist monasteries), Wu bestowed "spiritual names" on all his converts and decreed a degree of ascetic communalism. He also instituted the separation of men and women (and forbade tight-fitting blouses and makeup for women) but, like the Taiping "Heavenly King," cheerfully exempted himself. Many female followers were told to "receive God in nakedness" and to be "cleansed" and "blessed" by offering their bodies to Wu. Dozens were "called" (mengzhao) in this manner. Several illegitimate children were born. (Woe to the one-child policy!) Wu set at least two dates for the end of time, when the Established King would "overthrow the power of Satan" and usher in "a new heaven and a new earth." In 1995, he was arrested, convicted on cult charges, and executed.[47]

Wu's enterprise did not end, however. Two years before his death, a subordinate of his named Liu Jiaguo (1964–2003) had founded a splinter organization known as the Lord God Sect (Zhushenjiao), whose organization and teachings were modeled extensively on the original one. With the help of kinship ties, the group methodically developed an underground following in more than a dozen provinces that eventually grew to more than ten thousand. Like the Taiping Christians, the Lord God Sect created its own Ten Commandments that blended biblical moral teachings with exhortations of submission and self-sacrifice; in line with the dispensationalist teachings of the Little Flock, Liu announced that the third and last "age" was drawing to a close. There would be cosmic disasters, and then the visible "kingdom of the beast" with its "corrupt government . . . ruled by the Devil" would be overthrown; the Lord God would "ascend to his throne in Nanjing" (the "heavenly capital" of the Taiping rebels). In the meantime, the believers were warned not to hoard their money or grains at home but to "deposit" them in the "heavenly kingdom." Subsequently, the group's leaders reportedly collected more than three hundred thousand yuan of cash and twenty thousand kilograms of grains from their devotees. Liu also "bestowed the holy spirit" (through sex) on more than a dozen women and fathered six illegitimate children. He was arrested in 1998 and executed in 2003.[48]

In numerical strength, both the Established King and the Lord God Sect were minor affairs that were more or less brought under control (though not eliminated) once the founders and main leaders were arrested. Yet they pointed beyond themselves to the broader, sustained phenomenon of the cultic thrust in Chinese Protestantism during the late twentieth century that featured dire apocalypticism, opposition to the current political order, tight underground organization, and deification of spiritual leaders along with the typical claims of supernatural power. Three larger cultic groups, which appeared to have penetrated deeper into the religious life of the rural masses, arose during the same period. They were the Disciples' Society (Mentuhui), the Three Grades of Servants (Sanban Puren), and the Lightning out of the East (Dongfang Shandian). By the turn of the twenty-first century, they counted some two million followers. Ostensibly fundamentalist and unwavering in their adherence to biblical literalism, and yet strikingly innovative, they offer intimations of the future of popular Christianity in China. As was true with the Established King and the Lord God Sect, in all three cases, the original flame came from the Little Flock mystical eschatology transmitted through the Shouters in the early 1980s.

THE NARROW GATE IN THE WILDERNESS

The Disciples' Society, also known as the Narrow Gate in the Wilderness (Kuangye Zhaimen), was founded by Ji Sanbao (1940–1997), a farmer in the impoverished southern part of Shaanxi province. In 1977, a year after the tragic death of his two young children, Ji was converted by an underground TJC deacon. After his baptism, miracles began to happen. On one occasion, halfway through his prayer, he saw a shaft of heavenly light thrusting into his wooden chest (the grains storage) and pouring into it "a flood of wheat like water." In 1982, the Shouters' teachings reached southern Shaanxi and provided Ji with a sophisticated frame of cosmic meaning into which he could fit his potent religious experience initiated by the TJC.[49]

As elsewhere, the 1983 nationwide crackdown on the Shouters drove many of its activists in Shaanxi underground; it also eventually set Ji loose from the disrupted network of the banned sect. But he had mastered the dispensationalist syntax transmitted by the Shouters, and it would enable him to crack the apocalyptic code in the Bible on his own. By 1985, Ji began to build a following among the rural population. In 1989, he announced that God had spoken to him in person and installed him as his "prophet" and "stand-in" (*tishen*). Ji in turn appointed twelve "disciples," formalizing the establishment of the Disciples' Society. The group denounced the TSPM as the "wide gate" that "leads to destruction"; the Disciples' Society, which met in farmhouses or in fields, was the Narrow Gate in the Wilderness that "leads to life" (Matt. 7:13–14). In pamphlets such as *The Dream of the Kingdom of Heaven in Hanzhong* (*Hanzhong tianguomeng*), which located the cosmic regeneration in southern Shaanxi, Ji appeared as "the true Dragon, the Son of Heaven" (*zhenlong tianzi*). His more spiritual title as the end-time savior was "the Christ of the Third Redemption" (Sanshu Jidu)—the first two having been offered through Noah's ark and the Cross. Several dates were announced for the end of the world, which would be accompanied by "earthquakes, fire, floods, hail, plagues, and locusts." However, those who joined the society and dedicated themselves to preaching the Gospel would be spared the calamities. Miracles would also follow them: without medicine, the sick would be healed; without the use of fertilizer or pesticide, the faithful would have bumper crops.

Ji's followers were also taught to consume no more than two *liang*—one hundred grams—of grains each day as an expression of their repentance and spirituality. As a result, the group came to be nicknamed *erliang liang* (two *liang* of grains). As long as the believers remained under such spiritual discipline, their wheat and rice would become inexhaustible "grains of life" (*shengming liang*). In remote, mountainous areas of Shaanxi, Sichuan, and Hubei, the Disciples' Society succeeded in establishing its chief bases of operation. Each member was asked to bring at least ten relatives, friends, or neighbors into the group each month and was promised future "grains of life" in proportion to the number of new converts made. Proselytism was made easy with testimonies of faith healing and exorcism as well as generous group aid: "grains of charity" would be brought to the poor, or a free hand would be offered for farm work. The organization of the Disciples' Society—hierarchical, tight, and secretive from the beginning—also became increasingly sophisticated. Eventually, it even established its own underground "banks" and "post offices" to move funds and goods efficiently in the service of the Gospel.[50] The alarmed authorities in the three provinces began their crackdown on the group as early as 1990. In 1995, when it had expanded into fourteen provinces with more than 350,000 members, the Public Security system launched a nationwide campaign against the sect. However, neither the arrest of its core members nor the reported death of Ji Sanbao in an auto accident in 1997 was a deterrent to its continued growth. In the early 2000s, hundreds of thousands of people, most of them in China's northwest, still remained within the Narrow Gate in the Wilderness.[51]

THE THREE GRADES OF SERVANTS

Like "the Christ of the Third Redemption," Xu Shuangfu (1946–2006), the founder of the Three Grades of Servants, emerged from a humble, rural background. Born in southwestern Henan, Xu converted to Christianity in his childhood when the sickness of his mother brought the entire family into the church. At the age of twelve, he became helper to an invalid underground preacher, a former Jesus Family "parent," carrying him on his back as the evangelist made his rounds. Sometime after 1969, when the early paroxysms of the Cultural Revolution had given way to the doldrums of unrelieved poverty in the rural heartland of China, Xu joined a small group of wandering evangelists—several of whom were beggars with Jesus Family ties and were skilled in the art of fasting. (One boasted of a record of seventy-six days without food.) The group also claimed an abundance of spiritual gifts, including those of "tongues," healing, and exorcism. After 1975, Xu was arrested more than half a dozen times on charges of illegal itinerant preaching and "beguiling" and "defrauding" the masses; he reported having been "filled with the Holy Spirit" when Public Security personnel tortured him.

In 1980, Xu joined a loose coalition of anti-TSPM preachers of Henan who had been attracted to the Shouters' teachings. To his austere Jesus Family self-discipline was now added the inspiring theology of Watchman Nee. When the Shouters of Henan were scattered and hunted down in 1983, Xu fled into remote areas of rural Shaanxi where he carried on as an itinerant preacher and began setting dates for the end of the world. In the early 1990s, Xu drifted apart from his erstwhile comrades and developed his own secretive network that became known as the Three Grades of Servants. The name was distilled from the parable that Jesus told of the three servants who were respectively entrusted with five, two, and one talent according to their different abilities. At the top of the structure was Xu himself, the "great servant," who presided over the "small servants," his chief associates. At the provincial level, "handmaids" made up the third grade, who in turn supervised various levels of local "co-workers." The latter were held to a grinding daily schedule of gospel work and a merciless asceticism and could not visit family without permission. Submission to the higher levels of authority that culminated in Xu became the key to salvation. By the mid-1990s, the "great servant" had become the "physical master" of the believers.

By then he had also established in his network the trademark practice of "remission of sin through lashes." A minimum of forty lashes was decreed for spiritual lapses including drowsiness and homesickness. (Grave misdeeds, such as desertion or apostasy, could result in the breaking of arms or the severing of ankle tendons.) All this reminded one of the grim discipline in the Jesus Family, which was reinforced by Xu's own intimate experience of "the Cross"—the essence of Little Flock teachings that Xu claimed to have absorbed through the numerous beatings he received in police detention.[52] It also echoed the search for ascetic discipline outside the Protestant sectarian tradition: in Shandong province during the eighteenth century, members of the Catholic Confraternity of the Passion (Kuhui) had engaged in penitential practices that included self-flagellation, which "parallel[ed] . . . the Daoist practice of *zibo* (self-slapping) and Buddhist *zipu* (self-beating) found in China beginning in the late Han period."[53] With the help of followers disciplined in such a manner, Xu gradually built his network that reached across more than a dozen provinces and claimed a following of one million by the late 1990s. By dispatching skilled members to start businesses such as hair salons, restaurants, inns, and automobile repair shops, the sect also developed an extensive commercial enterprise at the disposal of the "great servant" (who purchased a Mercedes Benz and two plush apartments in Beijing in an emphatic renunciation of his childhood poverty). Meanwhile, eschatological warnings persisted in the sect, and new dates for the fiery destruction of the world were announced.[54]

THE LIGHTNING OUT OF THE EAST

For all the CCP repression of underground Christianity, it became clear to Xu Shuangfu during the late 1990s that the greatest force of darkness opposing the Three Grades of Servants was not the atheist state, but a rival millenarian Protestant sect that took shape in the early 1990s. Styled as the Lightning out of the East (also Eastern Lightning)—in reference to the same biblical passage (Matt. 24:27) in which the TJC had read its own cosmic destiny more than half a century earlier—the underground network was launched from Henan. Its founder, Zhao Weishan (1956?–), had been a core member of the Shouters in the northeastern province of Heilongjiang in the early 1980s. After the sect was outlawed there, Zhao fled to Henan where he was able to regroup and revitalize a number of former Shouters into a new network that, after 1993, evolved into the Lightning out of the East.[55]

In a possible reflection of his uncertain dominance during the early days of the sect, Zhao at first named seven senior members (most of them women) as God's "incarnations" (*huashen*), each embodying a divine attribute. Zhao himself personified divine "authority," while a woman surnamed Deng became Quanneng, or "the Almighty," the subsequent "female Christ" of the Second Coming. It was an ingenuous lineup, for Deng (her given name remains unknown) turned out to be an extraordinary personality. She had prolific visions; uttered profuse, strange, and mesmerizing prophecies; and exuded a peculiar charisma of her own while remaining fully under Zhao's control. She had failed the college entrance examination in 1990 and become mentally unstable, but her state reportedly much improved after she converted and joined the underground Shouters. Despite her unfulfilled dreams of a university education, her literacy was apparently not insignificant, for she soon began to pour out streams of prophecies that blended the incoherent and the indignant with the startling and the heartening. Her words were then recorded, edited, and compiled into several volumes by seven unmarried women whom Zhao appointed as "the seven stars" and "the seven Spirits" to serve "the female Christ." Zhao himself assumed the new office of "the high priest" (da jisi) to manage the emerging enterprise in her name. In *Xiao shujuan*, or *The Little Book*, which also reappeared under several other titles, Deng displayed her considerable command of the mystical, eschatological vocabulary bequeathed by the Little Flock. She announced the passage of the Age of Grace, the second period of human history that Jesus had inaugurated, and the dawning of the Age of the Kingdom with her own appearance.[56]

The claim may have been extravagant, but it required no great leap of imagination on her part: in transplanting premillennial dispensationalism (with its basic tripartite structure) from the West into Chinese soil more than half a century earlier, Watchman Nee not only secured for the Little Flock the preeminent place in God's end-time scheme, he also inadvertently—and continually—dangled in front of the eschatologically astute fresh messianic possibilities. Since the current age was soon to expire, a new cosmic age with its new revelations waited at the doorstep. Christ was to return at any moment. It took no more than acute despair, daring "revelations," and a profound contempt for worldly sense to usher in the millennium. Neither was her designation as "the female Christ" as novel as it seemed: the Shouters had freely promoted the faithful to Christhood on the basis of Philippians 1:21 ("for to me to live is Christ") and had reaped a harvest of "Christs" with Chinese surnames. Nor was her gender problematic in a Protestant community, official and unofficial, in which women made up about 80 percent of all the converts. The prevalence of Marian cults in underground Catholicism suggests that belief in a compassionate, female Christian deity is consistent with the worship of the Goddess of Mercy and the Mother of No-Birth in popular religion.[57] (In at least one documented case from the seventeenth century, a Catholic woman in Jinan, Shandong, who claimed to be able to summon rain with her prayers took the name of "the Mother of God" and built a following of two thousand people.)[58] In declaring that God had "returned to flesh" and that she, an "ordinary person," had been "possessed by the Spirit of God," Deng bypassed the potentially awkward theology of the virgin birth. It also rendered her divinity intelligible and in line with the tradition of spirit possession in folk religion. The sect pointed to Isaiah 41:2 ("who raised up the righteous man from the east"—the Chinese version makes no gender distinctions) as yet another biblical proof that the "lightning" must come from the east. "I descended in the east," she explained, "bringing Canaan to the people of the east."[59]

As the reincarnated divine, Deng had almost complete freedom to recast Christian theology in the mold of Chinese sensibility. Her direct commands replaced the Bible, which must not be allowed to "imprison" human understanding or to "usurp the position of God [herself]." She also threw out what was to her the incomprehensible doctrine of the Trinity, uniting the cumbersome, multiple godheads in her body instead. In a direct, earthy manner, Deng challenged the idea of a three-way division of the godhead that also seemed to float bodiless in a world of abstraction. "How old is the Holy Father?" she asked. "How old is the Holy Son? How old indeed is the Holy Spirit? What do they look like? How did they get separated? And how did they become united into one? . . . The God that you pray to all day—is he the big God, the second God, or the third God? . . . The God that is cut into three pieces . . . is he still one God?"[60]

A century and a half earlier, leaders of the Taiping Heavenly Kingdom had also shown a similar uneasiness with a triune deity. (Yang Xiuqing, the East King who assumed the title of the "Holy Spirit," had similarly inquired about the respective heights of God and Jesus as well as the lengths and colors of their beards.) Their solution had been to name Hong Xiuquan's top associates as separate mouthpieces for the Divine Persons.[61] For the followers of the Lightning out of the East, "the female Christ," though secluded and mysterious, out of sight and touch of all but Zhao Weishan and his inner circle, was the "real," or "realistic," God (Shijishen) in contrast to the distant, indistinct, and immaterial biblical deity. She had entered the hostile and dangerous land of the "great red dragon" to "redeem the poor and the suffering"; she will then also "conquer the entire universe" so that "all nations will come to worship me" and "all peoples will submit to my authority."[62]

Such a salvation required urgent, vigorous, and determined proselytism, before the terrifying collapse of the universe (originally set to occur in 1999). Families and properties must be left behind, money offered, obstructions of any kind removed, earthly rules suspended, and qualms of propriety banished. As the group expanded its membership aggressively among erstwhile Shouters and Little Flock communities and beyond them into congregations of other backgrounds, extraordinary techniques—including the lure of money and young women, blackmailing, kidnapping and brainwashing, as well as lynching and murder—were employed. Sophisticated infiltration of rival underground sects, at times using feigned defectors, was orchestrated.[63] By far the most intense war of faiths at the turn of the millennium was with the Three Grades of Servants, with which the Lightning out of the East traded denunciations of heresy. By the early 2000s, Zhao Weishan's enterprise was believed to be already one million strong. Zhao himself successfully fled the country in 2000 and subsequently obtained political asylum in the United States, where he set up an international headquarters for the group. The reported death of "the female Christ" in early 2005 did little to undercut the messianic exuberance of the movement.[64]

For the Three Grades of Servants, whose members defected to the Lightning out of the East in droves after the late 1990s, repeated strikes by the "Lightning" justified a matching wrathful response. Between 2002 and 2004, Xu Shuangfu's lieutenants masterminded at least sixteen fatal acts of "discipline" for defectors and suspected Lightning operatives across a broad stretch of spiritual battlefield from Heilongjiang in the north to Jiangxi in the south, and from coastal Shandong to the western provinces of Gansu and Sichuan. They included strangulation, drowning, stabbing, and burying alive. Biblical precedents were cited for the "righteous killings": hadn't Elijah ordered the slaughter of the prophets of Baal? Hadn't Samuel hewed Agag, king of the Amalekites, into pieces? In one grisly murder, eyes, ears, and nose were ripped from the victim. The authorities hunted down and captured Xu and several dozen associates in 2004. At least fifteen, Xu included, were later executed.[65] Outside the two dueling sects, competition for the souls of the country's marginalized millions continued with full force but generally without the same savagery. During the early 2000s, the unofficial Fangcheng Church and its affiliated networks alone claimed to be ten million strong.[66] By 2007, the total following of Protestant Christianity in China was likely more than fifty million, a majority of whom remained in the underground.[67]

"GRAINS OF LIFE": REFLECTIONS ON POPULAR CHRISTIANITY IN CONTEMPORARY CHINA

In 1998, Rev. Donald Argue, president of the National Association of Evangelicals in the United States, maintained that China might be experiencing "the single greatest Revival in the history of Christianity."[68] The swelling of the Protestant movement—and, to a lesser extent, the rise of millions in the underground Catholic Church—in contemporary China is undeniable, yet it was not a "revival" in the usual sense. Instead of bringing back to life a withered Western faith, the Chinese were fashioning a Christian faith that increasingly revealed continuities with indigenous folk religion, which also made a startling comeback during the same period, attracting some two hundred million worshipers at the turn of the twenty-first century.[69] Like the latter, popular Christianity in both its Protestant and Catholic forms often emphasized healing, miracles, and similar abilities to harness the power of the spiritual world to the struggles of common people. And just as one turned to Ma Zu, Niang Niang, the Dragon King, or other deities in popular religion in anticipation of a good spouse, a son (instead of a daughter), success in examinations, or escape from misfortunes, converts to Christianity have also accentuated the efficacy of their faith in promoting personal well-being.[70] As Richard Madsen points out, Catholics in rural communities have engaged in "quasi-magical practices" that owed little to Catholic doctrine.[71] The same held true for their Protestant counterparts. All this happened at a time when market reform downgraded public health and deprived the rural masses of the minimal protection once offered by the people's communes, leaving them to fend for themselves. By 1996, 90 percent of the peasants were without any form of health coverage.[72] In cities, migrant workers and laid-off employees of state-owned factories have likewise found themselves without a societal safety net.

Understandably, religion has filled the void that was left by the state. The explosive growth of new Protestant sects that gave vent to quasi-magical pursuits has coincided with the appearance of indigenous spiritual sects, most notably Falun Gong (Great Law of the Dharma Wheel) founded in 1992. Like more than twenty-four hundred associations of *qigong* (energy cultivation) that sprouted up across China after the 1980s to promote health and to find alternatives to expensive medical care, Falun Gong began as a form of *qigong* but developed into a syncretic religious movement by incorporating Buddhist and Daoist beliefs into the breathing exercise. By 1999, when the CCP unleashed its violent crackdown on the sect, it had already gained thirty million adherents.[73]

In addition to the precariousness of contemporary life for vast numbers of the Chinese populace—three hundred million or more remained below the poverty line at the beginning of the new century even as double-digit economic growth facilitated the emergence of a sizable middle class and catapulted many into conspicuous wealth—the collapse of Communist beliefs also hastened the search for alternative inspirations for life's struggles.[74] Even Ye Xiaowen, chief of the Religious Affairs Bureau of China's State Council, observed in Durkheimian terms in 1999 that both traditional Confucian values and the revolutionary ideology "formerly inculcated" by the CCP had fallen into disuse. As a result, a general "anomie" (*shifan*), or state of normlessness, along with a sense of loss and loneliness had become widespread in Chinese society.[75] As Madsen reminds us, the acute "crisis of meaning" in twentieth-century China deepened as recent reforms furthered inequalities and social dislocations as well as official corruption. China became a vast ideological market in which various faith traditions competed. Christianity in general, with its transcendent spiritual and moral message, proved to be able to "strengthen and fortify" people threatened by modernity. As a congregational religion, it also provided what one Chinese scholar aptly termed *jingshen danwei*, or a "work unit of the spirit," for those who craved to belong.[76]

Protestantism gained a further advantage, as noted by Alan Hunter and Kim-Kwong Chan, because of its inherent evangelistic impulse as well as the contemporary "prestige of the West"—an ironic twist in the church's tortuous relations with the latter. In fact, reactive nationalism against foreign dominance, which the Protestant community shared with the populace at large during the first half of the twentieth century, mostly disappeared in the Deng Xiaoping era (1978–1997). Protestantism emerged as a prized religious commodity on the strength of its attractive forms of worship, flexible and effective organization, and ability to grant "immense . . . worth to each individual."[77] It provided transcendent mean-ings for the suffering and pains in this world and reassurances of the unfailing love and protection of Jesus, who had also suffered. Beyond all this—outside the official church—popular, sectarian Christianity offered even more. For the destitute, the afflicted, and the frustrated living in the shadow of mocking wealth and abusive power, it prophesied an impending fiery end to the corrupt and unjust world and promised a complete deliver-ance in the coming millennial kingdom. It also guaranteed immediate, though often unverifiable, returns for spiritual investment (and monetary contributions) in the form of divine blessings, healing, exorcism, mutual aid, and elevated status in the spiritual hierarchy in addition to exclusive salvation. By offering Pentecostal ecstasies and "the communism of love" embedded in a secretive network of the faithful, it proved capable of sus-taining individuals who had otherwise been relegated to the margins, or counted among the "weak colonies" (*ruoshi qunti*), of Chinese society.[78]

In 2007 in northern Shaanxi, a journalist visited a Disciples' Society family in their three-hole cave dwelling, a typical farmer's home dug into the hillside on the loess plateau of northwestern China. Over the cave's entrance, the faded red of the painted slogan "Long Live the Chinese Com-munist Party" was still visible. Inside the cave, the couple with their heads wrapped in white turbans admitted that they had stopped singing songs about Chairman Mao—or visiting the local temple—for many years. In-stead, when they knelt on their *kang*, the heatable, platform bed, each day at dawn and at night, they faced a red cross on the cave wall. Their health had much improved since they believed in the "Christ of the Third Redemption," they claimed, as did a fellow member who had been left an invalid by polio but who reported lessened pain in her swollen knees after joining the sect. The couple's cave had also become a meeting point for local Disciples' Society devotees: in the dark of the night it burst into life at the arrival of kindred souls, who filled the mud courtyard with hymns set to the tunes of local folk songs. "What we need to do now is to spread the gospel," the husband said. "The more we preach, the more blessings we will get." With the anticipated amassing of the "grains of life," he added, he was not afraid of the calamities at the world's end. "At that time, even when others run out of grains, we will not starve."[79]

Afterword

FOR ALL THE PECULIARITIES of indigenous Chinese Protestantism, its main eschatological beliefs remain a tributary of a long flow of messianic Christianity. As an "adjunct of eschatology," Mircea Eliade writes, Christian millennialism has historically looked beyond the apocalypse—heralded by flood, famine, or war—to a new world that is "inexhaustibly fertile, harmonious, sanctified, and just." In its optimistic form known as postmillennialism, which parallels the "gentler rock of reformers," it sees the gradual expansion of the church and the progress of Christian civilization leading into the promised thousand-year reign of the Messiah.[1] What animated popular Chinese Protestantism during the past century, however, was the darker premillennialism, which foretold a fiery end of time before the Second Coming of Christ and his kingdom.

Leaders of the Chinese messianic movement did not, of course, invent the millenarian scheme. They merely inherited and adapted the eschatological thrust that is readily available in the Judeo-Christian tradition. Judaic messianic beliefs can be dated back to the eighth century BCE. They were later enriched by a Greek poetic imagination of comparable antiquity, which envisioned history as divinely ordered stages of general decline, and spawned such eschatological works as the Book of Daniel and the Revelation. The Christian religion, Harvey Cox notes, "began as an apocalyptic sect."[2]

Closely tied to the belief in the apocalypse (*apokalypsis*, the unveiling of the secret knowledge concerning the world's end) is the "collective effervescence" (to borrow Emile Durkheim's term) of the saved, which is as old as Christianity itself.[3] It was expressed through singing, "tongues," trances, and possibly dancing as well and served to forge the eschatological community of the first Christians. Felicitas D. Goodman maintains that "tongues," the passionate, often rhythmic, patter, constitute "one unit of an eschatological dyad."[4] A phenomenon that has been traced to an "altered state of consciousness," or "hyperaroused dissociation," glossolalia was recently shown (in brain imaging) to occur while the language centers and the frontal lobes—the thinking, willful part of the brain—remain "relatively quiet."[5] Likewise, trance is defined in the *Penguin Dictionary of Psychology* as "a condition of dissociation" characterized by "the lack of voluntary movement" or "automatisms in act and thought." Long before its induction was clinically proved to promote the production and release of endorphins—"natural opiates in the human brain"—it had been the specialization, or the "technique of ecstasy," of the shaman.[6]

Among Christians, a notable, early case of trance happened in the late second century when Montanus, a newly baptized Phrygian, burst into jubilant prophesying, in the voice of God, that Jesus would return soon and that the "New Jerusalem" would be established in Phrygia. Tertullian wrote that the "false prophet" Montanus "speaks in a trance . . . a delirium over which he has no control."[7] It is no surprise that as Christianity evolved from suppressed cult to established religion, end-time teachings, along with spontaneous ecstasies, also faded out of the church. As inspiration became its "institutionalized property," truth was dispensed to the masses through official rituals. It was only among the fringe, oppressed groups that apocalyptic effervescence and individual possession endured as a form of rebellion against authority, religious or secular.[8] Because of them, the Christian movement "never completely shed" its millennial disposition. Pentecostalism in recent history has been but a modern incarnation of the same ecstatic spirit of the first eschatological Christians.[9] "No faith is potent," Eric Hoffer reminds us in *The True Believer,* "unless it has a millennial component"—and a proper measure, we might add, of rapture.[10]

In *The Pursuit of the Millennium,* Norman Cohn shows that in Europe from the eleventh century on, especially in times of rapid social change, the millenarian impulse repeatedly defied both secular and ecclesiastical constraint and exploded into popular chiliastic movements. It drew its strength particularly from those on the margin of society—landless peasants, journeymen, unskilled workers, and vagabonds—who were left without the material and emotional support of traditional social groups such as kin, village communities, or guilds. In a state of chronic frustration, those people turned to prophets who provided them with a new frame of meaning and inspired in them "a wild enthusiasm born of desperation." In some cases, groups of laymen would form "quasi-monastic," egalitarian communities of common property in a return to the primitive Christian communalism described in Acts. And, time and again, the collective anxiety finally "discharged itself in a frantic urge to smite the ungodly" and to usher in the final Kingdom of lasting abundance and power.[11]

Outside Europe, in modern times, messianic movements, often inspired by Christianity, have risen among the people of Africa, the aboriginal populations of America and Oceania, and the Melanesians and Polynesians. Asia, from Indonesia and the Philippines to Vietnam, has provided fertile soil as well. Common to those groups, Vittorio Lanternari wrote, were such phenomena as a "prophet or guide" who received revelations from a Supreme Being or Spirit, the expectation of final "cataclysms and catastrophes," and, after the end of history, the regeneration of the world "in an age of abundance and happiness." Their rituals included "collective possessions, incantation, trances, and visions." In some of those places, prophetic movements also included the belief in the remaking of the existing social order, or the "the ejection of the white man," which paved the way for political emancipation or the overthrow of colonial rule.[12]

In modern China, the age-old messianic quest of Christianity with its undying ecstatic spirit has also drawn a profound response. It resonated with indigenous millenarianism, which likewise foretold a period of great cataclysms followed by the coming of a renewed world. As in the West, millennialism in China arose in antiquity. In the year 2 BCE, toward the end of the Western Han dynasty, an eschatological paroxysm centered on the mythic Queen Mother of the West (Xi Wangmu) took hold of many in the midst of a severe drought. Gripped by both "terror" and "ecstatic convulsion," thousands of people carrying the "wand" of the Queen Mother's "edict" swept through northwestern China. In the capital, people "ascended to the rooftops carrying torches, beat drums, and cried out in panic"; others sang and danced to the wand, sacrificed to the Queen Mother, and wore charms in order to escape death. Daniel L. Overmyer points out that by the first century CE, Xi Wangmu had evolved into a deity who lived in a huge palace built of precious stones on top of the Kunlun Mountains and bestowed peaches of immortality on those she favored.[13]

In the second century, a revealed Daoist text titled *The Scripture of Great Peace* (*Taiping jing*) painted a utopia of peace, equality, and communal sharing of all wealth. It became the vision of the unsuccessful Way of Great Peace (Taiping Dao), or Yellow Turban, Uprising in 184, which sought to destroy the Han order and establish a new dynasty with "great propitiousness all under heaven." After the collapse of Han, the growth of Buddhism as a popular faith nurtured the belief in the Maitreya Buddha—the Buddha of the future and the end-time savior who presides over a celestial realm of sweet dews, sparkling streams, precious jewels, heavenly music, and shapely "heavenly girls." Devotion to Maitreya began to spread among the lower class during the Western Jin period (265–316) and sparked the first of a long string of Buddhist sectarian revolts in 515.[14]

In the long run, the anticipation of the coming of Maitreya blended with the Daoist millenarian tradition to produce a basic popular eschatology. According to that belief, the Buddha of the future appears "at the nadir of cosmic disintegration" to save humanity and remake the world. By the fifth and sixth centuries, a "fundamental structure of destruction and renewal" had already emerged in indigenous Buddhist texts and was to continue down to the Qing dynasty.[15] Such an eschatology formed part of what C. K. Yang calls "diffused religion" in Chinese history, which arose particularly during interludes between major dynasties. In those times of civil strife, economic deterioration, social disintegration, and personal suffering, neither the once-dominant orthodox ideology nor the traditional pattern of social institutions remained adequate. It was in popular, often sectarian, religion that the masses found superhuman powers that "transcended the limits of man's earthly abilities" to wrestle with life's overpowering calamities.[16]

After the sixteenth century, various grassroots sects of Buddhism, including those in the White Lotus tradition, a Buddhist forerunner of popular Protestant sects of the twentieth century, centered their millenarian beliefs on the Mother of No-Birth (Wusheng Laomu).[17] The latter represented a crystallization of folk messianism that had begun in ancient China with the Queen Mother of the West. According to sectarian texts from the late Ming period (1368–1644), as the cosmic end approached, with chaos and destruction about to break loose, the Mother of No-Birth took pity on her children—the tortured, deluded mortals of this world who had "lost their native land" (*shixiang*) and were mired in wickedness. She promised to send down the Maitreya Buddha and provide a final chance for the faithful to be saved and to live a blissful life in a transformed world. That vision inspired the Eight Trigrams uprising of 1813.[18] The Taiping movement of the mid-nineteenth century, though enthralled by a different melody, swayed to the same salvationist rhythm. Mass beliefs in the eternal Mother survived down to the twentieth century. During the war-torn Republican period, they were incorporated into the teachings of several White Lotus offshoots that emerged alongside indigenous Protestant sects. Among them was the Way of Pervading Unity (Yiguandao), founded by a vagabond from Shandong who claimed to be the Maitreya Buddha dispatched by the Mother of No-Birth to cure sickness and lead humanity into the promised celestial beatitude.[19]

Though scorned by the literati, popular messianic beliefs in Chinese history actually mirrored an enduring utopian pursuit in the elite culture. As we have seen, *The Record of Rites* (*Liji*) of the Western Han dynasty had articulated the ideal of the Great Harmony (*datong*)—an orderly, communitarian society of love and material abundance, ruled by the virtuous and free from selfishness, crime, and exploitation (see Chapter 3). That dream had persisted through the centuries and, though not eschatological itself, had found its way into sectarian movements such as the Taiping Heavenly Kingdom. Toward the end of the Qing dynasty, Kang Youwei presented his platform for radical reform as a fulfillment of the Confucian vision of the Great Harmony.[20] In 1917, four years before he became a founding member of the CCP, an ambitious but frustrated young Mao Zedong, disenchanted with what he perceived to be the trivialities of "parliament," "constitution," "education," and the like, wrote, "the Great Harmony—that is my goal." As a first step toward that utopian society, both Mao and Yun Daiying, another CCP pioneer, planned to build "new villages" of love, egalitarianism, and shared property.[21] That vision helped inspire the Communist movement in China. For Mao, the Great Harmony that had eluded Kang Youwei finally dawned with the coming of Marxism and the establishment of the People's Republic of China.[22]

Among the lower class, excluded for the most part from such lofty pursuits, despair of this world frequently drove the afflicted and the oppressed into popular millenarian faiths. There in the religious underworld, traditional salvationist groups in China offered no less enchanting visions of a coming, regenerated world. Their religion, often inspired by charismatic lay leaders, anticipated the spirituality of popular Christianity in modern China. What Max Weber believed Confucianism had "expurgated" from Chinese life—the "orgiastic elements of animist religiosity" such as trances, divination, and dreams of the celestial palace, along with miraculous healing and exorcism—actually persisted outside religious and secular orthodoxy, shunned by the elite but unfazed by its disdain.[23] They luxuriated at the grassroots level and in the same soil that came to nourish the indigenous Christianity, beginning with Hong Xiuquan's dreams and revelations and the Taiping's collective leadership of spirit mediums. They also continued into the twentieth century among sectarian groups. Foreshadowing the charismatic practices of its Christian counterparts, traditional popular religion often featured spirit mediums who incarnated the deity in a state of trance to explain the past and foretell the future. It employed dramatic rituals of exorcism to cure the sick and to dislodge demons that were responsible for the "disorder" of disease, suffering, and death.[24] In the case of the Boxers, mass possession by gods—apotheosized heroes of popular culture such as the Monkey King and Lord Guan (Guanyu) along with other celebrated warriors from the *Romance of the Three Kingdoms*—was a patent means of healing and achieving invulnerability.[25]

For its part, independent, sectarian Protestantism in twentieth-century China also shared many basic characteristics of indigenous popular religion. In a parallel to earlier millenarian movements in the country, popular Christianity found its leadership primarily among the lower strata of the intelligentsia. The founders and leaders of the main Protestant sects held sway over their followers not merely on the strength of personal magnetism: in many cases they had acquired a level of education which, in a society that endowed the learned with moral influence and prestige, boosted the power of their personalities. As was the case in medieval Europe, where eschatological leaders tended to hail from what Cohn calls the "restless world of *déclassé* intellectuals and semi-intellectuals," or in traditional China, where popular religion was dominated by the "folk intellectuals" (as Overmyer puts it), most leaders of independent Protestant groups in modern China were also unfulfilled semi-intellectuals.[26] In their irreverence toward both the missionary Christianity of the pre-1949 period and to the Three-Self church since then, in their proffer of a "surer and smoother road" to salvation than institutionalized religion, one glimpses the unceasing rivalry between the "magician" and the "priest."[27] In the end, it was the unabashed usurpers of priestly power who managed to recast mission Christianity in a millenarian mold and breathe Chinese life into it.

As in traditional folk religion, which offered female adherents identity, status, and opportunities for leadership—an escape from the restrictions of patriarchal society—women were central to the rise of indigenous Christianity.[28] They were a main source of sectarian energy. Some pioneered in independent evangelism; others helped found or joined the inner leadership circle of sectarian groups, or became "spiritual mothers" to their leaders. Charismatic and visionary women were vital to the launching of the Jesus Family, the Bethel Band, the Little Flock, and some of the underground churches of contemporary China. On the other hand, the vigor, creativity, and ambition of individual women invariably ran up against entrenched male dominance in sectarian Christianity, which upheld traditional norms of patriarchy. The Little Flock's insistence on the covering of women's hair in worship and their subjection to male authority (without the niceties of Southern Baptists' call for the "servant leadership" of men) remains a stark reminder of the patriarchal habit of mind in mass Christianity in China.[29]

Like the eschatological Daoist and Buddhist sects of pre-modern China, or quasi-religious brotherhood associations such as the Triads (Tiandihui) that arose during the late imperial period, twentieth-century grassroots Christianity drew much of its following from the marginalized who were no longer able to find sustenance in their families, lineages, villages, or other traditional networks of support.[30] Many early members of the TJC, the Jesus Family, and the Spiritual Gifts Society were North China farmers who were fleeing banditry or famine or had drifted into cities because of rural hardships. Other sectarians were disenchanted revolutionaries, mission school graduates whose ambitions were loftier than their status, wandering fortune tellers, underpaid missionaries' helpers, bankrupt merchants, bandits, opium addicts, or those who found their lives otherwise wrecked and wasted. Similarly, in the late twentieth century, apocalyptic underground churches were a magnet for the disaffected from the surplus rural population and the urban "weak colonies" left behind by economic reforms as the safety nets of the Mao-era socialist state decayed or vanished.

As a whole, popular Chinese Protestantism has appealed to individuals whose personal crises, powerlessness, and helplessness cried out for Pentecostal intervention and eschatological redemption. Though not always poor and downtrodden, the majority of them were trapped in what some sociologists have termed "relative deprivation," which helps precipitate millenarian and sectarian movements.[31] Above and beyond the general otherworldly salvation promised by established churches, the masses who flocked into sectarian Christianity were able to find an ecstatic experience of the divine; free themselves from their frustrated, sinful, and worthless selves; build an exultant community separate from the corrupt, desolate world; and catch glimpses of their imminent, millenarian deliverance. It should be noted that such messianic beliefs rarely expressed themselves in defeating the evil in the present world, as the Taiping rebels attempted, but in escaping from it and transcending it in the radiant world about to dawn. As a result, it has fashioned a more sustainable messianism because of its failure, so far, to develop into a full-blown revolutionary chiliasm.

Looking beyond China, one finds that the rise of the Chinese church in our time is part of a phenomenal, global expansion of Christianity outside the West. By 2000, according to the *World Christian Encyclopedia,* there were more than 1.1 billion Christians in Latin America, Africa, and Asia—twice the total in Europe and more than five times that of North America. One hundred years earlier, 80 percent of the world's Christians were European or North American. Today, "60 percent of professing Christians live in the global South and East."[32] In the words of Andrew F. Walls, a "seismic shift in Christianity" occurred during the past century. In *The Next Christendom* (2002), Philip Jenkins also reminds us that the "era of Western Christianity has passed within our lifetimes, and the day of Southern Christianity is dawning."[33] The latter is clearly drawn toward Pentecostal ecstasies. The new churches that have attracted hundreds of millions of adherents worldwide "preach messages that, to a Westerner, appear simplistically charismatic, visionary, and apocalyptic. In this thought-world, prophecy is an everyday reality, while faith-healing, exorcism, and dream-visions are all basic components of religious sensibility."[34]

As is the case in China, the new gospel that features direct divine intervention in everyday life has appealed primarily to the poor in Africa, Latin America, and other parts of Asia—in both the rural areas and the megacities of the third world. The church has become a refuge for the marginalized, the sick, the desperate, and the forgotten. In the words of Harvey Cox, "sometimes the only thriving human communities in the vast seas of tar-paper shanties and cardboard huts that surround many . . . cities are the Pentecostal congregations." With spectacular names such as Mountain of Fire and Miracles and the no less fantastic promise of healing, prosperity, and protection from the precariousness of ordinary living and its "blackouts, robbery, disease, [and] corruption," the new churches have also drawn their following from a broad spectrum of social classes.[35]

Besides reshaping the global religious landscape, the new, predominantly charismatic Protestantism in both Latin America and Africa is also emerging as a political force. Throughout Africa, from Sudan to Ivory Coast, it is fueling the rivalry between Christian and Muslim populations. In Brazil, it proved capable of producing activists in a major political party and electing church members to the national congress.[36] Jenkins argues that the coming of "global Christianity" will possibly intensify the worldwide Christian–Muslim enmity, provoking civil wars and even sparking international conflicts in the form of "Christian crusades and Muslim jihads."[37]

Will Protestant Christianity also play a significant role in the political future of China? In *Jesus in Beijing: How Christianity Is Transforming China and the Global Balance of Power* (2003), David Aikman entertains the likelihood of "20 to 30 percent of China's population" becoming Christians within three decades. When that happens, "a Christian view of the world" will become "dominant . . . within China's political and cultural establishment." Such a "Christianized China" might cooperate with the United States on resolving thorny international issues and shoulder some of the "burdens" the latter has carried as a "benevolent global power." It would help "make the world safe for Christian missionary endeavor" and contribute vigorously to the enforcement of "international law," the fight against terrorism, and the prevention of "the proliferation of weapons of mass destruction."[38]

I do not see such a future. Despite the phenomenal growth of Christianity in twentieth-century China, it has not come to dominate the religious scene, which is still populated primarily by Buddhist, Daoist, and syncretic folk beliefs.[39] The underground church has in fact shown a greater tendency to absorb, and be absorbed by, popular religion than to replace it. More important, Chinese Christianity is, and will likely continue to be, primarily a religion of the masses, far from the center of political power. Like Mahayana Buddhism, which Arnold Toynbee characterized as the "church of the internal proletariat" and "politically incompetent," popular Christianity in China has generally shunned political activism, which has often alienated those who sought in the Christian faith inspirations for democracy and social justice.[40] Its eschatological bent and its exclusion from the political, social, and cultural pursuits of the elite have reinforced each other. As in the case of popular religious movements in pre-modern China, which were usually unable to complete their intellectual formulation and to find legitimate political or social expression, contemporary popular Christianity has been condemned to a similarly stunted political growth. Persecuted by the state, fractured by its own sectarianism, and diminished by its contempt for formal education (theological or otherwise), it will probably also remain, as sectarian religious groups did in the past, in the state of "intellectual decapitation."[41] The official church, on the other hand, has long accepted its status of subjugation to the state and shows neither the desire nor the ability to become a political force. As long as the one-party dictatorship continues, its general political passivity is unlikely to change.

What about the "cultural Christians"? The emergence since the 1980s of a small group of intellectuals—including writers, historians, philosophers, lawyers, artists, and activists in the democracy movement—who have either converted to or merely expressed interest in Christianity has kindled hopes among some evangelicals that Protestant elites may reshape the political and social landscape and play a vital role in China's advance toward civil society.[42] In *God Is Back: How the Global Revival of Faith Is Changing the World* (2009), John Micklethwait and Adrian

Wooldridge not only predict that "China could well be the world's biggest . . . Christian [nation]" by 2050, but also intimate that the emerging Chinese Christianity will be energized, perhaps spearheaded, by Westernized, educated, and enterprising urban Protestants. The book opens with the scene of a lively house church Bible study—complete with hymns downloaded to a laptop computer from the Internet and beamed onto the wall by a projector—in a comfortable Shanghai apartment. The meeting had drawn a small constellation of respectable local Protestants, including a "prominent academic," a manager of a state-owned enterprise, a handful of biotechnologists and ballet dancers, and "a pharmaceuticals executive who has just returned from a visit to New Jersey." They decried homosexuality and general immorality in Chinese society and were roused by a nationalist call to make China Christian in order to make it prosperous—while their BMWs waited outside the building. Micklethwait and Wooldridge present these Christians as a "cross-section of the 'new China.'"[43] However, in the absence of hard evidence supporting this view, one must regard such house church groups of successful, cosmopolitan Christians as not much more commonplace than their BMWs, and their embrace of Protestantism as no more revealing of the mainstream culture of contemporary China than Chiang Kai-shek's baptism in 1930 was of the spirituality of the Republican era.

The dream that Western Christianity would illuminate China's path to modernization is in fact an old one. It began with the late-nineteenth-century reformers and continued through the revolution of Sun Yat-sen. It also persisted amidst dubious nation-building efforts under the direction of the autocratic Methodist convert Chiang Kai-shek. Throughout that period, the warmth shown by the elite toward Christianity was largely one toward the midwife. The anticipated newborn was a unified and prosperous Chinese state.[44] In the end, it was Communism, not Christianity, that inspired the revolution that led to the founding of the People's Republic. With the decline of Marxist ideology, the current leaders look to nationalism, according to one official with the *People's Daily,* as "the only belief that can maintain China's unity and stability in a time of tumultuous change."[45] Meanwhile, China's quest for progress, power, and prestige involves increasingly broad, and decidedly pragmatic and secular, engagement with the outside world. Christianity has no better chance than Confucianism, which the CCP state in recent years has artificially resuscitated for tourism and as the core of Chinese nationalism, to become the guiding ideology for a future China.

On the other hand, as the new faith begins to spread among the young and the educated elite (with those aged between eighteen and forty accounting for more than a quarter of many urban congregations), a handful of Christian activists including democracy advocates and lawyers have joined the struggle to defend civil rights and to expand freedoms in China.[46] One recent study of Christianity in coastal China suggests that, in the long run, the church will have a positive effect on the country's democratization. It contends that two new urban groups of Protestant converts—the "bourgeois Christians" and the "educated, elite Christians"—rather than the rural church will play a central role in shaping the future of Chinese Christianity. They will seek representation and power, and introduce democratization, within the church and perhaps beyond.[47] My own views are less sanguine. Whatever contributions these Christians may make as inspired individuals, collectively they will play at best a marginal role in political liberalization in China, one that is proportional to their numerical strength and to their opportunities for political association. I believe that it is the Christianity of the masses (both rural and urban), not of the elite, that will imprint its character on the Chinese church in the future, as it has done in the past. Such a church will find itself energized not by political or social activism, but by the efficacy of its faith and by an apocalyptic triumph over a degenerate world.

Nevertheless, Christianity's gains among the upper strata of Chinese society, particularly the intellectuals, mean that elements of Western Protestant ideals, values, and idioms are finding their way, in however small measures, into the cultural synthesis of a future China. Historically, Buddhism in China completed a similar journey from inaccessible alien ideas, transmitted initially by the "superstitious and fickle" under conditions of much "ignorance," into elite Chinese culture.[48] By the Tang dynasty, eminent scholar-officials were breathing Buddhist transcendence and solace into the soul of Chinese poetry in works such as Wang Wei's "Stopping by the Incense-Filled Temple." The Song poet-statesman Su Dongpo would also write of his regular visits to Anguosi Temple in Huangzhou where, in deep contemplation, "I forgot both the world and myself, and found emptiness in both body and mind."[49] Will Christianity in China find devotees and apologists of comparable stature in the future?

That possibility does exist. In fact, an emerging circle of Protestant writers, thinkers, artists, and musicians, both inside China and living abroad, are already discovering refined literary and artistic expressions of their faith.[50] Among them is the Beijing-born, later New York–based, Shu Zhan, a graduate of the Central Conservatory of Music and an acclaimed performer of the two-stringed *erhu*, which had found its way into China from central Asia by the fifth century. She converted to Christianity after a tour of the United States in 1991 and began producing CDs of *erhu* Gospel music in 1999. Her masterful performance has coaxed the ancient, often mournful, instrument to pour out rich, caressing melodies of Chinese hymns such as "The Flowers of the Field" (*Yedi de hua*) written by Ye Weixin, a contemporary Taiwanese composer of sacred music.

In the long run, all this promises to transform elements of Protestant literature and art—which since the nineteenth century have often been snubbed by intellectuals because of their crudeness—into high culture. Yet even when that happens, the latter's predominantly secular bent will persist, as will its separation from the religious ethos of the masses.[51] It is also important to bear in mind that, in most cases, the imaginative flights into Christian redemption and solace in contemporary Chinese literary and artistic creations were also escapes from the cruel realities encountered on earth, be they crushed dreams of democracy or wrecked personal lives.[52] A parallel can be found in the turn to Buddhist wisdom on the part of Wang Wei and Su Dongpo as well as Xu Zhimo.[53] It is most likely that Christian themes and symbolism in literature and art will remain isolated, individual protests in the twilight of one's worldly career, not a battle cry with political potential.

The greatest political potential of Chinese Christianity will be found in the underground and among the masses. Historically, popular millenarian religion has displayed, along with eschatological anxieties, a volcanic energy that, unable to be drained through legitimate dissent or to find redress under repressive regimes, and beaten back into a habitual political disenchantment and numbness, did know of one way to discharge itself from time to time when it could no longer be contained—through violent eruption. In the Taiping Heavenly Kingdom movement, indigenized Protestantism had readily tapped into that tradition. The antagonism between the state and heterodox religion is rooted, of course, in the imperial tradition that bestowed the Mandate of Heaven on the ruler, who presided over both the political and the moral universe. Heterodox beliefs that offered salvation to, and demanded loyalty from, disenchanted social groups threatened both the authority and the moral prestige of the state and inevitably drew harsh, often violent, official suppression. That in turn radicalized religious movements and provoked popular uprisings.

The tension has continued under Communist rule. Richard Madsen reminds us that the Maoist state assumed the same "quasi-religious status" as it became not only an instrument of power but also "a representation of the moral order." In response, the unofficial Catholic Church has emerged as "a locus of passive resistance and insubordination" and has "at least the potential of becoming a nucleus of rural rebellion."[54] Similar conjectures about the underground Protestant church also began to emerge in the aftermath of the Tian'anmen crackdown of 1989 when an article published in an influential Hong Kong magazine called the church in China "a force of resistance that is growing in strength."[55] In August 2006, following the violent clash between police and the underground congregation in Xiaoshan over the demolition of its church, a *Time* magazine article observed, "Although Christians tend not to see themselves as revolutionaries, house churches have become one of China's few bulwarks against government power."[56]

Will popular Christianity inspire a violent uprising? Will "messianic theology eventually [breed] messianic politics"—an "iron law" that Mark Lilla believes was long ago uncovered by Thomas Hobbes?[57] Given the overwhelming power of the centralized state in contemporary China, there is little likelihood in the near future that a fragmented, however spirited, Christian movement will foment popular revolt. In the long run, one has to face that potential. Fundamentally, the answer depends primarily not on what happens within the Chinese church, but outside it—on whether or not Chinese politics, Chinese society, and Chinese life in general will evolve toward the rule of law, stability, and greater equality and "harmony," which the current leadership loudly champions, or will assume a beastly look, as pictured in Daniel and the Book of Revelation. In view of the CCP's reluctance to undergo fundamental political reform to confront the problems of Chinese society, one cannot discount the possibility that a major crisis would produce a deadly mingling of religious and political heterodoxy to spark an open flame of revolutionary chiliasm. As Susan Naquin reminds us, in popular millenarianism in Chinese history (with its "normally diffuse" but "potentially cohesive" organization), "believer and rebel" were merely "different phases of the same salvational process."[58] However, such a revolution, if it does break out, is unlikely to succeed, given the historical tendency of messianic movements in China toward utopian radicalism, internal strife, a plebian estrangement of the elite, and, ultimately, political incompetence. One would hope that the development of civil society in China would direct the energy as well as the anxiety and resentment of popular Christianity into secular politics and civic institutions. In the foreseeable future, however, chances for meaningful political reforms are slim, and the hostility between the state and the underground church is set to continue well into the twenty-first century.

NOTES

In citing works in the notes, I have generally used short titles. Works frequently cited are identified by the following abbreviations:

CCYB   *China Christian Year Book*
CMYB   *China Mission Year Book*
CR   *Chinese Recorder*
MRW   *Missionary Review of the World*
NYT   *New York Times*
ZJN   *Zhonghua Jidujiaohui nianjian*

EPIGRAPH

The epigraph is from T. S. Eliot, *Little Gidding*, No. 4 of *Four Quartets* (London: Faber and Faber, 1942), IV. The rest of the section runs as follows:

Who then devised the torment? Love.
Love is the unfamiliar Name
Behind the hands that wove
The intolerable shirt of flame
Which human power cannot remove.
    We only live, only suspire
    Consumed by either fire or fire.

INTRODUCTION

1. Howard W. French, "China Adds Restrictions in Effort to Shake the Faith of Independent Congregations," *NYT*, August 18, 2006; "Zhongguo Jidutu tong jingcha fansheng chongtu" (Chinese Christians Clash with Police),

BBC Chinese, August 1, 2006; China Aid Association, "Guanyu Zhejiang Xiaoshan jingfang qiangxing chaihui Dangshan tang de jinji shengming" (An Urgent Appeal Regarding the Forced Demolition of Dangshan
Church by the Police of Xiaoshan, Zhejiang), August 2, 2006, http://www
.peacehall.com/news/gb/china/2006/08/200608030623.shtml; Xiaoshan
house church leaders, interview. The incident took place in the township
of Dangshan. According to some of the sources, including those interviewed, thousands, not hundreds, of security officers were involved in
the raid. This is one of the many cases in which I had to reconcile differences in multiple sources. To prevent the notes from getting hopelessly
bloated, I have, in general, simply cited those sources without discussing
the minor differences and how I squared them.

2. Simon Elegant, "The War for China's Soul," *Time,* August 28, 2006, p. 40.
3. Dong Fang, "Zhejiang jingfang he dixia jiaohui chengyuan baoli chongtu"
   (Zhejiang Police Clash Violently with Underground Church Members),
   Voice of America, July 31, 2006; author's site visit and interview with Xiaoshan house church leaders, August 4, 2008. The new church in Hengpeng was completed in late 2005. Unapproved church constructions—
   and subsequent demolitions—have also been reported in other parts of
   the country. See press release archives of the China Aid Association at
   http://chinaaid.org.
4. Xiaoshan house church leaders, interview; Hong Kong–based evangelist
   and witness of the event (name omitted), interview, Fuzhou, August 2,
   2008. See also Dong Fang, "Zhejiang jingfang."
5. Gu Changsheng, *Zhongguo Jidujiao jianshi,* p. 97; U.S. Department of
   State, "International Religious Freedom Report" (2008); Brian Grim,
   "Religion in China on the Eve of the 2008 Beijing Olympics," Pew Forum
   on Religion & Public Life, May 7, 2008, http://pewresearch.org/pubs/
   827/china-religion-olympics; "Sons of Heaven," *Economist,* October 2,
   2008, http://www.economist.com/world/asia/displaystory.cfm?story_id=
   12342509. In 2006, the TSPM put the number of Chinese Protestants at
   more than 16 million. Current estimates of the numerical strength of the
   Protestant community vary considerably and run as high as 130 million.
   My own estimate of more than 50 million takes into account the facts that
   many house churches also register with the government and are already
   included in official figures, and that competing underground church
   groups tend to exaggerate their numbers and to lay claims to the same
   Protestant community in a given locality. See also Chapter 9, n.67. In
   2008, the Chinese Catholic Patriotic Association reported a total membership of 5.3 million and estimated that an additional 12 million Catholics
   worshiped in underground churches. See "The True Picture of China's
   Catholics," *Global Times,* April 22, 2009, http://en.huanqiu.com/www/
   english/opinion/top_photo/2009-04/426459.html.

6. Erik Eckholm, "China's Churches: Glad, and Bitter, Tidings," *NYT*, June 17, 1998.

7. Li Gangji, *Jiaowu jilue*, Part 3, pp. 21–22.

8. Jing Jing, "Daqin Jingjiao"; Wang Zhixin, *Zhongguo Jidujiao shigang*, pp. 37–41, 50; Charbonnier, *Christians in China*, pp. 24–30, 34, 50; Fairbank, *China: A New History*, p. 78. I consulted Charbonnier's work in rendering my own translation.

9. Wang Zhixin, *Zhongguo Jidujiao shigang*, p. 44; Charbonnier, *Christians in China*, pp. 67, 72–73, 76. During that period, Christianity survived among some tribes of Central Asia, including the Keraits, Onguts, Uighurs, Merkits, and Naimans. Recent archeological finds in Quanzhou suggest that a remnant Syrian Christianity community may have survived in China itself through the end of the Song Dynasty. See Wu Youxiong, "Yuandai Quanzhou," pp. 469–71.

10. Charbonnier, *Christians in China*, pp. 94, 100; Dawson, *Mongol Mission*, Appendix, pp. 73–76, 85–86; Weatherford, *Genghis Khan*, p. 152.

11. Komroff, *Travels of Marco Polo*, pp. 117–20. See also Standaert, *Handbook of Christianity in China*, pp. 80–82; S. N. C. Lieu, "Nestorians and Manichaeans on the South China Coast," *Vigiliae Christianae* 34 (1980): 72; Moule, *Christians in China before the Year 1550*, pp. 142–43.

12. Gillman and Klimkeit, *Christians in Asia before 1500*, p. 289; Latourette, *History of Christian Missions*, p. 65; Wang Zhixin, *Zhongguo Jidujiao shigang*, pp. 48–51.

13. See Moule, *Christians in China before the Year 1550*, pp. 250–51.

14. Standaert, *Handbook of Christianity in China*, p. 83; Charbonnier, *Christians in China*, pp. 107–9, 123–24; Latourette, *History of Christian Missions*, pp. 73–77. See also Wang Zhixin, *Zhongguo Jidujiao shigang*, pp. 61–62; Gu Changsheng, *Zhongguo Jidujiao jianshi*, pp. 20–24.

15. Charbonnier, *Christians in China*, pp. 132–33; Standaert, *Handbook of Christianity in China*, pp. 438–41.

16. Spence, *To Change China*, pp. 23–28; Wang Zhixin, *Zhongguo Jidujiao shigang*, pp. 91–104, 119–23.

17. Wang Zhixin, *Zhongguo Jidujiao shigang*, p. 129; Latourette, *History of Christian Missions*, pp. 126–29. See also Mungello, *Great Encounter*, p. 34. According to Mungello, "920 Jesuits . . . participated in the China mission between 1552 and 1800."

18. Gu Changsheng, *Zhongguo Jidujiao jianshi*, pp. 39–40; Latourette, *History of Christian Missions*, pp. 132–41, 146–48; Charbonnier, *Christians in China*, pp. 262–64.

19. Latourette, *History of Christian Missions*, pp. 174–75, 182–83. See also Entenmann, "Catholics and Society," p. 8, and Mungello, *Great Encounter*, p. 59, for a more positive assessment of the situation as Christianity was absorbed into, and transmitted within, the family structure.

20. Latourette, *History of Christian Missions*, pp. 212, 226.

21. Boynton and Boynton, *Handbook of the Christian Movement in China*, pp. v, ix, 304–35; Bates, "Gleanings," p. 96. By 1914, a total of 107 missionary societies were operating inside China.

22. Fairbank, *Missionary Enterprise*, pp. 2–3.

23. Cable, *Fulfillment of a Dream of Pastor Hsi*, p. 217.

24. Gu Changsheng, *Chuanjiaoshi*, p. 136. See also Cohen, *China and Christianity*, p. 275.

25. Lutz, *China and the Christian Colleges*, pp. 238–39, 252–54; Yeh, *Jindai Zhongguo de zongjiao pipan*, pp. 44–55; Latourette, *History of Christian Missions*, p. 697.

26. *CCYB* (1928), p. 9; Latourette, *History of Christian Missions*, p. 820. See also Boynton and Boynton, *Handbook of the Christian Movement in China*, p. ix; Grubb, *World Christian Handbook*, p. 249. Some of the 5,000 evacuees did return. In 1928, a total of 4,375 Protestant missionaries were reported; in 1949, the figure was about 4,000.

27. Fairbank, *Missionary Enterprise*, p. 1.

28. Cox, *Fire from Heaven*, p. 86.

29. Weber, *Religion of China*, p. 181.

30. See Sanneh and Carpenter, *Changing Face of Christianity*, Preface, p. vii.

31. Mungello, *Spirit and the Flesh in Shandong*, pp. 5–6, 140–41. See also Charbonnier, *Christians in China*, p. 238; Laamann, *Christian Heretics in Late Imperial China*, p. 3.

32. Jean-Paul Wiest, "Setting Roots: The Catholic Church in China to 1949," in Kindopp and Hamrin, *God and Caesar in China*, p. 91; Charbonnier, *Christians in China*, pp. 395–96; Madsen, "Catholic Church in China," p. 112.

33. See Boynton and Boynton, *Handbook of the Christian Movement in China*, pp. 202–3. The *China Christian Year Book*, published in the 1920s and 1930s by the Christian Literature Society for China, was primarily an annual report on Protestant developments put out by an editorial staff of Presbyterian, Baptist, and Methodist missionaries.

34. Troeltsch, *Social Teaching of the Christian Churches* 1: 82.

35. Cohn, *Pursuit of the Millennium*, p. 13.

36. See Cohn, *Pursuit of the Millennium*; Boyer, *When Time Shall Be No More*; Wacker, *Heaven Below*.

37. Bays, "Christianity and Chinese Sects," p. 123. See also Bays, "Indigenous Protestant Churches in China," pp. 128, 137.

38. Huntington, *Clash of Civilizations*, p. 66.

CHAPTER 1. IN SEARCH OF CHINESE CHRISTIANITY

1. Latourette, *History of Christian Missions*, pp. 213–14, 226.

2. Wickeri, *Seeking the Common Ground*, p. 37.

3. Boardman, *Christian Influence*, p. 42.

4. Waley as quoted in Lutz, "Grand Illusion," p. 50. See also Gu Changsheng,

Chuanjiaoshi, pp. 30–31; Latourette, *History of Christian Missions*, pp. 230, 274.

5. Li Zhigang, *Jidujiao*, pp. 61, 64, 244; Lutz, "Karl Gützlaff's Approach," pp. 269–71; Latourette, *History of Christian Missions*, p. 219.

6. Lutz and Lutz, "Invisible China Missionaries," p. 206; Lutz, "Karl Gützlaff's Approach," pp. 272, 275, 277; Li Zhigang, *Jidujiao*, pp. 64, 70–72.

7. Lutz, "Karl Gützlaff's Approach," p. 277. See also Lutz and Lutz, "Invisible China Missionaries," pp. 214–15; Li Zhigang, *Jidujiao*, p. 66. In her comments on a draft of this chapter, Lutz added, "Yet a number of Chinese Union members . . . gradually internalized the Christianity they were preaching. They founded several Christian congregations which became the core of the Hakka Christian church still existent today." For Tiandihui, see Ownby, "Heaven and Earth Society as Popular Religion," p. 1023.

8. Latourette, *History of Christian Missions*, pp. 226, 479.

9. See Spence, *God's Chinese Son*, pp. 89, 118, 133.

10. See Michael, *Taiping Rebellion* 1: 14–15.

11. See Chen Gonglu, *Taiping Tianguo lishi luncong*, pp. 64–67; Spence, *God's Chinese Son*, pp. 23–24.

12. Michael, *Taiping Rebellion* 1: 24–25; "The Taiping Heavenly Chronicle," in Michael, *Taiping Rebellion* 2: 56–66; Boardman, *Christian Influence*, p. 77. See also Spence, *God's Chinese Son*, p. 17.

13. "Gospel Jointly Witnessed and Heard by the Imperial Eldest and Second Eldest Brothers" (1860), in Michael, *Taiping Rebellion* 2: 9–10.

14. "Taiping Heavenly Chronicle," pp. 53–62.

15. "Appendix I: A Chronology of the Taiping Rebellion," in Michael, *Taiping Rebellion* 3: 1573–1611; Spence, *God's Chinese Son*, pp. 67–71.

16. Hung Jen-kan, "Hung Hsiu-Ch'üan's Background," in Michael, *Taiping Rebellion* 2: 7; Michael, *Taiping Rebellion* 1: 30.

17. Hong Xiuquan, "The Taiping Imperial Declaration" (1852), in Michael, *Taiping Rebellion* 2: 46; Spence, *God's Chinese Son*, pp. 80–81; Hunt, *Christian Millenarianism*, pp. 122–23.

18. Hung Jen-kan, "Hung Hsiu-Ch'üan's Background," pp. 4–5.

19. Michael, *Taiping Rebellion* 1: 35–36. See also Kojima Shinji, *Hong Xiuquan*, p. 52; Shih, *Taiping Ideology*, pp. 323, 328.

20. "Appendix I: A Chronology of the Taiping Rebellion," in Michael, *Taiping Rebellion* 3: 1573–1611; Michael, *Taiping Rebellion*, 1: 35–36.

21. Jen Yu-wen, *Qingshi Hong Xiuquan zaiji*, quoted in Li Zhigang, *Jidujiao*, p. 81. See also Spence, *God's Chinese Son*, pp. 76–77; Michael, *Taiping Rebellion* 1: 30; Boardman, *Christian Influence*, p. 118; Overmyer, *Folk Buddhist Religion*, p. 189.

22. Michael, *Taiping Rebellion* 1: 70; Spence, *God's Chinese Son*, p. 80. The Qing government estimated a total of more than three million Taiping rebels. See also Chen Gonglu, *Taiping Tianguo lishi luncong*, pp. 203, 207.

23. Spence, *God's Chinese Son*, p. 174. The Taiping segregation of sexes was

enforced from 1851 through 1855. See also Kojima Shinji, *Hong Xiuquan*, pp. 95–96.

24. "Tianchao tianmu zhidu," in Michael, *Taiping Rebellion* 2: 313–14.

25. Ibid., pp. 310, 314–15. See also Kojima Shinji, *Hong Xiuquan*, pp. 93–94. For the prototype of this hierarchical structure, see *Zhouli*, "Xiaguan Sima" (part 4 of 6), pp. 161–62.

26. Michael, *Taiping Rebellion* 2: 311; Kojima Shinji, *Hong Xiuquan*, pp. 101–10.

27. Michael, *Taiping Rebellion* 2: 232–35, 253–54.

28. Zeng Guofan as quoted in Spence, *Search for Modern China*, p. 178.

29. *ZJN* (1914) 1: 32–36; Latourette, *History of Christian Missions*, p. 366.

30. Zheng Yugui et al., eds., *Nanwang de licheng: Fujian Jidujiao sanzi daolu wushi nian* (The Unforgettable Journey: Fifty Years of Three-Self for Christianity in Fujian) (Fuzhou: Fujian sheng Jidujiao xiehui, 2001), p. 246; Wang Zhixin, *Zhongguo Jidujiao shigang*, p. 205; Dunch, *Fuzhou Protestants*, pp. 22–23.

31. Li Zhigang, *Jidujiao*, pp. 247–48; *CMYB* (1912), p. 220.

32. *ZJN* (1924), p. 77; *ZJN* (1927), p. 35; Tao Feiya and Liu Tianlu, *Jidujiaohui yu jindai Shandong shehui*, pp. 86–87.

33. Lutz and Lutz, "Invisible China Missionaries," p. 213; *Nanjing shenxue zhi*, August 1998, pp. 46–47.

34. Austin, "Missions Dream Team," p. 21; Cha, *Zhongguo Jidujiao*, p. 22. See also *CMYB* (1923), p. 242.

35. Taylor, *Pastor Hsi*, pp. 14–16, 20–21, 43, 46, 91, 96, 172; Austin, "Missions Dream Team," pp. 21–22.

36. Taylor, *Pastor Hsi*, pp. 182, 216; Taylor, *One of China's Scholars*, pp. 9–10. See also Wang Shenyin, "Xi Shengmo," p. 99; Latourette, *History of Christian Missions*, pp. 391, 434; Austin, "Missions Dream Team," p. 21.

37. Taylor, *Pastor Hsi*, pp. xvii, 170–75, 214–16.

38. Ibid., pp. 64–66, 172. See also *CMYB* (1924), p. 487; Austin, "Missions Dream Team," p. 22.

39. Taylor, *Pastor Hsi*, pp. 29, 45, 271–72, 289; Taylor, *One of China's Scholars*, pp. 9–10; Cha, *Zhongguo Jidujiao*, p. 24.

40. Taylor, *One of China's Scholars*, pp. 9–10.

41. Taylor, *Pastor Hsi*, pp. 225, 248–50, 274; Austin, "Missions Dream Team," p. 21.

42. Taylor, *Pastor Hsi*, pp. 172, 351, 354; Wang Shenyin, "Xi Shengmo" (Part 1), p. 99, (Continued), p. 125.

43. Xi Shengmo, *Xi Shengmo shige*, No. 19.

44. Ibid., No. 7. See also Austin, "Missions Dream Team," p. 22.

45. Taylor, *Pastor Hsi*, p. 351.

46. Austin, "Missions Dream Team," pp. 22–23.

47. Cable, *Fulfillment of a Dream of Pastor Hsi*, pp. 214–16.

48. D. E. Hoste, "Possible Changes and Developments in the Native Churches Arising Out of the Present Crisis," *CR* 31 (October 1900): 509–10.

49. "An Imperial Decree" of the Qing government, March 15, 1899, originally translated and published in the *North China Daily* (May 19, 1899), quoted in Broomhall, *Martyred Missionaries*, p. 309.

50. Broomhall, *Martyred Missionaries*, p. 311.

51. *ZJN* (1927), p. 35; Gu Weimin, *Jidujiao yu jindai Zhongguo shehui*, p. 450. See also Latourette, *History of Christian Missions*, p. 615; Xia Dongyuan, *Ershi shiji Zhongguo dabolan*, p. 30.

52. *ZJN* (1914), p. 12; *ZJN* (1927), p. 35. See also *CMYB* (1912), pp. 216–17; Zong Yao, "Shixi benshiji chu Shanghai Jidujiao," p. 121; Li Zhigang, *Jidujiao*, p. 249.

53. Gu Weimin, *Jidujiao yu jindai Zhongguo shehui*, pp. 450–51.

54. *CMYB* (1912), p. 217; Zong Yao, "Shixi benshiji chu Shanghai Jidujiao," pp. 118, 120; Yao Minquan, *Shanghai Jidujiao shi*, pp. 167–68.

55. Latourette, *History of Christian Missions*, p. 615; *ZJN* (1915), p. 147.

56. *ZJN* (1915), pp. 146–47; *ZJN* (1916), pp. [Xu] 114–20; *ZJN* (1925), pp. 68–73; Latourette, *History of Christian Missions*, p. 615.

57. *ZJN* (1925), pp. 68–73; Yao Minquan, *Shanghai Jidujiao shi*, p. 169; Latourette, *History of Christian Missions*, pp. 677–78.

58. Zong Yao, "Shixi benshiji chu Shanghai Jidujiao," pp. 118–22.

59. Alex R. Saunders, "The Problem of Reaching the Masses in China," *CR* 41 (March 1910): 204.

60. Latourette, *History of Christian Missions*, p. 673.

61. Ibid., p. 674.

62. W. Nelson Bitton, "Report of the Proceedings of the World Missionary Conference in Edinburgh from June 13th to 23rd," *CR* 41 (August 1910): 543; "Dr. Cheng Ching-yi," p. 692; Latourette, *History of Christian Missions*, pp. 677–78.

63. Lian Xi, *Conversion of Missionaries*, p. 135; *CMYB* (1913), p. 67. The same Chinese name Zhonghua Jidujiaohui was later adopted for the better-known interdenominational federation of mission churches—the Church of Christ in China—that emerged in 1927. See *CMYB* (1923), p. 334; Stauffer, *Christian Occupation of China*, p. 381.

64. Latourette, *History of Christian Missions*, pp. 620, 807; *ZJN* (1914), pp. 43–45. Other organizers of the Society included Yu Rizhang, Shi Meiyu (Mary Stone), and Cai Sujuan.

65. Bates, "Gleanings," p. 35; Latourette, *History of Christian Missions*, pp. 776–77, 807; *ZJN* (1934–1936), p. 143.

66. Rev. J. F. Love, "Relation of Doctrinal Soundness to Missionary Success," *Home and Foreign Fields*, October 1921, p. 6. See also Lian Xi, *Conversion of Missionaries*, pp. 134–35, 137.

67. Charles Ernest Scott, "Ding, the Apostle of Shantung," *MRW*, February 1911, pp. 125–27; *ZJN* (1914), p. 55. See also Cha, *Zhongguo Jidujiao*, pp. 107–8.

68. Bates, "Gleanings," p. 38; W. E. Taylor, "Evangelistic Movements among Students in China," *CMYB* (1916), p. 226–27.

69. *ZJN* (1914), pp. 43–45. See also Qu Zhengmin, "Meiguo zhanglaohui," pp. 256–57.

70. Latourette, *History of Christian Missions,* p. 620; Ding Limei, "Budaohui zhi banfa ji qingxing" (Methods and Current State of Evangelistic Meetings), *ZJN* (1914), pp. 53–57.

71. Lin Yutang, *From Pagan to Christian,* p. 233; Dunch, *Fuzhou Protestants,* pp. 158, 168.

72. Ding Limei, "Budaohui," pp. 53–57. See also Taylor, "Evangelistic Movements among Students in China," pp. 229–30.

73. Wu, *Yu Cidu,* pp. 23, 151–52; Kinnear, *Against the Tide,* p. 24.

74. Wu, *Yu Cidu,* pp. 36, 49–50, 87, 101–2, 106.

75. Ibid., pp. 62–63, 87, 101–5, 149–52.

76. *ZJN* (1914), pp. 29, 93; *ZJN* (1916), p. 229; *CR* 40 (May 1909): 292; Wu, *Yu Cidu,* pp. 152, 155–56, 164–71.

77. Wu, *Yu Cidu,* pp. 166–67. For the mission statement, see *CR* 47 (1916): 327.

78. *ZJN* (1924), p. 44. Other SVM leaders included Zhu Youyu, Jiang Changchuan, and Chen Jinyong. See *ZJN* (1914), pp. 43–45; Latourette, *History of Christian Missions,* p. 593; Taylor, "Evangelistic Movements among Students in China," pp. 227–231.

79. *ZJN* (1927), pp. 169–70; Wu, *Yu Cidu,* pp. 157–62; Qu Zhengmin, "Meiguo zhanglaohui," pp. 256–57.

CHAPTER 2. THE LIGHTNING OUT OF THE EAST

The epigraphs to this chapter are excerpted from D. E. Hoste, "Possible Changes and Developments in the Native Churches Arising Out of the Present Crisis," *CR* 31 (October 1900): 511; Wei Baoluo, *Shengling zhen jianzheng shu,* quoted in Wei Yisa, *Zhen Yesu Jiaohui,* pp. B22–B23.

1. Wei Yisa, *Zhen Yesu Jiaohui,* pp. C3, M8–M9; *CMYB* (1917), p. 102.

2. Wei Yisa, *Zhen Yesu Jiaohui,* pp. B20, M6; Chen Guangzao, "Zhen Yesu Jiaohui," pp. 3–5; Bays, "Indigenous Protestant Churches in China," pp. 130–32; Burgess, *New International Dictionary,* "China." Wei Enbo was baptized by "Ben Dexin," almost certainly the Chinese name of Bernt Berntsen (according to Bays). See also Lian Xi, "Messianic Deliverance," p. 434 n.10.

3. Ahlstrom, *Religious History,* pp. 819–21; Wacker, *Heaven Below,* pp. 3, 6. As a centerpiece of the modern popular eschatological movement, glossolalia can be traced back to the 1830s. During the 1820s, Edward Irving, minister of a Scotch Presbyterian chapel in London, preached about Christ's imminent return. Excommunicated by the London Presbytery for heresy in 1830, Irving won greater notoriety by encouraging glossolalia as one of the "signs and wonders" of the Last Days. See Boyer, *When Time Shall Be No More,* pp. 86–87.

4. Frodsham, *With Signs Following*, pp. 8–9. See also Ahlstrom, *Religious History*, pp. 820–21.

5. Wacker, *Heaven Below*, p. 45.

6. Bays, "Protestant Missionary Establishment," pp. 52–55. See also Boynton, *Directory of Protestant Missions in China*.

7. James A. Field Jr., "Near East Notes and Far East Queries," in Fairbank, *Missionary Enterprise*, p. 35.

8. *CMYB* (1910), "Statistics of the Work of Protestant Missions in China for 1909–1910."

9. Latourette, *History of Christian Missions*, pp. 601–2.

10. Wei Yisa, *Zhen Yesu Jiaohui*, pp. B18–B20, B22–B23, M4, M6.

11. Ibid., pp. C1–C6, D8, F12, F21, M6–M7. See also Chen Guangzao, "Zhen Yesu Jiaohui," p. 5. The TJC formally registered with the Beijing government in February 1918.

12. Wei Yisa, *Zhen Yesu Jiaohui*, pp. F1, F4, F11, H1; Bays, "Indigenous Protestant Churches in China," p. 134. I have used Bays's translation of "Wanguo gengzhengjiao bao."

13. Wei Yisa, *Zhen Yesu Jiaohui*, pp. B17, F1–F2, F11; Bays, "Indigenous Protestant Churches in China," pp. 134–35.

14. Wei Yisa, *Zhen Yesu Jiaohui*, pp. B19, C4, F1–F2. See also Zhen Yesu Jiaohui, *Shengling bao*, August 1926, pp. 2–3.

15. See Wei Yisa, *Zhen Yesu Jiaohui*, pp. B4, B20, M2, M7, M9.

16. Ibid., pp. F2–F3, M7.

17. Ibid., pp. C7–C11, M6. See also Bays, "Indigenous Protestant Churches in China," p. 134.

18. Wei Yisa, *Zhen Yesu Jiaohui*, pp. B17–B19, C4–C5, F13 (2), J1, J3, M12; F. P. Jones, *Church in Communist China*, p. 17. See also *CMYB* (1918), pp. 41–42.

19. Wei Yisa, *Zhen Yesu Jiaohui*, pp. F13 (2), J1, M12; *CMYB* (1923), pp. 242–43.

20. Wei Yisa, *Zhen Yesu Jiaohui*, pp. M12, J1–J2, D2, F14; Zhen Yesu Jiaohui, *Shengling bao* II, 2 (February 1927): 16.

21. Wei Yisa, *Zhen Yesu Jiaohui*, pp. C2, C21, M8–M10.

22. Latourette, *History of Christian Missions*, p. 598; Gu Changsheng, "Meiguo Anxirihui," pp. 11, 22–23.

23. Wei Yisa, *Zhen Yesu Jiaohui*, pp. C2, M19. See also Bays, "Indigenous Protestant Churches in China," pp. 132–33.

24. Wei Yisa, *Zhen Yesu Jiaohui*, pp. C11–C12, M9, M13.

25. Ibid., pp. C14–C15; Mao Zedong, "Hunan nongmin yundong," pp. 32–34. Guan Shengdi is a variant of Guangong, or Lord Guan.

26. Du Kaixu, "Zhen Yesu Jiaohui Maoping qidaosuo," pp. 141–46.

27. Deng Huagui and Sheng Daoyan, "Yanwo yidai de Zhen Yesu Jiaohui," p. 183.

28. Wei Yisa, *Zhen Yesu Jiaohui*, pp. C18, M10; Richard, *Forty-Five Years in China*, p. 310; Latourette, *History of Christian Missions*, p. 525. TJC teachings first reached Shanxi in 1919 when an unnamed student at a university

in Beijing was won over to the sect and carried the new faith back to his home province.

29. Wei Yisa, *Zhen Yesu Jiaohui*, pp. C19, M10. See also Latourette, *History of Christian Missions*, pp. 775–76; *CMYB* (1924), p. 486.

30. Wei Yisa, *Zhen Yesu Jiaohui*, pp. C34, C2; Gu Changsheng, "Meiguo Anxirihui."

31. Wei Yisa, *Zhen Yesu Jiaohui*, pp. C39–C41.

32. Yu Yucheng, interview, June 9, 2002.

33. Ibid.; Wei Yisa, *Zhen Yesu Jiaohui*, pp. C39–C41.

34. Lodwick, *Crusaders against Opium*, pp. 117, 178–79.

35. *CMYB* (1924), pp. 399–402. See also Madancy, *Troublesome Legacy of Commissioner Lin*, pp. 361–69.

36. Huang Zongrong, "'Zhen Yesu Jiao' zai Zhangpu," pp. 164–65; Chen Guangzao, "Zhen Yesu Jiaohui," pp. 12–15, 31. See also W. A. Graham Aspland, "Drug Traffic in China," *CMYB* (1923), p. 218; Lodwick, *Crusaders against Opium*, pp. 34–35, 136.

37. Wei Yisa, *Zhen Yesu Jiaohui*, pp. C1, C43; Chen Guangzao, "Zhen Yesu jiaohui," pp. 12–15.

38. Wei Yisa, *Zhen Yesu Jiaohui*, pp. C1, C39–C40, C59.

39. Ibid., pp. D2–D3, H1, H4, K3, M9.

40. Ibid., pp. G2, G14.

41. Ibid., pp. H5–H6; Xiong Songnian, "Xiangtan Zhen Yesu Jiaohui," pp. 253–54; Du Kaixu, "Zhen Yesu Jiaohui Maoping qidaosuo," pp. 138–48.

42. *CMYB* (1923), pp. 329–31; Wei Yisa, *Zhen Yesu Jiaohui*, pp. B21, D2–D3.

43. Wei Yisa, *Zhen Yesu Jiaohui*, pp. C22, C27.

44. Ibid., p. C22.

45. Cha, *Zhongguo Jidujiao*, p. 241; "Dr. Timothy Tingfang Lew," Lew, Papers.

46. "Dr. Cheng Ching-yi," pp. 692–93; Latourette, *History of Christian Missions*, p. 797.

47. *CMYB* (1923), p. 330; "Dr. Cheng Ching-yi," p. 693.

48. Wei Yisa, *Zhen Yesu Jiaohui*, pp. C22, C27.

49. *CMYB* (1923), p. 329. See also Lian Xi, *Conversion of Missionaries*, p. 159.

50. Latourette, *History of Christian Missions*, p. 798; "Dr. Cheng Ching-yi," p. 693; Cha, *Zhongguo Jidujiao*, pp. 121–26.

51. Cha, *Zhongguo Jidujiao*, p. 138; Latourette, *History of Christian Missions*, p. 628; "Dr. Cheng Ching-yi," p. 692.

52. NCC, *Annual Report* (1922–1923), pp. 36–39; *CMYB* (1923), p. 331; "Who's Who among Chinese Christian Leaders," *CCYB* (1936–1937), pp. 428–30; Wei Yisa, *Zhen Yesu Jiaohui*, pp. D9, J1–J5, M20.

53. NCC, *Annual Report* (1925–1926), pp. 163–69.

54. Wei Yisa, *Zhen Yesu Jiaohui*, pp. B4, B23; Chao, "Chinese Indigenous Church Movement," pp. 204–9; Latourette, *History of Christian Missions*, pp. 699, 819. See also *CCYB* (1931), p. 79.

55. Wei Yisa, *Zhen Yesu Jiaohui*, pp. J1–J9, C4, D7, M21. See also Wing-tsit Chan, *Religious Trends in Modern China*, pp. 162–68.

56. Wei Yisa, *Zhen Yesu Jiaohui*, pp. D5–D12, D21, J6; Bays, "Indigenous Protestant Churches in China," pp. 136–37.

57. *CCYB* (1934–1935), pp. 100–101.

58. Wei Yisa, *Zhen Yesu Jiaohui*, p. B3; Zhen Yesu Jiaohui, *Shengling bao*, August 1926, p. 7.

CHAPTER 3. THE JESUS FAMILY

The epigraph to this chapter is excerpted from Yesu Jiating, *Yesu Jiating shige*, No. 1. See also Tao Feiya, "Christian Utopia," pp. 84–85.

1. Billingsley, *Bandits in Republican China*, pp. 33–34, 217.

2. Wang Chao-hsiang, "Religious Elements in the Esoteric Societies of China," p. 762; Chan Wing-tsit, *Religious Trends*, pp. 163–64.

3. Ma Honggang, "Jieshao Zhongguo xinxing de jiaopai," p. 6; Wang Shen-yin, "Mazhuang 'Yesu Jiating' shimo," p. 90; Zhu Xin, "Wo suo renshi de Yesu Jiating," *Huhan* 47: 170–72; Tao Feiya, "Christian Utopia," pp. 42–47. See also "Tai'an diqu jiaohui xuexiao," p. 68.

4. Hanson to Ruth Ransom, Secretary of the Woman's Foreign Missionary Society, July 27, 1938, Dillenbeck, Biographical File.

5. Zhu Xin, "Wo suo renshi de Yesu Jiating," *Huhan* 47: 170; *Mazhuang Yesu Jiating*, p. 2; Wang Shenyin, "Mazhuang 'Yesu Jiating' shimo," p. 90; Tao Feiya, "Christian Utopia," pp. 47–48.

6. Woman's Foreign Missionary Society (WFMS) of the Methodist Episcopal Church, "Contract" signed with Dillenbeck, November 2, 1913; Bette James, Secretary of Chicago Training School for City, Home, and Foreign Missions, to WFMS, April 17, 1913; "Extracts from References." All from Dillenbeck, Biographical File.

7. Ma Honggang, "Jieshao Zhongguo xinxing de jiaopai," p. 6; Tao Feiya, "Christian Utopia," pp. 45, 47–48; *Mazhuang Yesu Jiating*, p. 2; Wang Shenyin, "Mazhuang 'Yesu Jiating' shimo," p. 111, n.2.

8. Tao Feiya, "Christian Utopia," pp. 50–51, 54; Wang Shenyin, "Mazhuang 'Yesu Jiating' shimo," p. 90. See also Wang Shih-peng (Wang Xipeng) and H. W. Spillett, "A Christian Communist Settlement in China," Missionary Research Library (Union Theological Seminary, New York), *Occasional Bulletin* 1, 13 (December 15, 1950): 1; Tai'anshi difang shizhi bangongshi, *Tai'an wuqiannian*, pp. 136–40; *CMYB* (1923), pp. 242–43.

9. Ma Honggang, "Jieshao Zhongguo xinxing de jiaopai," p. 6; Tao Feiya, "Christian Utopia," pp. 58–61. See also Xing You et al., "Taishan Gupin-yuan," pp. 200–228; Albus, *Twentieth-Century Onesiphorus*, pp. 23, 32–36, 143; *CMYB* (1914), "Directory."

10. Hanson to Ransom, July 27, 1938; Tao Feiya, "Christian Utopia," pp. 63–64.

11. Tao Feiya, *Zhongguo de Jidujiao wutuobang*, pp. 67–68; Albus, *Twentieth-Century Onesiphorus*, pp. 32–33.

12. Wang Shenyin, "Mazhuang 'Yesu Jiating' shimo," pp. 90–91, 96; Tao Feiya, "Christian Utopia," p. 66; *Mazhuang Yesu Jiating*, p. 2; Wang Xipeng, *Ji Yesu Jiating*, pp. 17, 21. See also Rees, *"Jesus Family,"* p. 14; Cha, *Zhongguo Jidujiao*, pp. 220–21. The name Yesu Jiating was first used by Jing for his own home in 1925 after he brought back his divorced wife.

13. See Tai'anshi difang shizhi bangongshi, *Tai'an wuqiannian*, pp. 147–49.

14. Wang Xipeng, *Ji Yesu Jiating*, pp. 15, 24; Zhu Xin, "Wo suo renshi de Yesu Jiating," *Huhan* 47: 175; Tao Feiya, "Christian Utopia," pp. 66, 91, 122; Wang Shenyin, "Mazhuang 'Yesu Jiating' shimo," p. 96. See also Jing Dianying to Li Dengfeng at Wuyuan Family, May 22, 1941, and Zhang Tianmin and Wang Yonglin, "Meiyimeihui yu Yesu Jiating zhi fenbiedian ji gaikuang" (Differences between, and a General Introduction to, the Methodist Episcopal Church and the Jesus Family), December 31, 1941, in Yesu Jiating, "Jiating shuxin." It appears that only a few leaders, including Jing himself, practiced complete *pochan*, the shedding of all private possessions before joining the Family.

15. *CCYB* (1932–1933), p. 188; Tao Feiya, "Christian Utopia," pp. 81–83; Wang Xipeng, *Ji Yesu Jiating*, p. 71.

16. Zhu Xin, "Wo suo renshi de Yesu Jiating," *Huhan* 47: 169; *Huhan* 49: 38–39; *Huhan* 51: 218.

17. Ibid., *Huhan* 51: 219–20; Jing Dianying, "Zeng Feng Lanxin yimeng bing xianjing xiezhen" (Verse written in honor of Feng Lanxin's Extraordinary Dreams), June 1940, in Jing Fuyin, *Lingyunji zhushi*, p. 121; Wang Xipeng, *Ji Yesu Jiating*, p. 54.

18. Jing Dianying, "Pin er le" (Joy in Poverty), in Jing Fuyin, *Lingyunji zhushi*, pp. 58–60. See also Yesu Jiating, "Sanshi nian lai de Yesu Jiating—Mazhuang laojia cheng renmin zhengfu yuanwen" (The Jesus Family in the Past Thirty Years: The Original Document Submitted to the People's Government by the Jesus Family at Mazhuang) (1950?), in Wang Xipeng, *Ji Yesu Jiating*, p. 15.

19. Cohen, *History in Three Keys*, pp. 96–97, 100. See also Esherick, *Origins of the Boxer Uprising*, pp. 216–19.

20. Cohen, *History in Three Keys*, pp. 96–97, 116–17.

21. During the 1930s, the Jesus Family attempted, but was unable to maintain, its theological training programs called Lingxiuyuan (the Court for Spiritual Retreat) and Daoxue Ban (the Class for the Study of the Way). See Dong Hengxin to Pentecostals in Yantai, n.d. (ca. 1940), in Yesu Jiating, "Jiating shuxin."

22. Yesu Jiating, "Fangzhou ge" (Song of the Ark), quoted in Wang Xipeng, *Ji Yesu Jiating*, p. 5.

23. Ma Xisha and Han Bingfang, *Zhongguo minjian zongjiao shi*, pp. 933,

1007–8, 1012; Naquin, *Millenarian Rebellion in China*, p. 10. See also Lev Deliusin, "The I-Kuan Tao Society," in Chesneaux, *Popular Movements and Secret Societies in China*, p. 227.

24. Ma Xisha and Han Bingfang, *Zhongguo minjian zongjiao shi*, pp. 1011, 1007. The incantation reads: "真空家鄉，無生父母，現在如來，彌勒我祖."

25. *Mazhuang Yesu Jiating*, p. 2. See also Wang Shenyin, "Mazhuang 'Yesu Jiating' shimo," p. 90; Tao Feiya, "Christian Utopia," p. 52.

26. Tao Feiya, "Christian Utopia," p. 82; *CMYB* (1924), pp. 487–88.

27. Rees, *"Jesus Family,"* pp. 34–35; *Mazhuang Yesu Jiating*, p. 9.

28. Li Ruijun, interview. Li, a former Jesus Family member, was elder of Bei Xinzhuang Church (renamed from Jesus Family) at the time of the interview.

29. Rees, *"Jesus Family,"* pp. 34–37; Zhu Xin, "Wo suo renshi de Yesu Jiating," *Huhan* 48: 281; Tao Feiya, "Christian Utopia," p. 88. The name of the hospital was Beijing Guoli Zhuchan Xuexiao Yiyuan.

30. Wang Xipeng, *Ji Yesu Jiating*, p. 64; Zhu Xin, "Wo suo renshi de Yesu Jiating," *Huhan* 50: 120.

31. Rees, *"Jesus Family,"* pp. 37–40; Wang Xipeng, *Ji Yesu Jiating*, pp. 64–65. See also Jing Zhendong, "Wo duiyu wushu wushen jiehun de baogao," pp. 41–42; *Mazhuang Yesu Jiating*, pp. 78–79; Tao Feiya, "Christian Utopia," pp. 88–89.

32. Clippings from Methodist Episcopal mission bulletins and branch reports, including correspondence from Dillenbeck and other reports on her life and service in Tai'an, Dillenbeck, Biographical File.

33. Hanson to Ransom, July 27, 1938; Hanson to "Dear Ones," from Tai'an, July 17, 1938, Dillenbeck, Biographical File.

34. Hanson to Ransom, July 27, 1938; biographical notes prepared by Louise Robinson of WFMS, Dillenbeck, Biographical File.

35. Romig, "Family of Jesus," pp. 7–8; Tao Feiya, "Christian Utopia," pp. 83, 98; Hanson to "Dear Ones."

36. See Tao Feiya, "Christian Utopia," pp. 88–89, 93; Wang Shenyin, "Mazhuang 'Yesu Jiating' shimo," pp. 94–95.

37. Yu, *Yejin tianming*, pp. 14, 78; Chang Zhifu, "Dui woxian 'Yesu Jiating' de tansuo," p. 153.

38. Zhang Tianmin and Wang Yonglin, "Meiyimeihui yu Yesu Jiating"; Rees, *"Jesus Family,"* p. 23; Zhu Xin, "Wo suo renshi de Yesu Jiating," *Huhan* 47: 176. In its later years, the Jesus Family also built a machine shop and an electrical department.

39. Jing Dianying to Li Dengfeng, May 22, 1941.

40. Rees, *"Jesus Family,"* pp. 101–2.

41. Tao Feiya, "Christian Utopia," pp. 89–90.

42. Romig, "Family of Jesus," pp. 5–6. See also *Shandong shengzhi*, p. 619; Sang Xujiu and Sun Bolong, "Shandong Zhonghua Jidujiao Ling'enhui," p. 1. See Chapter 4 for a discussion of the Spiritual Gifts Society.

43. Zhang Tianmin and Wang Yonglin, "Meiyimeihui yu Yesu Jiating."

44. *Mazhuang Yesu Jiating*, pp. 4, 18; Wang Xipeng, *Ji Yesu Jiating*, pp. 7, 24; Ma Honggang, "Jieshao Zhongguo xinxing de jiaopai," p. 8. See also Tao Feiya, "Christian Utopia," pp. 167–68. The Jesus Family did not institute fasting in its early years, but it became a more regular practice during the 1940s as economic hardships mounted.

45. Romig, "Family of Jesus," p. 2; Wang Shenyin, "Mazhuang 'Yesu Jiating' shimo," p. 101; Zhu Xin, "Wo suo renshi de Yesu Jiating," *Huhan* 48: 268–69.

46. Li Ruijun, interview.

47. Jing Zhendong, *Wo duiyu wushu wushen jiehun de baogao*, pp. 12, 38–39, 44; *Mazhuang Yesu Jiating*, p. 19; Jing Fuyin, interview. See also Tao Feiya, "Christian Utopia," p. 93. The statistics on marriages were from the period between 1942 and 1951.

48. *Mazhuang Yesu Jiating*, p. 19; Rees, *"Jesus Family,"* pp. 50–51; Wang Xipeng, *Ji Yesu Jiating*, pp. 33–34, 36.

49. Spence, *God's Chinese Son*, pp. 120–22, 171, 173.

50. Wang Xipeng, *Ji Yesu Jiating*, pp. 34–36. See also Wang Shih-peng and Spillett, "Christian Communist Settlement in China," p. 1. Wang's visit took place in 1949.

51. Yesu Jiating, *Xiangcun budao shige*, No. 132. See also Ma Honggang, "Jieshao Zhongguo xinxing de jiaopai," p. 8.

52. *Mazhuang Yesu Jiating*, pp. 5–6, 21; Li Ruijun, interview. See also Tao Feiya, *Zhongguo de Jidujiao wutuobang*, pp. 193, 195.

53. Rees, *"Jesus Family,"* p. 18.

54. Jing Dianying to Li Dengfeng, May 22, 1941; Li Ruijun, interview.

55. See *Mazhuang Yesu Jiating*, pp. 9, 23; Tao Feiya, *Zhongguo de Jidujiao wutuobang*, pp. 197–200.

56. Chen Gonglu, *Taiping Tianguo lishi luncong*, pp. 214–15.

57. Spence, *God's Chinese Son*, pp. 121, 225, 234. See also Kojima Shinji, *Hong Xiuquan*, p. 95. The Taiping regime dropped its forced separation of sexes in 1855.

58. See Dai Sheng, *Liji*, p. 285. I have used here the translation made by James Legge, with some minor modifications of my own.

59. Besides the Taiping Rebellion, such searches for an egalitarian society also included the Yellow Turbans uprising that broke out in 184 in pursuit of "the Way of Great Peace" (Taiping Dao), the uprisings in the northern Song dynasty led by Wang Xiaobo (993) and Fang La (1120), and the Republican revolution started by Sun Yat-sen in 1895. "Tianxia weigong" (the world . . . shared by all alike) became Sun's slogan.

60. See Tao Qian (Tao Yuanming, 365–427), "Taohuayuan ji" (The Spring of Peach Blossoms), circa 421.

CHAPTER 4. THE SMITTEN LAND

1. Crawford, *Shantung Revival*, p. 41. See also Cauthen, *Higher Ground*, p. 162.

2. Wang Shenyin and Yang Chengjing, "Linyi diqu Jidujiao fazhang gaishu" (A General Account of the Development of Christianity in the Linyi Area), *Cangshan wenshi ziliao* (Selected Literary and Historical Materials of Cangshan [County, Shandong Province]), No. 6 (1988): 182. See also Tao Feiya, "Christian Utopia," pp. 75–76.

3. *CCYB* (1932–1933), pp. 181–83, 186. See also Wang Mingdao, "Shengjing guangliang zhongde ling'en yundong"; *Shandong shengzhi*, p. 619; Tao Feiya, "Christian Utopia," p. 76.

4. Crawford, *Shantung Revival*, pp. 78–80.

5. Bates, "Gleanings," p. 79. See also "Indigenous Revival in Shantung," *CR* 62 (December 1931): 769.

6. *CMYB* (1916), "Statistics of the Work of Protestant Missions in China for the Year 1915."

7. *CCYB* (1926), pp. 151–52.

8. Boynton and Boynton, *Handbook of the Christian Movement in China*, pp. 40–47. See also C. Stanley Smith, "Modern Religious Movement," *CCYB* (1934–1935), p. 110.

9. Cauthen, *Higher Ground*, pp. 154, 162.

10. "Indigenous Revival in Shantung," pp. 768–72.

11. *ZJN* (1914), p. 29; Wu, *Yu Cidu*, pp. 122–23; Brewster, "Revivals," pp. 314–15; R. Goforth, *Goforth of China*, pp. 178, 181.

12. Yoo, *Korean Pentecostalism*, p. 80. See also Sung Won Yang, "Influence of the Revival Movement of 1901–1910," pp. 52–53, 64, 78.

13. Brewster, "Revivals," pp. 314–15; *CR* 40 (1909): 529; Brewster, *Modern Pentecost*, p. 8. See also Latourette, *History of Christian Missions*, p. 574; Wu, *Yu Cidu*, pp. 150, 153.

14. Zhang Fuji, *Xinghua Weili Gonghui shi*, pp. 204–9. See also Bates, "Gleanings," p. 39.

15. R. Goforth, *Goforth of China*, pp. 135, 177–78, 182–84, 187–88.

16. Ibid., pp. 190, 195, 199; Brewster, "Revivals," pp. 314–15.

17. J. Goforth, *"By My Spirit,"* p. 80.

18. Ibid., pp. 161–63; Brewster, "Revivals," pp. 313–15.

19. Feng Yuxiang, *Wode shenghuo*, p. 30; Bates, "Gleanings," pp. 88–89; Latourette, *History of Christian Missions*, p. 777.

20. Goforth and Goforth, *Miracle Lives of China*, p. 141; *CMYB* (1919): 281–85.

21. Ch'eng, *Marshal Feng*, pp. 21–22.

22. Goforth and Goforth, *Miracle Lives of China*, pp. 142–44; Sheridan, *Chinese Warlord*, p. 82, 243, 322 n.32. In 1929 Feng's army was 220,000 men strong.

23. Feng Yuxiang, "Address."

24. *CR* 54 (1923): 335.

25. Sheridan, *Chinese Warlord*, pp. 129, 135.

26. Bates, "Gleanings," pp. 89–90; Sheridan, *Chinese Warlord*, pp. 175, 130. See also *CR* 54 (1923): 335.

27. *CR* 54 (1923): 335; Sheridan, *Chinese Warlord*, p. 53.

28. Bates, "Gleanings," p. 89.

29. Sheridan, *Chinese Warlord*, p. 175.

30. Goforth and Goforth, *Miracle Lives of China*, pp. 152, 155; Holcombe, *Spirit of the Chinese Revolution*, pp. 73, 81; Sheridan, *Chinese Warlord*, pp. 186–87; Bates, "Gleanings," pp. 89–90.

31. *CR* 54 (1923): 336; Latourette, *History of Christian Missions*, p. 778.

32. Bates, "Gleanings," pp. 89–90.

33. Sheridan, *Chinese Warlord*, pp. 255, 259–60, 267.

34. Ibid., pp. 267–69, 281; Xing You, "Taishan Gupinyuan," pp. 207–8. See also Tao Feiya, "Christian Utopia," p. 80.

35. *ZJN* (1925), pp. 6–7.

36. Yu Yucheng, interview, 2003; Latourette, *History of Christian Missions*, pp. 703, 820.

37. Latourette, *History of Christian Missions*, p. 778.

38. Rawlinson as quoted in Carlberg, *China in Revival*, p. 21.

39. Crawford, *Shantung Revival*, p. 3.

40. Monsen, *Awakening*, pp. 21–29, 35–36.

41. Ibid., pp. 39–42.

42. Leslie T. Lyall, "Historical Prelude," in Monsen, *Awakening*, p. 21.

43. Carlberg, *China in Revival*, pp. 71–83; Monsen, *Awakening*, pp. 72, 77–78, 81–85; Crawford, *Shantung Revival*, p. 2.

44. Crawford, *Shantung Revival*, pp. 7–12, 16, 22.

45. Cauthen, *Higher Ground*, p. 152. See also Crawford, *Shantung Revival*, pp. 37, 41.

46. "A Spiritual Movement in China," *MRW* 56 (February 1933): 68.

47. "Indigenous Revival in Shantung," p. 768; Wang Shenyin and Yang Chengjing, "Linyi diqu Jidujiao." See also Bao Zhong, "Sishi nianlai," p. 115. Yang Rulin, one of the two founders, was a Presbyterian minister. The full name of the Pentecostal society was Zhonghua Yesujiao Ling'en Zilihui; that of the Independent Assemblies of God was Zili Shenzhaohui.

48. "Indigenous Revival in Shantung," pp. 767–68. See also "The New Spiritual Movement in Shantung," *CR* 63 (October 1932): 654.

49. Cauthen, *Higher Ground*, pp. 150, 159–60; "Spiritual Movement in China," p. 68.

50. Crawford, *Shantung Revival*, pp. 41, 44–48.

51. Among the few personal accounts in the Chinese language that date from the period are documents in the Tai'an Municipal Archives on the Jesus Family (whose revivalism overlapped with the broader Shandong Revival) and Sung, *Lingli jiguang*.

52. *ZJN* (1933), pp. 1–2. See also Xia Dongyuan, *Ershi shiji Zhongguo dabolan*, p. 374–79.

53. "Revival Movements in Manchuria: A Symposium," *CR* 64 (December 1933): 774, 778–81; Bates, "Gleanings," pp. 79–80.

54. Monsen, *Awakening*, pp. 39–42.

55. William H. Nowack as quoted in Carlberg, *China in Revival*, p. 136.

56. Thouless, *Introduction to the Psychology of Religion*, pp. 25–26.

57. "Indigenous Revival in Shantung," pp. 769–70.

58. Monsen, *Awakening*, p. 114.

59. Crawford, *Shantung Revival*, pp. 43–44.

60. "Indigenous Revival in Shantung," p. 770.

61. Geo. D. Wilder, "Congregationalists and Revivals," *CR* 67 (April 1936): 247.

62. "Spiritual Movement in China," p. 67; "Revival Movements in Manchuria," p. 776; "Indigenous Revival in Shantung," pp. 771–72.

63. *CCYB* (1934–1935), p. 99.

64. Sang Xujiu and Sun Bolong, "Shandong Zhonghua Jidujiao Ling'enhui"; *Shandong shengzhi*, pp. 619–20.

65. Tong Zhishan, "Jinan shi dongjiao Lingxiuyuan"; Pei Yufang, interview. The Jesus Family slogan in Chinese was "Huachu le huijie, quxiao le weifen."

66. "Spiritual Movement in China," p. 68.

67. "Indigenous Revival in Shantung," pp. 770–71.

68. "New Spiritual Movement in Shantung," p. 654.

69. "Revival Movements in Manchuria," p. 776. See also "New Spiritual Movement in Shantung," p. 654.

70. "Indigenous Revival in Shantung," pp. 769, 772.

71. "New Spiritual Movement in Shantung," p. 653. The Buddhist practice is called *sheshen ranzhi* (sacrifice the body by burning fingers).

72. "Revival Movements in Manchuria," p. 775.

73. Frank Rawlinson, "Trends among Chinese Protestants," *CCYB* (1932–1933), p. 88; Wang Feishao, "Ziboshi Jidujiaohui," pp. 235–36.

74. *CCYB* (1932–1933), p. 184.

75. Cauthen, *Higher Ground*, p. 154.

76. "Revival Movements in Manchuria," p. 776.

77. T. C. Chao (Zhao Zichen), "Religious Situation, 1930," in *CCYB* (1931), p. 71.

78. Zhao Zichen as quoted in Tao Feiya, "Christian Utopia," p. 78.

79. *CCYB* (1932–1933), pp. 181–83.

80. Yu, *Yejin tianming*, p. 20.

81. *CCYB* (1932–1933), p. 186.

82. D. H. Porter, "Secret Societies in Shantung," *CR* 17 (1886): 64–65, quoted in Chesneaux, *Secret Societies in China*, pp. 65–66.

CHAPTER 5. "ELUCIDATING THE WAY"

The epigraph to this chapter is excerpted from Xu Zhimo, "Changzhou Tianningsi wen lichan sheng" (1923). The English translation is from Spence, *Gate of Heavenly Peace*, p. 212, with minor alterations of my own.

1. *CCYB* (1932–1933), pp. 176–78. See also Bates, "Gleanings," p. 79.
2. *CCYB* (1934–1935), p. 109.
3. Wang Mingdao, *Wushi nian lai*, pp. 2–4.
4. Ibid., pp. 9–10.
5. Ibid., pp. 5, 10–11. The Dried Fish (*ganyu* 干魚) Alley was later renamed Sweet Rain (*ganyu* 甘雨) Alley. For a list of Wang's sermons and writings on such topics, see Wang Mingdao, *Wang Mingdao wenku*, vol. 1.
6. Wang Mingdao, *Wushi nian lai*, pp. 9, 12, 15, 18, 28, 34.
7. Ibid., pp. 28–30. See also Lyall, *Three of China's Mighty Men*, p. 105.
8. Wang Mingdao, *Wushi nian lai*, pp. 4, 33–38.
9. Ibid., p. 48. The verse is from Matthew 26:52.
10. Ibid., pp. 50–55.
11. Ibid., p. 56.
12. Ibid., pp. 57, 67, 70–71; Wang Mingdao, "Shengjing guangliang zhong de ling'en yundong," p. 107.
13. Wang Mingdao, *Wushi nian lai*, pp. 59–63.
14. Ibid., pp. 64, 66, 68–72. Wang drifted away from Pentecostalism under the influence of a missionary, "a Swedish old man" named Eric Pilquist. For Pilquist, see *CMYB* (1913), p. ccxiii; *CMYB* (1914), "Directory of Missionaries in China and Formosa."
15. Wang Mingdao, *Wushi nian lai*, pp. 85–90; Boynton and Boynton, *Handbook of the Christian Movement in China*, Introduction, p. ix; Latourette, *History of Christian Missions*, p. 820.
16. Wang Mingdao, *Wushi nian lai*, pp. 75, 85–88; Wang Mingdao, "Mengzhao de Jidian."
17. Wang Mingdao, "Renwo zhijian nianwu ze," pp. 119–28; Wang Mingdao, *Wushi nian lai*, pp. 85, 109. See also Lyall, *Three of China's Mighty Men*, pp. 114–15.
18. Wang Mingdao, *Wushi nian lai*, pp. 18, 74, 77–83.
19. Lian Xi, *Conversion of Missionaries*, pp. 10, 138.
20. Chen Tu-seu (Chen Duxiu), "Jidujiao yu Zhongguo ren" (Christianity and the Chinese People), trans. Y. Y. Tsu, *CR* 51 (July 1920): 454–55. See also N. Chang, *Guonei jin shinian lai zhi zongjiao sichao*, p. 192; Gu Changsheng, *Zhongguo Jidujiao jianshi*, p. 120.
21. Wang Mingdao, *Wushi nian lai*, pp. 77, 79.
22. Sun as quoted in Schiffrin, *Sun Yat-sen*, pp. 56–57.
23. Sun Yat-sen, "Using Religious Virtues to Remedy Political Inadequacies: The substance of a speech made on September 5, 1912, in response to a welcome by the churches of Peking," in Wei, Myers, and Gillin, *Prescriptions for Saving China*, pp. 88–89.
24. Cha, *Zhongguo Jidujiao*, pp. 143, 191.
25. Wang Mingdao, "Eshi zhong de husheng," p. 202; Wang Mingdao, "Yingdang bei zhouzu de ren," p. 54; Wang Mingdao, "Yigong you jige fuyin ne?" pp. 2–3.

26. Wang Mingdao, "Eshi zhong de husheng," p. 198; Spence, *Gate of Heavenly Peace,* pp. 240–41.

27. Wang Mingdao, "Eshi zhong de husheng," pp. 190–91, 202.

28. David Z. T. Yui (Yu Rizhang), "Present Tendencies in the Chinese Y.M.C.A.," in *CMYB* (1924), p. 158; "Some Modern Aspects of the Young Women's Christian Association in China," in *CMYB* (1924), p. 168.

29. NCC, *Annual Report* (1926–1927, 1927–1928); *CCYB* (1931), p. 345; *CMYB* (1924), pp. 402–3, 410, 416; *CCYB* (1929), pp. 222, 351, 359–61, 393.

30. J. C. Yen, "The Popular Education Movement," in *CMYB* (1924), pp. 309, 313; *ZJN* (1925), pp. 127–29; *CCYB* (1928), p. 29; Latourette, *History of Christian Missions,* pp. 781–82; Bates, "Gleanings," p. 38.

31. Yen, "Popular Education Movement," p. 310; *CCYB* (1928), p. 30; *CCYB* (1931), p. 353.

32. Henry T. Hodgkin, "The Forward Program of the National Christian Council," in *CMYB* (1924), pp. 150–51.

33. See Spence, *God's Chinese Son,* p. 55. For a look at rare, late-Qing literary talents among Protestants, see Cohen, *Between Tradition and Modernity,* pp. 58–61, 80, 232–33.

34. West, *Yenching University,* pp. 17–18. *Life Journal* was later renamed *Zhengli yu shengming,* or *Truth and Life.*

35. *ZJN* (1927), pp. 118–20; *CCYB* (1926), pp. 373–74; P. Wang, *Wenshe de shengshuai,* pp. 45–48, 62.

36. P. Wang, *Wenshe de shengshuai,* pp. 36–38, 47, 148; Peter Chen-Main Wang, "Contextualizing Protestant Publishing in China: The Wenshe, 1924–1928," in Bays, *Christianity in China,* p. 297. The formal dissolution of Wenshe came in 1930.

37. "Bible Stories through Chinese Eyes," *Asia: The American Magazine on the Orient* (December 1920): 1088–97.

38. *Life of Christ by Chinese Artists,* pp. 8–9, 20–21; Marie Adams, "A New School of Christian Art," *CR* (December 1938): 617.

39. Union Hymnal Committee, *Putian songzan,* pp. 1–14; *ZJN* (1928), p. III-1; "Dr. Timothy Tingfang Lew," Lew, Papers; West, *Yenching University,* pp. 61–62; Bates, "Gleanings," p. 50.

40. T. C. Chao (Zhao Zichen), "Tian'en ge," in Union Hymnal Committee, *Putian songzan,* No. 510.

41. T. C. Chao, "Qingchen ge," in Union Hymnal Committee, *Putian songzan,* No. 425.

42. Wang Mingdao, "Shenfang liuzei," pp. 26–27; Adams, "New School of Christian Art," p. 617.

43. Wang Mingdao, "Shenfang jiashifu," p. 33; Wang Mingdao, *Wushi nian lai,* pp. 93–94, 112, 171, 177–78.

44. Shi Meiling, *Liushisan nian,* pp. 16–17.

45. See Lyall, *Three of China's Mighty Men,* p. 95. The other two are Yang Shaotang and Watchman Nee.

CHAPTER 6. "FLAME FOR GOD"

1. *ZJN* (1933), p. 182; Huang Denghuang. *Gu'er zhifu*, p. 38.
2. *CCYB* (1932–1933), pp. 178–79.
3. Bethel Mission, *50th Anniversary*, pp. 3–4, 47–48; Boorman, *Biographical Dictionary of Republican China*; Stockwell-Mudd Libraries Special Collections: Chinese and American Methodist Women, http://www.albion.edu/library/specialcollections/exhibits/collins_exhibit4.asp. See also Kwok Pui-lan, *Chinese Women and Christianity*, pp. 117–18. Funds for the hospital were provided by Isaac Newton Danforth, a Chicago physician and friend of Shi's, in memory of his deceased wife Elizabeth Skelton Danforth.
4. Bethel Mission, *50th Anniversary*, pp. 3–4, 47–48; Boorman, *Biographical Dictionary of Republican China*; Yao Minquan, *Shanghai Jidujiao shi*, pp. 185–87.
5. Gih, *Twice Born*, pp. 14–24; Huang Denghuang, *Gu'er zhifu*, pp. 2–6, 14, 20.
6. Wilkes, *Dynamic of Service*, p. 16; Gih, *Twice Born*, p. 26; Wang Zhi, *Wang Zai jianzheng lu*, pp. 18–19, 33.
7. Gih, *Twice Born*, pp. 29, 31, 38; Bethel Mission, *50th Anniversary*, pp. 4–5.
8. Gih, *Into God's Family*, pp. 11–15, 35–40, 43–47; Zheng Xindao, "Taishan Gupinyuan," p. 95. The initial Bethel Band members included Lin Jingkang (Frank Lin), Li Daorong (Philip Lee), and Nie Ziying. Lin had attended the Fukien (Fujian) Christian University; Li was from Canton and had attended a Bible seminary.
9. Gih, *Into God's Family*, pp. 12–15. Phoebe Stone died in 1930.
10. Snow, *Red Star over China*, pp. 46–47, 50–51.
11. Stuart, *Fifty Years in China*, p. 155.
12. Xu Baoluo, *Cong buershiweike dao shenpu*, pp. 10, 15, 94–95, 103, 109–10.
13. Ibid., pp. 118–21, 143–45, 163–73.
14. Gih, *Twice Born*, p. 47.
15. Bethel Mission, *50th Anniversary*, p. 5. See also *CCYB* (1932–1933), p. 178.
16. Rev. James P. Leynse, Presbyterian Mission, Peiping, to *MRW*, Christmas 1932, in *MRW* 56 (February 1933): 71–72; Rev. and Mrs. James P. Leynse, "From an Evangelistic Report from China," *MRW* 56 (September 1933): 418.
17. Bethel Mission, *50th Anniversary*, p. 4; Gih, *Into God's Family*, p. 17; Sung, *Lingli jiguang*, pp. 68–70, 74–75; Liu Yiling, *Song Shangjie zhuan*, pp. 96–100.
18. Xie Yangping, *Jidutu budaotuan*, pp. 74–75, 81; Sung, *Lingli jiguang*, pp. 99–100, 159, 172, 186; Liu Yiling, *Song Shangjie zhuan*, p. 103.
19. Sung, *Lingli jiguang*, pp. 6–7, 12–13; *CMYB* (1919), p. 336; Liu Yiling, *Song Shangjie zhuan*, p. 58.
20. Sung, *Lingli jiguang*, pp. 15–17.
21. Ibid., pp. 16–19, 34; Schubert, *I Remember John Sung*, p. 19; Lyall, *Flame for God*, p. 27.

22. Sung, *Lingli jiguang*, pp. 18–20; Lyall, *Flame for God*, p. 31. Lyall mentions Sung's romantic affections for an unnamed fellow Chinese student. My own research in the student records of Union Theological Seminary for the early and mid-1920s yielded no female Chinese names. It is possible that she was enrolled at nearby Columbia University. In her interview with me in June 2001, Song Tianzhen, daughter of John Sung and editor of *Lingli jiguang*, admitted that she was unaware of the alleged episode and therefore was unable to either confirm or contradict Lyall's account. Sung only reluctantly agreed to marry Yu Jinhua as a matter of filial piety and regretted that decision on several occasions. See Sung, *Lingli jiguang*, p. 10; Liu Yiling, *Song Shangjie zhuan*, p. 93.

23. See Lian Xi, *Conversion of Missionaries*, p. 217; Ahlstrom, *Religious History*, pp. 911–13; De Plata, *Tell It from Calvary*, pp. 48–50.

24. See Sung, *Wode jianzheng*, pp. 51, 67.

25. Utley, *Why I Am a Preacher*, pp. 15–31, 44–45, 79, 85, 130–31; Sung, *Wode jianzheng*, p. 76; Sung, *Lingli jiguang*, p. 19; De Plata, *Tell It from Calvary*, p. 47. Utley's sermon on "rest" was delivered at a church in New York in 1930, but the same message was probably also included in her revival preaching in October 1926.

26. Lyall, *Flame for God*, p. 33; Schubert, *I Remember John Sung*, p. 94.

27. Sung, "Out of Modernism into God's Family," p. 58; Schubert, *I Remember John Sung*, pp. 20, 94; Sung, *Lingli jiguang*, p. 20; Sung, *Wode jianzheng*, 81; Lyall, *Flame for God*, pp. 34, 39. Fosdick allegedly replied, "Brother Sung . . . you need a rest."

28. Sung, *Wode jianzheng*, pp. 84–85; Sung, *Lingli jiguang*, pp. 19–21. See also Lyall, *Flame for God*, pp. 33, 37.

29. Bloomingdale Asylum discharge ledger for Sung, August 31, 1927, New York Weill Cornell Center Archives, New York, NY. The initial diagnosis appeared in the records of a meeting at the asylum on April 28, 1927, where Sung's case was discussed. The discharge ledger stated that his condition was much improved and that he was suffering from "psychosis with psychopathic personality."

30. Harry Emerson Fosdick to Henry Kingman of the Young Men's Christian Association of Tianjin, February 20, 1927, Fosdick Papers, Union Theological Seminary Library, New York.

31. Sung, *Wode jianzheng*, pp. 94–95; Sung, *Lingli jiguang*, pp. 28–29.

32. Gih, *Twice Born*, p. 53; Sung, *Lingli jiguang*, pp. 29–30; Liu Yiling, *Song Shangjie zhuan*, pp. 92–93. See also Latourette, *History of Christian Missions*, p. 698.

33. Sung, *Lingli jiguang*, pp. 61–63. For banditry in the border regions of Jiangxi and Fujian, see Billingsley, *Bandits in Republican China*, p. 36.

34. James Yen (Yan Yangchu), "New Life for the Rural Masses," *CR* 71 (June 1940): 366; Sung, *Lingli jiguang*, pp. 61–63, 67; Sung, *Wode jianzheng*, pp. 109–13; Lyall, *Flame for God*, pp. 56–58.

35. Schubert, *I Remember John Sung*, pp. 28–35; Sung, *Wode jianzheng*, pp. 113, 118; Sung, *Lingli jiguang*, pp. 68–71.

36. Sung, *Wode jianzheng*, pp. 116–17; Schubert, *I Remember John Sung*, pp. 53–55.

37. Yu Yucheng, interview, 2002. Yu, nephew of John Sung's wife, was a teen-age preacher trained by Sung in the late 1920s.

38. Lyall, *Flame for God*, p. 118; Schubert, *I Remember John Sung*, p. 44; Sung, *Lingli jiguang*, p. 151. Yu Yucheng, interview, 2003.

39. Yu, *Yejin tianming*, p. 51.

40. Schubert, *I Remember John Sung*, pp. 36, 93; Sung, *Lingli jiguang*, pp. 71–72, 94–97, 135.

41. Sung, *Lingli jiguang*, pp. 45, 66, 73, 75, 78–79, 83, 88; Liu Yiling, *Song Shangjie zhuan*, p. 167.

42. Sung, *Lingli jiguang*, pp. 76–81, 109, 138, 160, 162; Liu Yiling, *Song Shangjie zhuan*, p. 262. Sung's heart ailment in fact continued with him through his later life.

43. Sung, *Lingli jiguang*, pp. 58, 69, 105, 107, 112, 123–24, 134–35, 175, 180, 186, 226, 231, 238, 241; Schubert, *I Remember John Sung*, p. 62.

44. *CCYB* (1934–1935), pp. 107–8.

45. Sung, *Lingli jiguang*, p. 128.

46. H. R. Williamson, "Evangelistic Work in China To-day (Concluded)," *CR* 69 (September 1938): 449.

47. Sung, *Lingli jiguang*, pp. 105–7, 112, 175, 238; Lyall, *Flame for God*, p. 168; Guo Kechang and Zheng Suilan, *Xinjiapo Jidutu budaotuan*, pp. 29–30, 34; *Tongwenbao*, March, May, and October 1935. *Tongwenbao* was founded in June 1902 by the Presbyterian Mission. See *CMYB* (1910), pp. 348–49; *CCYB* (1928), p. 375.

48. See Billingsley, *Bandits in Republican China*, pp. 35, 250–53.

49. Sung, *Lingli jiguang*, pp. 89–102.

50. Ibid., p. 165. Sung's second meeting with Yu happened in May 1934. Yu died in January 1936. See also Z. S. Zia, "Indigenous Evangelism and Christian Unity," *CR* 67 (July 1936): 409.

51. Lyall, *Flame for God*, pp. 49, 145; Carlberg, *China in Revival*, pp. 185–86.

52. Zia, "Indigenous Evangelism and Christian Unity," p. 410.

53. Sung, *Lingli jiguang*, pp. 89, 97, 169, 217, 257.

54. Sung as quoted in Schubert, *I Remember John Sung*, p. 42.

55. Zia, "Indigenous Evangelism and Christian Unity," p. 409. See also *Tongwenbao*, October 1935, No. 41.

56. Sung, *Lingli jiguang*, pp. 74, 89.

57. Ibid., pp. 83, 88, 122, 153–55, 157; Schubert, *I Remember John Sung*, p. 39. See also *CCYB* (1934–1935), p. 99; Lyall, *Flame for God*, p. 112; Liu Yiling, *Song Shangjie zhuan*, p. 188.

58. Sung, *Lingli jiguang*, pp. 154, 157; Yu Yucheng, interview, 2003. According to Yu, correspondence from Sung's wife Yu Jinhua (Yu's aunt) in Shanghai

at the time of Sung's expulsion from Bethel revealed that many of the offerings were given directly to Sung and not to the group.

59. Bates, "Gleanings," pp. 78–79.

60. Sung, *Lingli jiguang*, pp. 119, 167; Schubert, *I Remember John Sung*, p. 46; Liu Yiling, *Song Shangjie zhuan*, p. 206.

61. He Shouliang, "Song Shangjie boshi," p. 66; Liu Yangfen (former Methodist Episcopal pastor in Fuzhou), interview, 2001; Schubert, *I Remember John Sung*, p. 46. Sung was *shiyong chuandao shi* (probationary preacher) in 1928. In 1929, he was appointed *budaoshi* (preacher).

62. Sung, *Lingli jiguang*, p. 116. The Reverend A. K. Reiton of Hong Kong baptized Sung by immersion in May 1932.

63. Ibid., p. 187; Lyall, *Flame for God*, pp. 141–42, 157–58, 204–5.

64. Sung, *Lingli jiguang*, p. 222; Liu Yiling, *Song Shangjie zhuan*, p. 236.

65. Schubert, *I Remember John Sung*, p. 42; Sung, *Lingli jiguang*, p. 167.

66. He Shouliang, "Song Shangjie boshi," p. 69; Liu Yangfen, interview, 2001. On May 5, 1938, Gowdy ordained Sung *zhangmu* (also *mushi*, officially "elder") in Fuzhou.

67. Sung, *Lingli jiguang*, pp. 244–46.

68. Ibid., pp. 247–55; Schubert, *I Remember John Sung*, p. 63.

69. Schubert, *I Remember John Sung*, p. 32; Sung, *Lingli jiguang*, pp. 8–9, 251, 284; Lyall, *Flame for God*, pp. 167, 175.

70. Sung, *Lingli jiguang*, pp. 77, 179.

71. Yu Yucheng, interview, 2002. The ship was on its way from Shanghai to Fujian. It did not sink as feared, and Yu Jinhua survived.

72. Sung, *Lingli jiguang*, pp. 169, 304–5, 311–14, 332; Lyall, *Flame for God*, p. 184.

CHAPTER 7. AWAITING RAPTURE

1. Sung, *Lingli jiguang*, p. 198; H. R. Williamson, "Evangelistic Work in China To-day" (Concluded), *CR* 69 (September 1938): 449.

2. John S. Barr, "Christian Activities in War-Torn China," *CR* 69 (September 1938): 418–19; "Mobile Hospitals and Wounded," *CR* 69 (May 1938): 271. See also Gu Changsheng, *Chuanjiaoshi*, p. 404.

3. Nee, *Women zai Jidu li*, pp. 323–24. See also Nee, *Ren de posui*.

4. Yu Chenghua as quoted in Yu Congjia, "Yu Chenghua yisheng yishi," p. 18.

5. Nee, "Yuchang laishi," pp. 314–19.

6. Jiang Shoudao, "Zuozhe shengping jianshi," p. 300; Cha, *Zhongguo Jidujiao*, p. 307; Roberts, *Understanding Watchman Nee*, p. 3.

7. Cha, *Zhongguo Jidujiao*, p. 308. See also Dunch, *Fuzhou Protestants*, pp. 62–69.

8. Kinnear, *Against the Tide*, p. 23; Dunch, *Fuzhou Protestants*, pp. 45–46.

9. Lin Heping, *En'ai biaoben*, p. 11; Kinnear, *Against the Tide*, pp. 23–25, 33.

10. Nee, "Wangshi de shushuo," pp. 21–22; Jiang Shoudao, "Zuozhe shengping

jianshi," p. 301; Kinnear, *Against the Tide*, pp. 46, 49; Wu, *Yu Cidu*, pp. 148, 183–84.

11. Kinnear, *Against the Tide*, p. 46; Lyall, *Three of China's Mighty Men*, pp. 53–54; Roberts, *Understanding Watchman Nee*, p. 13. See also Boynton, *Directory of Protestant Missions in China*, pp. 98–99, where Barber is listed under "Independent Missionaries" in Fuzhou.

12. Bebbington, *Evangelicalism in Modern Britain*, pp. 76–77, 94; Coad, *History of the Brethren Movement*, pp. 166–67; Kinnear, *Against the Tide*, p. 46; Lyall, *Three of China's Mighty Men*, p. 54; Li Ailian, *Paomao yu wuxian*, pp. 1–2; Ni Yulong, "Fuzhou Jidutujuji(hui)."

13. Randall, *Evangelical Experiences*, pp. 160–61. This teaching is a version of the Plymouth Brethren belief, to be discussed later in the chapter.

14. Margaret E. Barber, "Beiti" (Rapture), in Li Ailian, *Paomao yu wuxian*, p. 40; Nee, "Wangshi de shushuo," p. 22; Kinnear, *Against the Tide*, p. 46.

15. Nee, "Fujia yinyu," p. 84; Nee, "Wangshi de shushuo," pp. 21–22.

16. Wang Zhi, *Wang Zai jianzheng lu*, pp. 18–19; Cha, *Zhongguo Jidujiao*, pp. 270–72; R. Wright, *Chinese Steam Navy*, pp. 121, 145.

17. R. Wright, *Chinese Steam Navy*, pp. 133–34, 139–41.

18. Wang Zhi, *Wang Zai jianzheng lu*, p. 23; Nee, "Wangshi de shushuo," p. 25.

19. Kinnear, *Against the Tide*, p. 35; Cha, *Zhongguo Jidujiao*, p. 309; Bates, "Gleanings," pp. 40–43. See also *ZJN* (1914), Appendix, p. 15. According to that *ZJN* report, out of the three hundred students enrolled at Trinity College in 1914, only sixty-seven came from Christian families and twenty-eight were baptized.

20. Nee, "Wangshi de shushuo," pp. 26–28, 30–31, 43; Wang Zhi, *Wang Zai jianzheng lu*, p. 23; Kinnear, *Against the Tide*, p. 54.

21. See Gu Changsheng, *Chuanjiaoshi*, pp. 353–54; Latourette, *History of Christian Missions*, p. 697.

22. Cha, *Zhongguo Jidujiao*, p. 311; Kinnear, *Against the Tide*, pp. 89–90.

23. Nee, "Wangshi de shushuo," pp. 27–28.

24. Ni Yulong, "Fuzhou Jidutujuji(hui)"; Ni Yulong, interviews; Nee, "Wangshi de shushuo," pp. 36–37; Ren Zhongxiang, *Shanghai Jidutu Juhuichu*, p. 1. Nee's group was commonly referred to as Jidutu Juhuichu (or Jidutu Juhuisuo), which can also be rendered as the Christian Assembly Hall (or Meeting Place).

25. Lee, "Yiwei zai Jidu li de ren"; Zhang Qizhen, written response to author's questionnaire. The late Zhang, who graduated from Trinity College a year before Nee, served as the Fuzhou Christian Assembly leader after 1930. A literal translation of *Fuxingbao* (which began in late 1923) would be *The Revival*. Its English title echoed *A Witness and a Testimony*, the journal distributed by T. Austin-Sparks's Witness and Testimony Publishers in London.

26. Wang Zhi, *Wang Zai jianzheng lu*, pp. 34–35, 87.

27. Nee, "Fujia yinyu," pp. 84–92. The frustrated romance was with Zhang Pinhui, whom he would marry in 1934.

28. Ni Yulong, "Fuzhou Jidutujuji(hui)"; Kinnear, *Against the Tide*, pp. 65, 79; Cha, *Zhongguo Jidujiao*, p. 314.

29. Nee, "Fujia yinyu," pp. 81, 88, 93.

30. Price and Randall, *Transforming Keswick*, pp. 11–14, 46–47; Matthew and Harrison, *Oxford Dictionary of National Biography*. See also Kinnear, *Against the Tide*, p. 58; Nee, *Shuling de ren, Part I (1926)*, p. 25. Other writers whose works influenced Nee included G. H. Pember and Robert Govett.

31. Bebbington, *Evangelicalism in Modern Britain*, pp. 151–52; Matthew and Harrison, *Oxford Dictionary of National Biography*.

32. B. P. Jones, *Trials and Triumphs*, pp. 14, 16–17, 19, 26–27, 65, 91, 242–43. See also Price and Randall, *Transforming Keswick*, p. 157; Bebbington, *Evangelicalism in Modern Britain*, p. 175.

33. Penn-Lewis, *Awakening in Wales*, pp. 17, 160–65; Clive Price, "In the Land of the Welsh Revival," *Charisma & Christian Life*, December 1998, pp. 62–65.

34. B. P. Jones, *Trials and Triumphs*, pp. 132–33; Bebbington, *Evangelicalism in Modern Britain*, pp. 196–97; Matthew and Harrison, *Oxford Dictionary of National Biography*.

35. B. P. Jones, *Trials and Triumphs*, pp. 162–64, 193, 195, 200, 202, 212, 214–15, 287.

36. Ibid., pp. 242–43.

37. Chan, *Wode jiufu Ni Tuosheng*, p. 86; Nee, "Di sanci jianzheng," p. 72; Nee, "Wangshi de shushuo," p. 33.

38. Jiang Shoudao, "Zuozhe shengping jianshi," p. 300; B. P. Jones, *Trials and Triumphs*, p. 193.

39. Nee, "Di erci jianzheng," pp. 51–55; Chan, *Wode jiufu Ni Tuosheng*, p. 38; Nee, "Wangshi de shushuo," pp. 33–35; Jiang Shoudao, "Zuozhe shengping jianshi," p. 316. Nee's actual recovery from tuberculosis did not happen until the mid-1930s. See Kinnear, *Against the Tide*, pp. 101, 103, 105–7, 112, 142.

40. Nee, *Shuling de ren, Part I (1926)*, pp. 25–26, 68; Nee, *Shuling de ren, Part II (1928)*, pp. 14, 140–42, 438–39; Chan, *Wode jiufu Ni Tuosheng*, pp. 37–38.

41. Penn-Lewis, *Soul and Spirit*, p. 11; B. P. Jones, *Trials and Triumphs*, p. 287. See also Nee, *Shuling de ren, Part I (1926)*, p. 25. In his Introduction to the book, Nee made a general acknowledgment of his "liberal use" of the ideas of several Western Christian thinkers.

42. Nee, "Wangshi de shushuo," p. 34.

43. Tsai, *Queen of the Dark Chamber*, pp. 71–75.

44. Ibid., pp. 57–61, 71–75, 90, 115; Ren Zhongxiang, *Shanghai Jidutu Juhuichu*, pp. 2–3. In the 1930s, Cai contracted "pellegra and beri-beri" caused by malignant malaria in the marrow of her bones, which confined her to a dark chamber for the rest of her life.

45. Chen Zexin, *Wang Peizhen jianshi*, pp. 1–3; Wu, *Yu Cidu*, pp. 176–79. See also Boynton and Boynton, *Handbook of the Christian Movement in China*,

pp. 163, 168. The Chinese name of the school was Jinling Nüzi Shenxueyuan, which has been rendered in some English-language sources as
Ginling Theological Seminary for Women.

46. Boynton and Boynton, *Handbook of the Christian Movement in China,* Introduction, p. ix; Latourette, *History of Christian Missions,* p. 801; Wu, *Yu Cidu,*
p. 180. In 1920, 1,305 ordained Chinese and 1,268 ordained foreigners were
reported.

47. Chen Zexin, *Ni Tuosheng dixiong jianshi,* p. 29.

48. Nee, "Wangshi de shushuo," p. 35; Nee, "Di erci jianzheng," pp. 59, 62.
See also Wang Mingdao, *Wushi nian lai,* pp. 87–88.

49. Nee, "Feilatiefei," p. 351; Nee, "Wangshi de shushuo," p. 35; Lee, "Yiwei zai
Jidu li de ren."

50. Cohn, *Pursuit of the Millennium,* pp. 99–100; Boyer, *When Time Shall Be
No More,* p. 52. Joachim termed the three successive periods, respectively,
the Age of the Father (or of the Law), the Age of the Son (or of the Gospel),
and the Age of the Spirit. Several variations of this basic dispensational
system have emerged in modern times—developed by Pierre Poiret (1646–
1719), Isaac Watts (1674–1748), J. N. Darby (1800–1882), and C. I. Scofield
(1843–1921)—some of which identify seven rather than three divine-
instituted periods of human history. See Crutchfield, *Origins of Dispensationalism,* p. 211.

51. Baylis, *My People,* pp. 3–5, 31, 37; Krapohl, "Search for Purity," pp. 443–44,
447; Crutchfield, *Origins of Dispensationalism,* 217.

52. Scofield, *Scofield Reference Bible.* See its notes for Revelation 1:20 and Matthew 24:3. See also Ahlstrom, *Religious History of the American People,*
pp. 808–10.

53. Nee, "Wangshi de shushuo," p. 34; Nee, "Di erci jianzheng," p. 51; Nee,
"Jiaohui de zhengtong," p. 100.

54. Nee, "Feilatiefei," pp. 322–23, 351. Nee further explains, along the line of
the "partial rapture" eschatology developed by Panton, that this would be
the first rapture, granted to victorious Christians alone. The rest of the
Christians would be raptured, after the Great Tribulation, when Christ
returns.

55. Nee, "Wangshi de shushuo," p. 36; Lee, "Yiwei zai Jidu li de ren." See also
Hymns for the Little Flock.

56. Nee, "Wangshi de shushuo," p. 21; *CCYB* (1934–1935), p. 105; Nee, "Tongwen huikan yuanqi," p. 217; Lyall, *Three of China's Mighty Men,* pp. 61, 74.

57. Lyall, *Three of China's Mighty Men,* p. 139.

58. Nee, "Fuze dixiongmen de jijuhua," p. 223; Nee, "Wei tongwen huikan
tingkan," p. 232.

59. *CCYB* (1932–1933), p. 180.

60. *CCYB* (1934–1935), p. 105.

61. Zhang Runxian, "Zongpai shi zui'e shuo de jiepou" (A Dissection of the

"Denominationalism Is Sin" Theory), *Tongwenbao*, November 1935, No. 45, p. 5.

62. Zia, "Indigenous Evangelism and Christian Unity," *CR* 67 (July 1936): 409; Kinnear, *Against the Tide*, p. 140.

63. Zheng Zhengguang, interview. Zheng was a Little Flock elder in the Fuzhou congregation.

64. Zhang Qizhen, written response to the author's questionnaire; Zhang Qizhen, interviews, 1997; Kinnear, *Against the Tide*, pp. 127, 207; Lyall, *Three of China's Mighty Men*, p. 68. Unimpressed by Sung's exuberance onstage, some in the Little Flock offered to "test" the revivalist's "spirit," which did not amuse him.

65. Nee, "Jiaotong wenda," pp. 387–88; B. P. Jones, *Trials and Triumphs*, pp. 193, 200.

66. Nee as paraphrased, possibly quoted, in Kinnear, *Against the Tide*, p. 135.

67. Zhang Qizhen, interviews, 1997. See also Kinnear, *Against the Tide*, pp. 80–81, 129–30; Ren Zhongxiang, *Shanghai Jidutu Juhuichu*, pp. 4–5.

68. See Thornton Stearns, "Treatment of Tuberculosis of the Knee Joint in China," paper presented at the meeting of the China Medical Missionary Association, Shanghai, February 14, 1923; Sung, *Lingli jiguang*, p. 105; Kinnear, *Against the Tide*, pp. 113–14.

69. Jiang Shoudao, "Zuozhe shengping jianshi," p. 321; Chen Zexin, *Ni Tuosheng dixiong jianshi*, p. 52; Kinnear, *Against the Tide*, p. 131–33; Ren Zhongxiang, *Shanghai Jidutu Juhuichu*, p. 6; Zhang Qizhen, interviews, 1997; Lee, "Yiwei zai Jidu li de ren." Nee experienced his Spirit baptism at Stearns's summer house in Yantai. Both Stearns and Fischbacher later joined the Little Flock. For Fischbacher's earlier work in Shanxi and her turn to Pentecostalism, see Lyall, *Three of China's Mighty Men*, pp. 24, 28.

70. Jixu (Little Flock activist in Xianyou during the 1930s) to Zhang Qizhen, January 24, 1998, courtesy of Zhang Qizhen; Zhang Qizhen, interviews, 1997.

71. Li Ailian, *Paomao yu wuxian*, p. 4; Ni Yulong, "Fuzhou Jidutujuji(hui)."

72. Nee, "Wangshi de shushuo," pp. 39–40; Jiang Shoudao, "Zuozhe shengping jianshi," pp. 319–20; Baylis, *My People*, pp. 45–47, 71–72.

73. Baylis, *My People*, p. 74; Kinnear, *Against the Tide*, pp. 110–21; Xu Erjian, "Jiaohui 'difang lichang' jiaoxun zhi youlai."

74. Nee, "Wangshi de shushuo," pp. 39–40; Ren Zhongxiang, *Shanghai Jidutu Juhuichu*, pp. 5–6. During the early 1930s, Nee received financial support from the Ravenites.

75. Kinnear, *Against the Tide*, pp. 101, 119; Lyall, *Three of China's Mighty Men*, pp. 68–69.

76. B. P. Jones, *Trials and Triumphs*, pp. 293–97, 307.

77. Ren Zhongxiang, *Shanghai Jidutu Juhuichu*, p. 6; Xu Erjian, letter to Guangwu (given name), August 25, 1998, courtesy of Zhang Qizhen.

78. Kinnear, *Against the Tide*, p. 133.

79. Baylis, *My People*, pp. 75–77; Krapohl, "Search for Purity," p. 454.
80. Ren Zhongxiang, *Shanghai Jidutu Juhuichu*, pp. 4–5, 7–8.
81. Nee, *Gongzuo de zaisi*, pp. 22, 29, 42–43, 53, 81, 94, 207–9, 219.
82. Xu Erjian, "Jiaohui 'difang lichang' jiaoxun zhi youlai," p. 2.
83. Nee as quoted in Kinnear, *Against the Tide*, p. 143.
84. Guyon, *Xinxiang de moyao*, Jieyan (Introduction), pp. 1–4; Patricia A. Ward, "Madame Guyon and Experiential Theology in America," *Church History* 67, 3 (September 1998): 484.
85. Guyon, *Sweet Smelling Myrrh*, pp. 5, 43; Nietzsche, *Beyond Good and Evil*, p. 58.
86. Guyon, *Sweet Smelling Myrrh*, pp. 42–43.
87. Kinnear, *Against the Tide*, p. 58; B. P. Jones, *Trials and Triumphs*, pp. 16, 24.
88. Nee, "Wo zhu, wo zheng denghou ni zailin" (My Lord, I Am Waiting for Your Coming), in *Nian shiji Jidu weida de jianzhengren*; Nee, "Zhu ai chang-kuo gaoshen" (The Love of the Lord Is Wide, High, and Deep), quoted in Chen Zexin, *Ni Tuosheng dixiong jianshi*, p. 23; Yu Congjia, "Yu Chenghua yisheng yishi," p. 10.
89. Zhonghua Renmin Gongheguo Gong'anbu Diyiju, *Jidutu Juhuichu (Xiao-qun) Gaikuang*, p. 3; Shanghai Shi Renmin Jianchayuan, "Shanghai shi renmin jianchayuan qisushu" (The Indictment of the People's Procurator-ate of the City of Shanghai), 55 No. 3194, Shanghai, 1955, reprinted in Sze, *Ni Tuosheng xundao shi*, p. 97; Li Wenwei, "Guanyu Shi Bocheng," pp. 19–20; Zhang Qizhen, interviews, 1997; Tang Shoulin and Ren Zhongxiang, *Wei zhendao*, p. 225. Nudity scenes of Nee's two female "co-workers" were captured on a small cinecamera that he brought back from England in 1939.
90. Yu, *Yejin tianming*, p. 184; Lee, *Watchman Nee*, p. 314.
91. Nee, "Jiaohui de zhengtong," pp. 85, 99–105.
92. Zhou Xingyi, interview. According to the official estimate of the People's Republic of China, thirty-five million Chinese died during the Anti-Japanese War of 1937–1945. See http://english.people.com.cn/zhuanti/Zhuanti_451.html.
93. Ren Zhongxiang, *Shanghai Jidutu Juhuichu*, p. 30; Lyall, *Three of China's Mighty Men*, p. 64; Chan, *Wode jiufu Ni Tuosheng*, pp. 18, 26; Sze, *Ni Tuo-sheng xundao shi*, p. 5.

CHAPTER 8. THE INDIGENOUS CHURCH MOVEMENT THROUGH WAR AND REVOLUTION

The epigraph to this chapter is from *Bitan* (Penned Conversations) 1 (September 1941), reprinted in Ke Ling, *Ershi shiji Zhongguo jishi wenxue*, p. 145.

1. Lacy, *Great Migration and the Church in West China*, Preface; Grubb, *World Christian Handbook*, p. 127; Gu Changsheng, *Chuanjiaoshi*, p. 403.
2. Price, *China: Twilight or Dawn?* p. 107; Price, *Rural Church in China*, pp.

229–30. See also Cha, *Minguo Jidujiao shi,* pp. 237–50; Bates, "Gleanings," p. 100; Gu Changsheng, *Chuanjiaoshi,* p. 410.

3. Timothy Brook, "Toward Independence: Christianity in China under the Japanese Occupation, 1937–1945," in Bays, *Christianity in China,* pp. 331–33; Gu Changsheng, *Chuanjiaoshi,* p. 399. See also Grubb, *World Christian Handbook,* p. 134. According to Grubb, there were about fifteen hundred Protestant missionaries in occupied areas in late 1941.

4. Gu Changsheng, *Chuanjiaoshi,* pp. 403–7; Price, *China: Twilight or Dawn?* p. 124. Only St. John's University in Shanghai and West China Union University (already in Chengdu) did not leave their campuses.

5. Grubb, *World Christian Handbook,* p. 134.

6. John S. Barr, "Christian Activities in War-Torn China," *CR* 69 (September 1938): 414–28; Yao Minquan, *Shanghai Jidujiao shi,* pp. 217–18; Gu Weimin, *Jidujiao yu jindai Zhongguo shehui,* pp. 515–16, 524–25.

7. Grubb, *World Christian Handbook,* p. 249; Gu Changsheng, *Chuanjiaoshi,* pp. 415–16; Chao and Chong, *Dangdai Zhongguo Jidujiao,* Table 4, p. xxxii.

8. Grubb, *World Christian Handbook,* pp. 129–30; "Lines of Progress," *CR* 69 (November 1938): 538; Bates, "Gleanings," pp. 99–100. See also Chao and Chong, *Dangdai Zhongguo Jidujiao,* pp. xxxiv, 16 n.29, 21, 60. In early 1950, the NCC had issued two statistical reports of its own. According to the first, by 1949 the number of communicants in major churches—including the inflated figure of 125,000 for the TJC not cited in Grubb's or other previous statistics—was 773,862. In the second report, the total number of Protestant communicants in the country was given at 840,000, a "56 percent increase" over the 536,000 reported for 1936. That figure and the rate of increase have been cited in several works on Chinese Christianity. See Cha, *Minguo Jidujiao shi,* p. 293, and Gu Weimin, *Jidujiao yu jindai Zhongguo shehui,* p. 533. However, the 1936 figure did not include the TJC.

9. Xie Fuya, *Zi bianzi zhi dianzi,* pp. 10, 82–85; Cha, *Minguo Jidujiao shi,* p. 294. In the 1950s, the translation project was resumed at Drew University with the help of a small group of expatriate Protestant scholars and was scaled down to thirty-two volumes that were eventually published by the Hong Kong–based Chinese Christian Literature Council.

10. Barr, "Christian Activities in War-Torn China," p. 406.

11. Shen Derong, *Wu Yaozong xiaozhuan,* pp. 26–27.

12. NCC resolution as quoted in Price, *China: Twilight or Dawn?* p. 127.

13. Gu Changsheng, *Chuanjiaoshi,* pp. 417–21; Stuart, *Fifty Years in China,* pp. 191–92.

14. F. Wei, *Spirit of Chinese Culture,* pp. 160–72, as quoted in Price, *Rural Church in China,* pp. 239–40.

15. See Wei Yisa, *Zhen Yesu Jiaohui,* p. D19; Chen Guangzao, "Zhen Yesu Jiaohui," pp. 28, 43, 51.

16. Wei Yisa, *Zhen Yesu Jiaohui,* pp. C2–C3, F6, I10.

17. Du Kaixu, "Zhen Yesu Jiaohui Maoping qidaosuo," pp. 141–46.

18. Wei Yisa, *Zhen Yesu Jiaohui*, pp. C3, O1.

19. Ibid., pp. C2–C3, J1–J9, O1–O8, O11, O16, B24. The TJC had no precise figures for those living in Communist-controlled areas.

20. H. R. Williamson, "Evangelistic Work in China To-day (Concluded)," *CR* 69 (September 1938): 450.

21. Wei Yisa, *Zhen Yesu Jiaohui*, p. AZ6.

22. Tao Feiya, *Zhongguo de Jidujiao wutuobang*, pp. 92–95, 107–10.

23. *Mazhuang Yesu Jiating*, p. 4. The North China Christian Union (with its headquarters in Beiping) was established in late 1942.

24. Rees, *"Jesus Family,"* pp. 71–72.

25. Tao Feiya, *Zhongguo de Jidujiao wutuobang*, pp. 161–62; Rees, *"Jesus Family,"* p. 13; *Mazhuang Yesu Jiating*, p. 83; Romig, "Family of Jesus."

26. Jing Dianying, inscription for Zhao Hongji, 1946, in Jing Fuyin, *Lingyunji zhushi*, pp. 42–43.

27. "Jiating miao" (Wondrous Is the Family), quoted in Wang Shenyin, "Mazhuang 'Yesu Jiating' shimo," p. 93.

28. Tao Feiya, *Zhongguo de Jidujiao wutuobang*, pp. 162–64, 209.

29. Romig, "Family of Jesus," p. 4.

30. Ma Honggang, "Jieshao Zhongguo xinxing de jiaopai," p. 5. The figure of ten thousand included nonpermanent members and those who were otherwise loosely associated with the Jesus Family settlements. See also Qu Li, "Tancheng Yesujiao gaikuang," p. 178; Tao Feiya, *Zhongguo de Jidujiao wutuobang*, p. 115.

31. Wang Xipeng, *Ji Yesu Jiating*, pp. 17, 21; Tao Feiya, *Zhongguo de Jidujiao wutuobang*, pp. 185–86; F. P. Jones, *Church in Communist China*, p. 18. See also Romig, "Family of Jesus," p. 2.

32. Zhou Xinmin to Chang Zihua of Qingdao, July 24 (1938?), in Yesu Jiating, "Jiating shuxin."

33. See *Shandong shengzhi*, pp. 619–20.

34. Luo Xingsan, "Yantaishi Jidujiao Ling'enhui," pp. 235–36; Luo Xingsan, interview; Yu, *Yejin tianming*, p. 231.

35. Zhou Xinmin to Chang Zihua of Qingdao, July 24 (1938?); Pei Yufang, interview.

36. See Wang Feishao, "Ziboshi Jidujiaohui," p. 236.

37. Luo Xingsan, "Dongshan Yesu Jiating," p. 237; Yang Zhisheng, interview. Yang, who was in her early fifties at the time of the interview and a picture of health and happiness, was that orphaned baby girl.

38. Li Mingyao, "Lanzhou Yesu Jiating," pp. 174–78; Li Zirou, "Wo canjia 'Yesu Jiating' de qingkuang," pp. 155–57.

39. Bingle and Grubb, *World Christian Handbook*, pp. 141–42; Wang Xipeng, *Ji Yesu Jiating*, p. 21; F. P. Jones, *Church in Communist China*, p. 18.

40. Sun Yanli, "Wo suo renshi de Jiang Changchuan huidu," pp. 337–38; Zhao Zichen, *Xiyu ji*, pp. 1–4, 91–92.

41. Yu, *Yejin tianming*, pp. 223, 284.

42. Wang Zhi, *Wang Zai jianzheng lu*, pp. 53–54, 110; Lin Zhengye, *Zhai Fumin zhuan*, pp. 72–73.

43. Williamson, "Evangelistic Work in China To-day," p. 448.

44. See Z. K. Zia, "Chinese Evangelists in Modern China," *CR* 66 (January 1935): 46–48; Yu, *Yejin tianming*, p. 73.

45. Chen Renbing and Chen Meida, "Chen Chonggui mushi xiaozhuan," pp. 69–71, 76–78, 81–86; Bays, "Foreign Missions and Indigenous Protestant Leaders," pp. 147–48.

46. Chen Renbing and Chen Meida, "Chen Chonggui mushi xiaozhuan," pp. 87–88; Bays, "Foreign Missions and Indigenous Protestant Leaders," p. 152; Boynton and Boynton, *Handbook of the Christian Movement in China*, pp. 100–101; Yu, *Yejin tianming*, p. 216.

47. Yao Minquan, *Shanghai Jidujiao shi*, pp. 191–92; Yu, *Yejin tianming*, pp. 205, 319; Zia, "Chinese Evangelists in Modern China," p. 47.

48. Yu, *Yejin tianming*, pp. 201–5; Williamson, "Evangelistic Work in China To-day," p. 449; Luo Xingsan, interview. See also the following issues of *Tongwenbao:* October 1935, Nos. 38, 40; November 1935, Nos. 44, 46; August 1936, No. 30.

49. *Tongwenbao*, September 1936, No. 34.

50. See Yu, *Yejin tianming*, pp. 184–86, 192, 301, 320.

51. Zhao Junying, *Mantan wushinian lai*, pp. 5, 16–19, 25; Yu, *Yejin tianming*, pp. 202, 209.

52. Yu, *Yejin tianming*, pp. 169, 217, 221–22, 262; Zhao Junying, *Mantan wushinian lai*, pp. 18–19, 28. Budao Shizijun was later renamed Zhonghua Chuandaohui.

53. Yu, *Yejin tianming*, pp. 171–72, 224–29, 268.

54. Ibid., pp. 258–63, 276; Zhao Junying, *Mantan wushinian lai*, pp. 20–21. Those future church leaders included Watchman Nee's nephew Chen Zhongdao and Teng Jinhui.

55. Yin Renxian, *Shengguang zhiyin*, pp. 14, 21–22; Yu, *Yejin tianming*, pp. 225, 271–76.

56. Zhao Junying, *Mantan wushinian lai*, p. 19; Yu, *Yejin tianming*, pp. 234, 278–79.

57. Price, *Rural Church in China*, pp. 236–37.

58. See Yu, *Yejin tianming*, pp. 279–80, 284–87; Zhao Junying, *Mantan wushinian lai*, pp. 19–22. The core members of the Inter-Varsity Fellowship continued to draw their salaries from, and send their work reports to, the Seattle group of conservative Christians.

59. Lyall, *Come Wind, Come Weather*, pp. 10–11; Lyall, *Three of China's Mighty Men*, pp. 123–24.

60. Gih, *Church behind the Bamboo Curtain*, pp. 25–26; Huang Denghuang, *Gu'er zhifu*, pp. 62–63. In July 1947, Gih left the Bethel Mission and started an orphanage in interior China. See also Yu, *Yejin tianming*, p. 162.

61. Lyall, *Three of China's Mighty Men*, pp. 19–20, 24–28, 31, 34.

62. Wang Mingdao, *Wushi nian lai*, pp. 146–57, 179–81. The Chinese names of the league and the union were, respectively, Huabei Jidujiao Lianhe Cujinhui and Huabei Zhonghua Jidujiaotuan.

63. Lyall, *Three of China's Mighty Men*, pp. 124–26.

64. Gu Changsheng, telephone interview with the author, June 20, 2006. The first title appeared as *Yuanzidan yu shijie mori* (1948); *Time's Last Hour* was translated as *Lishi de moye* (1949).

65. Mao Dun, "Guxiang zaji," in Ke Ling, *Ershi shiji Zhongguo jishi wenxue*, pp. 20–21. *Shaobing ge* was traditionally attributed to Liu Bowen, military strategist and top advisor to Emperor Zhu Yuanzhang. *Tuibei tu*, dating possibly to the tenth century, was attributed to Li Chunfeng and Yuan Tiangang of the early Tang period. Li was allegedly pouring out a stream of prophecies on the rise and fall of dynasties when Yuan pushed his back to stop him, shouting "No giving away of Heaven's secret!" Hence the title *Tuibei tu*.

66. Yao Minquan, *Shanghai Jidujiao shi*, pp. 191–93, 197–200; Lu Chuanfang, interview with the author, Shanghai, June 20, 1997. Lu was an elder of the Spiritual Food Church.

67. Zhang Qizhen, interviews, 1997; Zhonghua Renmin Gongheguo Gong'anbu Diyiju, *Jidutu Juhuichu (Xiaoqun) Gaikuang*, p. 4; Kinnear, *Against the Tide*, pp. 163–64. Nee was accused of providing false information of the company's alleged losses (despite actual gains of more than US $100,000), prompting sell-offs of its stocks, which he bought back.

68. Kinnear, *Against the Tide*, p. 164; Huang Yushen, *Cong Hatonglu dao Nanyanglu*, p. 63. For the Little Flock's idolization of Nee, see Lee, *Watchman Nee*.

69. Nee's letter to the elders and deacons of the Shanghai Christian Assembly dated May 2, 1943, as quoted in Ren Zhongxiang, *Shanghai Jidutu Juhuichu*, p. 9.

70. Kinnear, *Against the Tide*, pp. 168–69. See also Brook, "Toward Independence," p. 333.

71. Shuiliu Zhishizhan, "Jinianwen"; Cha, *Zhongguo Jidujiao*, p. 330; Kinnear, *Against the Tide*, pp. 170, 177–78; Ren Zhongxiang, *Shanghai Jidutu Juhuichu*, p. 13; Lyall, *Three of China's Mighty Men*, p. 69.

72. Chen Biyin, interviews; Ren Zhongxiang, *Shanghai Jidutu Juhuichu*, p. 14. Chen was installed by Nee in 1948 as a Fuzhou elder.

73. Ren Zhongxiang, *Shanghai Jidutu Juhuichu*, pp. 10–14.

74. Nee, "Jinhou gongzuo de lu," pp. 253, 259–60.

75. Huang Yushen, *Cong Hatonglu dao Nanyanglu*, pp. 11, 68–69; Zhang Qizhen, interviews, 1997; Kinnear, *Against the Tide*, pp. 179–80.

76. Huang Yushen, *Cong Hatonglu dao Nanyanglu*, p. 63; Ren Zhongxiang, *Shanghai Jidutu Juhuichu*, pp. 14, 16, 19.

77. Nee, "Jinhou gongzuo de lu," p. 257; Ren Zhongxiang, *Shanghai Jidutu*

Juhuichu, pp. 19–20; Shen Chengyi (Yiyang collective farm member), interview with the author, Xiaoshan, August 4, 2008.

78. Huang Yushen, *Cong Hatonglu dao Nanyanglu*, p. 9; Lyall, *Three of China's Mighty Men*, p. 85.

79. Kinnear, *Against the Tide*, p. 158; Lyall, *Three of China's Mighty Men*, pp. 32–33.

80. Yu, *Yejin tianming*, pp. 191–92; Li Mingyao, "Lanzhou Yesu Jiating," p. 177.

81. Sze, *Ni Tuosheng xundao shi*, pp. 9–10; Li Wenwei, "Guanyu Shi Bocheng," pp. 1–2; Ren Zhongxiang, *Shanghai Jidutu Juhuichu*, pp. 15–16; Yao Minquan, *Shanghai Jidujiao shi*, p. 226.

82. "The Christian Manifesto," in F. P. Jones, *Documents of the Three-Self Movement*, p. 20; Chao and Chong, *Dangdai Zhongguo Jidujiao*, pp. 20–23, 22 n.50.

83. Gu Changsheng, *Zhongguo Jidujiao jianshi*, pp. 156–58, 160–65; Chao and Chong, *Dangdai Zhongguo Jidujiao*, pp. 26, 29–34, 78 n.30. See also Ling, *Changing Role of the British Protestant Missionaries*, p. 178. The full name of the initial Three-Self Committee was Zhongguo Jidujiao Kangmei Yuanchao Sanzi Gexin Yundong Weiyuanhui Choubei Weiyuanhui, or the Preparatory Committee of China Christian Resist America-Aid Korea Three-Self Reform Movement Committee. In 1954, it was renamed Zhongguo Jidujiao Sanzi Aiguo Yundong Weiyuanhui, or the Chinese Christian Three-Self Patriotic Movement Committee.

84. Price, *China: Twilight or Dawn?* p. 142; Shen Derong, *Wu Yaozong xiaozhuan*, p. 33.

85. Wu Leichuan as quoted in Kiang Wen-han, *Chinese Student Movement*, p. 126. See also West, *Yenching University*, pp. 167–69; Yu, *Yejin tianming*, pp. 266–68. Wu Leichuan was already moving in pro-Communist directions during the 1930s but died before the CCP victory.

86. J. Herbert Kane as quoted in Bays, "Foreign Missions and Indigenous Protestant Leaders," p. 159. See also Chen Renbing and Chen Meida, "Chen Chonggui mushi xiaozhuan," pp. 89–94.

87. Tao Feiya, *Zhongguo de Jidujiao wutuobang*, pp. 221–22.

88. Zhao Zichen, "Yanjing Daxue de zongjiao xueyuan," p. 112.

89. Wei Yisa, "My Self-Examination," pp. 63–65.

90. Nee, "Wo shi zenyang zhuan guolai de"; Ren Zhongxiang, *Shanghai Jidutu Juhuichu*, p. 22. Jia Yuming and Yang Shaotang also pledged their support for the Three-Self movement in 1951. See Chao and Chong, *Dangdai Zhongguo Jidujiao*, pp. 29–30.

91. Wang Mingdao, "Women shi weile xinyang," p. 64; Wang Mingdao as quoted in S. Wang, *You sishinian*, pp. 110–11.

92. *Mazhuang Yesu Jiating*, p. 9; Tao Feiya, *Zhongguo de Jidujiao wutuobang*, pp. 249–50, 259–61; Jing Fuyin, interview. See also Chao and Chong, *Dangdai Zhongguo Jidujiao*, p. 44. Jing died in Xi'an.

93. S. Wang, *You sishinian*, pp. 92, 98, 165–67; Chao and Chong, *Dangdai*

Zhongguo Jidujiao, pp. 82–84. Wang Mingdao "repented" of his "counter-revolutionary crimes" in September 1956 and was released. In 1958, he was rearrested and sentenced to life imprisonment.

94. Sze, *Ni Tuosheng xundao shi,* pp. 71–72; Luo Xingsan, interview.

95. Zhonghua Renmin Gongheguo Gong'anbu Diyiju, *Jidutu Juhuichu (Xiaoqun) Gaikuang,* pp. 4, 15; Ren Zhongxiang, *Shanghai Jidutu Juhuichu,* pp. 23–24, 26–29.

96. Li Wenwei, "Guanyu Shi Bocheng," p. 9.

97. Nee, letters to Zhang Pincheng, May 6, 16, and 22, 1972; Nee, letter to Ma Xingtao, May 22, 1972, reprinted in Lee, *Watchman Nee,* pp. 337–40. See also Kinnear, *Against the Tide,* p. 237.

98. Chen Guangzao, "Zhen Yesu Jiaohui," pp. 17–18; F. P. Jones, *Church in Communist China,* pp. 109–10; Chao and Chong, *Dangdai Zhongguo Jidujiao,* pp. 44, 102.

99. Gu Changsheng, *Zhongguo Jidujiao jianshi,* p. 164; Chen Guangzao, "Zhen Yesu Jiaohui," pp. 17–18. See also *Bridge* 76 (April 1996): 6–7, 10.

100. *Shandong shengzhi,* pp. 619–20; National Council of Churches (U.S.A.), "China Notes," October 1966, cited in Zhao Junying, *Mantan wushinian lai,* pp. 280–83; Gu Changsheng, *Zhongguo Jidujiao jianshi,* pp. 164–71.

101. Bingle and Grubb, *World Christian Handbook,* pp. 141–42. According to that report, the Protestant community in China (excluding the Jesus Family, the Little Flock, the Spiritual Gifts Society, and other small independent churches) claimed a baptized membership totaling around 936,000, of which 125,000 (an inflated number) belonged to the TJC and about 11,500 were affiliated with the China Christian Independent Church (Zilihui). The addition of the Jesus Family (10,000), the Little Flock (80,000), and the Spiritual Gifts Society, along with other small groups such as the Spiritual Food Church (Lingliangtang) for which no statistics are available, would bring the total of Chinese Protestants to about 1 million. See also Wei Yisa, "My Self-Examination," p. 60.

102. Zhao Zichen, *Xiyu ji,* pp. 43–44, 59–60. See also Ng, *Jidujiao yu Zhongguo shehui bianqian,* pp. 52–57. By the late 1940s, Zhao had returned to the teachings of social Christianity.

103. Zhao Junying, *Mantan wushinian lai,* p. 27.

CHAPTER 9. CRIES IN THE WILDERNESS

1. Gu Changsheng, "Wenhua Dageming." For the biblical theme of the Antichrist, see 1 John 2:18–22. In this chapter, apart from the specific sources cited below, I have also relied on my own encounter with, and knowledge of, both the Three-Self and unregistered churches since the 1980s, including personal interviews conducted in Fujian, Shandong, and Zhejiang in 2003, 2005, 2006, and 2008. To avoid causing potential harm to my sources, I have refrained from citing some of those interviews.

2. Gu Changsheng, *Zhongguo Jidujiao jianshi,* pp. 169–71; Gu Changsheng,

"Wenhua Dageming"; Chao and Chong, *Dangdai Zhongguo Jidujiao*, pp. 182–85. It should be noted that, in most cases of "persecution," religion was likely not the lone factor. Previous associations with the Nationalist government as well as one's social, economic, and family background and foreign connections tended to figure as well.

3. Chao and Chong, *Dangdai Zhongguo Jidujiao*, p. 191. See also Gu Changsheng, *Zhongguo Jidujiao jianshi*, pp. 170–71.

4. Gu Changsheng, "Wenhua Dageming."

5. U.S. Department of State, "International Religious Freedom Report" (2001); Barrett, Kurian, and Johnson, *World Christian Encyclopedia*, p. 17. According to the latter source, 35,778,000 people were affiliated with the "Chinese charismatic" church in 1995. See also Lambert, *China's Christian Millions*, pp. 19, 66.

6. Erik Eckholm, "China's Churches: Glad, and Bitter, Tidings," *NYT*, June 17, 1998; Robert Marquand, "In China, Pews Are Packed: Beijing Is Wary as Christianity Counts Up to 90 Million Adherents," *Christian Science Monitor*, December 24, 2003; Bays, "Chinese Protestant Christianity Today," p. 488. The total membership of the CCP at the end of 2000 was 64.5 million.

7. See Gu Changsheng, *Zhongguo Jidujiao jianshi*, pp. 166–67.

8. Chen Qiuxiang, interview with the author, Fuzhou, May 21, 2006; Lambert, *Resurrection of the Chinese Church*, pp. 18–19.

9. Chen Guangzao, "Zhen Yesu Jiaohui," pp. 50–51, 56–63. For the development of the TJC outside mainland China, see Rubinstein, *Protestant Community on Modern Taiwan*, pp. 126–28.

10. Chang Zhifu, "Dui woxian 'Yesu Jiating' de tansuo," pp. 152–62; *Bridge* 76 (April 1996): 5–6.

11. Zhang Yinan, "Shen de maoxianjia"; Li Musheng, *Shangshan zhi yao*, p. v; Aikman, *Jesus in Beijing*, pp. 67–69, 77. In the early 1970s, Zhang Rongliang was also apprenticed to Gao Yunjiu, a former Little Flock deacon. See also Lambert, *China's Christian Millions*, pp. 87–88.

12. "Rural Testimonies," *Bridge* 5 (May 1984): 8–10.

13. Lambert, *China's Christian Millions*, pp. 110–15.

14. Chao and Chong, *Dangdai Zhongguo Jidujiao*, pp. 302–3; S. Wang, *You sishinian*, pp. 236–39. See also Zhang Yinan, "Shen de maoxianjia."

15. "Resolution of the Third Chinese National Christian Conference" (October 1980), quoted in *Ching Feng* 24, 1 (March 1981): 79.

16. TSPM/China Christian Council, "Aiguo aijiao, tongxin maixiang xinshiji" (With Love for Our Country and Our Church, March toward the New Century), September 22, 2000, *Zhongguo Jidujiao wangzhan*; Ding Guangxun, *Ding Guangxun wenji*, Preface and p. 115; Gu Changsheng, *Zhongguo Jidujiao jianshi*, pp. 172–76.

17. TSPM/China Christian Council, "Aiguo aijiao"; "Zhongguo Jidujiao gaikuang" (An Overview of Chinese Christianity), 2003, *Zhongguo Jidujiao*

wangzhan; U.S. Department of State, "International Religious Freedom Report" (2001).

18. Li Ruijun, interview; observations of my own during the same visit.

19. See Chang Zhifu, "Dui woxian 'Yesu Jiating' de tansuo"; Lambert, *China's Christian Millions,* p. 62.

20. "Religious Problems in Hunan," *Bridge* 75 (February 1996): 3–4, 8–9; Chen Guangzao, "Zhen Yesu Jiaohui," p. 60.

21. Zhang Xiuxiu, biographical sketch of Ji Jianhong, *Zhongguo Jidujiao wangzhan.*

22. Adeney, *China: The Church's Long March,* p. 233; "Zhongguo Jidujiao gaikuang"; Lambert, *China's Christian Millions,* p. 48; Marquand, "In China, Pews Are Packed"; Eckholm, "China's Churches"; Joseph Kahn, "Violence Taints Religion's Solace for China's Poor," *NYT,* November 25, 2004. In 1995, the overall ratio of clergy to laity in TSPM churches was estimated to be 1 to 556. See Yang Fenggang, "Lost in the Market," p. 429.

23. See Hunter and Chan, *Protestantism in Contemporary China,* pp. 192–95; Zhang Yinan, "'Zhongguo jiating jiaohui."

24. Ye Xiaowen, "Xiejiao wenti de xianzhuang, chengyin yu duice" (The Problem of Heretic Cults: The Current State, Contributing Factors, and Our Strategy"), http://www.mingjing.org.cn/xgts/flgyxj/Part3/160.htm. Ye used the term *liumang wuchan jieji.*

25. *Bridge* 10 (March–April 1985): 3–4; Chen Guangzao, "Zhen Yesu Jiaohui," p. 61. See also Matthew 10:42. The Chinese term for the TJC baptismal rite is *dashuixi.*

26. Deng Zhaoming, "Recent Millennial Movements," pp. 17–18; Chen Guangzao, "Zhen Yesu Jiaohui," pp. 61–65; Gong'anbu Bangongting, "Xianyi rending de xiejiao"; "Linglingjiao," http://zaca.org.cn/info/content.asp?infoId=746&channelID=8.

27. "The Absurd 'Paradise,'" *Bridge* 71 (June 1995): 6–8; Lambert, *China's Christian Millions,* pp. 115–18, 123. CIM and the Christian and Missionary Alliance background were prominent in those tribal areas.

28. "Accounting for Differences: The Little Flock in Zhejiang," *Bridge* 16 (March–April 1986): 10–11; Lambert, *Resurrection of the Chinese Church,* pp. 86, 121, 160–61; Hunter and Chan, *Protestantism in Contemporary China,* p. 193.

29. Tang Shoulin and Ren Zhongxiang, *Wei zhendao,* p. 10; Daoren, *Difang Jiaohui,* pp. 35–44.

30. Tang Shoulin and Ren Zhongxiang, *Wei zhendao,* pp. 3–4, 161; Qin Jinggao, "Li Changshou sile"; Zheng Zhengguang and Ni Yulong, interviews. See also Li Bonan, "Jidujiao putaoshan huitang shilue," pp. 205–8. In 1943, Li suffered a nervous breakdown when the "evangelistic migration" he orchestrated landed him in a Japanese jail in Chefoo, where he was tortured.

31. Tang Shoulin and Ren Zhongxiang, *Wei zhendao,* pp. 8–11; Daoren, *Difang Jiaohui,* pp. 35–36, 44, 66–69.

32. "The Witness of a Former 'Yeller,'" *Bridge* 20 (November–December 1986): 9; Lambert, *Resurrection of the Chinese Church*, pp. 83–86, 160–61. For the establishment of connections between Little Flock congregations in Zhejiang and Henan, see Zhang Yinan, "Shen de maoxianjia," p. 6.

33. Li Changshou as quoted in Tang Shoulin and Ren Zhongxiang, *Wei zhendao*, pp. 10, 179, 196–97.

34. "Witness of a Former 'Yeller,'" p. 9; Tang Shoulin and Ren Zhongxiang, *Wei zhendao*, p. 178.

35. Qin Jinggao, "Li Changshou sile," pp. 214–15. See Isaiah 41:2 and Revelation 5:1–5 for the biblical references.

36. Tang Shoulin and Ren Zhongxiang, *Wei zhendao*, pp. 178–79, 211–12; Gong'anbu Bangongting, "Xianyi rending de xiejiao"; "Zhongguo jinnianlai chajin qudi xiejiao gaikuang" (An Overview of the Prohibition and Suppression of Heretic Cults in China in Recent Years), 2003, http://www .mingjing.org.cn/gnddxj/03-5.htm; Zhang Yinan, "Shen de maoxianjia." See Revelation 17:1 for descriptions of the "whore."

37. "China Sentences H. K. Bible Smuggler," *NYT*, January 28, 2002.

38. Zhang Yinan, "'Zhongguo jiating jiaohui'"; Zhang Yinan, "Shen de maoxianjia"; Aikman, *Jesus in Beijing*, pp. 87–89. See also Gong'anbu Bangongting, "Xianyi rending de xiejiao." The Weepers were also known as the Born-Again Sect (Chongshengpai) and the Total Scope Church (Quanfanwei Jiaohui).

39. Xie Moshan, "Jie Chongshengpai" (Exposing the Born-Again Sect), June 20, 1995, http://www1.bbsland.com/articleReader.php?idx=68504; Zhang Yinan, "'Zhongguo jiating jiaohui.'"

40. Gong'anbu Bangongting, "Xianyi rending de xiejiao"; "Zhongguo youyi Jidujiaohui zao zhenya" (Another Chinese Christian Church Suppressed), BBC Chinese, May 3, 2000; "Zhongguo jinnianlai chajin qudi xiejiao gaikuang." See also U.S. Department of State, "United States Policies in Support of Religious Freedom: Focus on Christians," July 22, 1997, http:// www.state.gov/www/global/human_rights/970722_relig_rpt_christian .html.

41. The China Gospel Fellowship is also known as Tanghe Jiaohui, named after its place of origin in southern Henan. The South China Church, also known as Huanan Fuyin Shituan, was founded in 1990 by Gong Shengliang (1952–), one of Xu Yongze's former associates among the Weepers. See Erik Eckholm, "Furor Over Death Sentences of 5 in Chinese Church Group," *NYT*, February 13, 2002; "Zhongguo 'xiejiao' sixing shangsu chenggong" (Chinese "Heretic Cult" Death Penalty Appeal Succeeds), *Duowei zhoukan* (Duowei Weekly), October 9, 2002. For Henan's reputation as a center of underground Christianity, see Lambert, *China's Christian Millions*, pp. 90, 227, 250.

42. Howard W. French, "Lives of Poverty, Untouched by China's Boom," *NYT*, January 13, 2008; Bates Gill and Sarah Palmer, "The Coming AIDS Crisis

in China," *NYT,* July 16, 2001; Chris Buckley, "AIDS-Afflicted Villagers Say Chinese Police Attacked Them," *NYT,* July 8, 2003.

43. Zhang Yinan, "Shen de maoxianjia"; Aikman, *Jesus in Beijing,* pp. 108–11, 271–74.

44. Lü Xiaomin, "Shen de ling gandong wo gaoge" (God's Spirit Inspired Me to Sing Loudly), March 12, 2007, http://zhidao.baidu.com/question/21489129 .html?fr=qrl3; Lü Xiaomin, "Jia'nan shixuan" (Selected Songs of Canaan), nos. 5, 8, 27, 34, 157, http://cannan.lingliang.org; Zhang Yinan, "Shen de maoxianjia."

45. "Zhongguo jiating jiaohui xinyang gaobai" (The Confession of Faith of House Churches in China), November 26, 1998, http://earlyrain.bokee .com/5415564.html; Zhang Yinan, "'Zhongguo jiating jiaohui'"; Zhang Yinan, "Shen de maoxianjia."

46. *Zhongguo fanxiejiao wang,* "Beiliwang" (Established King); Lambert, *China's Christian Millions,* pp. 142–43. See Luke 2:34 ("this child is set for the fall and rising again of many in Israel"). In the Chinese version, "set" is rendered as *beili,* or "established."

47. Gong'anbu Bangongting, "Xianyi rending de xiejiao"; *Zhongguo fanxiejiao wang,* "Beiliwang"; "Religious Problems in Hunan," *Bridge* 75 (February 1996): 11.

48. *Zhongguo fanxiejiao wang,* "Zhushenjiao" (Lord God Sect), May 5, 2007; Gong'anbu Bangongting, "Xianyi rending de xiejiao"; "Xiejiao 'Zhushenjiao' fumie" (Heretic Cult "Zhushenjiao" Destroyed), http://www.todayon history.com/11/10/d5926.htm; *Zhongguo fanxiejiao wang,* "Zhongguo dalu yi xiejiao 'jiaozhu' zuo zai Hunan fufa" ("Founder" of Mainland China Heretic Cult Executed in Hunan Yesterday), June 21, 2003.

49. Mentuhui, *Shanguang de lingcheng* (Shining Spiritual Journey), quoted in http://libanaba.ccblog.net/archives/2005/8460.html; Ma Yonghong, "Guanyu xiejiao 'Mentuhui' de xiangguang qingkuang" (The State of Affairs Related to the Heretic Cult "Mentuhui"), June 13, 2007, *Zhongguo fanxiejiao wang.*

50. Ma Yonghong, "Guanyu xiejiao 'Mentuhui'"; "Mentuhui" (The Disciples' Society), September 5, 2006, http://www.dlxg.gov.cn/fxj/display.asp?Id= 2093; Chen Yanhui, "Zhongguo xibu xiangcun 'xiejiao' diaocha" (An Investigation of "Heretic Cults" in the Rural West of China), June 30, 2007, *Zhongguo fanxiejiao wang.*

51. Gong'anbu Bangongting, "Xianyi rending de xiejiao"; "Zhongguo jinnian-lai chajin qudi xiejiao gaikuang"; "Zhongguo pan 'Mentuhui' chengyuan laogai" (China Sentences "Disciples' Society" Members to Reform through Labor), *Yeguang xinwen* (Latelinenews.com), January 11, 2002; Tianjin Anti-Cult Association, "Fangfan 'Mentuhui' jingshi jiaoyu xuanjiang tigang" (An Outline of Admonitory Education Materials on 'Disciples Society'), January 16, 2008, http://www.rbw.org.cn/article.aspx?i=uH2&ty=uuS& langu=f.

52. Deng Fei and Liu Zhiming, "Sanban Puren jiaohui'an zhuanti" (A Special Report on the Case of Three Grades of Servant Church), http://boxun.com/hero/2007/wanggz/79_1.shtml; Zhang Yinan, "Shenmi fuza de Xu Shengguang"; Zhuo Xuan, "Kuxiu dejiu de 'Sanban Puren'" (Salvation through Ascetic Devotions: Three Grades of Servants), http://cclw.net/gospel/new/sanbanpuren.htm.

53. Mungello, *Spirit and the Flesh in Shandong*, pp. 80–81.

54. Deng Fei and Liu Zhiming, "Sanban Puren jiaohui'an zhuanti"; Zhuo Xuan, "Kuxiu dejiu"; Gong'anbu Bangongting, "Xianyi rending de xiejiao"; "Zhongguo chujue 15 ming dixia jiaohui chengyuan" (China Executes 15 Underground Church Members), BBC Chinese, November 29, 2006.

55. Xue Feng, "Jiekai 'Dongfang Shandian' de zhen mianmu" (Unveiling the True Face of "The Lightning out of the East"), June 16, 2006, http://www.21sz.org/show.aspx?id=5435&cid=17; "'Dongfang Shandian' youhun weisi" (The Departed Soul of "The Lightning out of the East" Not Yet Dead), October 28, 2006, http://www.edzx.com/Article/Class9/Class15/200610/10629.html.

56. Wang Yongxin, *Zhendao shouce*, pp. 103–16; "Dongfang Shandian," http://www.pcchong.per.sg/2Heresy7a.htm; Xue Feng, "Jiekai 'Dongfang Shandian'"; Revelation 1:20, 3:1, 10:2.

57. For Marian cults, see Madsen, *China's Catholics*, pp. 88, 90, 242. For a discussion of the predominance of women in the Chinese church, see Aikman, *Jesus in Beijing*, p. 98.

58. Mungello, *Spirit and the Flesh in Shandong*, p. 6.

59. Dongfang Shandian, *Hua zai roushen xianxian*, p. 192; Dongfang Shandian, *Shengling xiang zhong jiaohui shuohua* (The Holy Spirit Speaks to the Churches), pp. 57–60, quoted in "Pouxi xiejiao zuzhi 'Dongfang Shandian'" (An Analysis of the Heretic Cult "The Lightning out of the East"), http://cclw.net/gospel/new/pxdfsd/htm/chapter02.html; "Dongfang Shandian."

60. Dongfang Shandian, *Hua zai roushen xianxian*, pp. 564, 1022, 1024–25.

61. See Spence, *God's Chinese Son*, pp. 229–33.

62. Gong'anbu Bangongting, "Xianyi rending de xiejiao"; Wang Yongxin, *Zhendao shouce*, p. 109; Dongfang Shandian, *Hua zai roushen xianxian*, pp. 192–93, 397–98. For "the great red dragon," see Revelation 12:3.

63. Dongfang Shandian, untitled printed directive addressed to "all church leaders" (*ge jiaohui dailing*) with a summary of "successful" and "failed" methods of proselytism, n.d. (early 2000s?); Wang Yongxin, *Zhendao shouce*, pp. 112–13; Chuandaoren, "Xiejiao 'Dongfang Shandian' de xin dongxiang" (New Developments of the Heretic Cult "The Lightning out of the East"), *Shengming jikan* (Christian Life Quarterly) 21 (March 2002). See also Lambert, *China's Christian Millions*, p. 134; "'Dongfang Shandian' ziliao xiaoji" (A Small Collection of Materials on "The Lightning out of the East"), *Jidutu shenghuowang* (Christian Life Net), http://cclw.net/gospel/

doubts.html; *Zhongguo fanxiejiao wang*, "Dongfang Shandian," http://www
.cnfxj.org/Html/xiejiaocn/2007–5/7/113256886.html.

64. Deng Fei and Liu Zhiming, "Sanban Puren jiaohui'an zhuanti"; "Pouxi
xiejiao zuzhi 'Dongfang Shandian'"; "'Dongfang Shandian' youhun weisi."

65. Deng Fei and Liu Zhiming, "Sanban Puren jiaohui'an zhuanti"; Kahn,
"Violence Taints Religion's Solace"; "Zhongguo chujue 15 ming dixia jiaohui chengyuan"; Zhuo Xuan, "Kuxiu dejiu de 'Sanban Puren.'" For biblical
killings, see 1 Kings 18:40 and 1 Samuel 15:33.

66. Lambert, *China's Christian Millions*, p. 66. See also Fu Xiqiu, "Jiating jiaohui lingxiu Zhang Rongliang beibu yu 'Duowei' wudao" (The Arrest of
House Church Leader Zhang Rongliang and the Misinformation on "Duowei"), *Da Jiyuan* (Epoch Times), December 10, 2004.

67. Wu Jiao, "Religious Believers Thrice the Official Estimate: Poll," *China
Daily*, February 7, 2007; U.S. Department of State, "International Religious Freedom Report" (2006–2008); Lambert, *China's Christian Millions*,
p. 19.

68. Argue as quoted in Eckholm, "China's Churches."

69. Wu Jiao, "Religious Believers Thrice the Official Estimate."

70. Ibid.; John Pomfret, "Old-Time Religion Popular Again in Rural China,"
Washington Post, August 24, 1998.

71. Madsen, *China's Catholics*, p. 101.

72. See Becker, *Chinese*, p. 227.

73. M. Chang, *Falun Gong*, pp. 1–4.

74. See French, "Lives of Poverty." The figure of three hundred million was
provided by the World Bank in December 2007.

75. Ye Xiaowen, "Xiejiao wenti."

76. Madsen, *China's Catholics*, pp. 9, 113, 138. See also Yang Fenggang, "Lost
in the Market," p. 439.

77. Hunter and Chan, *Protestantism in Contemporary China*, pp. 171–73.

78. For "the communism of love" as an attribute of religious sects, see
Troeltsch, *Social Teaching of the Christian Churches* 1: 82.

79. Chen Yanhui, "Zhongguo xibu xiangcun 'xiejiao' diaocha."

AFTERWORD

1. Eliade, *Encyclopedia of Religion* 9: 521–22, 524–25.

2. Cox, *Fire from Heaven*, p. 4. See also Cohn, *Pursuit of the Millennium*, p. 2;
Boyer, *When Time Shall Be No More*, pp. 21–26; Hesiod, *Works and Days*, in
The Poems of Hesiod, trans. R. M. Frazer (Norman: University of Oklahoma
Press, 1983), pp. 93–105.

3. Durkheim, *Elementary Forms of the Religious Life*, pp. 226–27; Landes,
Encyclopedia of Millennialism and Millennial Movements, p. 25.

4. Goodman, *Speaking in Tongues*, p. 87. See also Ehrenreich, *Dancing in the
Streets*, pp. 65–67, 85; Acts 2 in the New Testament.

5. Goodman, *Speaking in Tongues,* pp. 59–60, 160; Benedict Carey, "A Neuro-scientific Look at Speaking in Tongues," *NYT,* November 7, 2006.

6. Lewis, *Ecstatic Religion,* p. 34; Eliade, *Encyclopedia of Religion* 13: 202. See also Taves, *Fits, Trances, & Visions,* p. 357; Dawkins, *God Delusion,* p. 168. Dawkins suggests that "visionary religious experiences are related to temporal lobe epilepsy."

7. White, *From Jesus to Christianity,* pp. 413–14; Tertullian as quoted in Knox, *Enthusiasm,* p. 35.

8. Lewis, *Ecstatic Religion,* pp. 38, 118. See also Ehrenreich, *Dancing in the Streets,* p. 85.

9. Cox, *Fire from Heaven,* pp. 4, 90.

10. Hoffer, *True Believer,* pp. 9, 41.

11. Cohn, *Pursuit of the Millennium,* pp. 32, 207–8, 314–15.

12. Lanternari, *Religions of the Oppressed,* pp. ix, 240, 249.

13. Ban Gu, *Hanshu,* pp. 62, 238, 269. Of the relevant parts of *Hanshu,* "Aidi ji" (Records of the Ai Emperor) contains the following: "四年春，大旱。關東民傳行西王母籌，經歷郡國，西入關至京師。民又會聚祠西王母，或夜持火上屋，擊鼓號呼相惊恐。" Other reports on the incident are found in the parts titled "Tianwen zhi" (Annals of Astronomy) and "Wuxing zhi" (Annals of the Five Phases). The latter has: "其夏，京師郡國民聚會里巷阡陌，設張博具，歌舞祠西王母。又傳書曰: 母告百姓，佩此書者不死。" See also Overmyer, *Folk Buddhist Religion,* pp. 139–40; Ma Xisha and Han Bingfang, *Zhongguo minjian zongjiao shi,* pp. 66, 673. I consulted Overmyer's account in rendering my own translation.

14. Wang Qinghuai, *Zhongguo xiejiao shi,* pp. 69–72, 75–78; Ma Xisha and Han Bingfang, *Zhongguo minjian zongjiao shi,* pp. 36–42, 50–51, 55–56.

15. Overmyer, *Precious Volumes,* p. 17; Ma Xisha and Han Bingfang, *Zhongguo minjian zongjiao shi,* pp. 36–37; Overmyer, *Folk Buddhist Religion,* pp. 151–52.

16. C. K. Yang, *Religion in Chinese Society,* pp. 354–55.

17. Overmyer, *Religions of China,* p. 54. For the development of the White Lotus tradition, see Ma Xisha and Han Bingfang, *Zhongguo minjian zongjiao shi,* pp. 103, 118–25, 138–42, 152, 157. In the twelfth century, a new stream of popular Buddhist beliefs that focused on Amitabha and his "Pure Land" produced the White Lotus tradition. It featured a form of popular piety characterized by home-based worship, "halls of penance," and voluntary societies of devotees organized outside the monasteries. By the Ming dynasty, almost all the White Lotus sects had adopted millenarian beliefs.

18. Naquin, *Millenarian Rebellion in China,* pp. 2–3, 10–12; Ma Xisha and Han Bingfang, *Zhongguo minjian zongjiao shi,* pp. 507–8; Overmyer, *Precious Volumes,* p. 4.

19. For Yiguandao, see Lev Deliusin, "The I-Kuan Tao Society," in Chesneaux, *Popular Movements and Secret Societies in China,* pp. 226–28. See also Chan Wing-tsit, *Religious Trends in Modern China,* pp. 158–59, 162–67.

Besides Yiguandao, White Lotus offshoots also included the Big Sword
Society, the Small Sword Society, the Heavenly Gate Society, the Yellow
Society, and the resurgent Eight Trigrams Society. Other major religious
societies that emerged during the Republican period include the Society
of the Way (Daoyuan), the Society for the Common Good (Tongshanshe),
and the Society for the Intuition of the Good (Wushanshe). Still others,
such as the Union of World Religions (Shijie Zongjiao Datonghui), were
openly apocalyptic in their teachings and foretold specific times for the
end of the world. See Wang Chao-hsiang, "Religious Elements in the
Esoteric Societies of China"; Rawlinson, *Naturalization of Christianity in
China,* pp. 154–57.

20. See Spence, *Gate of Heavenly Peace,* pp. 64–68.
21. Mao Zedong to Li Jinxi, 1917, http://space.goiee.com/html/75/90875
    –41288.html. It contained the following: "彼時天下皆為圣賢，而無凡愚，
    可盡毀一切世法，呼太和之气而吸清海之波。孔子知此義，故立太平世為鵠，
    而不廢据亂、升平二世。大同者，吾人之鵠也。" See also Tao Feiya, *Zhong-
    guo de Jidujiao wutuobang,* p. 11.
22. Mao Zedong, "Lun renmin minzhu zhuanzheng," p. 1471.
23. Weber, *Religion of China,* p. 209. Such religiosity was already visible in the
    Taiping Dao Rebellion and the Five Pecks of Rice (Wudoumi) sect of the
    late Han period. Both groups used mass penance and "charmed water" in-
    stead of acupuncture or herbal medicine to cure diseases. See Ma Xisha
    and Han Bingfang, *Zhongguo minjian zongjiao shi,* pp. 5–7.
24. Overmyer, *Religions of China,* p. 52.
25. Esherick, *Origins of the Boxer Uprising,* pp. 216–19.
26. See Cohn, *Pursuit of the Millennium,* p. 318; Overmyer, *Folk Buddhist
    Religion,* pp. 64–65.
27. See Frazer, *Golden Bough,* p. 52.
28. See Overmyer, "Alternatives: Popular Religious Sects in Chinese Society,"
    p. 165; Naquin, *Millenarian Rebellion in China,* p. 41.
29. See Nee, "Mengtou de wenti," pp. 405–26. For biblical teachings on the
    covering of women's hair, see I Corinthians 11:5–6. Theologian E. S.
    Fiorenza hypothesizes that the Pauline head-covering rule arose from a
    male fear that women of Corinth were becoming too exuberant with their
    unbound hair and were coming too close to the hair-tossing practice in the
    ecstatic worship of oriental deities. See Ehrenreich, *Dancing in the Streets,*
    pp. 66–67. For a discussion of opportunities for (and limits of) women's
    leadership in mission Christianity, see Kwok Pui-lan, *Chinese Women and
    Christianity,* pp. 80–86.
30. For secret brotherhood associations, see Ownby, "Heaven and Earth
    Society as Popular Religion," pp. 1039–40.
31. See Bainbridge, *Sociology of Religious Movements,* p. 50; "Millennialism,"
    in Eliade, *Encyclopedia of Religion,* vol. 9.
32. Barrett, Kurian, and Johnson, *World Christian Encyclopedia,* p. 12; Sanneh

and Carpenter, *Changing Face of Christianity,* Preface, p. vii. In 2000, there were 335 million Christians in Africa, 307 million in Asia, 475 million in Latin America, 536 million in Europe, and 212 million in North America.

33. Andrew F. Walls, "Cross-cultural Encounters and the Shift to World Christianity," *Journal of Presbyterian History* 81, 2 (Summer 2003): 112; Jenkins, *Next Christendom,* pp. 2–3. See also Walls, *Cross-Cultural Process in Christian History,* pp. 30–32, 85.

34. Jenkins, *Next Christendom,* p. 8. See also Cox, *Fire from Heaven,* pp. 14–15. By the 1990s, Pentecostalism in its various forms had attracted more than four hundred million, accounting for almost a quarter of the world Christian population.

35. Cox, *Fire from Heaven,* pp. 15, 221; Somini Sengupta and Larry Rohter, "Where Faith Grows, Fired by Pentecostalism," *NYT,* October 14, 2003; Laurie Goodstein, "More Religion, but Not the Old-Time Kind," *NYT,* January 9, 2005. The largest megachurch in the world at the turn of the new millennium was the Yoido Full Gospel Church in Seoul that began as a prayer tent in a slum in 1958 but grew to include eight hundred thousand members by the 1990s.

36. Sengupta and Rohter, "Where Faith Grows"; Cox, *Fire from Heaven,* pp. 163–65.

37. Jenkins, *Next Christendom,* p. 13.

38. Aikman, *Jesus in Beijing,* pp. 285–87.

39. See Wu Jiao, "Religious Believers Thrice the Official Estimate: Poll," *China Daily,* February 7, 2007.

40. Arnold Toynbee as quoted in A. Wright, *Buddhism in Chinese History,* pp. 3, 106; Ron MacMillan, "House Church Struggles with New Converts," *Christianity Today,* August 20, 1990.

41. Overmyer, *Folk Buddhist Religion,* p. 65.

42. See Ka Lun Leung, "Cultural Christians and Christianity in China," *China Rights Forum,* No. 4, 2003: 28–31; Aikman, *Jesus in Beijing,* pp. 11, 230–31; Bays, "Chinese Protestant Christianity Today," pp. 498–500.

43. Micklethwait and Wooldridge, *God Is Back,* pp. 1–5.

44. See Lian Xi, "Western Protestant Missions and Modern Chinese Nationalist Dreams," *East Asian History* 32/33 (December 2006/June 2007).

45. Lin Zhibo, deputy director of the commentary department at the *People's Daily,* as quoted in "China Commentator Urges Tougher Line against Japan," Reuters, January 3, 2006.

46. Joseph Kahn, "Rivals on Legal Tightrope Seek to Expand Freedoms in China," *NYT,* February 25, 2007; Aikman, *Jesus in Beijing,* p. 11. See also Yang Fenggang, "Lost in the Market," p. 428.

47. Chen Cunfu, *Zhuanxingqi de Zhongguo Jidujiao,* pp. 51, 71, 73–74, 102, 118–19, 195.

48. A. Wright, *Buddhism in Chinese History,* pp. 32–35.

49. "Guo Xiangjisi" by Wang Wei (692?–761) ends with the following timeless

lines: "Towards dusk at the bend of a deserted pool / in meditation's calm I subdued the poisonous dragon [of passion]." See also Su Shi (Su Dongpo, 1037–1101), "Anguosi ji" (Remembering Anguosi Temple [in Huangzhou, Hubei]) (1084). At the temple, Su routinely "burned incense and sat in silent meditation."

50. See Yuan Zhiming, *Shizijia—Yesu zai Zhongguo*. Among the more articulate and accomplished contemporary Christian writers are Liu Xiaofeng and Yuan Zhiming himself.

51. A precedent for this can be found in Chinese Buddhism. See A. Wright, *Buddhism in Chinese History*, pp. 96–97. Wright points out that, after the Song dynasty (960–1279), the secular Neo-Confucian ideology "appropriated" elements of Buddhist thought while the upper class in general withdrew from the religion. The result was a "striking cleavage" in the modern period "between the rational ethic of the elite and the religious ethos of the peasantry."

52. See Yuan Zhiming, *Shizijia—Yesu zai Zhongguo*. Yuan's first religious work published in 1995 by the California-based Chinese Christian Mission was titled *Shile dadi dele tiankong* (*Losing the Good Earth, Gaining Heaven*). See also Zhang Boli, *Taoli Zhongguo* (1998). Its English version appeared as *Escape from China: The Long Journey from Tiananmen to Freedom* (New York: Washington Square Press, 2002).

53. Wang Wei composed his "Stopping by the Incense-Filled Temple" at a time when, disillusioned with the treacherous court politics but unable to retire, he led a "half official, half hermit" life. Su Dongpo, born into a Buddhist family, became deeply attached to Buddhism during his political exile in Huangzhou. See also lines from Xu Zhimo's poem excerpted at the beginning of Chapter 5.

54. Madsen, *China's Catholics*, pp. 34, 131.

55. Li Ming, "Jidujiao: zhengzai dalu zhuangda de fankang liliang" (Christianity: The Force of Resistance That Is Growing in Strength in the Mainland), *Cheng Ming*, September 1990.

56. Simon Elegant, "The War for China's Soul," *Time*, August 28, 2006, p. 43.

57. Lilla, "Politics of God." For a fuller discussion of the topic, see Lilla, *Stillborn God*, pp. 75–91.

58. Naquin, *Millenarian Rebellion in China*, pp. 2–3.

GLOSSARY

A'luoben (Alopen) 阿羅本
Bai Shangdi Hui 拜上帝會
Baoding 保定
Beiliwang 被立王
beiti 被提
Boteli Huanyou Budaotuan
    伯特利環游佈道團
Budao zazhi 佈道雜誌
Cai Sujuan 蔡蘇娟
Cansang Xuedaofang 蠶桑學道房
Changde 常德
Chefoo (Zhifu) 芝罘
Chen Bixi 陳碧璽
Chen Chonggui (Marcus Ch'eng)
    陳崇桂
Chen Duxiu 陳獨秀
Cheng Jigui 成寄歸
Cheng Jingyi (Cheng Ching-yi)
    诚静怡
Chenzhou 辰州
Chongshengpai 重生派
Ciqikou 磁器口
da jisi 大祭司
da yang 大洋
dangbu 黨部
Daoji Huitang 道濟會堂

Daoyuan 道院
dashuixi 大水洗
datong 大同
Dengshikou 燈市口
Dengzhou Wenhuiguan 登州文會館
desheng juhui 得勝聚會
Difang Jiaohui 地方教會
Ding Guangxun (K. H. Ting) 丁光訓
Ding Limei 丁立美
Dong Hengxin 董恆新
erliang liang 二兩糧
fachuan 法船
Fangcheng 方城
Feixian 費縣
Feng Yuxiang 馮玉祥
Fuhanhui 福漢會
fumushi 副牧師
Furen Daxue 輔仁大學
fuwang 父王
Fuxingbao 復興報
Fuyang 阜陽
fuyin yimin 福音移民
Gaiwuyan Jiao 改烏煙教
Gao Daling 高大齡
Gong Shengliang 龔聖亮
Gu Ren'en 顧仁恩

Guan Shengdi 關聖帝
Guo Duoma 郭多馬
Hanzhong tianguomeng 漢中天國夢
Hengpeng 橫蓬
Hong Rengan 洪仁玕
Hong Xiuquan 洪秀全
Hua Jiuzhu 華救主
Hua Xuehe 華雪和
Huabei Jidujiao Lianhe Cujinhui
    華北基督教聯合促進會
Huabei Shenxueyuan 華北神學院
Huabei Zhonghua Jidujiaotuan
    華北中華基督教團
Huaibei 淮北
huashen 化身
Huhanpai 呼喊派
hukou 戶口
Hunan Shengjing Xueyuan
    湖南聖經學院
hutu 糊塗
Ji Jianhong 季劍虹
Ji Sanbao 季三保
Ji Zhiwen (Andrew Gih) 計志文
Jia Yuming 賈玉銘
jiandu 監督
Jiang Changchuan 江長川
jiangtong 降僮
jiao'an 教案
jiaochulai 交出來
Jidutu Huitang 基督徒會堂
Jidutu Juhuichu 基督徒聚會處
Jidutu Juhuisuo 基督徒聚會所
Jidutu Lingxiuyuan 基督徒靈修院
jiebian 劫变
Jinanshi Dongjiao Lingxiuyuan
    濟南市東郊靈修院
Jing Dianying 敬奠瀛
Jinling Daxue 金陵大學
Jinling Nüzi Shenxueyuan
    金陵女子神學院
jinshi 进士
Jixin Jiti Nongchang 基信集體農場
Kuangye Zhaimen 曠野窄門
kuhui 苦會

Kupai 哭派
laojia 老家
leyuan wanzi 樂園丸子
Li Changshou (Witness Lee) 李常受
Li Daorong 李道榮
Li Jinxi 黎錦熙
Li Musheng (Li Tian'en) 李慕聖
Li Tian'en 李天恩
Li Xiaofeng 李曉峰
Li Yuanru 李淵如
Li Zongren 李宗仁
Liang Fa 梁發
lianlu 煉爐
Liji 禮記
Lin Heping 林和平
Lin Jingkang 林景康
Lin Yutang 林語堂
ling'en dahui 靈恩大會
Ling'enhui 靈恩會
Linggongtuan 靈工團
Lingguangbao 靈光報
Lingliangtang 靈糧堂
Linglingjiao 靈靈教
Lingshi jikan 靈食季刊
lingtong 靈統
Lingxiuyuan 靈修院
Linyi 臨沂
Lishi de moye 歷史的末頁
Liu Bowen 劉伯溫
Liu Jiaguo 劉家國
Liu Shoushan 劉壽山
Liu Tingfang 劉廷芳
Lu Hongnian 陸鴻年
Lü Xiaomin 呂小敏
Luo Wenzao (Gregory Lopez) 羅文藻
Ma Zhaorui 馬兆瑞
Mawei 馬尾
Mazhuang 馬莊
mengzhao 蒙召
Mentuhui 門徒會
Miyang (Biyang) 泌陽
mu 畝
Nanchang 南昌
Nanyuan 南苑

Ni Tuosheng (Watchman Nee) 倪柝聲
Nie Ziying 聶子英
peilinghui 培靈會
Penglai xianjing 蓬萊仙境
Pingdingshan 平頂山
pingmin qianzi ke 平民千字課
Pingyuan 平原
pochan 破產
Putian songzan 普天頌贊
qiushen futi 求神附體
Quanfanwei Jiaohui 全範圍教會
Quanguo Jidutu Daxuesheng
    Lianhehui
    全國基督徒大學生聯合會
Quanshi liangyan 勸世良言
Quan-Zhang Zhanglao Dahui
    泉漳長老大會
Randengfo 燃灯佛
renge jiuguo 人格救國
Rongcheng 容城
ruoshi qunti 弱勢群體
san jie 三劫
Sanshu Jidu 三贖基督
sanzi 三自
Shaanxi 陝西
Shandong Chou'en Chuandaohui
    山東酬恩傳道會
Shandong Zhonghua Jidujiao
    Ling'enhui Zonghui
    山東中華基督教靈恩會總會
Shanxi 山西
Shaobing ge 燒餅歌
Shenghua Yaochang 生化藥廠
shengli 聖篱
Shengling bao 聖靈報
Shengmingshe 生命社
Shengtu Xinyong Chuxushe
    聖徒信用儲蓄社
Shengxiandao 聖賢道
shengyuan 生員
Shenzhaohui 神召會
Shi Chengzhi (Phoebe Stone) 石成志
Shi Meiyu (Mary Stone) 石美玉
shifan 失範

Shijie Zongjiao Datonghui
    世界宗教大同會
Shijishen 實際神
shiwai taoyuan 世外桃園
shixiang 失鄉
Shizhao yuebao 時兆月報
Shu Zhan 舒展
Shuiliu Zhishizhan 水流執事站
Song Shangjie (John Sung) 宋尚節
Sun Zhanyao 孫瞻遙 (孫占堯?)
Tai'an 泰安
Taiping Dao 太平道
Taiping Tianguo 太平天國
Taishan Jiaoyangyuan 泰山教養院
Tao Yuanming 陶淵明
Tengxian 滕縣
Tianchao tianmu zhidu 天朝田畝制度
Tiandihui 天地會
Tianmuhui 天母會
Tianzhaoju 天召局
tishen 替身
Tongchuan fuyin zhenlibao
    通傳福音真理報
Tongshanshe 同善社
Tongwenbao 通問報
Tongxian 通縣
Tuibei tu 推背圖
Wang Mingdao 王明道
Wang Peizhen 汪佩真
Wang Yuansong 王元松
Wang Zai (Leland Wang) 王載
Wanguo gengzhengjiao bao
    万國更正教報
Wei Baoluo 魏保羅
Wei Enbo (Wei Baoluo) 魏恩波
Wei Yisa (Isaac Wei) 魏以撒
Wei Zhuomin (Francis Wei) 韋卓民
Weifang 濰坊
Weishan 微山
Weixian (Weifang) 濰縣
Wenshe yuekan 文社月刊
Wu Xikao 武錫考
Wu Yangming 吳揚明
Wu Yaozong (Y. T. Wu) 吳耀宗

Wudoumi 五斗米

Wushanshe 悟善社

Wusheng Laomu 無生老母

wuwei 無為

Wuxunjie zhenlibao 五旬節真理報

Xi Shengmo 席胜魔

Xi Wangmu 西王母

Xi Zizhi (Xi Shengmo) 席子直

Xiang-Ya 湘雅

Xiao shujuan 小書卷

xiao tiantang 小天堂

xiaochu baibing 消除百病

Xiaoqun 小群

Xiaoshan 蕭山

xiaozai jie'e 消災解厄

Xie Fuya (N. Z. Zia) 謝扶雅（謝乃壬）

Xie Honglai 謝洪賚

Xie Songgao (Z. K. Zia) 謝頌羔

xiejiao 邪教

Xinghua 興化

Xinxinhui 信心會

xiqi zhi ai 希奇之愛

xixin gemian 洗心革面

Xu Baoluo 徐保羅

Xu Sanchun 徐三春

Xu Shengguang 徐聖光

Xu Shuangfu (Xu Shengguang) 徐雙富

Xu Wenku (Xu Shengguang) 徐文庫

Xu Yongze 徐永澤

Xu Zhimo 徐志摩

xunxing ganshi 巡行干事

yamen 衙門

Yan Xishan 阎锡山

Yan Yangchu (James Yen) 晏陽初

Yang Rulin 楊汝霖

Yang Shaotang 楊紹唐

Yang Xiuqing 楊秀清

Yantai Haijun Xuexiao 煙臺海軍學校

Ye Fusheng 耶复生

Yelikewen 也里可溫

Yenching (Yanjing) 燕京

Yesu Dayuan 耶穌大院

Yesu Jiating 耶穌家庭

Yiguandao 一貫道

Yiyang 弋陽

Yizhoufu 沂州府

youwu xiangtong 有無相通

Yu Chenghua 俞成華

Yu Cidu (Dora Yu) 余慈度

Yu Guozhen 俞國楨

Yu Jinhua 余錦華

Yu Ligong 于力工

Yu Rizhang 余日章

Yuanzidan yu shijie mori 原子彈與世界末日

Yun Daiying 惲代英

Zaishangzhu 在上主

Zhang Banaba 張巴拿巴

Zhang Boling 張伯苓

Zhang Dianju (Zhang Banaba) 張殿舉

Zhang Lingsheng 張靈生

Zhang Pincheng 張品玶

Zhang Qizhen 張啟珍

Zhang Rongliang 張榮亮

Zhao Junying (Calvin Chao) 趙君影

Zhao Shiguang 趙世光

Zhao Weishan 趙維山

Zhao Zichen (T. C. Chao) 趙紫宸

Zhen Yesu Jiaohui 真耶穌教會

Zhenli Shengling Xuexiao 真理聖靈學校

zhenlong tianzi 真龍天子

Zhijiang Daxue 之江大學

Zhili 直隸

Zhong Leyuan 中樂園

Zhongguo Budao Shizijun 中國佈道十字軍

Zhongguo Fuyang Jiaohui 中國阜陽教會

Zhongguo Jidujiao Kangmei Yuanchao Sanzi Choubei Weiyuanhui 運動委員會籌備委員會 Gexin Yundong Weiyuanhui 中國基督教抗美援朝三自革新

Zhongguo Jidujiao Sanzi Aiguo
   Yundong Weiyuanhui
   中國基督教三自愛國運動委員會
Zhongguo Jidujiao Xiehui
   中國基督教協會
Zhongguo Jidujiaohui 中國基督教會
Zhongguo Jidutuhui 中國基督徒會
Zhongguo Tianzhujiao Aiguohui
   中國天主教愛國會
Zhongguo Yesujiao Zilihui
   中國耶穌教自立會
Zhonghua Fuyin Tuanqi
   中華福音團契
Zhonghua Guizhu Yundong
   中華歸主運動
Zhonghua Guonei Budaohui
   中華國內佈道會
Zhonghua Guowai Budaotuan
   中華國外佈道團
Zhonghua Jidujiao Xiejinhui
   中華基督教協進會

Zhonghua Jidujiaohui 中華基督教會
Zhonghua Mengfu Jiaohui
   中華蒙福教會
Zhonghua Minguo Guominjun
   中華民國國民軍
Zhonghua Pingmin Jiaoyu
   Cujinhui 中華平民教育促進會
Zhonghua Xuesheng Lizhi
   Chuandaotuan
   中華學生立志傳道團
Zhonghua Yesujiao Ling'en Zilihui
   (Ling'enhui)
   中華耶穌教靈恩自立會
Zhou Xingyi 周行義
Zhou Zhiyu 周志禹
Zhushenjiao 主神教
zibo 自搏
zipu 自撲
zizhi, ziyang, zichuan
   自治 、自養、自傳
Zuo Shunzhen 左順真

BIBLIOGRAPHY

Abbott, Paul R. "Revival Movements." *China Christian Year Book* (1932–1933), pp. 175–92.

Adeney, David H. *China: The Church's Long March.* Ventura, Calif.: Regal Books/ Overseas Missionary Fellowship, 1985.

Ahlstrom, Sydney E. *A Religious History of the American People.* New Haven, Conn.: Yale University Press, 1972.

Aikman, David. *Jesus in Beijing: How Christianity Is Transforming China and the Global Balance of Power.* Washington, D.C.: Regnery, 2003.

Albus, Harry J. *Twentieth-Century Onesiphorus: The Story of Leslie M. Anglin and the Home of Onesiphorus.* Grand Rapids, Mich.: William B. Eerdmans, 1951.

Anderson, Robert M. *Vision of the Disinherited: The Making of American Pentecostalism.* New York: Oxford University Press, 1979.

Austin, Alvyn. "Missions Dream Team." *Christian History* 52 (November 1996): 19–23.

Bainbridge, William Sims. *The Sociology of Religious Movements.* New York: Routledge, 1997.

Ban Gu (d. 92) 班固. *Hanshu* I 漢書 (上) (The History of the Western Han Dynasty). In *Siku quanshu, Shibu—disi ji,* compiled by Ji Xiaolan.

Bao Zhong 鮑忠. "Sishi nianlai zhi Nanjing Jidujiaohui" 四十年來之南京 基督教會 (Christian Churches in Nanjing in the Past Forty Years). In *Jinling shenxueyuan sishi zhounian jinian tekan* 金陵神學院四十週年紀念特刊 (Special Commemorative Volume for the Fortieth Anniversary of the Founding of Nanjing Theological Seminary). *Jinling shenxue zhi* 26 (November 1950): 107–25.

Barnett, Suzanne Wilson, and John King Fairbank, eds. *Christianity in China: Early Protestant Missionary Writings*. Cambridge, Mass.: Harvard University Press, 1985.

Barrett, David, George T. Kurian, and Todd M. Johnson, eds. *World Christian Encyclopedia*. 2nd ed. New York: Oxford University Press, 2001.

Bates, M. Searle. "Gleanings from the Manuscripts of M. Searle Bates: The Protestant Endeavor in Chinese Society, 1890–1950." Unpublished manuscript, edited by Cynthia McLean. New York: National Council of Churches of Christ in the U.S.A., 1984.

Baylis, Robert H. *My People: The History of Those Christians Sometimes Called Plymouth Brethren*. Wheaton, Ill.: Harold Shaw Publishers, 1995.

Bays, Daniel H. "Chinese Protestant Christianity Today." In *Religion in China Today*, edited by Daniel L. Overmyer. Cambridge and New York: Cambridge University Press, 2003.

————. "Christian Revival in China, 1900–1937." In *Modern Christian Revivals*, edited by Edith L. Blumhofer and Randall Balmer. Urbana and Chicago: University of Illinois Press, 1993.

————. "Christianity and Chinese Sects: Religious Tracts in the Late Nineteenth Century." In *Christianity in China: Early Protestant Missionary Writings*, edited by Suzanne Wilson Barnett and John King Fairbank.

————, ed. *Christianity in China: From the Eighteenth Century to the Present*. Stanford, Calif.: Stanford University Press, 1996.

————. "Foreign Missions and Indigenous Protestant Leaders in China, 1920–1955: Identity and Loyalty in an Age of Powerful Nationalism." In *Missions, Nationalism, and the End of Empire*, edited by Brian Stanley and Alaine Low. Grand Rapids, Mich.: William B. Eerdmans, 2003.

————. "Indigenous Protestant Churches in China, 1900–1937: A Pentecostal Case Study." In *Indigenous Responses to Western Christianity*, edited by Steven Kaplan. New York: New York University Press, 1995.

————. "The Protestant Missionary Establishment and the Pentecostal Movement." In *Pentecostal Currents in American Protestantism*, edited by Edith L. Blumhofer, Russell P. Spittler, and Grant A. Wacker. Urbana and Chicago: University of Illinois Press, 1999.

Bays, Daniel H., and Grant Wacker, eds. *The Foreign Missionary Enterprise at Home: Explorations in North American Cultural History*. Tuscaloosa and London: University of Alabama Press, 2003.

Bebbington, David W. *Evangelicalism in Modern Britain: A History from the 1730s to the 1980s*. London: Unwin Hyman, 1989.

Becker, Jasper. *The Chinese*. Oxford: Oxford University Press, 2000.

Bethel Mission of China. *50th Anniversary of Bethel Mission of China, 1920–1970*. Hong Kong, 1970.

Billingsley, Phil. *Bandits in Republican China*. Stanford, Calif.: Stanford University Press, 1988.

Bingle, E. J., and Kenneth G. Grubb, eds. *World Christian Handbook*. 1952 ed. London: World Dominion Press, 1952.

Boardman, Eugene Powers. *Christian Influence upon the Ideology of the Taiping Rebellion, 1851–1864*. Madison: University of Wisconsin Press, 1952.

Boorman, Howard L., ed. *Biographical Dictionary of Republican China*, Vols. 1–4. New York: Columbia University Press, 1967.

Boyer, Paul. *When Time Shall Be No More: Prophecy Belief in Modern American Culture*. Cambridge, Mass.: Harvard University Press, 1992.

Boynton, Charles L., ed. *Directory of Protestant Missions in China, 1917*. Edited for the China Continuation Committee. Shanghai, 1917.

Boynton, Charles L., and C. D. Boynton, eds. *Handbook of the Christian Movement in China under Protestant Auspices*. Shanghai: National Christian Council of China, 1936.

Brewster, William N[esbitt]. *A Modern Pentecost in South China*. Shanghai: Methodist Publishing House, 1909.

———. "Revivals." *China Mission Year Book* (1910), pp. 313–19.

Bridge: Church Life in China Today. Nos. 1–20 (1983–1986), 71–86 (1995–1997). Hong Kong: Tao Fong Shan Ecumenical Centre.

Broomhall, Marshall, ed. *Martyred Missionaries of the China Inland Mission*. New York: Fleming H. Revell, 1901.

Burgess, Stanley M., ed. *The New International Dictionary of Pentecostal and Charismatic Movements*. Rev. and exp. ed. Grand Rapids, Mich.: Zondervan, 2002.

Cable, A. Mildred. *The Fulfillment of a Dream of Pastor Hsi: The Story of the Work in Hwochow*. London: Morgan & Scott, 1917.

Carlberg, Gustav. *China in Revival*. Rock Island, Ill.: Augustana Book Concern, 1936.

Cauthen, Eloise Glass. *Higher Ground: Biography of Wiley B. Glass Missionary to China*. Nashville, Tenn.: Broadman Press, 1978.

Cha, James Shih-Chieh (Zha Shijie) 查時傑. *Minguo Jidujiao shi lunwenji* 民國基督教史論文集 (A Collection of Essays on the History of Christianity during the Republican Period). Taipei: Yuzhou guang, 1993.

———. *Zhongguo Jidujiao renwu xiaozhuan* 中國基督教人物小傳 (Concise Biographies of Important Chinese Christians). Taipei: China Evangelical Seminary Press, 1983.

Chan, Stephen C. T. (Chen Zhongdao) 陳終道. *Wode jiufu Ni Tuosheng* 我的舅父倪柝聲 (My Uncle, Watchman Nee). Petaluma, Calif.: Chinese Christian Mission, 1982.

Chan Wing-tsit (Chen Wenjie). *Religious Trends in Modern China*. New York: Columbia University Press, 1953.

Chang, Maria Hsia. *Falun Gong: The End of Days*. New Haven, Conn.: Yale University Press, 2004.

Chang, Neander C. S. (Zhang Qinshi) 張欽士. *Guonei jin shinian lai zhi zongjiao sichao* 國內近十年來之宗教思潮 (Religious Thought in China in the Last Ten Years). Beijing: Chinese Language School, 1927.

Chang Zhifu 常志富. "Dui woxian 'Yesu Jiating' de tansuo" 對我縣 "耶穌家庭" 的探索 (An Exploration of the "Jesus Family" in Our County). Weishan wenshi ziliao 微山文史資料 (Literary and Historical Materials of Weishan [County]) Vol. 2 (May 1988): 152–62.

Chao, Jonathan T'ien-en (Zhao Tian'en) 趙天恩. "The Chinese Indigenous Church Movement, 1919–1927: A Protestant Response to the Anti-Christian Movements in Modern China." PhD diss., University of Pennsylvania, 1986.

———, ed. *Zhenli yiduan zhenwei bian* 真理異端真偽辯 (Discerning Truth from Heresies: A Critical Analysis of the Alleged and Real Heresies in Mainland China). Taipei: CMI Publishing, 2000.

Chao, Jonathan (Zhao Tian'en) 趙天恩, and Rosanna Chong (Zhuang Wanfang) 莊婉芳. *Dangdai Zhongguo Jidujiao fazhan shi* 當代中國基督教發展史 (A History of Christianity in Socialist China, 1949–1997). Taipei: CMI Publishing, 1997.

Charbonnier, Jean-Pierre. *Christians in China: A.D. 600 to 2000*. Translated by M. N. L. Couve de Murville. San Francisco: Ignatius Press, 2007.

Chen Biyin 陳必蔭. Interviews with the author. Fuzhou, July 1997.

Chen Cunfu 陳村富. *Zhuanxingqi de Zhongguo Jidujiao: Zhejiang Jidujiao ge'an yanjiu* 轉型期的中國基督教—浙江基督教個案研究 (Chinese Christianity in a Period of Structural Transformation [of Society]: A Case Study of Christianity in Zhejiang). Beijing: Dongfang chubanshe, 2005.

Chen Gonglu 陳恭祿. *Taiping Tianguo lishi luncong* 太平天國歷史論叢 (Essays on the History of Taiping Heavenly Kingdom). Guangzhou: Guangdong renmin chubanshe, 1995.

Chen Guangzao 陳光藻. "Zhen Yesu Jiaohui zonghui ji bufen shengxian jiaohui jianshi" 真耶穌教會總會及部分省縣教會簡史 (A Brief History of the General Assembly of the True Jesus Church and Its Member Churches in Some of the Provinces and Counties). True Jesus Church pamphlet printed in Fujian, 1999.

Chen Renbing 陳仁柄 and Chen Meida 陳美大. "Chen Chonggui mushi xiao-zhuan" 陳崇桂牧師小傳 (A Brief Biography of Pastor Chen Chonggui). In *Huainian Chen Chonggui mushi* 懷念陳崇桂牧師 (In Remembrance of Pastor Chen Chonggui). Shanghai: Zhongguo Jidujiao Sanzi Aiguo Yundong Weiyuanhui, 1991.

Chen Zexin 陳則信. *Ni Tuosheng dixiong jianshi* 倪柝聲弟兄簡史 (Meet Brother Nee, or A Brief Biography of Brother Ni Tuosheng). Hong Kong: Fuyin shufang, 1973.

———. *Wang Peizhen jianshi* 汪佩真簡史 (A Brief Biography of Wang Peizhen). 1974. Enlarged ed. Hong Kong: Jidutu chubanshe, 1982.

Ch'eng, Marcus (Chen Chonggui). *Marshal Feng—The Man and His Work*. Shanghai: Kelly & Walsh, 1926.

Chesneaux, Jean. *Secret Societies in China in the Nineteenth and Twentieth Centuries.* Translated by Gillian Nettle. Ann Arbor: University of Michigan Press, 1971.

———, ed. *Popular Movements and Secret Societies in China, 1840–1950.* Stanford, Calif.: Stanford University Press, 1972.

The China Christian Year Book (CCYB). Vols. 1–21 (1926–1935). Shanghai: Christian Literature Society for China. Vols. 1–13 (1910–1925) were published as the *China Mission Year Book (CMYB)* (annually, suspended 1920–1922). Vols. 14–21 (1926–1939) were under the title the *China Christian Year Book* (annually, 1928–1929; biennially, 1926–1927, 1931–1939).

The Chinese Recorder (CR). Vols. 31–70 (1900–1939). Shanghai.

Coad, F. Roy. *A History of the Brethren Movement.* Paternoster Press, 1968.

Cohen, Paul A. *Between Tradition and Modernity: Wang T'ao and Reform in Late Ch'ing China.* Cambridge, Mass.: Harvard University Press, 1974.

———. *China and Christianity: The Missionary Movement and the Growth of Chinese Antiforeignism, 1860–1870.* Cambridge, Mass.: Harvard University Press, 1963.

———. *History in Three Keys: The Boxers as Event, Experience, and Myth.* New York: Columbia University Press, 1997.

Cohn, Norman. *The Pursuit of the Millennium: Revolutionary Messianism in Medieval and Reformation Europe and Its Bearing on Modern Totalitarian Movements.* 1957. 2nd ed. New York: Harper Torchbooks, 1961.

Cox, Harvey. *Fire from Heaven: The Rise of Pentecostal Spirituality and the Reshaping of Religion in the Twenty-first Century.* Reading, Mass.: Addison-Wesley, 1995.

Crawford, Mary K. *The Shantung Revival.* Shanghai: China Baptist Publication Society, 1933.

Crutchfield, Larry. *The Origins of Dispensationalism.* Lanham, Md.: University Press of America, 2002.

Culpepper, C. L. *The Shantung Revival.* Dallas: Evangelism Division, Baptist General Convention of Texas, 1971.

Dai Sheng 戴聖 (Western Han dynasty 西漢), ed. *Liji* 禮記 (The Record of Rites), "Liyun" 禮運 (The Development and Usages [or Conveyance] of the Rites). In *Siku quanshu, Jingbu—diyi ji,* compiled by Ji Xiaolan.

Daoren 禱人. *Difang Jiaohui—sishinian lai de huigu yu qianzhan* 地方教會—四十年來的回顧與前瞻 (The Local Church: The Past Forty Years and the Future). Taipei: Mingming chubanshe, 1990.

Davenport, F. M. *Primitive Traits in Religious Revivals.* New York: Macmillan, 1905.

Dawkins, Richard. *The God Delusion.* Boston: Houghton Mifflin, 2006.

Dawson, Christopher, ed. *The Mongol Mission: Narratives and Letters of the Franciscan Missionaries in Mongolia and China in the Thirteenth and Fourteenth Centuries Translated by a Nun of Stanbrook Abbey.* New York: Sheed and Ward, 1955.

De Plata, William Robert. *Tell It from Calvary*. New York: Calvary Baptist Church, 1972.

Deng Huagui 鄧華貴 and Sheng Daoyan 盛道炎. "Yanwo yidai de Zhen Yesu Jiaohui" 燕窩一帶的真耶穌教會 (The True Jesus Church in the Yanwo Area). *Honghu wenshi* 洪湖文史 (Literature and History of Honghu), No. 4 (December 1988): 181–83.

Deng Zhaoming. "Recent Millennial Movements on Mainland China: Three Cases." *Bridge: Church Life in China Today* 80 (December 1996): 15–24.

Dillenbeck, Nora M. Biographical File. United Methodist Church Archives, Madison, New Jersey.

Ding Guangxun 丁光訓 (K. H. Ting). *Ding Guangxun wenji* 丁光訓文集 (Collected Works of Ding Guangxun). Nanjing: Yilin chubanshe, 1998.

Dongfang Shandian 東方閃電 (The Lightning out of the East). *Hua zai roushen xianxian* 話在肉身顯現 (The Word Manifested in the Flesh). Chenxing chubanshe 晨星出版社 (Morning Star Press), n.d. (mid-1990s?).

"Dr. Cheng Ching-yi." Editorial. *Chinese Recorder* 70 (December 1939): 689–95.

Du Kaixu 杜開許. "Zhen Yesu Jiaohui Maoping qidaosuo gaikuang" 真耶穌教會茅坪祈禱所概況 (A Brief Survey of the Maoping True Jesus Church Prayer House). *Zigui wenshi ziliao* 秭歸文史資料 (Literary and Historical Materials of Zigui), No. 6 (December 1988): 138–48.

Dunch, Ryan. *Fuzhou Protestants and the Making of a Modern China, 1857–1927*. New Haven, Conn.: Yale University Press, 2001.

———. "Protestant Christianity in China Today: Fragile, Fragmented, Flourishing." In *China and Christianity: Burdened Past, Hopeful Future*, edited by Stephen Uhalley and Xiaoxin Wu.

Durkheim, Emile. *The Elementary Forms of the Religious Life*. Translated by Joseph Ward Swain. London: George Allen & Unwin, 1915.

Durnbaugh, Donald F., et al., eds. *The Brethren Encyclopedia*. Philadelphia: Brethren Encyclopedia, 1983.

Ehrenreich, Barbara. *Dancing in the Streets: A History of Collective Joy*. New York: Metropolitan Books, 2007.

Eliade, Mircea, ed. *The Encyclopedia of Religion*. New York: Macmillan, 1987.

Entenmann, Robert E. "Catholics and Society in Eighteenth-Century Sichuan." In *Christianity in China: From the Eighteenth Century to the Present*, edited by Daniel H. Bays.

Esherick, Joseph W. *The Origins of the Boxer Uprising*. Berkeley and Los Angeles: University of California Press, 1987.

Fairbank, John King. *China: A New History*. Cambridge, Mass.: Harvard University Press, 1992.

———, ed. *The Missionary Enterprise in China and America*. Cambridge, Mass.: Harvard University Press, 1974.

Feng Yuxiang (Feng Yu Hsiang) 馮玉祥. "Address Delivered by Feng Yu Hsiang (the Christian General) to the North China Union Language School, Peking, China," February 27, 1923. Translated by George L. Davis. Pamphlet. Southern

Baptist Theological Seminary Library Special Collections, Louisville, Kentucky.

———. *Wode shenghuo* 我的生活 (My Life). Shanghai: Jiaoyu shudian, 1947.

Frazer, James George. *The Golden Bough: A Study in Magic and Religion.* 1922. Reprint. New York: Macmillan, 1934.

Frodsham, Stanley. *With Signs Following: The Story of the Pentecostal Revival in the Twentieth Century.* Springfield, Mo.: Gospel Publishing House, 1946.

Gernet, Jacques. *China and the Christian Impact: A Conflict of Cultures.* Translated by Janet Lloyd. Cambridge: Cambridge University Press, 1985.

Gih, Andrew (Ji Zhiwen, Andrew Gee). *The Church behind the Bamboo Curtain.* London. Marshall, Morgan & Scott, 1961.

———, comp. *Into God's Family: The Life Stories and Messages of China's Famous Bethel Evangelistic Bands.* Edited by J. Edwin Orr. London: Marshall, Morgan & Scott, 1937.

———. *Twice Born—and Then? The Life Story and Message of Andrew Gih, Bethel Mission, Shanghai.* London: Marshall, Morgan & Scott, 1936.

Gillman, Ian, and Hans-Joachim Klimkeit. *Christians in Asia before 1500.* Ann Arbor: University of Michigan Press, 1999.

Goforth, Jonathan. *"By My Spirit."* London and Edinburgh: Marshall, Morgan & Scott, 1929.

Goforth, Rosalind. *Goforth of China.* Grand Rapids, Mich.: Zondervan, 1937.

Goforth, Rosalind, and Jonathan Goforth. *Miracle Lives of China.* New York and London: Harper & Brothers, 1931.

Gong'anbu Bangongting 公安部辦公廳 (The Office of the Department of Public Security). "Xianyi rending de xiejiao zuzhi qingkuang" 現已認定的邪教組織情況 (The Situation regarding the Organization of Confirmed Heretic Cults). May 10, 2000. http://www.zhengqi.org.cn/zhengcefagui/xiejiaojiyouhaiqi gongchuli/20070205/1242.html.

Goodman, Felicitas D. *Speaking in Tongues: A Cross-Cultural Study of Glossolalia.* Chicago: University of Chicago Press, 1972.

Grubb, Kenneth G., ed. *World Christian Handbook.* London: World Dominion Press, 1949.

Gu Changsheng 顧長聲. *Chuanjiaoshi yu jindai Zhongguo* 傳教士與近代中國 (Missionaries and Modern China). Shanghai: Shanghai renmin chubanshe, 1981.

———. Interviews and conversations with the author, Orleans, Massachusetts, and by phone, 1997–2007.

———. "Meiguo Anxirihui zai Zhongguo 美國安息日會在中國, 1902–1950" (The American Seventh-Day Adventist Church in China, 1902–1950). Unpublished manuscript, 1987.

———. "Wenhua Dageming dui zongjiao de yingxiang" 文化大革命對宗教的影響 (The Influences of the Cultural Revolution on Religion). *Shijie zhoukan* 世界週刊 (*World Journal Weekly*), July 21, 1996.

———. *Zhongguo Jidujiao jianshi* 中國基督教簡史 (A Concise History of Christianity in China). Monterey Park, Calif.: Evergreen, 1999.

Gu Weimin 顧衛民. *Jidujiao yu jindai Zhongguo shehui* 基督教與近代中國社會 (Christianity and Modern Chinese Society). Shanghai: Shanghai renmin chubanshe, 1996.

Gu Zhijie 顧致潔. Interview with the author. Jinan, Shandong, October 7, 2003.

Guo Kechang and Zheng Suilan 郭克昌 鄭遂藍, eds. *Xinjiapo Jidutu budaotuan jinxi jiniankan* 新嘉坡基督徒佈道團金禧紀念刊 (Singapore Christian Evangelistic League Golden Jubilee Souvenir Magazine). Singapore: Singapore Christian Evangelistic League, 1985.

Guyon, Jeanne-Marie Bouvier de La Motte. *Sweet Smelling Myrrh: The Autobiography of Madame Guyon,* edited by Abbie C. Morrow. 1898. Reprint. Salem, Ohio: Schmul Publishing, 1996.

———. *Xinxiang de moyao* 馨香的沒藥 (Sweet Smelling Myrrh). Translated by Yu Chenghua. Shanghai, 1938. Reprint. Hong Kong: Elim, 1983.

He Shouliang 何受良. "Song Shangjie boshi yisheng de lingcheng" 宋尚節博士一生的靈程 (The Spiritual Journey of Dr. Song Shangjie). In *Jidutu budaotuan wushi zhounian jinian tekan, 1936–1986,* edited by Xie Yangping.

Hoffer, Eric. *The True Believer: Thoughts on the Nature of Mass Movements.* New York: Harper & Row, 1951.

Holcombe, Arthur N. *The Spirit of the Chinese Revolution.* New York: Alfred A. Knopf, 1930.

Huang Denghuang 黃燈煌. *Gu'er zhifu—Ji Zhiwen mushi zhuan* 孤兒之父—計志文牧師傳 (Father of the Orphans: A Biography of Pastor Ji Zhiwen). Taipei: Tian'en chubanshe, 1996.

Huang Yushen 黃漁深. *Cong Hatonglu dao Nanyanglu: zhi Ni Tuosheng xiansheng qifeng gongkai de xin* 從哈同路到南陽路—致倪柝聲先生七封公開的信 (From Hatong Road to Nanyang Road: Seven Open Letters to Mr. Ni Tuosheng). n.d. (1949/1950?) Reprint. Hong Kong: Lingshi chubanshe (Spiritual Rock Publishers), 1998.

Huang Zongrong 黃宗榮. "'Zhen Yesu Jiao' zai Zhangpu chuanbo" 真耶穌教在漳浦傳播 (The Spread of the True Jesus Church in Zhangpu). *Zhangpu wenshi ziliao* 漳浦文史資料 (Literary and Historical Materials of Zhangpu [county, Fujian province]), No. 9 (June 1990): 164–66.

Hunt, Stephen, ed. *Christian Millenarianism: From the Early Church to Waco.* Bloomington: Indiana University Press, 2001.

Hunter, Alan, and Kim-Kwong Chan. *Protestantism in Contemporary China.* Cambridge: Cambridge University Press, 1993.

Huntington, Samuel P. *The Clash of Civilizations and the Remaking of World Order.* New York: Touchstone, 1996.

Hymns for the Little Flock: A Few Hymns and Some Spiritual Songs Selected 1856 for the Little Flock. Denver: Wilson Foundation, 1881.

Jenkins, Philip. *The Next Christendom: The Coming of Global Christianity.* Oxford: Oxford University Press, 2002.

Ji Xiaolan (Qing dynasty) 紀曉嵐 (清), comp. *Siku quanshu* 四庫全書 (The Complete Library of Four Treasuries), *Jingbu—diyi ji* 經部 第一輯 (Classics: Vol. 1), and *Shibu—disi ji* 史部 第四輯 (History: Vol. 4), edited by Qi Yusheng 齊豫生 and Guo Zhenhai 郭鎮海. Beijing: Zhongguo wenshi chubanshe, 1999.

Jiang Shoudao 江守道. "Zuozhe shengping jianshi" 作者生平簡史 (A Short History of the Life of the Author [Watchman Nee]). In Nee, *Ni Tuosheng zhushu quanji* (Complete Works of Watchman Nee) 33: 300–329.

Jing Fuyin 敬福音. Interview with the author. Jinan, Shandong, October 8, 2003.

———, comp. and ed. *Lingyunji zhushi* 靈韻集註釋 (Annotations on "Lingyunji" [Collections of Spiritual Rhymes by Jing Dianying]). Vol. 1. Jinan: Privately printed, n.d. (1980s?).

Jing Jing 景淨. "Daqin Jingjiao liuxing Zhongguo bei" 大秦景教流行中國碑 (Memorial of the Introduction into China of the Luminous Religion from Syria). CE 781.

Jing Zhendong 敬振東. "Wo duiyu wushu wushen jiehun de baogao" 我對於五叔五嬸結婚的報告 (My Report Concerning the Marriage of the Fifth Uncle [Jing Dianying] and Fifth Aunt [Chen Bixi]). Pamphlet published by Yesu Jiating in 1950. Bureau of Archives, Tai'an City, Shandong Province.

Jinling shenxue zhi 金陵神學誌 (Nanjing Theological Review). 1986–1996. The journal was renamed *Nanjing shenxue zhi* 南京神學誌 in 1998. Its English name remains unchanged.

Jones, Brynmor Pierce. *An Instrument of Revival: The Complete Life of Evan Roberts, 1878–1951.* South Plainfield, N.J.: Bridge, 1995.

———. *The Trials and Triumphs of Jessie Penn-Lewis.* North Brunswick, N.J.: Bridge-Logos, 1997.

Jones, Francis Price. *The Church in Communist China: A Protestant Appraisal.* New York: Friendship Press, 1962.

———, ed. *Documents of the Three-Self Movement: Source Materials for the Study of the Protestant Church in Communist China.* New York: National Council of the Churches of Christ in the U.S.A., 1963.

Ke Ling 柯靈, ed. *Ershi shiji Zhongguo jishi wenxue wenku diyi ji (1900–1949)— Minsu juan: Tiantang yu diyu* 20世紀中國紀實文學文庫第一輯 (1900–1949 年) 民俗卷：天堂與地獄 (A Treasury of Twentieth-Century Chinese Non-fiction. No. 1 [1900–1949]—Volume on Folk Culture: Heaven and Hell). Shanghai: Wenhui chubanshe, 1997.

Kiang Wen-han (Jiang Wenhan). *The Chinese Student Movement.* Morningside, N.Y.: King's Crown Press, 1948.

Kindopp, Jason, and Carol Lee Hamrin, eds. *God and Caesar in China: Policy Implications of Church-State Tensions.* Washington, D.C.: Brookings Institution Press, 2004.

Kinnear, Angus I. *Against the Tide: The Story of Watchman Nee.* 1973. Rev. ed. Fort Washington, Pa.: Christian Literature Crusade, 1974.

Knox, Ronald A. *Enthusiasm: A Chapter in the History of Religion.* New York: Oxford University Press, 1950.

Kojima Shinji 小島晉治. *Hong Xiuquan* 洪秀全. Translated into Chinese by
Cheng Zhiping 成之平 and Luo Yu 羅宇. Xi'an: Sanqin chubanshe, 1990.

Komroff, Manuel, ed. *The Travels of Marco Polo*. New York: Liveright, 1926.

Krapohl, Robert H. "A Search for Purity: The Controversial Life of John Nelson
Darby." PhD diss., Baylor University, 1988.

Kwok Pui-lan. *Chinese Women and Christianity, 1860–1927*. Atlanta, Ga.: Scholars
Press, 1992.

Laamann, Lars Peter. *Christian Heretics in Late Imperial China: Christian Incul-
turation and State Control, 1720–1850*. London and New York: Routledge, 2006.

Lacy, G. Carleton. *The Great Migration and the Church in West China: Reports of
a Survey Made under the Auspices of the Nanking Theological Seminary and the
National Christian Council of China*. Shanghai: Thomas Chu & Sons, 1941.

Lam, Wing-hung (Lin Ronghong) 林榮洪. *Fengchao zhong fenqi de zhongguo
jiaohui* 風潮中奮起的中國教會 (Chinese Theology in Construction). Hong
Kong: Tien Dao Publishing House, 1980.

Lambert, Tony. *China's Christian Millions*. 1999. Rev. and updated ed. Oxford:
Monarch Books, 2006.

———. *The Resurrection of the Chinese Church*. Wheaton, Ill.: Overseas Missionary Fellowship, 1994.

Landes, Richard A., ed. *Encyclopedia of Millennialism and Millennial Movements*.
New York: Routledge, 2000.

Lanternari, Vittorio. *The Religions of the Oppressed: A Study of Modern Messianic
Cults*. Translated by Lisa Sergio. New York: Alfred A. Knopf, 1963.

Latourette, Kenneth Scott. *A History of Christian Missions in China*. New York:
Macmillan, 1929.

Lee, Witness (Li Changshou) 李常受. *Watchman Nee: A Seer of the Divine Revelation in the Present Age*. Anaheim, Calif.: Living Stream Ministry, 1991.

———. "Yiwei zai Jidu li de ren—Ni Tuosheng dixiong niandai jilue" 一位在基
督裡的人—倪柝聲弟兄年代記略 (A Man in Christ—A Chronicle of Main
Events in the Life of Watchman Nee). Unpublished typescript amended by
Ni Yulong. n.d. (1990s).

Lew, Timothy T. (Liu Tingfang). Papers, Missionary Research Library, Union
Theological Seminary, New York.

Lewis, I. M. *Ecstatic Religion: A Study of Shamanism and Spirit Possession*. 3rd ed.
London and New York: Routledge, 2003.

Li Ailian 黎愛蓮 (M. L. S. Ballord), comp. *Paomao yu wuxian—He Shou'en de
gushi he tade shige quanji* 拋錨於無限—和受恩的故事和她的詩歌全集 (An-
chored in Infinity: The Story of Margaret E. Barber and a Complete Collection
of Her Hymns). Fuzhou, 1930.

Li Bonan 李伯南. "Jidujiao putaoshan huitang shilue" 基督教葡萄山會堂史略
(A Brief Historical Account of the Christian Church at Putaoshan). *Yantai
wenshi ziliao* 煙臺文史資料 (Literary and Historical Materials of Yantai) 3
(October 1984): 205–8.

Li Gangji 李剛己, ed. *Jiaowu jilue* 教務記略 (A Brief Chronicle of Missionary Affairs). 1905. Reprint. Shanghai: Shanghai Shudian, 1986.

Li Mingyao 李明曜. "Lanzhou Yesu Jiating yu Zhonghua Jidujiaohui de shimo" 蘭州耶穌家庭與中華基督教會的始末 (An Account of the Jesus Family and the Church of Christ in China at Lanzhou). *Gansu wenshi ziliao xuanji* 甘肅文史資料選輯 (Selected Literary and Historical Materials of Gansu) 31 (April 1990): 174–78.

Li Musheng 李慕聖. *Shangshan zhi yao* 上山之钥 (The Key to Ascending the Mountain). Alhambra, Calif.: Chinese Christian Testimony Ministry, 2001.

Li Ruijun 李瑞君. Interview with the author. Mazhuang, Shandong, June 1, 2002.

Li Shixiong and Fu Xiqiu, eds. *Religion and National Security in China: Secret Documents from China's Security Sector*. Bayside, N.Y.: Committee for Investigation on Persecution of Religion in China, 2002.

Li Wenwei 李文蔚. "Guanyu Shi Bocheng zhu *Ni Tuosheng xundaoshi* yishu weifan shishi de cankao ziliao (zhaiyao)" 關於史伯誠著《倪柝聲殉道史》一書違反史實的參考資料（摘要）(Reference Materials Concerning Historical Untruths in *The Martyrdom of Watchman Nee* by Shi Bocheng [A Synopsis]). Privately printed pamphlet. 1998.

Li Zhigang 李志剛. *Jidujiao yu jindai Zhongguo wenhua lunwenji* 基督教與近代中國文化論文集 (A Collection of Essays on Christianity and Modern Chinese Culture). Taipei: Yuzhou guang, 1989.

Li Zirou 李子柔. "Wo canjia 'Yesu Jiating' de qingkuang" 我參加 "耶穌家庭" 的情況 (How I Joined the "Jesus Family"). *Gansu wenshi ziliao xuanji* 甘肅文史資料選輯 (Selected Literary and Historical Materials of Gansu) 31 (April 1990): 155–57.

Lian Xi. *The Conversion of Missionaries: Liberalism in American Protestant Missions in China, 1907–1932*. University Park: Pennsylvania State University Press, 1997.

———. "A Messianic Deliverance for Post-Dynastic China: The Launch of the True Jesus Church in the Early Twentieth Century." *Modern China* 34, 4 (October 2008): 407–41.

———. "The Search for Chinese Christianity in the Republican Period (1912–1949)." *Modern Asian Studies* 38 (October 2004): 851–98.

The Life of Christ by Chinese Artists (Wozhu shengchuan tu—huashi huamiao 我主聖傳圖—華師畫描). Westminster, S.W.: Society for the Propagation of the Gospel, 1938.

Lilla, Mark. "The Politics of God." *New York Times,* August 19, 2007.

———. *The Stillborn God: Religion, Politics, and the Modern West*. New York: Alfred A. Knopf, 2007.

Lin Heping 林和平. *En'ai biaoben* 恩愛標本 (An Object of Grace and Love). Shanghai, 1943.

Lin Yutang. *From Pagan to Christian*. Cleveland and New York: World, 1959.

Lin Zhengye (J. S. Linn) 林證耶. *Zhai Fumin zhuan* 翟輔民傳 (The Life of Dr. R. A. Jaffray). 1962. Rev. ed. Hong Kong: China Alliance Press, 1981.

Ling, Oi Ki. *The Changing Role of the British Protestant Missionaries in China, 1945–1952.* London: Associated University Presses, 1999.

Liu, Kwang-Ching, and Richard Shek, eds. *Heterodoxy in Late Imperial China.* Honolulu: University of Hawaii Press, 2004.

Liu Yangfen 劉揚芬. Interviews with the author. New York City, July 25, 2001; by telephone, March 19, 2003.

Liu Yiling (Liu Yih Ling) 劉翼凌. *Song Shangjie zhuan* 宋尚節傳 (Life of John Sung). Hong Kong: Christian Witness Press, 1962.

Lodwick, Kathleen L. *Crusaders against Opium: Protestant Missionaries in China, 1874–1917.* Lexington: University Press of Kentucky, 1996.

Lü Xiaomin 呂小敏. "Jia'nan shixuan" 迦南诗选 (Selected Songs of Canaan). http://cannan.lingliang.org.

Luo Xingsan 羅星三. "Dongshan Yesu Jiating" 東山耶穌家庭 (The Jesus Family of Dongshan [District]). *Zhifu wenshi ziliao* 芝罘文史資料 (Literary and Historical Materials of Cheefoo) 4 (April 1989): 237.

———. Interview with the author. Yantai, Shandong, October 12, 2003.

———. "Yantaishi Jidujiao Ling'enhui" 煙臺市基督教靈恩會 (The Christian Spiritual Gifts Society of Yantai City) *Zhifu wenshi ziliao* 芝罘文史資料 (Literary and Historical Materials of Cheefoo) 4 (April 1989): 235–36.

Lutz, Jessie G. *China and the Christian Colleges, 1850–1950.* Ithaca, N.Y.: Cornell University Press, 1971.

———. *Chinese Politics and Christian Missions: The Anti-Christian Movements of 1920–28.* Notre Dame, Ind.: Cross Cultural Publications, 1988.

———. "The Grand Illusion: Karl Gützlaff and Popularization of China Missions in the United States during the 1830s." In *United States Attitudes and Policies toward China: The Impact of American Missionaries,* edited by Patricia Neils. Armonk, N.Y.: M. E. Sharpe, 1990.

———. "Karl Gützlaff's Approach to Indigenization: The Chinese Union." In *Christianity in China: From the Eighteenth Century to the Present,* edited by Daniel H. Bays.

Lutz, Jessie G., and R. Ray Lutz. *Hakka Chinese Confront Protestant Christianity, 1850–1900.* Armonk, N.Y.: M. E. Sharpe, 1998.

———. "The Invisible China Missionaries: The Basel Mission's Chinese Evangelists, 1847–1866." *Journal of the International Association for Mission Studies* 12 (October 1995): 204–27.

Lyall, Leslie T. *Come Wind, Come Weather: The Present Experience of the Church in China.* Chicago: Moody Press, 1960.

———. *Flame for God: John Sung and Revival in the Far East.* 1954. Reprint. London: Overseas Missionary Fellowship, 1972.

———. *Three of China's Mighty Men.* London: Overseas Missionary Fellowship, 1973.

Ma Honggang 馬鴻綱. "Jieshao Zhongguo xinxing de jiaopai 'Yesu Jiating'" 介紹中國新興的教派 "耶穌家庭" (An Introduction to the "Jesus Family," a New Sect in China). *Xiejin yuekan* 協進月刊 (The National Christian Council of China Monthly), October 16, 1948, pp. 5–10.

Ma Xisha 馬西沙 and Han Bingfang 韓秉方. *Zhongguo minjian zongjiao shi* 中國民間宗教史 (A History of Folk Religion in China). Shanghai: Shanghai renmin chubanshe, 1992.

MacGillivary, D. *A Century of Protestant Missions in China (1807–1907), Being the Centenary Conference Historical Volume.* Shanghai: American Presbyterian Mission Press, 1907.

Madancy, Joyce A. *The Troublesome Legacy of Commissioner Lin: The Opium Trade and Opium Suppression in Fujian Province, 1820s to 1920s.* Cambridge, Mass.: Harvard University Press, 2003.

Madsen, Richard. "Beyond Orthodoxy: Catholicism as Chinese Folk Religion." In *China and Christianity: Burdened Past, Hopeful Future,* edited by Stephen Uhalley and Xiaoxin Wu.

———. "The Catholic Church in China: Cultural Contradictions, Institutional Survival, and Religious Renewal." In *Unofficial China: Popular Culture and Thought in the People's Republic,* edited by Perry Link, Richard Madsen, and Paul G. Pickowicz. Boulder, Colo.: Westview Press, 1989.

———. *China's Catholics: Tragedy and Hope in an Emerging Civil Society.* Berkeley and Los Angeles: University of California Press, 1998.

Mao Dun 茅盾. "Guxiang zaji" 故鄉雜記 (Hometown Miscellanies). *Xiandai* 現代 (Modern Times), Vol. 1, Nos. 2, 3, 4 (June, July, August 1932). In *Ershi shiji Zhongguo jishi wenxue,* edited by Ke Ling.

Mao Zedong 毛澤東. "Hunan nongmin yundong kaocha baogao" 湖南農民運動攷察報告 (Investigative Report on the Peasant Movement in Hunan), March 1927. In *Mao Zedong xuanji* (Selected Works of Mao Zedong) 1: 12–44.

———. "Lun renmin minzhu zhuanzheng" 論人民民主專政 (On the People's Democratic Dictatorship), June 30, 1949. In *Mao Zedong xuanji* (Selected Works of Mao Zedong) 4: 1468–82.

———. *Mao Zedong xuanji* 毛澤東選集 (Selected Works of Mao Zedong). 4 vols. Beijing: Renmin chubanshe, 1991.

Martin, W. A. P. *A Cycle of Cathay, or China, South and North, with Personal Reminiscences.* New York: Fleming H. Revell, 1896.

Matthew, H. C. G., and Brian Harrison, eds. *Oxford Dictionary of National Biography.* Oxford: Oxford University Press, 2004.

Mazhuang Yesu Jiating gexin jingguo 馬莊耶穌家庭革新經過 (An Account of the Revolutionary Transformation of the Jesus Family of Mazhuang). Shanghai: Tianfeng chubanshe, 1953.

Michael, Franz. *The Taiping Rebellion: History and Documents.* 3 vols. Seattle: University of Washington Press, 1971.

Micklethwait, John, and Adrian Wooldridge. *God Is Back: How the Global Revival of Faith Is Changing the World.* New York: Penguin Press, 2009.

Monsen, Marie. *The Awakening: Revival in China (1927–1937), a Work of the Holy Spirit*. 1959. Translated from the Norwegian by Joy Guinness. London: China Inland Mission, 1961.

Moule, A. C. *Christians in China before the Year 1550*. 1930. New York: Octagon Books, 1977.

Mungello, D. E. *The Great Encounter of China and the West, 1500–1800*. Lanham, Md.: Rowman & Littlefield, 1999.

———. *The Spirit and the Flesh in Shandong, 1650–1785*. Lanham, Md.: Rowman & Littlefield, 2001.

Nanjing shenxue zhi 南京神學誌 (Nanjing Theological Review). 1998–2007.

Naquin, Susan. *Millenarian Rebellion in China: The Eight Trigrams Uprising of 1813*. New Haven, Conn.: Yale University Press, 1976.

National Christian Council of China (NCC). *Annual Report* (1922–1923, 1925–1926, 1927–1928). Shanghai.

Nee, Watchman (Ni Tuosheng) 倪柝聲. "Di erci jianzheng" 第二次見證 (The Second Testimony). 1936. In *Ni Tuosheng zhushu quanji* 33: 49–63.

———. "Di sanci jianzheng" 第三次見證 (The Third Testimony). 1936. In *Ni Tuosheng zhushu quanji* 33: 65–73.

———. "Feilatiefei—zhongxin Xiaoqun" 非拉鐵非—忠心小群 (Philadelphia—The Faithful Little Flock). 1927. In *Ni Tuosheng zhushu quanji* 14: 321–77.

———. "Fujia yinyu" 負架吟語 (Moanings of the Cross-Bearer). 1923. In *Ni Tuosheng zhushu quanji* 33: 79–92.

———. "Fuze dixiongmen de jijuhua" 負責弟兄們的幾句話 (A Few Words from the Brothers in Charge). 1934. In *Ni Tuosheng zhushu quanji* 33: 223.

———. *Gongzuo de zaisi* 工作的再思 (Rethinking Our Missions, or Concerning Our Missions). 1938. In *Ni Tuosheng zhushu quanji* 8: 15–250.

———. *Jiaohui de zhengtong* 教會的正統 (The Orthodoxy of the Church). 1945. Vol. 6 of *Ni Tuosheng zhushu quanji*.

———. "Jiaotong wenda" 交通問答 (Questions and Answers in Fellowship). 1926–1927. In *Ni Tuosheng zhushu quanji* 11: 369–421.

———. "Jinhou gongzuo de lu" 今後工作的路 (The Road Ahead for Our Work). 1948. In *Ni Tuosheng zhushu quanji* 8: 251–66.

———. "Mengtou de wenti" 蒙頭的問題 (The Issue of Head-Covering). 1948. In *Ni Tuosheng zhushu quanji* 4: 405–26.

———. *Ni Tuosheng zhushu quanji* 倪柝聲著述全集 (Complete Works of Watchman Nee). 33 vols. Hong Kong: Manna Publisher, 1995.

———. *Ren de posui yu ling de chulai* 人的破碎與靈的出來 (The Brokenness of Man and the Release of the Spirit). Collection of sermons delivered between 1943 and 1952. In *Ni Tuosheng zhushu quanji* 9: 81–190.

———. *Shuling de ren* 屬靈的人 (The Spiritual Man), Part I (1926). Vol. 15 of *Ni Tuosheng zhushu quanji*.

———. *Shuling de ren* 屬靈的人 (The Spiritual Man), Part II (1928). Vol. 16 of *Ni Tuosheng zhushu quanji*.

———. "Tongwen huikan yuanqi" 通問彙刊緣起 (The Origin of the *Intelligencer Digest*). 1933. In *Ni Tuosheng zhushu quanji* 33: 217–22.

———. "Wangshi de shushuo" 往事的述說 (The Narration of Things Past). 1932. In *Ni Tuosheng zhushu quanji* 33: 19–40.

———. "Wei tongwen huikan tingkan zhi tonggongmen de yifeng xin" 為通問彙刊停刊致同工們的一封信 (A Letter to the Co-Workers Regarding the Suspension of the *Intelligencer Digest*). 1935. In *Ni Tuosheng zhushu quanji* 33: 229–33.

———. "Wo shi zenyang zhuan guolai de" 我是怎樣轉過來的 (How I Turned Around). Public address to Little Flock associates. Shanghai, August 20, 1951.

———. *Women zai Jidu li yijing sile* 我們在基督裡已經死了 (We Are Already Dead in Christ). Collection of sermons delivered in English between 1938 and 1942 and translated into Chinese. In *Ni Tuosheng zhushu quanji* 28: 303–28.

———. "Yuchang laishi zhuban de quanneng" 預嘗來世諸般的權能 (A Foretaste of the Powers in the Next World). Sermon delivered in Shanghai in 1940. In *Ni Tuosheng zhushu quanji* 29: 311–19.

Ng, Lee Ming (Wu Liming) 吳利明. *Jidujiao yu Zhongguo shehui bianqian* 基督教與中國社會變遷 (Christianity and Social Change in China). 1980. Reprint. Hong Kong: Chinese Christian Literature Council, 1990.

Ni Yulong 倪玉隆 (Jing Xing 儆醒). "Fuzhou Jidutujuji(hui) chuqi qingkuang jianjie" 福州基督徒聚集(會)初期情況簡介 (A Brief Introduction to the Beginnings of Fuzhou Christian Assembly). Manuscript dated April 10, 1993, and made available to the author. Subsequently published without the original footnotes in *Jiecai zhong* 芥菜種 (Mustard Seed) 10 (December 23, 1995): 12–14.

———. Interviews with the author. Fuzhou, July 1997.

Nian shiji Jidu weida de jianzhengren (The Great Witness to Christ in the Twentieth Century). Collection of hymns written by Watchman Nee. Little Flock publication, n.d. (1980s?).

Nietzsche, Friedrich. *Beyond Good and Evil*. Translated by Marianne Cowan. South Bend, Ind.: Gateway Editions, 1955.

Overmyer, Daniel L. "Alternatives: Popular Religious Sects in Chinese Society." *Modern China* 7, 2 (April 1981): 153–90.

———. *Folk Buddhist Religion: Dissenting Sects in Late Traditional China*. Cambridge, Mass.: Harvard University Press, 1976.

———. *Precious Volumes: An Introduction to Chinese Sectarian Scriptures from the Sixteenth and Seventeenth Centuries*. Cambridge, Mass.: Harvard University Press, 1999.

———, ed. *Religion in China Today*. Cambridge and New York: Cambridge University Press, 2003.

———. *Religions of China: The World as a Living System*. San Francisco: HarperSanFrancisco, 1986.

———. "The White Cloud Sect in Sung and Yuan China." *Harvard Journal of Asiatic Studies* 42, 2 (December 1982): 615–42.

Overmyer, Daniel L., et al. "Chinese Religions—The State of the Field, Part II, Living Religious Traditions: Taoism, Confucianism, Buddhism, Islam and Popular Religion." *Journal of Asian Studies* 54, 2 (May 1995): 314–95.

Ownby, David. *Brotherhoods and Secret Societies in Early and Mid-Qing China: The Formation of a Tradition.* Stanford, Calif.: Stanford University Press, 1996.

———. "The Heaven and Earth Society as Popular Religion." *Journal of Asian Studies* 54, 4 (November 1995): 1023–46.

Pei Yufang 裴玉芳. Interview with the author. Jinan, Shandong, October 6, 2003.

Penn-Lewis, Jessie. *The Awakening in Wales and Some of the Hidden Springs.* New York: Fleming H. Revell, 1905.

———. *Soul and Spirit: A Glimpse into Bible Psychology.* Leicester: Overcomer Book Room, n.d. [1910s].

Porterfield, Amanda. *Healing in the History of Christianity.* New York: Oxford University Press, 2005.

Price, Charles, and Ian Randall. *Transforming Keswick.* Carlisle, Cumbria, UK: OM Publishing, 2000.

Price, Frank Wilson. *China: Twilight or Dawn?* New York: Friendship Press, 1948.

———. *The Rural Church in China: A Survey.* New York: Agricultural Missions, 1948.

Qin Jinggao 秦鏡高. "Li Changshou sile" 李常受死了 (Li Changshou Is Dead). *Huhan* 呼喊 (Shout) 83 (November 1997): 205–20.

Qu Li 瞿理. "Tancheng Yesujiao gaikuang" 郯城耶穌教概況. *Tancheng wenshi ziliao* 郯城文史資料 (Literary and Historical Materials of Tancheng [County]) 4 (October 1987): 169–78.

Qu Zhengmin 曲拯民. "Meiguo zhanglaohui he Shandong zilihui shilue" 美國長老會和山東自立會事略 (A Brief Account of the American Presbyterian Church and Shandong Independent Church). *Shandong wenshi ziliao xuanji* 山東文史資料選輯 27 (October 1989): 239–61.

Randall, Ian M. *Evangelical Experiences: A Study in the Spirituality of English Evangelicalism, 1918–1939.* Carlisle, Cumbria, UK: Paternoster, 1999.

Rawlinson, Frank [Joseph]. *Naturalization of Christianity in China.* Shanghai: Presbyterian Mission Press, 1927.

Rees, D[avid] Vaughan. *The "Jesus Family" in Communist China: A Modern Miracle of New Testament Christianity.* London: Paternoster, 1959.

Reilly, Thomas H. *The Taiping Heavenly Kingdom: Rebellion and the Blasphemy of Empire.* Seattle: University of Washington Press, 2004.

Ren Zhongxiang 任鐘祥. *Shanghai Jidutu Juhuichu jianshi* 上海基督徒聚會處簡史 (A Brief History of Shanghai Christian Meeting Places). Shanghai: Shanghai shi Jidujiao Sanzi Aiguo Yundong Weiyuanhui, 1996.

Richard, Timothy. *Forty-Five Years in China, Reminiscences.* New York: Frederick Stokes, 1916.

Roberts, Dana. *Understanding Watchman Nee.* Plainfield, N.J.: Haven Books, 1980.

Romig, Theodore F. "The Family of Jesus." *Occasional Bulletin.* Missionary Research Library, Union Theological Seminary, New York. Vol. 1, No. 11 (October 23, 1950).

Rubinstein, Murray A. *The Protestant Community on Modern Taiwan: Mission, Seminary, and Church.* Armonk, N.Y.: M. E. Sharpe, 1991.

Sang Xujiu 桑敘九 and Sun Bolong 孫伯隆. "Shandong Zhonghua Jidujiao Ling'enhui zonghui shijie" 山東中華基督教靈恩會總會史介 (An Introduction to the History of the General Assembly of Shandong Chinese Christian Spiritual Gifts Society). Unpublished paper, Jinan, Shandong, n.d. (1980s).

Sanneh, Lamin, and Joel A. Carpenter, eds. *The Changing Face of Christianity: Africa, the West, and the World.* New York: Oxford University Press, 2005.

Schiffrin, Harold Z. *Sun Yat-sen and the Origins of the Chinese Revolution.* Berkeley: University of California Press, 1968.

Schubert, William E. *I Remember John Sung.* Singapore: Far Eastern Bible College Press, 1976.

Scofield, C. I., ed. *The Scofield Reference Bible.* 1909. New and improved edition. New York: Oxford University Press, 1917.

Seventh-day Adventist Encyclopedia. Rev. ed. Vol. 10. Washington: Review and Herald, 1976.

Shandong shengzhi: shaoshu minzu zhi, zongjiao zhi 山東省志—少數民族志宗教志 (Chronicles of Shandong Province: Minorities and Religion). Vol. 78. Shandong renmin chubanshe, 1997.

Shen Derong 沈德溶. *Wu Yaozong xiaozhuan* 吳耀宗小傳 (A Brief Biography of Wu Yaozong). Shanghai: Zhongguo Jidujiao Sanzi Aiguo Yundong Weiyuanhui, 1989.

Sheridan, James E. *Chinese Warlord: The Career of Feng Yu-hsiang.* Stanford, Calif.: Stanford University Press, 1966.

Shi Meiling 施美玲. *Liushisan nian: yu Wang Mingdao xiansheng zhailu tongxing* 六十三年—與王明道先生窄路同行 (Sixty Three Years: Walking on the Narrow Road with Mr. Wang Ming Dao). Hong Kong: Lingshi chubanshe, 2001.

Shih, Vincent Y. C. *The Taiping Ideology: Its Sources, Interpretations, and Influences.* Seattle: University of Washington Press, 1967.

Shuiliu Zhishizhan 水流執事站 (Living Stream Ministry). "Jinianwen" 記念文 (A Memorial [upon the death of Li Changshou]). Leaflet printed by the Living Stream Ministry, Anaheim, California, June 15, 1997.

Snow, Edgar. *Red Star over China.* 1938. Rev. and enl. ed. New York: Grove Press, 1968.

Song Tianzhen 宋天真. Interviews with the author. Brooklyn, New York, June 2001.

Spence, Jonathan D. *The Gate of Heavenly Peace: The Chinese and Their Revolution, 1895–1980.* New York: Viking Penguin, 1981.

———. *God's Chinese Son: The Taiping Heavenly Kingdom of Hong Xiuquan*. New York: W. W. Norton, 1996.

———. *The Search for Modern China*. 2nd ed. New York: Norton, 1999.

———. *To Change China: Western Advisers in China*. New York: Little, Brown, 1969.

Standaert, Nicolas, ed. *Handbook of Christianity in China, Volume One: 635–1800*. Leiden: Brill, 2001.

Stauffer, Milton T., ed. *The Christian Occupation of China: A General Survey of the Numerical Strength and Geographical Distribution of the Christian Forces in China Made by the Special Committee on Survey and Occupation, China Continuation Committee, 1918–1921*. Shanghai: China Continuation Committee, 1922.

Stuart, John Leighton. *Fifty Years in China: The Memoirs of John Leighton Stuart, Missionary and Ambassador*. New York: Random House, 1954.

Sun Yanli 孫彥理. "Wo suo renshi de Jiang Changchuan huidu" 我所認識的江長川會督 (Bishop Jiang Changchuan as I Know Him). In *Shanghai de zongjiao* 上海的宗教 (Religions of Shanghai), edited by Shi Hongxi 石鴻熙. Shanghai: Shanghai shi Zhengxie wenshiziliao bianjibu, 1996.

Sung, John (Song Shangjie, Sung Shang-chieh, Sung Siong Ceh) 宋尚節. *Lingli jiguang* 靈歷集光 (Gleanings of My Spiritual Experience). Lost and recovered diaries of John Sung, edited by Levi Tianzhen Song (daughter). Hong Kong: Eng Yu Evangelical Mission, 1995.

———. "Out of Modernism into God's Family." In *Into God's Family*, compiled by Andrew Gih.

———. *Wode jianzheng* 我的見證 (My Testimony). 1933. Hong Kong: Bellman House, 1991.

Sunquist, Scott W. ed. *A Dictionary of Asian Christianity*. Grand Rapids, Mich.: William B. Eerdmans, 2001.

Sweeten, Alan Richard. *Christianity in Rural China: Conflict and Accommodation in Jiangxi Province, 1860–1900*. Ann Arbor: University of Michigan Press, 2001.

Sze, Newman (Shi Bocheng) 史伯誠. *Ni Tuosheng xundao shi* 倪柝聲殉道史 (The Martyrdom of Watchman Nee). Culver City, Calif.: Testimony Publications, 1995.

"Tai'an diqu jiaohui xuexiao gaikuang" 泰安地區教會學校概況 (A General Survey of Church Schools in the Tai'an Area). *Tai'an wenshi ziliao* 泰安文史資料 (Literary and Historical Materials of Tai'an) 2 (October 1987): 66–74.

Tai'anshi difang shizhi bangongshi 泰安市地方史誌辦公室 (Tai'an City Office of Local Chronicles), edited by *Tai'an wuqiannian dashiji* 泰安五千年大事紀 (Chronicles of Five Thousand Years of Tai'an). Tai'an: Shandong sheng ditu chubanshe, 2001.

Tang Shoulin 唐守臨 and Ren Zhongxiang 任忠祥. *Wei zhendao jieli zhengbian (bochi Li Changshou de yiduan xieshuo)* 為真道竭力爭辯 (駁斥李常受的異端

邪說) (Contending for the Faith: A Refutation of the Heresies of Li Chang-shou). Shanghai: Shanghai shi Jidujiao jiaowu weiyuanhui, 1983.

Tao Feiya 陶飛亞. "A Christian Utopia in China: A Historical Study of the Jesus Family (1921–1952)." PhD diss., Chinese University of Hong Kong, 2001.

———. *Zhongguo de Jidujiao wutuobang: Yesu Jiating (1921–1952)* 中國的基督教烏托邦—耶穌家庭 (A Christian Utopia in China: Jesus Family, 1921–1952). Hong Kong: Chinese University Press, 2004.

Tao Feiya 陶飛亞 and Liu Tianlu 劉天路. *Jidujiaohui yu jindai Shandong shehui* 基督教會與近代山東社會 (Protestantism in Modern Shandong). Jinan: Shandong daxue chubanshe, 1994.

Taves, Ann. *Fits, Trances, & Visions: Experiencing Religion and Explaining Experience from Wesley to James*. Princeton, N.J.: Princeton University Press, 1999.

Taylor, M. Geraldine (Mrs. Howard Taylor). *One of China's Scholars: The Culture and Conversion of a Confucianist*. London: Morgan and Scott, 1900.

———. *Pastor Hsi (of North China): One of China's Christians*. New York: Fleming H. Revell, 1903.

Thouless, Robert H. *An Introduction to the Psychology of Religion*. 3rd ed. Cambridge: Cambridge University Press, 1971.

Tong Zhishan 佟至善. "Jinan shi dongjiao Lingxiuyuan (Jidujiaotu Lingxiuyuan) shiliao cankao" 濟南東郊靈修院 (基督教徒靈修院史料參考) (Historical Documents for Reference Concerning the Court for Spiritual Retreat [Christians' Court for Spiritual Retreat] in the Eastern Suburb of the City of Jinan). Unpublished manuscript, June 19, 1985, Jinan, Shandong.

Tongwenbao 通問報 (*The Chinese Christian Intelligencer*). Shanghai, 1935–1936.

Troeltsch, Ernst. *The Social Teaching of the Christian Churches*. 2 vols. Translated by Olive Wyon. 1931. Reprint. Louisville, Ky.: Westminster/John Knox Press, 1992.

Tsai, Christiana. *Queen of the Dark Chamber: The Story of Christiana Tsai As Told to Ellen L. Drummond*. Chicago: Moody Press, 1953.

Uhalley, Stephen, and Xiaoxin Wu, eds. *China and Christianity: Burdened Past, Hopeful Future*. Armonk, N.Y.: M. E. Sharpe, 2001.

Union Hymnal Committee, ed. *Putian songzan* 普天頌贊 (Hymns of Universal Praise). Shanghai: Jidujiao wenyi chubanshe, 1936.

U.S. Department of State, "International Religious Freedom Report" (2001–2008). http://www.state.gov.

Utley, Uldine. *Why I Am a Preacher: A Plain Answer to an Oft-Repeated Question*. New York: Fleming H. Revell, 1931.

Wacker, Grant. *Heaven Below: Early Pentecostals and American Culture*. Cambridge, Mass.: Harvard University Press, 2001.

Walls, Andrew F. *The Cross-Cultural Process in Christian History*. Maryknoll, N.Y.: Orbis Books, 2002.

Wang, Peter Chen-Main (Wang Chenmian) 王成勉. *Wenshe de shengshuai—ershi niandai Jidujiao bensehua zhi ge'an yanjiu* 文社的盛衰 (The Flourishing and the Decline of the National Christian Literature Association of China:

A Case Study of the Indigenization of Christianity in the 1920s). Taipei: Yuzhou guang, 1993.

Wang, Stephen C. H. (Wang Changxin) 王長新. *You sishinian* 又四十年 (Wang Ming-Dao: The Last Forty Years). Ontario: Canada Gospel Publishing House, 1997.

Wang Chao-hsiang (Wang Zhaoxiang). "Religious Elements in the Esoteric Societies of China." Translated by F. R. Millican, *Chinese Recorder* 58 (December 1927): 757–66.

Wang Feishao 王費劭. "Ziboshi Jidujiaohui de lishi yange" 淄博市基督教會的歷史沿革 (The Historical Development of the Christian Churches in Zibo City) *Zibo wenshi ziliao xuanji* 淄博文史資料選輯 (Selected Literary and Historical Materials of Zibo) 1, n.d. (1980s): 227–39.

Wang Mingdao (Wang Ming-Tao) 王明道. "Eshi zhong de husheng" 惡世中的呼聲 (A Voice Crying in a World of Evils). 1928. In *Wang Mingdao wenku* 2: 189–204.

———. "Mengzhao de Jidian" 蒙召的基甸 (The Gideon Who Heard the Call). 1927. In *Wang Mingdao wenku* 6: 1–17.

———. "Renwo zhijian nianwu ze" 人我之間廿五則 (Twenty-five Rules in Interpersonal Relations). 1936. In *Wang Mingdao wenku* 1: 111–60.

———. "Shenfang jiashifu" 慎防假師傅 (Watch Out for False Masters). 1935. In *Wang Mingdao wenku* 7: 33–40.

———. "Shenfang liuzei" 慎防綹賊 (Watch Out for the Thieves). 1929. In *Wang Mingdao wenku* 7: 23–27.

———. "Shengjing guangliang zhong de ling'en yundong" 聖經光亮中的靈恩運動 (The Spiritual Gifts Movement Seen in the Light of the Bible). 1933. In *Wang Mingdao wenku* 4: 93–112.

———. *Wang Mingdao wenku* 王明道文庫 (Treasures of Wang Ming Tao). 7 vols. 1977. Reprint. Taiwan: Conservative Baptist Press, 1998.

———. "Women shi weile xinyang" 我們是為了信仰 (We, Because of Faith). 1955. In *Wushi nian lai*, Appendix.

———. *Wushi nian lai* 五十年來 (The Past Fifty Years). 1950. Rev. ed. Hong Kong: Bellman House Publishers, 1993.

———. "Xiandai jiaohui de banghe" 現代教會的棒喝 (A Club and a Loud Shout for the Modern Church). 1927. In *Wang Mingdao wenku* 2: 237–53.

———. "Yigong you jige fuyin ne?" 一共有幾個福音呢？(How Many Gospels Are There?). 1932. In *Wang Mingdao wenku* 7: 1–7.

———. "Yingdang bei zhouzu de ren" 應當被咒詛的人 (The One Who Should Be Cursed). 1947. In *Wang Mingdao wenku* 7: 50–59.

Wang Qinghuai 王清淮, et al. *Zhongguo xiejiao shi* 中國邪教史 (A History of Heresies in China). Beijing: Qunzhong chubanshe, 2007.

Wang Shenyin 王神蔭. "Mazhuang 'Yesu Jiating' shimo" 馬莊耶穌家庭始末 (The Beginning and the End of the "Jesus Family" in Mazhuang). *Shandong wenshi ziliao xuanji* 山東文史資料選輯 17 (1984): 89–111.

———. "Xi Shengmo he ta chuangzuo de shengshi" 席勝魔和他創作的聖詩 (Xi Shengmo and the Hymns He Composed). Part 1. *Jinling shenxue zhi* 9 (Resumed) (November 1988): 99–103; (Continued from Part 1) *Jinling shenxue zhi* 11 (Resumed) (February 1990): 124–27.

Wang Xipeng 汪錫鵬. *Ji Yesu Jiating* 記耶穌家庭 (An Account of the Jesus Family). Shanghai: Zhonghua Jidujiao Xiejinhui, 1950.

Wang Yongxin 王永信. *Zhendao shouce* 真道手冊 (A Handbook of the True Way). Enl. ed. Argyle, Tex.: Dashiming zhongxin, 2000.

Wang Zhi (Wilson Wang) 王峙. *Wang Zai jianzheng lu* 王載見證錄 (Leland Wang). Taipei: Zhongxin yinwubu, 1980.

Wang Zhixin (Wang Chih-hsin) 王治心. *Zhongguo Jidujiao shigang* 中國基督教史綱 (History of Christianity in China). Hong Kong: Chinese Christian Literature Council, 1959.

Weatherford, Jack. *Genghis Khan and the Making of the Modern World.* New York: Three Rivers Press, 2004.

Weber, Max. *The Religion of China: Confucianism and Taoism.* Translated by Hans H. Gerth. Glencoe, Ill.: The Free Press, 1951.

———. *The Sociology of Religion.* 1922. Translated by Ephraim Fischoff. Boston: Beacon Press, 1963.

Wei, Francis C. M. (Wei Zhuomin). *The Spirit of Chinese Culture.* New York: Scribner, 1947.

Wei, Julie Lee, Ramon H. Myers, and Donald G. Gillin, eds. *Prescriptions for Saving China: Selected Writings of Sun Yat-sen.* Translated by Julie Lee Wei et al. Stanford, Calif.: Hoover Institution Press, 1994.

Wei Baoluo (Wei Enbo) 魏保羅. *Shengling zhen jianzheng shu* 聖靈真見證書 (The True Witnesses of the Holy Spirit) (Collected autobiographical essays of Wei Baoluo). 2 vols. Tianjin: Zhen Yesu Jiaohui, 1919. Excerpted in *Zhen Yesu Jiaohui chuangli sanshi zhounian jinian zhuankan,* edited by Wei Yisa.

Wei Yisa (Isaac Wei) 魏以撒, ed. "My Self-Examination." *Tianfeng,* February 23, 1952. In *Documents of the Three-Self Movement: Source Materials for the Study of the Protestant Church in Communist China,* compiled and translated by Francis P. Jones.

———. *Zhen Yesu Jiaohui chuangli sanshi zhounian jinian zhuankan* 真耶穌教會創立三十週年紀念專刊 (Commemorative Volume on the Thirtieth Anniversary of the Founding of the True Jesus Church). Nanjing: Zhen Yesu Jiaohui, 1948.

Wenshi ziliao xuanji 文史資料選輯 (Selected Literary and Historical Materials), 1961–1964, 1982–1990. Beijing: Zhongguo wenshi chubanshe.

West, Philip. *Yenching University and Sino-Western Relations, 1916–1952.* Cambridge, Mass.: Harvard University Press, 1976.

White, L. Michael. *From Jesus to Christianity.* New York: HarperCollins, 2004.

Wickeri, Philip L. *Seeking the Common Ground: Protestant Christianity, the Three-Self Movement, and China's United Front.* Maryknoll, N.Y.: Orbis Books, 1988.

Wilkes, A[lphaeus] Nelson Paget. *The Dynamic of Service*. London: Japan Evangelistic Band, 1925.

Wright, Arthur F. *Buddhism in Chinese History*. Stanford, Calif.: Stanford University Press, 1959.

Wright, Richard N. J. *The Chinese Steam Navy, 1862–1945*. London: Chatham,
2000.

Wu, Silas (Wu Xiuliang) 吳秀良. *Yu Cidu: ershi shiji Zhongguo jiaohui fuxing de
xianqu* 余慈度——二十世紀中國教會復興的先驅 (Dora Yu: Harbinger of Chris-
tian Church Revival in 20th-century China). Boston: Pishon River, 2000.

Wu Yaozong 吳耀宗 (Y. T. Wu, John Wu), ed. *Jidujiao yu xin Zhongguo* 基督教與
新中國 (Christianity and New China). Shanghai: Association Press of China,
1940.

Wu Youxiong 吳幼雄. "Yuandai Quanzhou liangfang Jidujiao (Jingjiao) mubei
yanjiu" 元代泉州兩方基督教 (景教) 墓碑研究 (A Study of Two Yuan-Dynasty
Christian [Luminous Religion] Tombstones in Quanzhou). In *Quanzhou gang
yu haishang sichou zhilu* 泉州港與海上絲綢之路 (The Quanzhou Port and the
Maritime Silk Road). Edited by Lin Zuyi 林祖乙, Shi Yongkang 施永康 et al.
Beijing: Zhongguo shehui kexue chubanshe, 2003.

Xi Shengmo 席勝魔. *Xi Shengmo shige* 席勝魔詩歌 (Hymns by Xi Shengmo).
Nos. 2, 7, 9, 11, 14, 19, 27, 44, 55, 56. In "Xi Shengmo he ta chuangzuo de
shengshi (Xi Shengmo and the Hymns He Composed)," edited by Wang
Shenyin.

Xia Dongyuan 夏東元, ed. *Ershi shiji Zhongguo dabolan* 二十世紀中國大博覽
(A Chronicle of Twentieth-Century China). Changchun: Jilin renmin chubanshe, 1994.

Xiaoshan 蕭山 house church leaders (names omitted). Interview with the
author. Xiaoshan, Zhejiang, August 4, 2008.

Xie Fuya (N. Z. Zia) 謝扶雅. *Zi bianzi zhi dianzi* 自辮子至電子 (From Pigtail
to Electron). Hong Kong: Chinese Christian Literature Council, 1992.

Xie Yangping 謝仰平, ed. *Jidutu budaotuan wushi zhounian jinian tekan,
1936–1986* 基督徒佈道團五十週年紀念特刊 (Commemorative Volume on
the Fiftieth Anniversary of the Founding of the Christian Preaching Band,
1936–1986). Sibu, Malaysia: Sibu Methodist Church, 1986.

Xing Jun. *Baptized in the Fire of Revolution: The American Social Gospel and the
YMCA in China, 1919–1937*. Bethlehem, Pa.: Lehigh University Press, 1996.

Xing You 興友 et al. "Taishan Gupinyuan jiqi chuangshi zhe Anlinlai" 泰山
孤貧院及其創始者安臨來 (Taishan Home for the Orphaned and the Poor
[Home of Onesiphorus] and Its Founder Leslie M. Anglin). *Shandong wenshi
ziliao xuanji* 山東文史資料選輯 24 (December 1987): 200–228.

Xiong Songnian 熊松年. "Xiangtan Zhen Yesu Jiaohui jiankuang" 湘潭真耶穌
教會簡況 (A Brief Survey of the True Jesus Church of Xiangtan). *Xiangtan-
xian wenshi* 湘潭縣文史 (Literature and History of Xiangtan County [Hunan
Province]) 1 (December 1985): 250–54.

Xu Baoluo (Paul Xu) 徐保羅. *Cong buershiweike dao shenpu—Xu Baoluo mushi huiyi lu* 從布爾什維克到神仆—徐保羅牧師回憶錄 (From a Bolshevik to God's Servant: The Memoirs of the Reverend Paul Xu). Taipei: Yuzhou guang, 1995.

Xu Erjian (Herald Hsu) 徐爾建. "Jiaohui 'difang lichang' jiaoxun zhi youlai" 教會地方立場教訓之由來 (The Origin of the Teaching on the "Principle of Locality" in the Church). Privately printed and distributed pamphlet. West Hills, Calif., n.d. (late 1990s).

Yamamoto, Sumiko. *History of Protestantism in China: The Indigenization of Christianity*. Translated by John Wisnom. Tokyo: Toho Gakkai (Institute of Eastern Culture), 2000.

Yang, C. K. *Religion in Chinese Society: A Study of Contemporary Social Functions of Religion and Some of Their Historical Factors*. Berkeley: University of California Press, 1961.

Yang, Sung Won. "The Influence of the Revival Movement of 1901–1910 on the Development of Korean Christianity." PhD diss., Southern Baptist Theological Seminary, 2002.

Yang Fenggang. "Lost in the Market, Saved at McDonald's: Conversion to Christianity in Urban China." *Journal for the Scientific Study of Religion* 44, 4 (2005): 423–41.

Yang Zhisheng 楊致聖. Interview with the author. Yantai, Shandong, October 12, 2003.

Yao, Kevin Xiyi. *The Fundamentalist Movement among Protestant Missionaries in China, 1920–1937*. Lanham, Md.: University Press of America, 2003.

Yao Minquan 姚民權. *Shanghai Jidujiao shi, 1843–1949* 上海基督教史 (A History of Christianity in Shanghai, 1843–1949). Shanghai: Shanghai shi Jidujiao Sanzi Aiguo Yundong Weiyuanhui, 1994.

Yeh, Solomon (Ye Renchang) 葉仁昌. *Jindai Zhongguo de zongjiao pipan—feiji yundong de zaisi* 近代中國的宗教批判—非基運動的再思 (Religious Criticism in Modern China: Rethinking the Anti-Christian Movement). Taipei: Christian Arts Press, 1987.

Yesu Jiating (Jesus Family) 耶穌家庭. "Jiating shuxin" 家庭書信 (Collected Family Letters) (1942). Bureau of Archives, Tai'an City, Shandong Province.

———. *Xiangcun budao shige* 鄉村佈道詩歌 (Songs for Village Evangelism). 1942.

———. *Yesu Jiating shige* 耶穌家庭詩歌 (Songs of the Jesus Family). Tai'an, Shandong: Jesu Jiating, 1940.

Yin Renxian 尹任先. *Shengguang zhiyin: Yin Renxian meng'en sanshi nian de jianzheng* 聖光指引—尹任先蒙恩三十年的見證 (The Holy Light Guiding: Yen Renxian's Testimony of Thirty Years of Grace). Hong Kong: Tiandao shulou, 2001.

Yoo, Boo-Woong. *Korean Pentecostalism: Its History and Theology*. Frankfurt am Main: Verlag Peter Lang, 1988.

Yu, Leekung (Yu Ligong) 于力工. *Yejin tianming: Yu Ligong kan Zhongguo fuyin zhenhan* 夜盡天明—于力工看中國福音震撼 (The End of the Night and the

Dawning of the Day: The Earthshaking Gospel in China through the Eyes of Yu Ligong). Taipei: Ganlan jijinhui, 1998.

Yu Congjia 俞崇架. "Yu Chenghua yisheng yishi" 俞成華醫生軼事 (Episodes in the Life of Dr. Yu Chenghua). Pamphlet printed by the author (son of Yu Chenghua). San Diego, California, 1997.

Yu Yucheng 余玉成. Interviews with the author. Putian, Fujian, June 9, 2002, and September 29, 2003.

Yuan Zhiming 遠志明, scriptwriter and ed. *Shizijia—Yesu zai Zhongguo* 十字架—耶穌在中國 (The Cross—Jesus in China). Documentary film. Petaluma, Calif.: China Soul for Christ Foundation, 2003.

Zhang Fuji 張福基, ed. *Xinghua Weili Gonghui shi* 興化衛理公會史 (A History of the Xinghua Conference of the Methodist Episcopal Church). Xinghua (Putian), Fujian: Xinghua Weili Gonghui, 1947.

Zhang Qizhen 張啟珍. Written response to questionnaire on the Little Flock sent out by the author. Edited by Ni Yulong. May 1996.

———. Interviews with the author. Fuzhou, July 1997 and June 1999.

Zhang Shuyuan 張淑遠. Interview with the author. Jinan, Shandong, October 6, 2003.

Zhang Yinan 張義南. "Shen de maoxianjia Zhang Rongliang" 神的冒險家張榮亮 (Zhang Rongliang: Adventurer for God). March 10, 2007. http://shengshan .org.cn/bbs/redirect.php?fid=9&tid=176&goto=nextnewset.

———. "Shenmi fuza de Xu Shengguang" 神秘複雜的徐聖光 (The Mysterious and Complex Xu Shengguang). July 24, 2006. http://jesus.bbs.net/bbs/12/ 1377.html.

———. "'Zhongguo jiating jiaohui xinyang gaobai' beijing" "中國家庭教會信仰 告白" 背景 (The background of "The Confession of Faith of House Churches in China") August 16, 2007. http://loves7.com/38817/viewspace-30285.html.

Zhang Yufang 張玉芳. Interview with the author. Jinan, Shandong, October 8, 2003.

Zhao Junying (Calvin Chao) 趙君影. *Mantan wushinian lai Zhongguo de jiaohui yu zhengzhi* 漫談五十年來中國的教會與政治 (An Informal Discussion of the Chinese Church and Politics in the Past Fifty Years). Taipei: Zhonghua gui- zhu xiehui, 1981.

Zhao Zichen 趙紫宸 (T. C. Chao). *Xiyu ji* 繫獄記 (My Experience in Prison). Hong Kong: Chinese Christian Literature Council, 1969.

———. "Yanjing Daxue de zongjiao xueyuan" 燕京大學的宗教學院 (The School of Religion at Yenching University). *Wenshi ziliao xuanji* 文史資料選輯 (Se- lected Literary and Historical Materials) 15, 43 (1964): 94–113.

Zhen Yesu Jiaohui 真耶穌教會 (The True Jesus Church). *Shengling bao* 聖靈報 (The Holy Ghost). Vols. 1–2 (1926–1927).

Zheng Xindao 鄭新道. "Taishan Gupinyuan" 泰山孤貧院 (Taishan Home for the Orphaned and the Poor [Home of Onesiphorus]). *Tai'an wenshi ziliao* 泰安文史資料 (Selected Literary and Historical Materials on Tai'an) 2 (October 1987): 88–102.

Zheng Zhengguang 鄭證光. Interview with the author. Fuzhou, July 1997.

Zhongguo fanxiejiao wang 中國反邪教網 (China Anti-Cult Net). http://www .cnfxj.org.

Zhongguo Jidujiao wangzhan 中國基督教網站 (Website of Chinese Christianity). http://www.ccctspm.org/history/important/2008/617/08617526.html.

Zhonghua Jidujiaohui nianjian (ZJN) 中華基督教會年鑒 (The China Church Year Book). Vols. 1–13 (1914–1937). Shanghai: Commercial Press.

Zhonghua Renmin Gongheguo Gong'anbu Diyiju 中華人民共和國公安部第一局 (The First Bureau of the Department of Public Security of the People's Republic of China). *Jidutu Juhuichu (Xiaoqun) Gaikuang* 基督徒聚會處 (小群) 概況 (An Overview of the Christian Meeting Place [The Little Flock]). August 1955.

Zhou Xingyi 周行義. Interview with the author. Shanghai, June 1997.

Zhouli 周禮 (Rites of the Zhou Dynasty, attributed to Ji Dan [Duke of Zhou]). In *Siku quanshu, Jingbu—diyi ji*, compiled by Ji Xiaolan.

Zhu Xin 朱信. "Wo suo renshi de Yesu Jiating: jieshao yu pinglun" 我所認識的耶穌家庭—介紹與評論 (The Jesus Family That I Know: Introductory and Critical Notes). *Huhan [jikan]* 呼喊 (季刊) (Shout [Quarterly]) 47 (January 1987): 168–79; 48 (March 1987): 264–81; 49 (May 1987): 34–51; 50 (July 1987): 119–29; 51 (January 1988): 214–25.

Zong Yao 宗堯. "Shixi benshiji chu Shanghai Jidujiao de zili yundong" 試析本世紀初上海基督教的自立運動 (A Tentative Analysis of the Movement toward Independent Christianity in Shanghai in the Early Part of This Century). In *Zongjiao wenti tansuo* 宗教問題探索 (Probings into the Question of Religion). Edited by Shanghai shehui kexueyuan zongjiao yanjiusuo (Institute for Research on Religion, Shanghai Academy of Social Sciences) and Shanghai shi zongjiao xuehui (Shanghai Association for Religious Studies). Shanghai: 1988.

Abbott, Paul, 85–86
Advent Testimony and Preparation Movement, 163
Age of the Church (or Grace), 168, 178
Age of the Kingdom, 156, 168, 227. *See also* premillennial dispensationalism
Age of the Law, 168
American Board of Commissioners for Foreign Missions, 27
Anglin, Leslie, 68, 94
Anti-Christian Federation, 160
Anti-Christian Movement, 7, 137, 160
antiforeignism: and indigenous church, 9, 41, 170, 188; and Western missions, 7, 32, 109, 116, 133
Anti-Religious Federation, 161
Anti-Rightist campaign, 201–2
apocalypticism, 234; in indigenous churches, 10, 15–16, 179, 192, 218, 221–23, 226; in popular culture, 193, 290n19; in revivals, 86, 99, 102. *See also* eschatology; messianism; millenarianism
Apostolic Faith Mission, 46
Austin-Sparks, T. (Theodore), 174–76, 272n25
Azusa Street Revival, 45–46, 164

Back-Pushing Sketches (Tuibei tu), 193, 280n65
Balcombe, Dennis, 220
banditry, 65, 69, 125, 142, 145, 152; and revivals, 88, 95–96, 101–3, 107, 131, 148
Barber, Margaret E., 157–58, 161, 163–64, 173–74, 177
Bells, Ruth, 162
Berntsen, Bernt, 46, 256n2
Bethel Band (Bethel Worldwide Evangelistic Band; Boteli Huanyou Budaotuan), 131–33, 136–37, 145–46, 148–50, 190
Bethel Mission, 132–34, 145, 150, 192
Bible Teachers Training School for Women, 167
Blessed Church of China (Zhonghua Mengfu Jiaohui), 219
Boat of the Dharma (*fachuan*), 73
Boxer Uprising, 7, 31–32, 35, 37, 58, 64, 88, 111; spirit possession in, 72–73, 106, 238
Buddhism, Chinese, 4, 34, 108, 181, 206, 221, 242, 244–45; popular, 52, 105, 166, 179, 226, 231, 236; sectarian, 15, 107, 236, 239

Cai Sujuan (Christiana Tsai), 166–67, 255n64, 273n44
Calvary Baptist Church (New York), 140
Cambridge Seven, 28, 30–31
Carlberg, Gustav, 97
Catholic Church, Chinese, 4–5, 11–12, 31, 52, 151, 204–5, 230; Catholic Patriotic Association, 197; Catholic University in Beiping (Furen Daxue), 124; contemporary, 2, 227, 230, 246, 250n5; indigenization of, 11, 124, 205, 226–28
Centenary Missionary Conference (1907), 34, 36–37
Chen Bixi, 75–76
Chen Chonggui (Marcus Ch'eng), 92, 188–89, 198, 202
Chen Duxiu, 118
Cheng Jigui, 189
Cheng Jingyi, 35–36, 40–41, 43, 58–60, 111, 123, 130
Chiang Kai-shek, 94, 101, 119, 134, 141, 148, 165, 243
China Christian Council (Zhongguo Jidujiao Xiehui), 210
China Christian Independent Church (Zhongguo Yesujiao Zilihui), 32–34, 41, 131, 187, 282n101
China Church Year Book (Zhonghua Jidujiaohui nianjian), 48
China Continuation Committee, 35–36, 57–58, 60
China for Christ Movement (Zhonghua Guizhu Yundong), 36
China Gospel Fellowship (Zhonghua Fuyin Tuanqi), 219, 285n41
China Inland Mission (CIM), 7, 28–31, 60, 158, 208, 284n27; and indigenous Christianity, 75, 99, 133, 162, 170, 172, 189–92, 197–98
Chinese Christian Church (Zhonghua Jidujiaohui, also Zhongguo Jidujiaohui), 33–34, 36
Chinese Christian Union (Zhongguo Jidutuhui), 32, 113
Chinese Communist Party (CCP; Communists), 7, 118, 134–35, 148, 166, 191, 195–96, 237, 246; appeal of, 134–35, 184–85, 198, 203; and mission

churches, 95, 101, 166, 182, 191–92; religious policies, 197, 204–7, 209–10, 231
Chinese Home Missionary Society (Zhonghua Guonei Budaohui), 36, 189
Chinese Native Evangelical Crusade (Zhongguo Budao Shizijun), 191
Chinese Overseas Mission (Zhonghua Guowai Budaotuan), 188
Chinese Student Volunteer Movement for the Ministry (Zhonghua Xuesheng Lizhi Chuandaotuan), 37, 105
Chinese Union (Fuhanhui), 19–21, 253n7
Christ of the Third Redemption (Sanshu Jidu), 223–24, 232
Christian and Missionary Alliance, 135, 161, 188–89, 194, 284n27
Christian Assembly (Jidutu Juhuichu). See Little Flock
Christian Bible Institute (Jidutu Lingxiuyuan), 189
Christian Faith Collective Farm (Jixin Jiti Nongchang), 196. See also Little Flock
Christian Manifesto, 197–98
Christian Tabernacle (Jidutu Huitang), 112, 117, 129, 171, 193, 201
Christianity in China: future of, 241–47; independence, search for, 26–27, 31–34, 41, 43, 105, 138, 168; indigenization of, 2, 9, 16, 26, 34, 87, 202–3, 230; in Ming dynasty, 5; and modernization, 6–7, 38, 119, 243; political potential, 245–47; in Qing dynasty, 5–6, 11, 15–17, 26–27, 31, 33; and social elite, 118–19, 122–23, 243–45; in Song dynasty 251n9; in Tang dynasty, 3–5; in Yuan dynasty, 4–5. See also Catholic Church, Chinese; indigenous churches; mission churches; underground Christianity
Christianity in global South and East, 11, 240–41
Church of Christ in China (Zhonghua Jidujiaohui), 8, 118, 124, 171, 180, 187
communalism: in indigenous churches, 15, 65, 187, 192, 195–96, 211; in popular religion, 236; in underground Christi-

anity, 221–22. *See also* Jesus Family; True Jesus Church

Communism. *See* Chinese Communist Party

Confraternity of the Passion (Kuhui), 226

Court for Spiritual Retreat (Lingxi-uyuan), 104

Cuiying Middle School, 67–68

"cultural Christians," 242–45

Cultural Revolution, Christianity during, 11, 202, 204–5, 207–9

Daoism, 4, 10, 34, 226, 231, 236, 239, 242

Darby, J. N. (John Nelson), 168–69, 173–74

denominational churches. *See* mission churches

Dillenbeck, Nora (Lin Meili), 67–69, 76–77, 83

Ding Guangxun (K. H. Ting), 210

Ding Limei, 37–38, 105, 189, 191

Disciples' Society (Mentuhui), 222–24, 232

Document No. 19 (1982), 210

Dong Hengxin, 75, 200

Door of Hope, 121

Eastern Lightning. *See* Lightning out of the East

ecstasy: in indigenous Christianity, 2, 9–10, 15, 77, 109, 140, 214, 232; in revivals, 85, 137, 144; 172, 174, 216; in popular religion, 235; religious, 234, 290n29; in Southern Christianity, 240

Eddy, Sherwood, 38, 40, 89, 119

Eight Trigrams, 73–74, 107, 237, 290n19

Elizabeth Skelton Danforth Memorial Hospital, 132, 268n3

end-time theology. *See* apocalypticism; eschatology; messianism; millenarianism

eschatology: Christian, 158, 163–64, 168–69, 233–34, 238–39, 256n3; in indigenous churches, 2, 10, 14–15, 25, 76, 155, 193–94; in popular religion, 235–37, 245; in underground Christianity,

204, 207, 214–16, 223, 226–27, 242. *See also* apocalypticism; messianism; millenarianism

Established King (Beiliwang), 221–22

Evangelism (Budao zazhi), 189

exorcism: in indigenous churches, 15, 28, 48, 51, 99, 135, 147, 220; in popular religion, 15, 238; in underground Christianity, 207, 209, 215, 224–25, 232

faith healing: in indigenous churches, 15, 28, 99, 189, 201, 208–9; in Pentecostalism, 45–46, 241; in popular religion, 238; in underground Christianity, 207, 209, 215, 219–21, 224–25, 230, 232. *See also* Sung, John

Falun Gong, 231

Fangcheng Church (Fangcheng Jiaohui), 208–9, 218–20, 230

"female Christ," 226–29

Feng Yuxiang, and Home of Onesiphorus, 94; as militarist, 92, 101, 188; and missionaries, 89–95; patriotism of, 92–93; religion of, 89–91, 93–94, 116, 188, 208; and the Soviet Union, 93–94

Fischbacher, Elizabeth, 172, 275n69

Fosdick, Harry Emerson, 139, 141, 269n27

Gao Daling, 53, 56–57, 62

Glass, Wiley B., 86, 106

glossolalia (speaking in "tongues"), 45–46, 234; 256n3; in indigenous churches, 15, 76, 115, 186, 192; in revivals, 9, 85, 99, 104, 106, 146, 172; in underground Christianity, 209, 220, 225. *See also* Jesus Family; True Jesus Church

Goddess of Mercy (Guanyin), 52, 105, 227

Goforth, Jonathan, 88–90, 93

Good Words to Admonish the Age (Quan-shi liangyan), 22, 122

Gowdy, J., Bishop, 151–52, 271n66

Great Depression, and missions, 96, 99

Great Harmony (*datong*), 64, 83–84, 185, 237–38

Great Leap Forward, 202, 204, 208

Great Tribulation, 158, 168–69, 219, 274n54. *See also* premillennial dispensationalism

Greer, Lillian, 77, 79

Gu Changsheng, 193, 204

Gu Ren'en (John Ku), 189, 201

Guo Duoma, 55–56, 62

Gützlaff, Karl, 19–21

Guyon, Madame (Jeanne-Marie Bouvier de la Motte Guyon), 176–77

Hakka, 21, 23, 209, 253n7

Hansen, Sophie, 46

Hanson, Perry O., 67–68, 77

Heavenly Invitation Office (Tianzhaoju), 29, 55

"heretic cult" (*xiejiao*), 218

Home of Onesiphorus, 68–69, 78, 94, 134

Hong Rengan, 23

Hong Xiuquan, 21–25, 81, 83, 122, 228, 238. *See also* Taiping Heavenly Kingdom

Honor Oak Fellowship, 174

Hoste, D. E., 30–31, 42, 162

house churches. *See* underground Christianity, contemporary

Hua Xuehe, 215

Hughes, Jennie V., 132, 145, 150, 162

Hunan Bible Institute, 189

Hymns of Universal Praise (*Putian song-zan*), 124–25

independent churches. *See* indigenous churches

indigenous (independent) churches: apocalypticism in, 9, 14–15; background of members, 33, 238–40; characteristics, 202; in Communist era, 198, 200, 211; development of, 11, 27, 31–34, 41, 53, 135, 182–83, 202, 240; and nationalism, 12, 14, 32–33, 105, 202; wartime, 187, 193; women and, 239. *See also* Christianity in China: independence, search for; Jesus Family; Little Flock; Spiritual Gifts Society; True Jesus Church; underground Christianity, contemporary

Inter-Varsity Christian Fellowship of China, 190–92, 279n58

Jaffray, Robert A., 188

Jesuits, 5–6, 251n17

Jesus Family (Yesu Jiating), 9; apocalypticism, 73, 82; arranged marriages, 80–81; background of members, 77–78, 184; and CCP, 185, 198; communal life in, 64, 69–70, 78, 80–83; development of, 65, 69, 78, 80, 184–85, 208, 211, 282n101; disbanded, 200; as haven, 69, 184–85; influence of, 79, 104, 186–87, 195–96, 198; leadership, 75–77; organization of, 69, 78; Pentecostalism in, 15, 64–65, 68–73, 77, 82; sexual segregation, 80; and Spiritual Gifts Society, 186

Ji Jianhong, 211

Ji Sanbao, 223–24

Ji Zhiwen (Gih, Andrew), 132–33, 136, 150, 190, 192

Jia Yuming, 189, 192, 202, 281n90

Jiang Changchuan (Kiang Ch'ang-ch'uan), 187, 256n78

Jing Dianying: and Communism, 64, 185; conversion to Christianity, 65–67; end-time beliefs, 70, 73, 76; and Dillenbeck, Nora, 67, 76–77; and Home of Onesiphorus, 68–69; on Jesus Family, 64, 70, 72–73, 78, 185; as leader, 68–69, 76–78, 81–83, 94, 200; and Pentecostalism, 68; and Western missions, 67–69. *See also* Jesus Family

Joachim of Fiore, 168

Jones, Francis P., 181

Kang Cheng (Ida Kahn), 132, 142–44

Kangxi, Emperor, 5–6

Keswick Holiness (Higher Christian Life) movement, 163–64, 172, 176

Korean Revival (1907), 87–88, 164

Land of the Peach Blossoms (land beyond the "spring of peach blossoms"), 84, 108, 185

"Land System of the Heavenly Dynasty." (*Tianchao tianmu zhidu*), 24–25

Larson, I. V., 98

Li Changshou (Witness Lee), 195, 197, 216–19, 221, 284n30

Li Daorong, 136, 150

Li Shuqing, 87

Li Tian'en (Li Musheng), 208, 218

Li Yuanru (Ruth Lee), 166–67, 174, 201

Li Zongren, 184

Liang Fa (Liang Afa), 17, 22

Liang Qichao, 120

liberalism (modernism), theological, 9, 60–61, 86, 117–19, 189–90, 202–3, 210

Life Fellowship (Shengmingshe), 123

Life of Christ by Chinese Artists, 124

Lightning out of the East (Dongfang Shandian; Eastern Lightning), 222, 226–29

Lin Heping, 156–57

Lin Yutang, 38

Little Flock (Xiaoqun; Christian Assembly; Local Church): background of members, 170, 196; and CCP, 196–97, 200–201; contemporary, 1, 207–8, 211, 216–17, 229; "evangelistic migration" (*fuyin yimin*), 195–96; growth of, 160, 166–68, 170–71, 174, 178, 196, 201, 282n101; "hand over" movement in, 195–96; influence of, 155, 197, 215, 222–23, 225, 227; and mission churches, 161, 170–71; organization, 174, 176, 196; patriarchal tradition in, 239; and Pentecostalism, 15, 172–73; and Plymouth Brethren, 173–74, 177–78; roadside evangelism, 160, 197. *See also* Nee, Watchman

Liu Daosheng, 102

Liu Jiaguo, 222

Liu Tingfang (Timothy Tingfang Lew), 58, 60, 123–25, 128–29

Living Stream Ministry, 217

Lobenstine, Edwin C., 35, 59

Local Church (Difang Jiaohui). *See* Little Flock

London Missionary Society (LMS), 6, 17, 43, 60, 111, 122; and indigenous churches, 26–27, 35

Lord God Sect (Zhushenjiao), 222

Lü Xiaomin, 220

Luce, Henry Winters, 37

Luo Wenzao (Gregory Lopez), 11, 13

Ma Zhaorui, 98

Maitreya Buddha, 73–74, 236–37

Manchurian crisis (1931), 101, 137, 148. *See also* Mukden Incident

Manchurian Revival (1908), 88, 95

Mao Zedong, 53, 135, 142, 232, 237–38, 290n21

Marian cults, 227

Mass Education Movement, 121, 142. *See also* National Popular Education Association

Mateer, Calvin, 37

Maxwell, Arthur S., 193

May Thirtieth Incident, 61, 92, 116, 133–34, 138, 161

McPherson, Aimee Semple, 140, 153

messianism, 246; in indigenous churches, 8, 11, 14–16, 183, 186, 188, 240; modern, 235; in popular religion, 209, 237, 247; in underground Christianity, 205, 214, 227, 229; in Western tradition, 233–35. *See also* millenarianism

Methodist Episcopal Church: and indigenous Christianity, 67–69, 79, 90, 119, 145, 151–52, 157–58, 161; missions, 39, 88, 95, 111, 132, 138, 142; and Pentecostalism, 68–69, 77

Meyer, F. B. (Frederick Brotherton), 163–65

millenarianism: in indigenous churches, 14–16, 25, 30, 39, 41, 73, 200; in popular religion, 15–16, 73–74, 107, 235–38, 246–47; in underground Christianity, 206, 214, 226, 232; in Western Christianity, 15, 233–35. *See also* apocalyptism; messianism; premillennial dispensationalism

Milne, William, 17

mission churches: and CCP, 191–92, 197–98; development of, 6, 8, 21, 167, 181, 282n101; and indigenization of Christianity, 33, 36–37, 40, 57, 60–61, 109–10, 121–27, 133, 181–82; and nationalism, 3, 61–62, 95–96, 160–61, 181;

mission churches (*continued*)
and revivals, 85, 87, 98–99, 101;
during wartime, 179–80, 191–92
"missionary case" (jiao'an), 7, 32, 58
modernism, theological. *See* liberalism,
theological
Monsen, Marie, 85, 96–98, 102, 218
Montanus, 234
Morrison, Robert, 6, 8, 17–19, 34
Mother of No-Birth (Wusheng Laomu),
62, 74, 227, 237
Mott, John R., 35, 37–38, 40, 89, 93, 124
Mukden Incident, 76, 148, 181. *See also*
Manchurian crisis

Nanjing Incident (1927), 7–8, 95, 134,
165–67
Nanking (Nanjing) Theological Semi-
nary, 179, 181, 210
Narrow Gate in the Wilderness (Kuangye
Zhaimen; Disciples' Society), 223–24,
232
National Christian Conference (1922),
57
National Christian Council of China
(Zhonghua Jidujiao Xiejinhui; NCC),
8, 57, 59–61, 109, 119, 179–81, 197; and
indigenization of Christianity, 61, 86,
122–23; and Nationalist-Communist
rivalry, 180, 182; and social reform, 118,
121, 148
National Christian Literature Association
(Zhonghua Jidujiao Wenshe), 122–24
National Christian Service Council for
Wounded Soldiers in Transit, 155, 180
National Free Christian Church of
China, 33
National People's Army of the Republic
of China (Zhonghua Minguo Guomin-
jun), 92
National Popular Education Association
(Zhonghua Pingmin Jiaoyu Cujinhui),
121–22. *See also* Mass Education
Movement
Native Land of True Emptiness, 74
Nee, Watchman (Ni Tuosheng), 10, 40,
155–58, 165, 194, 201; eschatology of,
163, 165, 168–70, 177–78, 274n54; and

Jessie Penn-Lewis, 163–65; and John
Sung, 171; and Keswick movement,
163, 176; and Little Flock (Christian
Assembly), 155, 160, 166–68, 170, 172,
194–96, 201; and Margaret E. Barber,
157–58, 163, 173; and mission churches,
156, 158, 161–63; and Pentecostalism,
164, 171–73; and Plymouth Brethren,
10, 168–70, 172–74, 178; *Rethinking
Our Missions* (*Gongzuo de zaisi*), 174,
197; scandals, 177, 194–95; on TJC, 171;
and TSPM, 200; "truth of the Cross,"
155–56, 165; and Wang Mingdao, 168,
170; and Wang Zai, 159–61, 171. *See also*
Little Flock
Nestorians, 3–4
Ni Tuosheng. *See* Nee, Watchman
Nie Ziying (Lincoln Nieh), 133–36, 150
"No Room in the Inn," 124, 126, 129
North China Association of Chinese
Christian Churches, 34
North China Christian Union (Huabei
Zhonghua Jidujiaotuan), 184, 187, 193,
278n23
North China Theological Seminary, 40,
70, 105, 189
Northern Expedition, 7–8, 61, 94–95,
119, 161, 165, 167
Nowack, William H., 102

opium refuges, of Xi Shengmo, 8, 29, 31;
of TJC, 55

Panton, David M., 157–58
Peking Union Medical College, 139, 170,
186
Penn-Lewis, Jessie, 163–65, 170–74, 177,
189; end-time teachings, 164; and
Pentecostalism, 164
Pentecostalism, 45, 140, 164, 234, 240–
41; in indigenous churches, 9, 15, 115,
172–73, 186, 194, 202; Pentecostal
missions in China, 43, 46–47, 68, 86,
114–15; and revivals, 76, 85–86, 94,
98–107, 146–47. *See also* Jesus Family;
Spiritual Gifts Society; True Jesus
Church; underground Christianity
Plymouth Brethren, 10, 168–70, 177–78

premillennial dispensationalism, 10, 168–69, 190, 194, 216, 227
premillennialism, 9, 45, 163, 190, 233
Presbyterian Tengchow College (Dengzhou Wenhuiguan), 27, 37, 189
Price, Frank W., 179, 191–92, 198

Quanzhou-Zhangzhou Presbyterian Assembly (Quan-Zhang Zhanglao Dahui), 26
Queen Mother of the West (Xi Wangmu), 235–37
Queen of the Dark Chamber, 166

"rapture" (beiti): 71, 107, 154, 158, 168–69, 173, 178, 216. See also premillennial dispensationalism
Ravenites, 173–74, 275n74
Rawlinson, Frank Joseph, 91–93, 95
Record of Rites (Liji), 237
Red Spears, 69
Rees, David Vaughan, 75
"restoration of educational rights," 7, 161
Ricci, Matteo, 5–6
Rites Controversy, 5
Roberts, Issacher J., 20, 23
Robertson, C. H., 38, 119

Saints' Credit and Savings Society (Shengtu Xinyong Chuxushe), 68–69
Schubert, William E., 145, 151, 153
Scofield, Cyrus Ingerson, 169
Scripture of Great Peace (Taiping jing), 236
sectarianism: in indigenous churches, 11–12, 14–15, 51, 65, 68, 196, 238–40, 242; in popular religion, 16, 236–37; in underground Christianity, 207, 211, 214, 216, 218, 220–21, 232
"self-government, self-support, and self-propagation" (zizhi, ziyang, zichuan), 11, 197. See also Three-Self Patriotic Movement
Sesame Seed Cake Song (Shaobing ge), 193
Seven Chinese Prophecies (Zhongguo yuyan qizhong), 193
Seventh-Day Adventist Church, 50–52, 54, 57, 193, 207
Shandong Evangelistic Association of

the Grateful (Shandong Chou'en Chuandaohui), 27
Shandong Revival, 9, 85–87, 96–107, 115, 146–47, 171–72; affinity to popular religion, 105–6; and church schisms, 99, 104–5; institutionalization of, 103–4; missionaries and, 97–101, 105–7; and nationalism, 98, 105. See also Spiritual Gifts Society
Shengxiandao (the Way of the Sages and the Worthies), 74
Shi Meiyu (Mary Stone), 132–33, 145, 157, 167, 255n64
Shouters (Huhanpai), 195, 216–19, 221, 223, 225–27, 229
Shu Zhan, 245
Signs of the Times (Shizhao yuebao), 52. See also Seventh-Day Adventist Church
Silkworm and Mulberry-Tree House for the Learning of the Way (Cansang Xuedaofang), 69
Snow, Edgar, 134
Social Gospel, 9, 110, 121–22, 142, 148, 190, 198
Society of the Way (Daoyuan), 65, 290n19
Song Shangjie. See Sung, John
Songs of Canaan, 220
Soong Mayling (Song Meiling), 119
South China Church (Huanan Jiaohui), 219, 285n41
Spirit Boxers, 72. See also Boxer Uprising
spirit possession: in indigenous Christianity, 23, 54, 71–72, 103, 228; in popular religion, 9, 53, 55, 72–73, 147, 209, 228, 238
Spirit-Spirit Sect (Linglingjiao), 215
Spiritual Action Team (Linggongtuan), 192, 205
Spiritual Food Church (Lingliangtang), 194, 211, 282n101
Spiritual Gifts Society (Ling'enhui), 79, 85, 98–101, 103, 202, 239, 282n101; communalism in, 186; and Jesus Family, 104, 186; and mission churches, 104–5, 186; organization of, 103–4, 185–86
Spiritual Light (Lingguangbao), 162, 166

St. John's University, 6, 38, 60, 277n4
Stearns, Thornton, 172, 275n69
Stone, Mary. *See* Shi Meiyu
Stone, Phoebe (Shi Chengzhi), 133–34
Straton, John R., 139–40
Stuart, John Leighton, 37–38, 135
Student Volunteer Movement for Foreign Missions (U.S.), 37
Sun Yat-sen, 27, 33, 119, 141–42, 144–45, 157, 159
Sun Zhanyao, 99, 104
Sung, John (Song Shangjie), 10; apocalyptism of, 141, 144, 146, 148, 154–55; and Bethel Band, 145–46, 150; faith healing, 146–47, 151, 153; and Harry Emerson Fosdick, 139, 141; against "idolatry" of Sun Yat-sen, 141–42, 144–45; nationalism of, 138–39, 145, 148–50; nervous breakdown, 139–41; and Pentecostalism, 146; against Social Gospel, 142, 148; in Southeast Asia, 151, 153; style of preaching, 137–38, 144–45, 149–53; and theological liberalism, 139–41, 145–46; and Uldine Utley, 140; at Union Theological Seminary, 139–41; and Western missions, 145, 149–52; and Yu Rizhang, 148
Sweet Smelling Myrrh, 176–77

Taiping Heavenly Kingdom, 2, 21–26; charismatic religion in, 23–24, 238; egalitarianism in, 24–25, 81, 83; and indigenization of Christianity, 8, 24, 92, 222, 228; millenarianism in, 23, 25, 84, 237, 240, 245; sexual segregation in, 24, 81, 83
Taylor, James Hudson, 28–30, 158
Three Grades of Servants (Sanban Puren), 222, 224–26, 229
Three-Self Patriotic Movement (TSPM), 11, 197–98, 205–6, 210–11; indigenous churches and, 200–202, 211; TSPM churches, 206, 212, 242; underground Christianity and, 12, 206–7, 214–16, 239
To Tsai Independent Church (Daoji Huitang), 27
"tongues," speaking in. *See* glossolalia

trance, 234. *See also* ecstasy; Pentecostalism
Triads (Tiandihui), 21, 239
Trinity College (Fuzhou), 160–61, 272n19
True Jesus Church (Zhen Yesu Jiaohui; TJC; Universal Correction Church): and Adventists, 51–52, 54; apocalyptism in, 9, 42, 47, 50, 52, 54, 63, 201; basic doctrines, 48–49, 56–57; communalism in, 50–51; in Communist era, 200–202, 207–8, 211; divisions within, 62; faith healing in, 43, 48, 51, 53–54, 202, 215; glossolalia, 43, 48, 50, 51–53, 55; growth of, 9, 47–48, 50–56, 62–63, 183–84, 282n101; *Holy Ghost (Shengling bao)*, 183; and mission churches, 47–49, 54, 58, 183–84; and nationalism, 47–50, 54, 62; and NCC, 57–59, 61; and opium addiction, 53–55; organization of, 49, 56–57; Pentecostalism in, 47, 49–56, 62, 183, 207; and underground Christianity, 207–8, 215. *See also* Wei Enbo

underground Christianity (house churches), contemporary: apocalyptism in, 206–7, 215–18, 220–23, 226, 242; appeal of, 214, 220, 223–24, 230–32; and Communist state, 207–9, 214, 218–19, 221–24, 229; among ethnic minorities, 209; growth of, 2, 11, 205–10, 214–19, 226, 230, 242, 250n5; Jesus Family and, 208, 224–25; Little Flock and, 207–8, 215–16, 222–23, 225, 227; messianism in, 209, 214, 221–23, 226–29, 232; opposition to TSPM, 206, 211–12, 214–15, 218, 223, 225; Pentecostalism in, 206–7, 209, 214–16, 218, 220, 225, 232; and popular religion, 207, 209, 225–26, 228, 230, 242; sectarian tendency in, 206–7, 214, 218, 221, 229; TJC and, 207–8, 215, 223
Union Theological Seminary (New York), 139–41
Universal Correction Church (Wanguo Gengzhengjiao). *See* True Jesus Church
Utley, Uldine, 140, 153

Verbiest, Ferdinand, 5

Wang Mingdao: apocalypticism of, 115, 120–21, 129–30; and Communist state, 200–201, 210, 221; as independent preacher, 116–17, 129, 193, 200–201; and indigenous Christianity, 9–10, 129, 193, 221; and mission churches, 111–18, 129–30, 150; patriotism of, 113–14; and Pentecostalism, 114–15; and Social Gospel, 9, 118, 120; *Spiritual Food Quarterly* (*Lingshi jikan*), 123, 129; and theological liberalism, 117–18
Wang Peizhen (Peace Wang), 166–67
Wang Yuansong, 208
Wang Zai (Leland Wang), 133, 159–60, 161–162, 171, 188
Way of Great Peace (Taiping Dao), 236, 290n23
Way of Pervading Unity (Yiguandao), 237
Weepers (Kupai), 218–19
Wei Enbo (Wei Baoluo, Paul Wei): apocalypticism of, 42; and founding of TJC, 43, 47–48; and Pentecostal mission, 43, 47, 49. *See also* True Jesus Church
Wei, Francis (Wei Zhuomin), 182
Wei Yisa, 54, 56–57, 62, 183, 200–201
Welsh revival, 87, 164
Wenshe. *See* National Christian Literature Association
White Lotus tradition, 73–74, 236–37, 289n17
Wilkes, A. Paget, 133
World Missionary Conference (1910), 35
World Student Christian Federation, 160
Wu Leichuan, 198
Wu Yangming, 221
Wu Yaozong (Y. T. Wu), 198–200, 210

Xi Shengmo (Xi the Overcomer of Demons), 27–31
Xie Fuya (N. Z. Zia), 181
Xie Honglai, 32, 113
Xu Baoluo (Paul Xu), 135
Xu Jinhong, 157
Xu Shuangfu, 224–26
Xu Yongze, 218–19
Xu Zhimo, 109, 120, 245

Yang Shaotang, 192–93, 202, 205, 281n90
Yang Xiuqing, 23, 228
Yen, James (Yan Yangchu), 121–22, 142, 182. *See also* Mass Education Movement; National Popular Education Association
Yenching University, 6, 106, 113, 135, 142, 170, 180, 187; and indigenization of Christianity, 123, 125, 198, 202–3; and Jesus Family, 198
Yin Renxian, 191
YMCA (Young Men's Christian Association), 7, 118; and indigenization of Christianity, 32, 36–37, 60, 113, 181; and Social Christianity, 36, 40, 119–22, 138, 180, 198; and theological liberalism, 117, 119–20
Yu Chenghua, 156, 177
Yu Cidu (Dora Yu), 38–40, 157, 167
Yu Guozhen (Yu Zongzhou), 32–33, 41, 131
Yu Ligong, 190
Yu Rizhang (David Z. T. Yui), 36, 59–60, 119, 123, 148, 255n64
YWCA (Young Women's Christian Association), 92, 119–21, 180

Zhang Banaba (Barnabas Zhang; Zhang Dianju), 50, 54–55, 57, 62
Zhang Boling (Chang Po-ling), 60
Zhang Lingsheng, 50, 62
Zhang Rongliang, 208, 218, 220–21, 283n11
Zhao Junying (Calvin Chao), 189–92, 203
Zhao Shiguang (S. K. Chow, Timothy Chao), 189, 194
Zhao Weishan, 226–29
Zhao Zichen (T. C. Chao), 60, 106, 123, 125, 187, 198, 202–3
Zhou Xingyi, 178
Zhou Zhiyu, 189
zibo, 226
zipu, 226
Zuo Shunzhen, 75–76, 81, 83